A SOCIOLOGY OF SPIRITUALITY

The emergence of spirituality in contemporary culture in holistic forms suggests that organised religions have failed. This thesis is explored and disputed in this book in ways that mark important critical divisions. This is the first collection of essays to assess the significance of spirituality in the sociology of religion. The authors explore the relationship of spirituality to the visual, individualism, gender, identity politics, education and cultural capital. The relationship between secularisation and spirituality is examined and consideration is given to the significance of Simmel in relation to a sociology of spirituality. Problems of defining spirituality are debated with reference to its expression in the UK, the USA, France and Holland. This timely, original and well structured volume provides undergraduates, postgraduates and researchers with a scholarly appraisal of a phenomenon that can only increase in sociological significance.

THEOLOGY AND RELIGION IN INTERDISCIPLINARY
PERSPECTIVE SERIES IN ASSOCIATION WITH THE
BSA SOCIOLOGY OF RELIGION STUDY GROUP

BSA Sociology of Religion Study Group Series editor:
Pink Dandelion and the publications committee

Theology and Religion in Interdisciplinary Perspective Series editors:
Douglas Davies and Richard Fenn

The British Sociological Association Sociology of Religion Study Group began in 1975 and provides the primary forum in Britain for scholarship in the sociology of religion. The nature of religion remains of key academic interest and this series draws on the latest worldwide scholarship in compelling and coherent collections on critical themes. Secularisation and the future of religion; gender; the negotiation and presentation of religious identities, beliefs and values; and the interplay between group and individual in religious settings are some of the areas addressed. Ultimately, these books reflect not just on religious life but on how wider society is affected by the enduring religious framing of human relationships, morality and the nature of society itself.

This series is part of the broader *Theology and Religion in Interdisciplinary Perspective Series* edited by Douglas Davies and Richard Fenn.

Other titles published in the BSA Sociology of Religion Study Group Series

Materializing Religion
Expression, Performance and Ritual
Edited by Elisabeth Arweck and William Keenan
ISBN 978-0-7546-5094-2 (HBK)

Reading Religion in Text and Context
Reflections of Faith and Practice in Religious Materials
Edited by Elisabeth Arweck and Peter Collins
ISBN 978-0-7546-5482-7 (HBK)

Religion, Identity and Change
Perspectives on Global Transformations
Edited by Simon Coleman and Peter Collins
ISBN 978-0-7546-0450-1 (HBK)

A Sociology of Spirituality

Edited by

KIERAN FLANAGAN
University of Bristol, UK

PETER C. JUPP
University of Durham, UK

ASHGATE

Published by
Ashgate Publishing Limited
Gower House
Croft Road
Aldershot
Hampshire GU11 3HR
England

Ashgate Publishing Company
Suite 420
101 Cherry Street
Burlington, VT 05401-4405
USA

Ashgate website: http://www.ashgate.com

British Library Cataloguing in Publication Data
A sociology of spirituality. – (Theology and religion in interdisciplinary perspective)
1. Religion and sociology
I. Flanagan, Kieran, 1944– II. Jupp, Peter C. III. British Sociological Association.
Sociology of Religion Study Group
306.6

Library of Congress Cataloging-in-Publication Data
A sociology of spirituality / edited by Kieran Flanagan and Peter C. Jupp.
        p. cm. – (Theology and religion in interdisciplinary perspective series)
    Includes index.
    ISBN-13: 978-0-7546-5458-2 (hardcover : alk. paper)
1. Religion and sociology. 2. Spirituality. I. Flanagan, Kieran, 1944– II. Jupp, Peter C.

    BL60.S6285 2007
    306.6–dc22

2006022471

ISBN 978-0-7546-5458-2

Printed and bound in Great Britain by MPG Books Ltd, Bodmin, Cornwall.

*Kieran Flanagan dedicates this book to Michael Robertson,
parish priest, librarian and a man of great sagacity*

*Peter C. Jupp dedicates this book to his wife Elisabeth and his sons
Edmund and Miles; and to the congregation of Westgate Church,
Peterborough, for all its teamwork in Christian ministry*

Contents

List of Tables

List of Contributors

Steve Bruce is Professor of Sociology and Head of the School of Social Science at the University of Aberdeen. He studied at the University of Stirling and previously taught at The Queen's University of Belfast, Northern Ireland. He was elected a Fellow of the British Academy in 2003 and a Fellow of the Royal Society of Edinburgh in 2005 and has been a member of both the 2001 and 2008 Research Assessment Exercise panels for Sociology. He has written extensively on the nature of religion in the modern world and on the links between religion and politics. His most recent book is *Paisley: Religion and Politics in Northern Ireland* (2006).

Paul Chambers is a Research Fellow in the Centre for Border Studies at the University of Glamorgan, Wales. A sociologist of religion, he is the author of *Religion, Secularization and Social Change in Wales* (2005) and has written extensively on aspects of the Christian religion and identity in Wales, the relationship between religion and politics, and latterly on Welsh Muslims. He has also been active in the relatively new field of congregational studies, being a co-contributor to *Congregational Studies in the UK* (2004) and *Studying Local Churches: A Handbook* (2005).

André Droogers is Professor of Cultural Anthropology with special reference to Anthropology of Religion and Symbolic Anthropology, at the Vrije Universiteit, Amsterdam. He is Director of the Hollenweger Center for the Interdisciplinary Study of Pentecostal and Charismatic Movements, and General Editor of the online journal *PentecoStudies*. His numerous publications address various themes, such as Pentecostalism, syncretism, religion and play, the changing worldviews in The Netherlands, and religion and power. With Sidney M. Greenfield he edited a collected volume of essays, *Reinventing Religions, Syncretism and Transformation in Africa and the Americas* (2001). He is the coordinator of research programmes on changing worldviews in The Netherlands and on conversion careers and culture politics in Global Pentecostalism.

Kieran Flanagan is a Reader in Sociology at the University of Bristol. Between 1997 and 2000, he was Chair of the British Sociological Association Sociology of Religion Study Group. With Peter C. Jupp, he has edited *Postmodernity, Sociology and Religion* (1996) and *Virtue Ethics and Sociology: Issues of Modernity and Religion* (2001). His latest book is *Seen and Unseen: Visual Culture Sociology and Theology* (2004) and he is completing *Sociology in Theology: Reflexivity and Belief* for publication in 2007.

Richard W. Flory is Associate Professor of Sociology at Biola University and a Research Associate in the Center for Religion and Civic Culture at the University of Southern California. With Donald Miller, he was editor of *GenX Religion* (2000) and is author of *Finding Faith: The Spiritual Quest of the Post-Boomer Generations* (2008). He has created two interactive, multi-media art gallery installations: with Donald Miller and Daniel Callis, 'Finding Faith: Christianity in a New Generation' (2003), and with Daniel Callis, 'The Postmodern Metropolis: Los Angeles, Tijuana and Las Vegas' (2004). His research has been supported by grants from the Louisville Institute, the Pew Charitable Trusts, the Lilly Endowment, and Biola University.

Giuseppe Giordan is a Lecturer in Sociology at the University of Valle d'Aosta. He is a member of the Board of the Italian Sociological Association: Section on the Sociology of Religion, and Book Review Editor of *Religioni e Società*. His main works include: *Valori e cambiamento sociale. Definizioni operative e modello esplicativo* (2001); *Dall'uno al molteplice. Dispositivi di legittimazione nell'epoca del pluralismo* (2003); and *Identity and Pluralism. The Values of the Postmodern Time* (2004). He is editing a collection *Tra religione e spiritualità. Il rapporto con il sacro nell'epoca del pluralismo*. His current interests are the sociology of religion, the interaction between religion and spirituality and the relationship between sociology and theology.

Mathew Guest is a Lecturer in Theology and Society in the Department of Theology and Religion at Durham University. His main research interests are in the relationship between evangelicalism and modern/postmodern culture, the inter-generational transmission of religious values, and he has written extensively on the sociology of contemporary Christianity and Christian community. He has co-edited (with Karin Tusting and Linda Woodhead) *Congregational Studies in the UK: Christianity in a Post-Christian Context* (2004), is the co-author (with Douglas Davies) of *Bishops, Wives and Children: Spiritual Capital Across the Generations* (2007), and is the author of *Evangelical Identity and Contemporary Culture: A Congregational Study in Innovation* (2007).

Paul Heelas is Professor in Religion and Modernity in the Department of Religious Studies at Lancaster University. The author of *The New Age Movement* (1996) and the co-author of *The Spiritual Revolution* (2005), he is currently completing *Spiritualities of Life*. He was the Principal Applicant for the grant which funded 'The Kendal Problem', an exploration of religion and spirituality in a particular locality. At present, he is planning further empirical research focusing on spirituality within mainstream institutions.

Peter R. Holmes completed his doctorate at the University of Birmingham and is a Lead Reviewer for the Community of Communities project of the Association of Therapeutic Communities and the Royal College of Psychiatrists. His recent works include: *Letting God Heal* (2000) and *Becoming More Human: Exploring the Interface of Spirituality Discipleship and Therapeutic Faith Community* (2005). With Susan Williams, he has also co-edited *Changed Lives* (2005) He specialises in therapeutic community in a faith context, healing personal positive change and group process. He is a member of the Chartered Management Institute and a professional trainer focusing on leadership, emotional intelligence (EQ) and team-building. His latest work is *Trinity in Human Community: Exploring Congregational Life in the Image of the Social Trinity* (2006).

Peter C. Jupp is Golders Green Foundation Research Fellow in the Department of Theology and Religious Studies at the University of Durham, and is a United Reformed Church minister. He was Convenor (Secretary) of the BSA Sociology of Religion Study Group 1991–94. His special interest is in the history and sociology of death. He was Director of the National Funerals College, 1992–97. He is a founding co-editor of the quarterly journal, *Mortality* and has co-edited a number of books in the field, including *Interpreting Death* (1997) and *Death in England: An Illustrated History* (1999). His *From Dust to Ashes: cremation and the British Way of Death* was published in 2006. He is Chairman of the Council of the Cremation Society of Great Britain.

Donald E. Miller is Firestone Professor of Religion at the University of Southern California and Executive Director of the Center for Religion and Civic Culture at USC. He is the author/editor of seven books, including, *The Case for Liberal Christianity* (1981), *Writing and Research in Religious Studies* (1992), *Homeless Families: The Struggle for Dignity* (1993), *Survivors: An Oral History of the Armenian Genocide* (1993), *Reinventing American Protestantism* (1997), *GenX Religion* (2000) and *Armenia: Portraits of Survival and Hope* (2003). He is currently writing a book on global Pentecostalism with Tetsunao Yamamori, based on interviews and observations in twenty developing countries.

Ivan Varga is Professor Emeritus of Sociology, Queen's University, Kingston, Canada and Honorary President of Research Committee 22 (Sociology of Religion) of the International Sociological Association. He is also a member of the Editorial Board of *International Sociology*. He is author or editor/co-editor of four books and has contributed 30 chapters in books published in Canada, Czechoslovakia, France, Hungary, Poland, the United Kingdom, and Yugoslavia. He has taught in Germany (Visiting Professor at the Universities of Konstanz and Bielefeld), Hungary and Tanzania before settling in Canada. He was also Visiting Professor at University of Roma Tre and Senior Fellow, Centre for the Study of World Religions, Harvard University.

Peter Versteeg is a Post-doctoral Research Fellow at the Department of Social and Cultural Anthropology of the Vrije Universiteit Amsterdam, where he also completed his PhD dissertation entitled: *Draw Me Close: An Ethnography of Experience in a Dutch Charismatic Church* (2001). He has done fieldwork on religion in The Netherlands since 1993 and has written on such topics as exorcism, charismatic Christianity and Christian spirituality. Currently, he is working on a comparative research projection of changing Protestant liturgies and experience.

David Voas is Simon Research Fellow at the University of Manchester, where he works in the Cathie Marsh Centre for Census and Survey Research. After studying at the London School of Economics and the University of Cambridge he spent a number of years outside academic life, returning in 1998. His work often involves using survey data to study religious change in modern societies; his articles are published in *Sociology*, the *British Journal of Sociology*, the *American Sociological Review*, and elsewhere. He has been awarded several grants by the Economic and Social Research Council, most recently for a study of 'Local culture and the maintenance and transmission of religious practice'.

Linda Woodhead is Professor of Sociology of Religion at Lancaster University. She is currently Head of the Department of Religious Studies, and has been elected as Chair of the British Sociological Association's Sociology of Religion Study Group from 2006–09. Her recent publications include: *The Spiritual Revolution* (with Paul Heelas, 2004); *An Introduction to Christianity* (2004); *A Very Short Introduction to Christianity* (2004); and has co-edited with Kendall Soulen, *God and Human Dignity* (2006).

Acknowledgements

The editors warmly thank the contributors to this volume for their endless patience and efficiency in handling queries and in re-drafting their contributions. We would also like to thank members of the BSA Sociology of Religion Study Group for their interest and support in the production of this volume. Especial thanks are due to Dr Peter Gee, the Convenor, and Dr Ben Pink Dandelion, the Publication Officer of the Group.

Kieran Flanagan would like to thank Mrs Jackie Bee and Ms Elaine Escott in the Department of Sociology at the University of Bristol for much support and help with word processing queries. He would also like to express his gratitude to the Faculty Computing Service at the University of Bristol for their rapid, patient and efficient support. Both editors wish to mark their appreciation of Professor Gregor McLennan, who is in charge of the forthcoming Research Assessment Exercise for the Department of Sociology at the University of Bristol for his close, but kindly interest in the collection and its eventual publication. They also thank Miss Edith Coole of Westgate Church, Peterborough for help with proof-reading. Finally, we would like to offer a special word of thanks to Sarah Lloyd, our editor at Ashgate, who has been most supportive and helpful.

Kieran Flanagan and Peter C. Jupp

Introduction

Kieran Flanagan

If sociology is to maintain its distinctive function as an academic discipline, it has to display finesse in matching concepts to the cultural needs of the day. As tools that encapsulate facets of the social, concepts magnify sensibilities, anxieties and needs in ways that capture the sentiments of a moment. Thus, in the 1990s, concepts of identity, risk and globalisation came to the fore. These terms became the focus of much sociological interest and concern. They acted as keys and opened up other boxes in the discipline's depository. It is in the forging of concepts that sociology finds its depth and true vocation. Might spirituality be the conceptual key that opens many cultural doors? Omens for such a concept to be put to sociological use hardly seem propitious.

The term is most unlikely to be found in the index of sociological works, even those devoted to religion. Anyhow, as a discipline, sociology tends to hunt for religion as a dead entity not as a living enterprise. Spirituality might present an alluring image to sociology, but hardly one to conjure with by a discipline dedicated to higher analytical matters. As a term, spirituality betokens matters of the spirit world, issues of animism, ecstasy, magic and spells that sociology tends to treat with the utmost reserve, if not disdain. These are will-o'-the-wisp the enlightened forces of modernity have long blown away. But spirituality does not only relate to supernatural forces; it bears on the recognition and pursuit of matters of ultimate concern that lie beyond the limits of the corporeal and the social. As a member of the humanities, sociology is called to affirm matters of the spirit. In doing so, it confronts a conundrum peculiar to the discipline. The modernity that facilitated the birth of sociology is infused with capacities to kill the spirit. This was a matter of deep perplexity to Weber, Simmel and Durkheim. The de-spiritualisation of culture was something they prophesied to a discipline denied the means of resisting what seems for many the inevitable fate of modernity.

Spirituality signifies an indispensable dimension of what it is to be human. In the spirit, the social actor finds ambition, animation and exultation that all move and mobilise the self to reach beyond itself, to find powers that make humans small divinities pursuing destinies that transcend the mundane necessities of the immediate and the temporal. In reaching to surpass, the limits of self-endeavour become horribly plain. The actor sees what to grasp but the reaching eludes. Spirituality is not only about what is beyond human limits; it is the sensibility of incompleteness in the journeying. For something so intangible, spirituality produces its own tangibilities felt and known by those with the wisdom to quest and perhaps to find. Those with spiritual powers know what it is to be touched by them. Yet, oddly, those who come closest to the realms of spirituality seem to be struck dumb in articulating adequately what they feel they discerned. Oracles, prophets and seers exercising spiritual powers of vision belong to worlds of anthropology, but also to those sociology inhabits. These powers bear reflection in mysticism and meditation. They come to be embodied in Weber's notion of charisma, the wild card that wields such authority.

But who 'owns' these powers? Are they of magic, or theology? Who channels these and who is authorised to do so? More importantly, who defines what spirituality is? Does it require reference to some ecclesial authority or to some social ordering, or is its authentic location in the hinterland of the individual where the self finds its ultimate destination, its own unique source of transcendence? Perhaps sociology is wise in its customs to keep the issue of spirituality at bay? As a phenomenon, spirituality is something subjective, experiential, non-rational, unverifiable and serendipitous in its eruptions, all properties an enlightened sociology finds difficult to transpose into the ordering argot of the discipline.

Spirituality partly overlaps with theology, but also belongs to religion in terms of channelling, reproducing and stipulating uses and forms of incorporation; it relates to what is proper to metaphysics, its cold study, but also to the needs of the self for an inner warmth, something mysteriously supplied; it realises emotions whose testimonies are persuasive but also profoundly inexact; it inheres in the social in the subjective realms of appropriation, but then its external manifestations provide an objective facet in the frames that cradle its coming and manifest its infusion to each and all; yet it is available to some but then decidedly unavailable to others, either due to denial or incapacity to discern; its expression can be remarkably and mysteriously variable; and finally, it lies within the realm of technique, in manipulations that place the self by its own efforts into the laps of the gods, but for others it is a transcendent phenomenon, one whose ultimate source lies outside self-endeavour, in a God who comes and goes with Divine discretion. Spirituality is of the ultimate, but also the supernatural. Both seem melded together, but then for others they are separate, belonging to different compartments of life and beyond. Universal and highly specific, outside time, yet within it and confined to realms of the social or the self, chasing spirituality around the sociological table is like trying to squeeze mercury with a nutcracker. Yet, despite all these paradoxes, mysteries and conundrums sociology needs to attend to spirituality. It has a habit of springing up in terrains very proper to sociological concerns.

As the social unsettles in modernisation and progress, these unsettlements generate sensibilities of inadequacy which only spirituality can heal, embody and transcend. Culture is but a shell awaiting spiritual fillings, a point that seems subject to endless rediscovery. Thus, many movements vie to mix ingredients in culture and to place these advantageously to harness distinctive spiritual powers best fitted for the needs of the times. This lends an adjectival property to spirituality. Thus, expressed in Celtic varieties, in feminism or in New Age, spirituality gives vent to ultimate aspirations and is the propulsion that moves them from insignificance of cultural station to dalliances with higher matters.

Collective memory invokes a sense of loss, of nostalgia for times of a golden age when the gods touched the rims of culture and made them spin in animation and exultation. As modernity moves memory on, an increasing awareness arises that in the cultural cracks effected by progress, something of the spirit has escaped. Paradoxically, the powers of modernity to destroy the gods produce forces that seek their resuscitation. The genius of modernity to wrap displacement with the colours of liberty is matched by angsts it generates over the price demanded for being dressed by the light of reason. Something has been misplaced in the displacements wrought by modernity hence its concerns with Diaspora, exile and alienation. What modernity took with the one hand is given back with the other. It consoles for what it took, and it offers to re-invent what it discarded. Dalliances with modernity invite hope of recovery of what it inadvertently destroyed.

A curious outcome of modernity is the sense of floating on a sea of culture with no tides and no sensibilities of ebb and flow. Life in the dead sea of modernity generates its own revolts but also its own projects of recovery. These are familiar. The neo-Gothic revival and the Romantic movements are cases in point. Revival and redemption spring from the movements of modernity and these find expression in the emergence of nationalism.

Seeking to heal displacement and standing for the recovery of the spirit of a nation crushed by the engines of colonisation, cultural nationalism expresses the brokenness of a people but invites hope for their healing. The Celtic revival, of drama and poetry that served to kindle fires of insurrection, summoned ghosts from the Irish past. These past heroes and heroines came to strut again on the field of culture, in song, saga and sentiment, all serving to revitalise a people whose spirit had been extinguished by the light of progress: British rule in Ireland. In his quest for renewal and creativity, Yeats felt bound to 'to fling his soul/Upon the growing gloom' (cited in Heaney 1991: 788). Heaney suggests that in the poetry of Yeats is to be found the power of 'knitted thought'. It is to experience again 'the force of what he called "the spiritual intellect's great work"' and perhaps to find what he sought in his nationalism, 'an ideal if unattainable "Unity of Being"' (Heaney 1991: 790). Married to the notion of the nation, the spirit moved in ways reason alone could not.

It is in appeal to memory that the spiritual finds its greatest powers. It calls society back to reverence what should be marked as sacred, to what needs honouring and commemorating, if the highest manifestations and ambitions of a culture are to be sustained (Misztal 2004: 67–84). When what is of the highest ideal is proclaimed, spirituality is invoked to clothe the rhetoric and to give persuasion to appeals to the sublime. This can occur in the most secular of realms, in Irish history in its purest republican mode. An illustration of this appears in Emmet's famous speech from the dock in Dublin, made before being sentenced to death by hanging for leading an insurrection that failed in 1803. His justification was not based on an appeal to the cold clammy claims of reason but to the spirituality that animated the blood of the nation. Invoking an appeal to destiny, he claimed to fulfil one by his death. He spoke of his ministry now ended, of the lamp of his life being nearly extinguished, and of the prospect of being parted from 'everything that was dear to me in this life, and for my country's cause with the idol of my soul, the object of my affections' (Edwards et al. 1968: 83). Until his country was free, he proclaimed, nobody could write his epitaph.

The duty to write accurate inscriptions in the proper circumstances of a post-colonial existence became an imperative that ricocheted down through Irish history.

The call to martyrdom was made by appeal to spiritual rhetoric that infused nationalism and converted it into an irresistible force. Paradoxically, his appeal to a common citizenship and to the edicts of French republicanism involved acceptance of the tenets of secularisation that facilitated their formulation, yet to accomplish their ends the powers, forces and rhetoric of spirituality had to be invoked to give motive force to his vision. This property of paradox can be found at the heart of sociology itself. Spirituality supplies a vision the light of reason reveals only darkly. Pushed to its limits, sociology might study spirituality, but it hardly seems to have aspirations to embody it. Yet this would be to miss sociology's own perorations on its own destiny, and these Weber famously supplied in his essay 'Science as a Vocation'.

There the need is affirmed to meet '"the demands of the day", in human relations as well as in our vocation' (Weber 1946: 156). This calling is 'plain and simple, if each finds and obeys the demon who holds the fibers of his very life' (Weber 1946: 156). It is perhaps typical that Weber should make dark descent to the demon within as the ultimate reference point for the calling of sociology. As Weber is to the gloomy side of spirituality, Simmel is to its light, a point explored in Varga's chapter in this collection. Simmel had the most marked concern with spirituality of all the founding fathers of the discipline and this is evident in his essays on religion (Simmel 1997). Weber, however, is supplying something different in his approach to spiritual matters, the way sociology is caught in bleak outcomes where it is a symptom of a state of affairs it is fated to analyse but never to redeem. It is like modernity – sociology unsprings what it cannot close.

Like Simmel, Weber's concerns were directed to the de-spiritualisation of culture. At the end of *The Protestant Ethic*, Weber encapsulates well the world sociology faces, where the ascetic justification for stewardship had passed, and material goods have 'inexorable power over the lives of men' in ways without precedent. 'Victorious capitalism' has won and needed Calvinist warrant no more. But then, 'the rosy blush of its laughing heir, the Enlightenment, seems also to be irretrievably fading, and the idea of duty to one's calling prowls about in our lives like the ghost of dead religious beliefs'. The detachment of a duty of calling from the highest spiritual and culture values leads to the abandonment of its justification and so Weber gloomily characterised the last stage of this cultural development as the victory of 'specialists without spirit, sensualists without heart; this nullity imagines that it has attained a level of civilization never before achieved' (Weber 1930: 181–2). The sense that there is something cadaverous about modernity finds apt and more recent expression in Carroll's recent dirge (2004). Yet Weber also dealt with resuscitations of the spirit, most notably in his notion of charisma. His formulation of this gift of the spirit comes close to traditional Christian formulations of spirituality (Fyffe 1920: 808–10). Matters of the spirit and soul were also of deep concern to Durkheim, and these are subsumed under his notions of piacular rites and collective effervescence.

If postmodernity is the maturation of modernity, an unexpected outcome has been the quest for enchantment, for a 'magicing' of the spirit (Flanagan 1996). One needs only to refer to the books and films on Harry Potter or to *The Lord of the Rings* as examples of this trend in popular culture. In its wider remit, sociology might be more receptive to the spiritual than some might think.

A sociology of spirituality encompasses many concerns of the wider discipline of sociology itself and some of these are well represented in the collection. The self, embodiment, identity, visual culture, responses to postmodernity in diverse forms of seeking, the spiritual interests of Simmel, gender, relationships with other disciplines, notably theology all point to issues of enormous sociological and cultural importance. These issues are matters of debate of the moment and this collection, utilising contributors with a very broad span of interests and positions, hopes to illuminate a topic of unfolding importance. How has it come to pass that spirituality might be considered a sociological term of the moment?

Because spirituality is such a difficult term to define, it can provide a broad junction for many concepts of sociological interest to pass across. Spirituality illuminates facets of culture in ways other concepts cannot supply. In addition, spirituality has become a topic of unavoidable sociological interest. It seems to express and fulfil the cultural needs of the moment.

First, the traits of postmodernity, the nihilism and cynicism that marked concerns in the 1990s, have now encountered limits of disbelief; hence the turn to hope, to trust and to the need to consider matters of ultimate veracity. This present cultural moment seems populated with too many false gods, icons and supposedly charismatic figures, who are very often creatures of the public relations industry. The millennium celebrations also brought matters of the ultimate into focus, but above all the terrorist attack of 9/11 intensified a sense that the spiritual did count. This was an event that many witnessed and many found themselves at a loss before such an event so tragic and which they seemed powerless to prevent or to counter. Civil arrangements were rattled and unreflected routines were cast asunder. Matters seem to have become increasingly contingent, not in the manner of armchair speculations of sociology, but in the lives of the citizenry. The rise of religious fundamentalism in the Middle East and in the West and worries about the environment and climate change added to a sense of how diminutive the self had become in the face of forces that increasingly had a potential to engulf.

The turn to interest in spiritual matters reflects an earlier turning, one that shaped the images and priorities of the counterculture some 40 years earlier. Partly a Romantic movement, but also a revolt against the artificiality of modernity, the counterculture had a strong spiritual dimension to its questings and the unsettlements it reflected. Since then, culture has become more complicated and more confused.

The culture landscape has changed utterly and what was predicted by Adorno and Benjamin in the 1930s has been intensified and speeded up in a diversity of technological forms, such as the Internet, in ways they could never envisaged. Rootless, restless, and operating alone, with solace a scarcity, the self has come to stand as the only certainty, the only entity deserving of ultimate exploration when what seemed of enduring significance in the social has been fractured brick by brick. In peering through the gaps to see, there seems little to discern, hence the imperative to cultivate an interior gaze, to search for matters of enduring and ultimate concern in the most obvious place – within the self.

Secondly, this interior questing is linked to the growing importance of the body as a cultural and symbolic entity, a site of increasing sociological significance. This consciousness of embodiment leads to sensibilities of spirituality (Beckford 2003: 206–9). Yet, oddly, for some, this spiritual enlargement occurred *despite* organised religion – not *because* of it. Indeed, these new forms of spirituality operate often outside organised religions and mark a vote of no confidence in the latter's capacity to provide authentic channels for the spiritual. In one sense, secularisation has won. Organised religion has been weakened greatly. Yet, spirituality does not seem to have suffered the same fate. It has become the solace of soul survivors who journey outside organised religion. They find their own uses for spirituality and make their own destinies. Thus, spirituality is increasingly treated as a force, a resource of self-empowerment and expressiveness, democratised and available to all. In the quest for health of body and soul, the holistic opportunities presented by spirituality are available for the self to appropriate and to find its own criteria of validation within. Holistic spirituality offers the self the prospect of ultimate self-mastery through technique though, as in the case of Calvinism and capitalism, the prime casualty is again the ascetic. These notions of spirituality as an ultimate resource are by no means confined to the individual; they emerge also in institutions.

This trend is well illustrated in an advertisement in the *Church Times* (26 November 2004) for the post of 'Inter-faith and Spiritual Care Manager' in a high secure hospital. Duties included developing service provision for and appraisal of the spiritual needs of service users, carers and staff. In addition, the manager would be responsible 'for the assigned Chapel, Mosque and other places identified for the purpose of Spiritual Care'. The wording of the advertisement is significant. The term chaplain no longer appears, the implication being that the cure of all souls is no longer an exclusive preserve of the Established Church in England. But there is another implication that the state Church is delivering the 'wrong' spirituality, one that is out of kilter with the needs and expectations of the times. There is an increasing realisation in the health services in the United Kingdom that staff who cure and heal, but who cannot utilise the services of Christian clergy, need to make their own provisions to cope with matters pertaining to spirituality. Suffering, death, depression, healing and anxiety have inescapable spiritual dimensions and these emerge, especially in the practice of nursing. Reflection, meditation, well-being and the management of grief have become nursing skills where spirituality is mobilised as a coping mechanism both for the nurses and their patients (Robinson et al. 2003).

This institutionalisation of spiritual provision illustrates the degree to which holistic spirituality is not just a matter of the self and the culture of individualism that facilitates its basis. Even though detached from religion, and indeed a replacement of it, spirituality in its corporate and institutional appropriations risks evolving into a virtual religion (Flanagan 2004: 14–41). These appropriations of spirituality from organised religions are not the result of some accident or some serendipitous outcome of secularity. These involve a define strategy of replacement of organised religion, notably Christianity in the United Kingdom, particularly in sectors of education and health care.

As Christianity continues to weaken in large parts of the United Kingdom, this has provided an opportunity to affirm non-sectarian and inclusive values. Spirituality is an important aspect of this strategy, for it can be sold as warding off the dangers of religionism but also filling the vacuum that emerges from the decline of religion (Wright 2000: 84–9). In the vacuum left by institutional religion, the need to develop alternative sources for spirituality in the classroom have become more self-evident. Ironically, the one sector of education seemingly exempt from these concerns with spirituality is higher education. Academic theology, that might have given witness to the spiritual needs of the secular university, seems to have adjusted too well to the landscape to do so (Flanagan 1996: 89–99; D'Costa 2005).

Thirdly, as these new forms of spirituality emerge, issues have arisen over who owns these, by what authority do they operate and according to what criteria are they to be evaluated. These new forms place sociology in a novel situation of having to arbitrate on the forms through which spirituality is channelled. Increasingly, there is in operation what Brown (1997) terms a 'spiritual commerce'. In this trade, clients need enablers, those who can tap in and turn on spiritual powers. These diviners can sell bogus wares in a spiritual marketplace, entrapping the theologically witless and those seeking quick fix spiritual solutions for their restless souls. In this regard, the privatisation of spirituality enables psychology to replace theology as the arbiter on practice and wholeness. The outcome can be less than satisfactory, producing what Carrette and King describe as 'the new *cultural prozac*', a sedative that renders spirituality ripe for capitalist plucking. Ironically, what they suggest is that 'in the very act of freeing the mind from the dogma of religion, consumers [have] now entered the thought-control of individualism' (Carrette and King 2005: 77). They go on to add that privatised spirituality 'fails to acknowledge the interdependence of the self within community and the ethical necessity of countering the abuses of power within market societies' (Carrette and King 2005: 78)

Sociologists sympathetic to the emergence of holistic spirituality tend to accept by default the notion it portrays of organised religions as being incapable of meeting the spiritual needs of present Western society in all its sophistications. It would come as a great surprise to many adherents of organised religions that their practices, beliefs and traditions yielded no spiritual fruit. Holistic spirituality attracts many adherents who have been displaced by choice or circumstance from organised religions. In making their own destinies, their tales and testimonies inevitably attract more sociological attention than those who stay in ecclesial homes and seemingly have no need to quest alone. As in many other areas, spirituality too has its own politics. There are also other manifestos in town.

Catholicism can still make claims for spirituality as life in the Holy Spirit and the channelling of Divine grace through sacraments and sacramentals. It has its own schools of spiritual direction and formation, deep repositories of wisdom and many virtuosi worthy of emulation. Lives lived in spiritual edification seek to engage with God, not the self. Spiritual paths based on monastic life can be pursued in the routines of everyday life (Taylor 1989). Other great world religions such as Buddhism, Islam and Judaism have matching tales and testimonies and stores of wealth and experience about how to pursue spiritual excellence. Yet, despite this wealth of testimony and tradition, there is a feeling that paths to spiritual enlightenment have been colonised by academic disciplines. In chapter 1, Holmes displays the scale and width of academic interests in spirituality. Increasingly, to seek spiritual wisdom, one searches the shelves of *Borders* for guidance.

Fourthly, for the past 40 years, there has been a fascination with the dark side of spirituality in horror films, such as *The Omen* (1976) and its successors. In this regard, it might seem the devil had all the best films. Dracula sucked blood and stole spiritual identities with ghastly impunity to the delight of many teenagers. The Hollywood dream machine moved into the provision of nightmares for the credulous with haunted houses, grave stealing and every horror that would excite the spiritual imagination. Somehow, the spirituality of the night had won over the forms of manifestation more fitted for the day. Set in ecclesial culture in the 1970s, the neo-Gothic seemed to be a barrier to reaching into modernity. Unfortunately, in treating the neo-Gothic as unfit to bear the light of belief, theologians passed it over to the entertainment industry that managed to see profits looming from the dark. What theologians cast as irrelevant, the carpetbaggers of culture found deeply relevant. These cultural forms of spiritual darkness might well be treated as innocuous, yet their emergence coincided with loss of a capacity in Catholicism to instil fear and trembling in its flock – theologians passed such a grim task over to the entertainment industry.

As postmodernity pointed to a void in the 1990s, there was a sense of danger in the emptiness, an awaiting that came into focus as a matter of concern with the Millennium commemorations. Another ghost emerged in the 1980s that underlay the emergence of spirituality. Its appearance divided critics of society. At one level, religious fundamentalism offered a praiseworthy resistance to the vacuity of modernity, but at another level it posed a threat to its basis. The zeal of Islam in matters of sexuality generated profound discomfort, as did the creationism of Evangelical groups who sought to impose their views in sectors of education. Somehow society seemed to be going back to go forward. The past shrouded in the ethos of spirituality keeps coming back unpredictably and frequently.

This is well illustrated in the publicity and controversy surrounding the book and the film of *The Da Vinci Code*. Selling over 40 million copies, as one writes in May 2006, with the film version looking likely to have an equally large cultural impact, the book attacks the truth of the Gospels in ways that have uniquely captured the public imagination. The significance of the book lies in the opportunity it offers each reader to believe that Christianity is a conspiracy not so much against reason as against history, that its God was no god, and that the lonely quest of those outside ecclesial cultures to find their own spirituality is justified. That the book is a work of fiction is beside the point; it affirms what many are desperate to believe, that the clutches of Christianity grip no more. Perhaps there are some with wit who will go back to the Gospels or investigate Gnosticism on a website. Yet, whatever the outcome, the book slays a crucial facet of secularity: indifference. Christianity is showing plenty of evidence of fighting back against a conspiracy of disbelief. The charge of incredulity made against Christianity is turned around and directed to those who believe in the veracity of *The Da Vinci Code* and who make a pilgrim's progress around Europe to see its landmarks. Other forms of emergence of spirituality have attracted sociological interest for what they indicate about the state of culture and the movements of identity and identification within it. In this regard, culture itself is taking some odd turns.

Since the mid-1990s, spirituality has emerged as an American concern, notably in the works of Wade Clark Roof and Robert Wuthnow. But it is a spirituality cast in a particular form and derived from particular cultural circumstances. It is a specific brand of spirituality, one that reflects an uncoupling from institutional religion and builds on American traditions of self-improvement. It embodies a pioneering spirit, combined with an expectation that spirituality should be meaningful, moving and expressive, notions derived from influences of Eastern religions and forms of mysticism. Pragmatism and Protestantism underlie these new forms of spirituality, but any notion that these forms of spirituality are peculiarly American is undermined by the noteworthy study of Kendal, England, published after the conference upon which this collection is based. The Kendal Project asserted that holistic spirituality (the shorthand for new forms, loosely connected to New Age religions) is set to replace institutional religion (Heelas and Woodhead 2005). They provide their own reflections on the study in Chapters 3 and 6. But in looking at Census statistics, the state of religion in parts of the United Kingdom is rather contradictory.

For the first time since 1851, the 2001 census of England, Wales and Scotland collected information on religious affiliation and some contradictions were revealed in its findings. In the overall table, on religion in England and Wales, 72 per cent (37.3 million) respondents declared themselves to be Christian, a figure decidedly at odds with the 4 million or so who could be treated as weekly churchgoers. But the other surprising figure related to New Age religions where only 904 in England and Wales defined themselves accordingly.[1] The figures on self-declared Christians might reflect desirability rather than actual affiliation, a cultural claim to identity, or a highly inflated degree of agnosticism. Yet, without further research, one can only take these self-declarations at face value. These two sets of figures, one too high and the other too low, underline the importance of the Kendal study but also some of the criticisms made of its methodology and inferences in Chapter 2 by Voas and Bruce in this collection.

The miniscule numbers declaring themselves members of New Age religions are perplexing. There are reasons for thinking that New Age religions have peaked in interest. It is notable that Heelas, who pioneered much sociological work on New Age religions, downplays linkages with these in his treatment with Woodhead of holistic spirituality (Heelas and Woodhead 2005). Is holistic spirituality an outcome of New Age religion or is it an entirely separate development, a particular response to present social circumstances? If holistic spirituality has outgrown its New Age period of exuberance, how should sociology respond? A recent Vatican document on New

---

1   2001 Census Commissioners table (M275) supplied by the Office for National Statistics.

Age religions and their forms of spirituality provided some pointers for sociological consideration (Pontifical Council for Culture 2003).

Although the intention of the document is theological, it grasps an important point, that these new forms of spirituality express a cultural moment or tendency. The New Age is a child of contemporary culture but it also expresses an old heresy, one of the second and third centuries – Gnosticism. Alternative spiritualities are by no means new and have lineages that go back to the eighteenth century. Many of the factors affecting present treatments of holistic spirituality can be traced back to the late 1960s and early 1970s, when a counterculture established an agenda in the USA that profoundly, if not fatefully, reshaped the main churches (Oppenheimer 2003).

It might be argued that capitulation to these insurrectionary forces destabilised organised religion, so that in seeking to modernise (seemingly without apparent limit) a condition of anomie emerged. A symbolic violence was effected, and a process of internal secularisation commenced, unrecognised, but whose growth seems irresistible, all of which set expectations that spiritual endeavour did not need an ecclesiastical cradle for nurture and growth. Spiritual seeking could be undertaken unfettered by institutional constraints. Given the uncertainty that descended on Catholicism after Vatican II, it is not surprising that many Catholics left to forge their spiritual destinies elsewhere and alone.

In dealing with holistic spirituality, sociology faces a dual problem, of an endless diversity of forms of channelling and expression of a phenomenon that is also uniquely resistant to a common and acceptable definition. Is sociology to treat this infinite aggregate of beliefs and practices as a religion, even though for many, it represents a form of emancipation from the constraints of one? Is holistic spirituality simply a response to cultural circumstances and is nothing more than a form of leisure or therapy devoid of deeper theological significance? Even if holistic spirituality operates outside the ambit of religion, it still demands sociological scrutiny for the cultural needs it fulfils. If these new forms of spirituality reflect a restlessness of the self, deriving their mandate from individualism, is the social, in terms of capital and bonding, rather than religion, the prime casualty of such solitary expressiveness? Clearly, holistic spirituality, as with other forms, is incomplete without a wider ambit or setting to which it can be attached. This is the endemic problem of spirituality: it demands contextualisation. But if spirituality is contextualised, by what set of presuppositions is its significance to be read and understood? Whatever its good intentions, there are dysfunctional properties to the pursuit of holistic spirituality.

The quest for the spiritual located within, and strictly in reference to the interior, might mark an egoism that subtracts from the social. The present Pope identified one of the most pernicious effects of a philosophy of egoism that it produces a set 'of strategies to reduce the number of those who will eat at humanity's table' (Pontifical 2003: 20). Similar worries over the effects of holistic spirituality on the social fabric have also emerged in Judaism (Sacks 2005). In this regard it might seem that the present Pope and Durkheim have made an unexpected alliance over the status of the social and the state of the communal basis of religion in the face of competition from holistic spirituality.

The trouble with spirituality is that its opacity admits too much but precludes too little. It can be attached to religion but it can also operate in detached forms. Zinnbauer et al. (1997: 551, 561) are right to argue that in looking at spirituality as separate from religiousness, the new forms have taken many properties from the latter and notably in regard to matters of the sacred. The sacred is one property that compromises efforts to separate spirituality from religiousness (Seidlitz et al. 2002). As long as the sacred hovers around matters of spirituality, then a potential for realisation will always be there. This suggests that holistic spirituality might well be a refuge from organised religion, but that its aggregate always signifies a potential to be harnessed into one. The pitfalls spirituality presents, of its indefinite locations in culture, the individual, organised religion, and its potential to be about the ultimate or about the supernatural, or about God or gods, or none at all, should not preclude its study and sociological appreciation. Spirituality is simply too important a topic in present culture to be left out of sociological account.

In 2002, spirituality was proposed as a theme for a future annual conference of the British Sociological Association Sociology of Religion Study Group. The conference was held in 2004 at the University of Bristol. Papers were sought on spirituality in relation to the classical tradition, civics and education, conversion, emotion and healing, authority and ritual, relationships to other disciplines, and images and models of the afterlife. The conference attracted over 70 delegates, with a significant number from overseas. The conference was greatly assisted by a plenary paper by Professor Jéan Seguy, who might well be described as the father of French sociology of religion. Drawing from his published works, his paper 'Sociology and Spiritualities: the French case' opened out a vision of disciplinary possibilities. Unfortunately, owing to limits of space, we have been only able to publish a selection of the 34 papers given.

As a sociological venture into an unknown territory, the use of the indefinite article in the title of the collection suggests hesitancy over how to characterise an elusive phenomenon, such as spirituality. Although the notion of spirituality is profoundly indefinite, there is an expectation that a sociological collection on the topic should have definite and identifiable properties. In seeking a sociological voice for the topic, the editors are all too aware of the plethora of literatures in adjacent areas, such as theology, religious studies, anthropology and psychology, to name a few. At a time when a premium is placed on interdisciplinary work, it might seem perverse to work the issue of spirituality back into a specific discipline: sociology.

The axis of the collection moves around the location of spirituality either as a phenomenon that operates outside organised religion, or within. This issue of contextualisation generates distinctive sociological issues regarding the cultural basis of the phenomenon, its ebb and flow, but also questions of channelling and authority. Is spirituality something free floating and individualised, as in the case of holistic spirituality, or is it a property of organised religion, the site where it authoritatively belongs? A further question emerges. Is the rise of holistic spirituality due to a failure to spiritualise by organised religion and to that degree is an outcome of forces of secularisation? If there is a seeking and questing in culture, how is sociology to arbitrate on this process?

The ordering of the contributions to the collection reflects these points. The first half of the collection presents six essays that deal with spirituality on the outside of organised religion. The second half casts spirituality in the direction of organised religion, notably Islam, Catholicism and more diffuse forms of Christianity. In the conclusion, the editors reflect on the openings spirituality offers to sociology for further research. It is a topic in the ascendant and its implications have many sociological ramifications. The contributors to the collection have made notable efforts to reflect on a new territory for sociology that is well worth mapping and exploration.

In Chapter 1, Holmes, drawing on an extensive bibliography, amply illustrates the interdisciplinary nature of spirituality. In his assessment of spirituality in seven disciplinary areas, the problem of its definition is raised early. He seeks to characterise spirituality in ways that operate adjacent to Christianity, arguing that disillusionment with material values, loss of religious faith and scepticism regarding 'success' have given rise to societal interests in spirituality that are reflected in academic discourse. But Holmes raises an intriguing question as to whether spirituality is by definition something multi-disciplinary, or is some form of disciplinary specialisation required? In his assessment of how disciplines formulate concerns with spirituality, some seem better placed than others to deal with it. As a topic, spirituality relates closely to psychology, medicine and health care and education but less clearly to sociology. In fact he suggests that sociology lags behind these. This tardiness in relation to the topic is itself a sociological question as to why sociology has been immune to movements in adjacent disciplines that have taken on board the implications of spirituality.

The Kendal study by Heelas and Woodhead of holistic spirituality can be treated as a new landmark in the sociology of religion in the United Kingdom. It was a detailed study of holistic spirituality and its practice in a town in the North West of England. The premises of the study rested on the recent subjective turn in culture, the rise of individualism and the growth of expressivism in a marketplace of practice. The claim by Heelas and Woodhead that these new forms of spirituality are set to displace organised religion, notably in Christianity has aroused considerable debate. While acknowledging the significance of the study, Voas and Bruce offer criticisms of the assumptions of the Kendal study regarding the notion of spirituality used, how it is measured and what they conceive to be methodological flaws in the research.

Their criticisms centre on the counting of holistic spiritual activities and on multiple attendances that inflate incidences of practice. They claim that self-interpretation and self-accounting conflate practices, that are really therapeutic or leisure activities, into notions of spiritually. To confirm this point, they note that few of the activities listed in the Kendal Project are clearly spiritual and also that few relate to matters of the supernatural or the sacred. They assert that arguments for secularisation remain intact and are not affected by claims regarding the emergence of 'new' forms of holistic spirituality. In their interpretation, the transmission of holistic spirituality is in similar demographic terms of plight to organised religion and so they argue that the projections of Woodhead and Heelas regarding its replacement are misplaced. In short, they feel the importance of alternative forms of spirituality has been exaggerated. Whatever the case, they suggest that the constituencies involved in holistic spirituality need to be explored further.

As the Principal Applicant for the grant that funded 'The Kendal Problem', Heelas in Chapter 3 reflects on the criticisms of Voas and Bruce. His detailed, careful and constructive response adds much to understanding a topic, holistic spirituality, whose sociological significance can only increase. He meets head on some of the points of criticism Voas and Bruce raise – the difficulties of comparing the holistic milieu with the congregational domain; of estimating the numbers in Kendal involved in these forms of spirituality; the methodological problems of multiple participants; and the issue of what constitutes the spiritual. Central to Heelas's defence of the project is the subjectivisation thesis and this forms a crucial basis for understanding the advent and expansion of holistic spirituality. A prospect is offered of limitless realisation and many seek to accept what it offers. In his chapter, especially in its second half, Heelas defends the authenticity of holistic spirituality, the self-awareness of its practitioners, its relevance to youth, and above all the affirming and humanising ethos of a concern with the spirit. Holistic spirituality is defended as autonomous and separate from Christianity. A rather different view of the link between new forms of spirituality and Christianity emerges in Chapters 4 and 5.

Droogers and Versteeg draw their contributions from a research programme entitled 'Between Secularisation and Sacralisation' undertaken in the Department of Social and Cultural Anthropology at the Free University of Amsterdam. In Chapter 4, Droogers, who directs the programme, provides an overview of its research as undertaken by postgraduates. Unfortunately, there is no equivalent to this programme in the United Kingdom. Droogers's chapter is especially valuable in drawing out a justification for a qualitative approach to the study of religion and spirituality, building on the quantitative approaches of his Dutch colleagues in the sociology of religion. His account of 'relay writing' as a means of working out the focus of the research programme will be of interest. The notion of secularisation as the motive force of individualism is well made, but Droogers's chapter draws attention to an important point. Individualism might well emerge as a property of postmodernity, but its genesis also lies in cultural and religious traditions, a point Droogers draws out specifically in relation to The Netherlands.

A particular attraction of the two chapters is the way they handle the domestic responses of the Churches to secularisation and to competition from alternative forms of spirituality. Assimilation and accommodation mark their responses, in particular affirming the liberal basis of Dutch Catholicism. There is a stimulating untidiness to the findings from the five research programmes that conveys a sense of contact with their ecclesial tribes. The contribution from Droogers links back to some themes that emerged in the Kendal study, but he suggests that the Dutch experience is somewhat different. He points to the growth of 'individual repertoires' that operate both inside *and* outside religious institutions. His main lesson drawn from The Netherlands is that secularisation and sacralisation operate together in a paradoxical way, so that institutional religion is undermined by the former but in the latter can be found a quest to experience religiosity. Thus a rather different but complex and paradoxical notion of spirituality emerges. The tales of self-accounting about spirituality require further investigation. Droogers's plea is for both methodologies, quantitative and qualitative to be involved in this venture. The strengths of the programme in drawing attention to what it is easy to miss are well illustrated in the companion piece from Versteeg in Chapter 5.

Versteeg's chapter deals with Catholicism and the variety of spiritualities that operate within its ambit, mainly catered for by religious orders, whose traditions might be deemed more orthodox in terms of the forms of spirituality they have hitherto recognised. His chapter is concerned with what he terms marginal spirituality in the context of secularisation. This underlines an important point of the collection, that the location of spirituality greatly affects the type, style and form of verification employed, whether by the self or others. Versteeg's chapter illustrates well the competition that occurs between differing forms of spirituality and how they are blended in a liberal ethos of religious orders reformulating their goals and seeking to keep connected to a culture that is perhaps changing in ways they do not approve. The methodological reflections in the chapter will be noted.

Versteeg confronts an issue the previous three chapters do not consider – Christian spirituality. His interest is in Catholic retreat centres, and the spiritual formation and guidance these give. The market-based nature of contemporary spirituality is well illustrated in his chapter. An issue starts to emerge, touched on in Chapters 2 and 3 – that the clients for these centres tend to be predominantly middle aged, middle class and female. Again, the issue of transmission emerges in the notion of living off a spiritual capital (in this case of Catholicism) but of not being committed to it as an investment in its growth. Clients are seeking a personalised spirituality. Versteeg has a useful section on techniques of self-experience that illustrates well how formation is undertaken and how spiritual growth is developed. The 'this worldly' form of spirituality (as he terms it) uncovered in these centres focuses on the self and to that degree takes on holistic, expressive forms that echo the values uncovered in the Kendal study. The theological end of spirituality in these centres emerges as inchoate, unfocused, and indeed, marginalised.

The point Holmes made in Chapter 1, regarding the unevenness of response of academic disciplines, also applies in relation to gender. Earlier in Chapter 2, Voas and Bruce observed the significance of the holistic milieu for women. In her Chapter 6, Woodhead investigates the issue of gender further. Drawing from the Kendal study, she seeks a purely sociological account for this gender imbalance in holistic spirituality. As she suggests in the introduction to her chapter, the issue involves relatively uncharted territory. She claims there was a gender-blindness in the theoretical frameworks used to interpret the findings of the Kendal study. The subjective turn marks an expansion of cultural expectations. This coincides with changes in the relation of work to leisure, but in ways that are to the benefit of males, not females. The outlets open to males in leisure activities that give vent to their needs of expressiveness are unavailable to females. Holistic spirituality offers women the means of exploring an identity in cultural circumstances they can control. Thus, in this milieu they can discover subjective fulfilments and satisfactions unavailable elsewhere. As Woodhead suggests, beauty, health and self-identity are entities that lead to 'deeper' realms of the psyche and the soul. The needs of identity holistic spiritualities supply partly account for the gender imbalance in their appropriation. In the milieu of holistic spiritualities, women can find a 'safe' place to explore matters of identity and emotion. A rather different connection between women, spirituality and identity is explored in Chapter 7.

This chapter marks a turn in the collection towards the pursuit of spirituality within organised religion, in this case Islam. Chambers is concerned with the civil rights of Islamic women who wish to veil in public. In wearing the *hijab* or headscarf, these women seek to express spiritual values in the identity they present in European societies where civil rights are enshrined. In exercising these rights, these women, notably in France and Holland come into conflict with assumptions regarding the expression of religion in civil and educational institutions and in the workplace. In France, since the Revolution, secularisation has been a crucial political value, and the State exercises zeal in marking limits to the display of religious symbols in the public arena. These limitations conflict with Islamic rights for free religious expression and veiling has come to symbolise these hopes and expectations. Chambers explores the conflicts between the two cultures, providing a novel twist to the agenda of politics of spirituality.

The issue of embodiment and spirituality starts to emerge in this chapter, when Chambers uses the notions of boundaries drawn from Mary Douglas to express how these women make their mark and express their spiritual and symbolic sensibilities. The notion of 'frontier bodies' is well related to the politics of spiritual identity. Chambers suggests that these issues point to wider questions of the state and spirituality. These direct sociological attention away from matters of subjectivity and individualism that mark the emergence of holistic spirituality. By resetting spirituality in the context of an organised religion, Chambers illustrates how the pursuit of identity has communal implications that can elicit state intervention. These issues of spirituality and communal identity are linked to matters of immigration and ethnicity thus providing a topical turn to the second part of his chapter. His contribution drives the issue of spirituality on to more familiar sociological landscapes. Their exploration might signify present necessities imposed on sociology that seem alien to its traditional concerns. But Varga's assessment of Simmel overturns this sociological prejudice against the incorporation of spiritual matters into its disciplinary domain.

Often regarded as the 'fourth man' of sociology, Simmel's star, of late, has been in the ascendant as his status is increasingly recognised as a progenitor of postmodernity and the provider of theoretical gifts to notable sociologists such as Bauman, Bourdieu and Goffman, to name a few. Using his own translations from the German, Varga provides a scholarly appraisal of the significance of spirituality in Simmel's sociology. In his notion of form and content, the notion of spirituality emerges and more specifically, as Varga demonstrates in the distinctions Simmel makes between religion and religiosity. Notions of individualism that emerged in previous chapters take on a different turn in the context of Simmel. The embodiment that emerges in Chapter 6 and that comes to the fore in Chapter 7 can be linked to the subjective sense of experience Simmel's notion of religiosity yields, an issue Varga explores in his chapter.

The value of Varga's chapter lies in how he links Simmel's notion of religiosity to contemporary debates on spirituality. He also draws out well how Simmel connects spirituality to social relationships, marking the possibility of a sociological turn away from the interior inspections of holistic spirituality. In his section on religion and postmodernity, Varga shows how issues raised by a linkage of these were anticipated by Simmel in his approach to subjective *and* objective facets of culture. It is in this area that contemporary questions of spirituality belong and these can lead in a theological direction and away from purely matters of religion. As Varga concludes, the spirituality that concerned Simmel emerged from cultural circumstances that made inescapable demands to consider the transcendent and the ultimate. Despite the forces of secularisation, these imperatives persist and as suggested earlier are embedded in the ambitions of sociology to be something more than a mere science in terms of what it stands to envision. But this generates a question that puzzles Giordan.

In Chapter 9, he ponders on how '"spirituality" has moved from the shadowy realms of theology to become a "fashionable" sociological concept'. As with Flanagan, in Chapter 12, he works from within the ambit of Catholic theology, but in the case of Giordan, his concern is with the 'particular' case of Italian Catholicism. There is a fresh quality to Giordan's perspectives as these are formulated within the ambit of Italian sociology of religion. The notion of spirituality generates a dilemma of choice for sociology as to which end to start the analysis from. Are holistic forms of spirituality the extra-mural activities of the disaffected who voluntarily cast themselves into ecclesial exile, and are therefore to be treated as creatures of disenchantment, or are these heroic seekers who quest alone, who feel more painfully the pulse of culture and are to be regarded as worthy travellers journeying to new horizons for enchantment?

Giordan links the emergence of spirituality to what he terms the 'crisis' of the concept of religion as it is reset in the context of globalisation, pluralism and the flow of recent events that have so unsettled. Contrary to the implicit assumptions of adherents of holistic spirituality, Giordan does not see spirituality as a crisis of disconnection from organised religion, but rather as yielding strategies of connection in re-arrangements wrought by the forces of secularisation. In this regard, his contribution bears on similar points made by Droogers in Chapter 4. As with others in the collection, Giordan links spiritual revivals in the present to efforts to rehumanise Western society that seems progressively to be ordered according to de-humanising considerations. He well indicates that the 'return' to spirituality within organised religions such as Catholicism is by no means new, but is endemic in its traditions. The dilemmas these 'returns' effect are by no means new. But what is new is the sociological realisation of the importance of spirituality emerging as a cultural need in Italian society, a point only grasped as recently as 2003.

In Giordan's perspective, spirituality is attached to religion, but in an unofficial almost residual form, where Catholicism can still make claims on Italian cultural sensibilities and the needs of identity that underpin these. To illuminate this state of affairs, Giordan invokes a wonderfully apt concept of Garelli, 'scenario religion'. This refers to a blunting of the significance of religion and its power to command. The term refers to a crisis of appropriation of what Giordan terms symbolic capital. The concept could be twinned with notions of 'implicit religion' and Davie's 'vicarious memory'. It is as if organised religion has slipped into the background; it is part of the fabric of culture, but its weave makes no demands for interpretation, scrutiny or commitment. In his account, spirituality and religion, contrary to the claims of the Kendal Project, are to be understood as interconnected. Somehow, alternative forms of spirituality face sterner tests in a Catholic ethos than in more individualistically prone Protestant settings.

As in the case of the Dutch contributions, one senses a struggle to find new interpretative categories to make sense of a rapidly shifting cultural and religious landscape where spirituality has emerged as an unexpected, pervasive and characterising phenomenon. The dilemmas of the individual and the institution, of the needs of objectivity and the urges of subjectivity, are not new, as Giordan reminds us. The present novelty lies in the problem of reconciling traditional forms of spirituality with current cultural needs to find and to secure their own authentic versions. Giordan's conclusion can be usefully contrasted to the insights of Versteeg in Chapter 5.

The interconnection between religion and spirituality that yields a resource of power is well explored in Chapter 10. Drawing from a wider study of the children of leading Anglican clergy, notably Bishops, Guest introduces an important concept – spiritual capital. Verter's term is of enormous importance, for it facilitates the placement of spirituality in the heart of sociology itself, not least in building on the insights of Bourdieu in regard to the reproduction of culture. Again, the location of spirituality is within a theology, this time Anglicanism, though the interpretative framework Guest uses, derives from Bourdieu whose borrowings from Catholicism to formulate his sociology are increasingly well known. Guest carefully tracks the evolution of capital from economics into a sociological realm where it is given a social dimension, one that Bourdieu elaborates into cultural, symbolic and religious forms. From these, Guest sets out to consider how 'religious' capital evolves into a 'spiritual' version.

For his project, Guest treats the transmission of spiritual capital less in terms of a crisis but more as a means of clarifying values and cultural traits that are passed on to the children of clergy. His approach to transmission is far more definite than is the case with other contributors in the collection. Spirituality within an organised religion is treated as a definite form of empowerment, one that shapes and accounts for the subject matter of the wider study. Guest's highly useful appraisal of spiritual capital articulates an institutional dimension to spirituality, one that can be contrasted to the more individualised forms of use that tend to dominate the early contributions in the collection.

The application of spiritual capital to understanding clerical families and their children forms the last and substantial part of his contribution. The positive and empowering properties of spiritual capital, but also its negative effects, are well considered. Again the individualism associated with versions of spirituality is qualified by this account, which explores the altruism of clerical vocation and its effects on children, where those outside the family seem to have first claim on charity. The blurring of the public and private spheres in the clerical households is well covered, again qualifying notions of their strict separation in other treatments of spirituality. The link between spiritual capital, identity and the voluntary sector suggests a communal dimension to spirituality that is deserving of further exploration. Guest treats spirituality as a liquid resource taken from institutions but in part embodying a tradition. His methodological reflections on the study might be profitably linked to others in the collection, notably in Chapters 2–5. In the collection, therefore, four substantial research projects that relate to spirituality are given close readings.

Little sociological attention has been given to testimonies that illustrate the questing dimensions of spirituality. The neglect of these is odd given the close links between the seeking of identity and the questing involved in spirituality. This neglect might emerge from the hegemony holistic spirituality increasingly exercises in the sociology of religion, where conversions to organised religion and the seeking of faith within it are rendered invisible.

In Chapter 11, Flory and Miller fill a gap, by looking at the contrasting journeys of the post-Boomer generation in the USA. Drawing from rich qualitative material (and therefore supplying a useful complement to Droogers's contribution in Chapter 4), Flory and Miller divide their seekers into two types – Reclaimers and Innovators. Their stories are well illustrated. Often liberal theologians are perplexed at the conservative movements of the younger generation, many of whom are dismissed as trading in trivia and nostalgia. Flory and Miller do much to destroy such stereotypes. The spiritual questing of these Reclaimers relates to a need to find a point of stability in the flux of life. Their spiritual quests reflect a recovery of tradition, notably in liturgy which caters for their visual and ritual needs. The indefiniteness of postmodern life and the rootlessness of their culture, with its endless capacities for experimentation, generate an emptiness that can be resolved by a rooting in tradition. The very elements of subjectivity and expressiveness that takes a turn into holistic spirituality can also effect movement in the opposite direction, as in the case of these Reclaimers in California. As portrayed by Flory and Miller, they see something new in the older forms of liturgy of the Orthodox and Anglican Churches that connects to wider traditions of Christianity. Many of the Reclaimers are journeying from what Flory and Miller term 'seeker friendly' movements and from user-friendly Evangelical churches. The Reclaimers seem fatigued with experimentation, and perhaps in Wuthnow's terms seek to return to a dwelling within which to place their spiritual seeking. Whereas commitment is a problem for those in holistic spirituality, for the Reclaimers it represents a solution. The Reclaimers seem to be seeking something ascetic and demanding, and in traditional forms of organised religion it would appear that they find their spiritual needs well fulfilled.

The other group, the Innovators, represent an equally fascinating form of spiritual questing. As with the Reclaimers, they also prefer small size congregations. Both ideal types find a need for an 'inward experiential and outward expression of the spiritual'. Again what is striking is the concern with the visual, cast not in traditional forms, as for the Reclaimers, but in ways that utilise a wider variety of technological resources. The sense of bonding and need of each for the other is common to both ideal type forms of spirituality. Both indicate a common response to a felt loss of social capital. Unlike the Reclaimers, the Innovators seem almost indifferent to their worshipping settings. Oddly, their visual expectations do not move in that direction. Non-institutional and non-hierarchical, Innovators seem to abhor the authority in their spiritual forms that the reclaimers seek.

In their notion of embodied spirituality, Flory and Miller seek to move beyond past notions of individualistic spiritualities and into communal settings. In this context, embodiment is given a social ambit. This reflects an outward dimension to their seeking and questing in what Flory and Miller term 'expressive communalism'. The term is useful in adding a social layer to expressiveness and displacing it from the overly self-centred treatments that mark holistic spiritual emphases. The making sense of a faith in shifting cultural circumstances is what stands out in this contribution. In both ideal types, the seeking is very definitely within the ambit of Christianity. In different ways, both are seeking renewal but also a purification of practice of spirituality in a culture whose assumptions are stacked against such ambitions and their realisation. The emergence of what Flory and Miller term 'expressive communalism' points to a new form of spirituality that is well worth further sociological exploration. Many of these concerns with the communal dimension to spirituality and to its response to the social, what is in the visual, are pursued in the last chapter.

In this chapter, Flanagan is concerned with the rise of visual culture, where character is formed through seeing. Concerns with the moral responsibilities of ways of seeing have arisen in the past decade at the same time as concerns with holistic spirituality have impinged on sociological awareness. Yet both movements have emerged simultaneously, but with no connection proffered between either. Flanagan seeks to remedy this deficiency by using a notion of visual spirituality. This medieval term bridges the divide between visual culture and spirituality. The term exposes a defect of holistic forms of spirituality that makes them unfit for reconciliation with the demands of visual culture. The defect lies in the exaggerated stress which holistic spirituality lays on interior questing. The detachment of this questing from religion accelerates this sense of disconnection from the exterior world. On the side of the Reclaimers of the last chapter, Flanagan's approach complements that of Flory and Miller. His ambitions of reclamation relate to a wider canvas, that of Catholicism, where for him the pictures requisite for visual spirituality are best hung. It is only in religion that the eye takes on a social flesh necessary for seeing visual spirituality. The term straddles the interior and the exterior in the ways of seeing it generates.

The worlds of heaven and hell seem to impinge little on religious sensibilities of the present and, in consequence, images that animate and give focus to exercises in visual spirituality have become pallid and insufficient for those who wish to see to believe. Fear has been taken out of the visual as it relates to the invisible. Far from being outside sociology, the dilemmas of visual spirituality, of seeing this world and darkly the other world lie at the heart of the issues raised in Weber's *Protestant Ethic*. These are of enduring sociological significance.

Flanagan argues that holistic spirituality, whilst affirming individualism and a detachment of questing from the ambit of organised religion, leaves it at risk of re-appropriation into virtual forms of religion, notably those of corporate capitalism. The escape into the interior and from religion leaves spirituality in difficulties unfit for the expectations of a life in a culture where alertness to the visual shapes and governs forms of expression to an increasing degree.

Like Varga in Chapter 8, Flanagan uses Simmel to affirm a living basis to religion one infused with spirituality. Visual spirituality presupposes a capacity, a disposition to see, and, like Guest in Chapter 10, Flanagan employs the notion of spiritual capital as the resource for the exercise of habitus. He argues that ill-considered efforts to modernise have left the spiritual capital of Catholicism depleted. In addition, the spiritual dimensions to theology have been neglected. Nevertheless, he feels there are changes for the better in recent efforts of Catholicism to rehabilitate and to recast its notions of spirituality. Like Flory and Miller, he suggests that there is a compelling dimension to the visual in modern culture that generates spiritual needs. The seemingly endless capacity of organised religion to re-invent its traditions and to follow Giordan in Chapter 9, to respiritualise their basis, suggests that new forms of culture can present old images in a new light, Tarkovsky's film, on *Andrei Rublev*, the Russian icon painter being a case in point. The face on the icon is seen in the context of a religion and it is this that supplies incentives to be alert, to see and to believe.

In presenting this collection to readers, we hope that the work of the contributors bears fruit and that much will be found in the issue of spirituality that is well deserving of sociological attention and further study.

Bibliography

Beckford, J.A. (2003), *Social Theory and Religion*, Cambridge: Cambridge University Press.

Brown, M.F. (1997), *The Channelling Zone: American Spirituality in an Anxious Age*, Cambridge: Harvard University Press.

Carrette, J. and R. King (2005), *Selling Spirituality: The Silent Takeover of Religion*, London: Routledge.

Carroll, J. (2004), *The Wreck of Western Culture: Humanism Revisited*, Melbourne: Scribe.

D'Costa, G. (2005), *Theology in the Public Square: Church, Academy and Nation*, Oxford: Blackwell.

Edwards, Dudley O., G. Evans, I. Rhys and H. MacDairmid (1968), *Celtic Nationalism*, London: Routledge and Kegan Paul.

Flanagan, K. (1996), *The Enchantment of Sociology: A Study of Theology and Culture*, Basingstoke: Macmillan.

Flanagan, K. (2004), *Seen and Unseen: Visual Culture, Sociology and Theology*, Basingstoke: Palgrave Macmillan.

Fyffe, D. (1920), 'Spirituality', in Hastings, J. (ed.), *Encyclopaedia of Religion and Ethics*, vol. 11, Edinburgh: T. and T. Clark, pp. 808–10.

Heaney, S. (1991), 'William Butler Yeats (1865–1939)', in S. Deane (ed.), *The Field Day Anthology of Irish Writing*, vol. II, Derry: Field Day Publications, pp. 783–90.

Heelas, P. and L. Woodhead (2005), *The Spiritual Revolution: Why Religion is Giving Way to Spirituality*, Oxford: Blackwell.

Misztal, B. (2004), 'The Sacralisation of Memory', *European Journal of Social Theory*, 7(1): 67–84.

Oppenheimer, M. (2003), *Knocking on Heaven's Door: American Religion in the Age of the Counterculture*, New Haven: Yale University Press.

Pontifical Council for Culture (2003), 'Jesus Christ the Bearer of the Water of Life: A Christian Reflection on the "New Age"', http://www.vatican.va/roman_curia/pontifical_ councils/interrelg/index.htm

Robinson, S., K. Kendrick and A. Brown (2003), *Spirituality and the Practice of Healthcare*, Basingstoke: Palgrave Macmillan.

Sacks, J. (2005), *To Heal a Fractured World: The Ethics of Responsibility*, London: Continuum.

Seidlitz, L., A.D. Abernethy, P.R. Duberstein, J.S. Evinger, T.H. Chang and B.L. Lewis (2002), 'Development of the Spiritual Transcendence Index', *Journal for the Scientific Study of Religion*, 42(3): 439–53.

Simmel, G. (1997), *Essays on Religion* (trans. H.J. Helle), New Haven: Yale University Press.

Taylor, B.C. (1989), *Spirituality for Everyday Living: An Adaptation of the Rule of St Benedict*, Collegeville, MN: The Liturgical Press.

Weber, M. (1930), *The Protestant Ethic and the Spirit of Capitalism* (trans. T. Parsons), London: Unwin.

Weber, M. (1946) 'Science as a Vocation', in H.H. Gerth and C. Wright Mills (eds and trans.), *From Max Weber: Essays in Sociology*, New York: Oxford University Press, pp. 129–56.

Wright, A. (2000), *Spirituality and Education*, London: RoutledgeFalmer.

Zinnbauer, B.J., K. Pargament, B. Cole, M.S. Rye, E.M. Butter, T.G. Belavich, K.M. Hipp, A.B. Scott and J.L. Kadar (1997), 'Religion and Spirituality: Unfuzzing the Fuzzy', *Journal for the Scientific Study of Religion*, 36(4): 549–64.

Chapter 1

Spirituality: Some Disciplinary Perspectives

Peter R. Holmes

There is an increasing realisation that belief in an authentic, tangible, spiritual reality is now widespread and more, significantly, is occurring outside the main Christian churches. Thus, Hay and Hunt (2000), researching among the UK un-churched, noted a significant numerical growth, from 29 per cent in 1987 to 55 per cent in 2000, in those who believe spirituality is something to be found in their own personal experience. Allied to this rise is a growing number who indicate an awareness of evil. This rose from 12 per cent to 25 per cent (Hay and Hunt 2000: 13). Postmodern people are now looking beyond religion for their spirituality (Young-Eisendrath and Miller 2000b). In our lifetime in the social sciences we have moved from a position where it was unfashionable to talk about spiritual reality to the present day: Now among the un-churched it is increasingly acceptable to speak of one's own spirituality, one's personal journey and experiences (Drane 2002).

This growth of spiritual awareness is reflected in a diversity of academic disciplines that also seem to capture a cultural moment, one of increasing significance. This chapter explores the emergence of spirituality in some of these disciplines through an exploration of some of their literatures. Before looking at spirituality within disciplinary settings, a number of questions emerge.

First, we must decide whether we believe in the existence of spirituality, and if we do then the academic question is whether it is possible to study it at all. Many have traditionally seen spirituality as a *mystery*. If we do see spirituality this way, then we have a choice. Either we acknowledge we cannot study it *directly* because of its intangibility. Alternately, we accept the study of spirituality at a corporeal level, but only through its *outcomes* and *symptoms*. In accepting this latter option we are also acknowledging that current academic tools are unable to study the incorporeal essence of spirituality. In this chapter, seven disciplinary areas are selected, all well illustrating the emergence of interest in spirituality. Some of these areas are broad academic domains like sociology, while others are more specific subjects like medicine and health care within the human sciences. Before proceeding to these disciplines, the problem of defining spirituality needs to be laid out.

Defining Spirituality and Understanding its Complexity

The need to find *a* definition of spirituality first became obvious to me over 30 years ago when I previously encountered Schaeffer's effort to define what it meant to be human and spiritual in contemporary society (Schaeffer 1972). Traditionally I had seen God as spiritual, and us as created in His image. But up until that time I had found few definitions of human make up within traditional Christianity that upheld this spiritual aspect of our personhood. I felt that to be human was to be spiritual, after the *Holy Spirit*, but at that time this was not something one could easily read about. Although traditional definitions of the spiritual nature of human personhood do already exist in the Church (Fitzpatrick and Wellmuth 1259 [1949]) today the landscape has changed dramatically. The canvas is now much broader. What has happened is that spirituality as a domain has broken away from its traditional religious moorings. The reason is that the concept of spirituality has begun to appear in numerous academic and professional disciplines, all outside traditional religion. This is happening in fields as diverse as nursing and social theory. Attempts at a single definition are therefore increasingly problematic, because any definition must take account of many disciplines, numerous research methodologies and an increasing range of domains of practice.

One of the outcomes of this growth of interest in spirituality is that even traditional Christianity now needs to fit into this new picture. An example of this emerges in Ballard's exploration of the place of the Bible within this new spirituality (Ballard 2003). Another example that explores how traditional Christian communities need to redefine what is now meant by spirituality is the Iona Document (Armirtham and Pryor 1991). Schneiders (1993: 10–15) found that the more she worked at the theoretical elaboration of this new field of spirituality studies the more serious and complicated the questions became. She explored spirituality from the traditional Christian private and personal perspective and related it to more contemporary fields such as psychology and anthropology, noting on the way that this new interest is more ontological and existential than academic.

As with others who have explored the topic of spirituality, one seems some distance from writing a definition that is adequate (Holmes 2005). This task is being made increasingly difficult because very little comparative research is being done between the various emerging spiritualities in Western culture. So this chapter must be viewed as a work in progress. Personally I am in two minds whether we can achieve *a* definition or now even need one. Seeking a definition that is all encompassing would obscure the diversity of disciplinary approaches that make the topic so interesting. Spirituality might well be a topic that by its very nature defies any single definition.

Even while we are struggling to define this spirituality, the domain continues to grow and mature (see Sutcliffe and Bowman 2000). As spirituality grows it seems increasingly to defy efforts to treat it as a single discipline with a single definition. As Sutcliffe and Bowman note, spirituality is finding its own gurus and even eccentric exponents. Hazarding a definition of spirituality, one can treat it (very inadequately) as the human search for meaning, particularly relationally, and that for many today this incorporates a supernatural/corporeal dimension that suggests many of us have discovered we are more than our physical biology.

Within the Church there is no doctrine of human spirit or spirituality. This lack inhibits our visualising and practicing spirituality as a valid relational aspect to faith. The Church's failure could well be one of the reasons why we have seen such an increase of interest in the subject. Though having said that, the Hebrew concept of 'body–spirit' unity based on Genesis 3 suggests a holistic view of human make-up, an equality and a balance in the two aspects of our one nature. Body and spirit co-exist and co-mingle within one another in our one holistic nature. This Hebrew model contrasts with the idea that spirituality is the good 'core' to human nature, as the Greeks tended to see it.

But there are other benefits to seeing human nature as having a spiritual aspect. The notion of body-spirit unity enables us to look beyond our physical nature to our spiritual nature. Such a view also sets humanity apart from other species, thereby giving human personhood an implicit deep value, of being in God's image. This in turn suggests the possibility that we can all be greater than who we are now, thus releasing us from the constraints of material circumstances. In reaching beyond ourselves, the notion of the human spirit also suggests the possibility of a supernatural life for all of us, both personally and together. The possibility is offered of our being able to connect with others at more subliminal levels than mere words and body functions. Spirituality also suggests at least two stories exist between us and not just a physical one. In clinical work, this idea of connecting at emotional spiritual levels can be particularly helpful, especially when looking at male and female conflict. The idea of human spirituality also gives us a platform for engaging with spiritual reality while at the same time suggesting we all have the ability to write a history greater than our human lifetime.

These reflections led me to a profound shift in self-understanding: that human nature, body and spirit, is constant, whether seen from Scripture or from outside the Church. We are all in the same place, with the same deep human need to understand more clearly why we exist. But this spirit-body model of human nature helps us to understand better that the contemporary search for spirituality involves all people being on a similar spiritual journey.

The mapping of this domain of spirituality and human spiritual nature is still in early stages. Yet, almost every religion in the world, as well as every culture, would recognise a spiritual dimension to human make-up, and/or the presence of a spiritual reality, or value systems that are 'spiritual'. In contemporary society, there has been a profound shift in understanding of the notion of the spiritual one. Heelas formulates this well when he observes that the religious (for God) is giving way to the spiritual (for life) (Heelas 2002: 358).

Some argue that spirituality is not much different to emotional phenomena like love, hate, trust and forgiveness. Its very nature is something experienced but 'unseen', therefore defying more pragmatic traditional empirical research such as that shaped by positivism. As the dominant paradigm in the twentieth century, it has made meaningless research into an intangible reality like spirituality. However, this has not stopped numerous ideas emerging over the last 20 years, suggesting how one can study spirituality, both in religious (Kinerk 1981 *passim*) and non-religious contexts.

Hay and Hunt (2000: 41) suggest that outside certain religious contexts spirituality is still inchoate, not yet having a developed language. Even where it is developing, it is often doing so within the confines of specific academic or professional disciplines (for example nursing or business), where it tends to reflect the language and expectations of a particular discipline. Thus, spirituality has now entered a series of boxes, discrete and with distinct argots. Can these argots be applied across contexts and disciplines, or should we seek to build a single new language from out of these diverse fields, a uniquely distinctive argot for spirituality?

Views differ, but Sheldrake suggests spirituality must be studied in the context of its culture, implying that any serious study of spirituality therefore needs to be multi-disciplinary. To study spirituality in a particular cultural context requires the use of a hermeneutical or interpretive framework (Sheldrake 1999: 69). Such an approach could take it outside any single academic domain. Is this feasible? How would we tackle this? What academic framework would we use?

This question is made more complicated in that most people have an ontological and existential priority of living spirituality, rather than academically studying it – playing the clarinet rather than learning its theory or manufacture. Spirituality generates an emancipatory interest in becoming more human. This has meant that much of the time we see a strict separation of the academic and the personal. Can these aspects of spirituality be combined? If so, how? Can spirituality be both learned, clinically applied and also lived? To make this possible we need to find marking criteria to assess progress in spiritual maturing and its wholeness. If this expectation were to be applied in a university context, would it be possible to fail a student for not attaining what is believed by the teacher to be greater spiritual maturity? There is another dimension to spirituality that Goddard (1995) has explored.

He suggests that in the West, spirituality is developing along two lines. The first relates to the metaphysical, focusing on the supernatural, but also often incorporating belief in a higher being. The second is also metaphysical, but carrying for many a belief in the 'solid' nature of reality, recognising human personhood as having a spiritual nature, and maybe even admitting to a spiritual reality, though often dismissing a Creator (Goddard 1995: 808–15). We have to work with this bifurcation, but should we try to keep it together? By doing so would we enrich the subject? It is to be argued that the central ground is to be held that allows spirituality to be both material and incorporeal, because part of the apparent failure of Western Christianity has been its study as a metaphysical, sterile and historic phenomenon, rather than as personally relevant, salugenic or positively transformative. 'Salugenic' refers to the sense of wholeness that induces healthy living as opposed to sickness (pathogenic).

Fragmentation is further encouraged by the rise in alternative philosophies of knowledge, encouraging more interpretive and reflexive research. So can we find any basic principles for effectively researching spirituality across these emerging fields, or do they vary too much? Perhaps we need to develop a new set of research tools for the study of this subject, but if so, where will they come from? Traditional definitions of spirituality are no longer helpful, and new ones tend to remain discrete to the subject or to the discipline of which they are part. No one academic domain or discipline seems equipped to meet this emerging diverse challenge, within so many diverse fields.

Contemporary Spirituality as Emerging in Academic Disciplines

The genesis of these disciplinary concerns regarding spirituality rests on a complex range of values and changes in contemporary society, including disillusionment with 'success', the loss of religious faith, and the growing interest in values other than those that are material. The 1960s saw two important processes emerging in Europe and the USA – a questioning of traditional church-based seeker spirituality; and people outgrowing the values of the early scientific era (Tracy 2004).

If academic study is about making sense of some of these shifts, why are some academic disciplines more amenable to spirituality than others? One reason might be the nature of the discipline and its closeness to the human search for meaning. For example nursing, one of the fields with a maturing spirituality, daily confronts issues like suffering and death. Also, within domains like business we are no longer dealing only with 'success', but increasingly with the human need for 'significance'. By contrast, in other areas such as philosophy, the emergence of spirituality as a significant matter of consideration is less easy to discern.

With this chaotic uneven emergence of spirituality across a range of disciplines one of the key questions emerging is whether multi-disciplinary approaches to research are better than a more discrete-within-a-discipline approach. These options are being debated on a number of websites, for example on (http://dmoz.org/Science/Social_Sciences/Psychology/Psychology_and_religion). This web reference looks at issues of the integration of spirituality in these fields. Another indication of the rising significance of these matters is that world-class research institutes are now financing research on the 'galvanizing of mind, religion and spirituality' (Templeton Research Lectures 2005–07) (See http://www.metanexus.net/lectures/winners/penn.html). Yet, overall, such expressions of research interest seem random and spasmodic, although academic interests in spirituality veer towards multi-disciplinary approaches and ideals. But such ambitions seem premature without some study of how specific disciplines formulate notions of spirituality and fit these to their needs and expectations.

Psychology

Spirituality in psychology is now a significant area (Young-Eisendrath and Miller 2000a). Behind the spiritual journey of most of us is the human search for meaning. 'Why am I here?' Carl Rogers eventually distilled this quest into two simple questions, 'Who am I, really?' and 'How can I become myself?' (Fairchild 1978: 212). These questions point to the ontogenetic in all of us, our sense of finitude on the one hand

and what lies beyond our capacity to live on the edges of personal consciousness (Grof 1975). Spiritless psychology has awakened in many the conviction that we are more than our biology, having capacity, experience and hunger for supra-sensible reality. The scientific loss of human spirituality has led to a loss of our value of human life (Christians 1998). May provided an early recognition of this need for a spirituality in psychotherapy (1974). But now we have gone much further, with calls for an integrated spiritual gestalt in psychology and religion (Prasinos 1992). To date this call is primarily unanswered though there are some exceptions (Gorsuch 2002).

Consciousness studies are often described as the heart of what it means to be human, offering similar challenges as faced by those studying spirituality (Searle 1998), but also here a mature understanding is still needed (Andresen and Forman 2000). Connected with consciousness studies is the whole area of connatural experience. An inexplicable dimension to this is blindsight, the remarkable skill developed by blind people to see 'visually' (Weiskrantz 1986). This simple experiment, along with countless others, suggests we are more than our natural senses. But how do we measure this *more*?

Part of the answer may be in supra-sensibility, where spirituality touches into areas such as near death experience (NDE), extra sensory perception (ESP), and the paranormal (a key 'New Age' area with its own substantial literature). A recognition of consciousness leads into numerous directions, including our awareness that spirituality for many of us only exists as we live and experience it.

In psychology, there have been paradigms of measurement that have evolved. Thus, concerns with the measurement of IQ have led to interests in EQ, emotional intelligence, which within Christianity has traditionally been linked with our spirituality (Allender and Longman 1994). But EQ is yesterday's song, as we are now into SQ, spiritual intelligence (Zohar and Marshall 2000; 2004). They define SQ as the intellectual spiritual drive or human capacity to ask 'fundamental' or 'ultimate' questions. The authors suggest we live in a culture that is spiritually dumb, characterised by materialism, expediency, and narrow self-centredness, lack of meaning and dearth of commitment. Spiritual intelligence is part of the reaction against these values, being essential to their recovery in a shallow dumb age (Zohar and Marshall 2004).

However, SQ is merely a part of the much wider interest in personal uniqueness, the desire for connectivity, 'self-help' (Hannaford 1998: 42–61), and the growing spirituality of the human potential movement (Puttick 2000). These concerns mark an interface between psychology and sociology, since personal identity must be shared and reinforced relationally. Yet traditional quantitative and individualistic research approaches within psychology struggle for the language and methodology to address this aspect of human spirituality, as they also do in medicine and health care.

Medicine and Healthcare

The rise of interest in spirituality in the health sciences has been dramatic, both in the United States (Miller 1999) and in the UK (Orchard 2001). For some years, healthcare professionals have been arguing that spirituality needs to become a key component in health promotion (Bensley 1991; Miller and Thoresen 1999) and in the treatment of mental of serious mental illness (Lindgren and Coursey 1995). Interest in spirituality is also emerging in occupational therapy (Enquist et al. 1997), while a growing body of research is connecting spirituality, moral choices and human health (Gushee 2004).

But this rise has not been evenly spread across all fields of healthcare. In some areas, such as nursing, interest in spirituality has developed rapidly. This is probably not surprising, given that nurses need a practical spiritual context for illness, suffering, death and healing. Nursing is calling for an awakening of spirit in clinical practice (Burkhardt and Nagai-Jacobson 1994), often focusing around spiritual distress and how to work with it (Burnard 1987). Martsolf and Mickley (1998) outline the range of theories being developed and used, while Carson (1989) marks out a multi-faith approach to spirituality in regard to nursing practice. Likewise, specific areas of nursing, such as those dealing with maternity are discovering the significance of spirituality (Hall 2003). Others such as Neuman (1989: 16) adopted 'the spiritual variable' as part of her model, describing it as an 'energy force' which Pierce and Hutton (1992) have expanded. This trend in nursing reflects part of a much wider cultural mood swing that now permits us to talk about issues of life and death, the human spirit, and the cost of science being spiritless (Dossey 1998).

Many people's personal journey to seek positive change is in part a reaction to the psychotropic medication culture, which is proving not all good, inducing its own iatrogenesis, or 'man made' illnesses (Illich 1990: 11). These new sicknesses include dependency disorders, poly-pharmacy, and the negative side effects of medication, alongside new diseases like MRSA. Consequently, many are moving away from traditional pharmacological medication (James 1997) and seeking solace in alternative medicine and its spirituality (Weil 2003). These concerns are key aspects of New Age (Heelas 1996; Hanegraaff 1998: 525ff; Hannaford 1998). Therefore, we are seeing an 'esoteric renaissance', with the growing field of esoteric studies and hermeticism (www.esalenctr.org/display/ren.cfm).

What is becoming clearer is that increasing numbers of people now believe that spirituality is a key health contributor in itself (Koenig 1999). In some circles, this is now known as 'spiritual health'. We have moved from merely treating disease in a discrete way, to beginning to look at the whole person in the context of their environment and taking more serious account of *all* these factors in defining illness and treatment. Spiritual beliefs and values are part of this healing wholeness approach. Against this background, there has been a crucial shift in the provision of spiritual care. Thus, in hospitals and other medical settings, spirituality is no longer the domain of chaplains (Carr 2001) or spiritual directors. These settings are using similar basic tools as psychotherapists to help create spiritual health (Ganje-Fling and McCarthy 1991). These concerns with spiritual health are beginning to be both defined and measured (Ellison 1983; Chapman 1987). O'Connor et al. (2002) gives us an overview of these trends from 1962, while Scott and Bergin (1997) offer a helpful introduction to their significance.

In psychotherapy, spirituality is also becoming a key element for many (Izzard 2003). Some, like Spezzano and Garguilo (1997) focus on psychoanalysis, where spirituality still does not have a unified understanding (see Schermer 2003). Using research tools from one specific discipline, such as within medicine and health care, is proving a challenge in other disciplines. For instance, in psychotherapy and in psychoanalysis, two distinct fields, we see a number of views of spirituality and its research emerging and not just one or two definitions or research tools. But this has not stopped the rise of medical ethical holism and its spiritual dimension becoming a core part of treatment, for instance, of dependency disorders (Miller 1998). Interest in spirituality is spreading into other areas of psychology, for instance in dealing with those with learning disabilities (Swinton 2001).

Alongside this new holism is the field of psychophysiology where there is a realisation that the human spirit and body co-mingle, and that damage or healing in one is often mirrored in the other (Cacioppo et al. 1993). Emotion and its spirituality is becoming more accepted as a contributor in many illnesses. Healing the human spirit of say, revenge or bitterness, in turn allows the body to heal itself of numerous related organic disorders. Some are calling this field 'spiritual body language', though in the past it has been described by a friend Dr John Jelfs as 'the voice of illness' (see Siegel 1991; Jobst et al. 1999). Such a psychosomatic connection, as it used to be called, is not new. Old Testament Scripture often connects sin to physical consequences. In this regard, sin can be treated as a spiritual disease (Thompson 1905). Such a theme is carried through to modern times (Wright 1999) though, to the Church's shame, the concept today is more popular outside than within the church (Myss 1996).

Connected to this is the new field of pre-cognition. It deals with forms of response that arise for some, *before* they are presented with stimuli. This is one aspect of neuro-theology, now being called by some 'presponse' (Bierman and Radin 1999). Probably connected to this in ways not yet fully understood are 'subtle energies', chakras and auras that can be harnessed for health. One recent example focused on Glastonbury (Bowman 2000). Spirituality is gaining ground as part of this shift. However this renewed interest in healing spirituality is little shared within Western Christian orthodox religion.

Religion

Some people are disillusioned with traditional Christian religion despite gallant efforts by Christian authors such as Callen (2001). The contemporary church has largely failed to develop authentic clinical transformational spiritualities. This has encouraged alternative spiritualities to mature outside the Church. The Church has in part given away spirituality by retaining its historic shape (Fox 1981). One of the early surveys noting the health of spiritual belief outside the Church was undertaken by Hardy (1979). Postmoderns are now seeking what Heelas denotes as 'expressive spirituality' (Heelas, 2000, 2004; Schreiter 2001). Estep suggests that Vygotsky's developmental theory processes spirituality better than traditional religion, because traditional development theories have proven inadequate in accounting for spirituality. Meanwhile, Vygotsky's (2002: 143) theory of human nature provides a new perspective emphasising the interrelationship between the development of mind *and* its embodiment in social interaction.

Christianity's single historic intrinsic private domain for spirituality has in part been it's undoing, defying the diversity of contemporary spiritualities. Its emphasis on knowing *about* God rather than *knowing* God has left it sterile and unconvincing. But a range of other factors have also contributed to its undoing, such as the Church's suspicion of emotion, its immutable God, and its Augustinian discomfort with a God who is too present in our world (Holmes 2006).

Blaming the Church entirely for this shift is, of course, too simplistic. Other alternatives to traditional Christian contemplation have been successful since the Beatles' pilgrimages East. These and the popularisation of Eastern meditative practices now have a positive mystical edge in many people's minds. Likewise, although we may not have seen an increase in atheism, there is greater interest in Wikka, the Occult and the paranormal (Bruce 2000). Harry Potter and the Hobbits seem to have contributed to this shift in interest in spirituality. There is a range of publications on the writings of Rowling and Tolkien in bookshops. Similarly, Buddhism remains a huge sub-culture here in the West. Suzuki (1983) is a good introduction to this trend, and Christmas Humphries introduced popularised knowledge about this religion to the West in the 1950s. Various forms of Hinduism have also come to Europe, mainly through immigrants and converts from the West. Islam and Judaism also offer mature spiritualities that seem more appealing to some than what Christianity can supply (Green 1987; Lerner 1994).

Currently, we are seeing a wholesale abandonment of the traditional Church and its historic spiritualities. The post war baby boom and Gen X (Beaudoin 1998) have looked elsewhere, finding what they are looking for in other traditional religions and in a range of alternative spiritualities outside religion, often within New Age. In some ways this situation is similar to the field of anthropology.

Anthropology

Anthropology is the study of people and their cultures. With its rich tradition of interest in ritual, and its experience and long tradition of collecting data, it has learnt to account for experiences, which participants express in the context of spiritual reality. However, it has often responded by rationalising these 'primitive' practices, so denying the legitimacy of the culture's own belief system (Turner 1994). Recent developments in ethnography are challenging this imperialism, striving to offer a methodology and style of representation that retains 'true' validity alongside an interpretation that participants would themselves recognise (Brewer 2000). For instance, Arweck and Stringer (2002) wrestle with the methodological and ethical conflicts of insider-outsider accounts of religion, raising questions such as, can outsiders ever research a spirituality in which they have not themselves become participants.

Toynbee (1948) suggested that spiritual teaching provides the seed from which a civilisation develops. If this is so, anthropology is well placed to help identify these emerging spiritual principles and values. Anthropology and religion will always be connected, as religion is part of most cultures. But the emergence of spirituality as its own domain is beginning to redefine research in both religion and anthropology, because both traditionally deal with ultimate values and the way people handle these.

At the other extreme we are beginning to learn about *techno-spirituality*, how spirituality relates to our high technology age (www.greenflame.org/archives/2003/10/28/technospirituality.php). Others are calling it cyber-spirituality. Although spirituality is emerging in a high-tech global way, we are only just beginning to understand both its role and significance. Some are suggesting that the emergence of interests in spiritualities will help to usher in a new golden age for anthropology (Glazier 1997). Because anthropology has always dealt with how people live their religion, the emergence of spirituality outside of religion means the whole field is open to new research. Anthropology, it is argued, is the most obvious contender to study their understandings. However, just as other disciplines lack a theoretical framework for their exploration of spirituality, anthropology is still some distance away from a *theory of spiritual anthropology*. But spirituality is now appearing in most areas of anthropological research, while the spiritual nature of personhood is becoming a matter of increasing importance (Gilder 1998). Other domains are opening out where spirituality is emerging as a matter of concern. These interests are driven by legislation and education is a case in point.

Education

In educational discourse the idea of spirituality has re-emerged as an important element. Having been relegated for many years to Religious Education (RE) and to corporate acts of worship, spirituality is now accepted as being present across the curriculum. It is linked with the need to nurture core values, and also to new requirements of citizenship education. Such demands call for an integration of spirituality into the broader classroom curriculum. For an early definition of spirituality see the Discussion Papers from the Department for Education and Science (1977) and the National Curriculum Council (1993). More recently Miller (2000) has linked spirituality, the soul and education together, and treated these as part of a spiritual curriculum. The most recent Ofsted (Office for Standards in Education) definition reads as follows:

> Spiritual development is the development of the non-material element of a human being, which animates and sustains us and, depending on our point of view, either ends or continues in some form when we die. It is about the development of a sense of identity, self-worth,

personal insight, meaning and purpose. It is about the development of a pupil's 'spirit'. Some people may call it the development of a pupil's 'soul'; others as the development of 'personality' or 'character'. (Ofsted 2004: 12)

We have also been seeing an increasing focus on the process of learning itself, and on learning to learn, rather than simply on learning outcomes (Crick 2002). To help this integration, major works have appeared on the spiritual development of the child and adolescent (Roehlkepartain et al. 2005). Increasingly, these issues form part of general introductions to the sociology of education (Ball 2000).

National Curriculum documentation describes pupil attainment as consisting of *both* learning and achievement *and* personal development. It requires schools to 'deliver the spiritual, moral, social and cultural development of pupils', as well as cognitive learning outcomes. In addition, it refers to the consensus in values such as truth, which emerged from the National Forum for Values in Education and the Community (1996). Ofsted reports on each of these four areas of personal development in its inspection of schools, not only in relation to RE and worship, but also in respect of school culture, ethos and the whole curriculum. These changes have emerged throughout the 1990s in response to societal concerns about values but also to the overwhelming global changes characteristic of postmodernity. Statutory assessment of spiritual development fuels the debate about spirituality, calling for a new language, new methodology and a means of supporting personal and communal spirituality (Fullan 1993; 1999). The notion of spirituality is both important and problematic in contemporary education.

Wright argued that the contemporary consensus on spiritual pedagogy is actually framed within the modernistic thought forms that it is seeking to counter. It is dependent on a particular spiritual tradition arising from Western culture's response to the fragmentation of the narratives of modernity. Thus it reflects the flaws of the very culture it seeks to undermine (Wright 1998: 68). The dominant discourse of spirituality in education can nurture children in a single, closed view of spirituality, a form of benign paternalism that makes research complex. These issues are now beginning to be addressed.

Why education has such a benign attitude to spirituality is intriguing. It might simply be because it is driven by education within a multi-ethnic culture like UK. But, by contrast, it could be because education has traditionally always taken some responsibility for religious teaching, with some of its roots in traditional Christianity. What is more likely, though, is that the rise of spirituality as a domain in its own right has resonated within the field of education, thereby finding a home.

Outside school education we have also seen a resurgent interest in spirituality, as a taught subject now on the agenda of pre-adolescents (Bosacki 2002), and in universities and Bible colleges, as well as in adult education (Fenwick et al. 2001). But such a favourable climate does not exist in some other disciplines.

Sociology

The field of sociology is different from any other, not least in its breadth and scope. Sociology is well placed to offer social comment about spirituality, alongside consideration of appropriate research methods. But sociology appears to be lagging behind areas such as education, nursing and psychotherapy in its consideration of spirituality. Perhaps this reflects a mistaken belief that spirituality is personal and private and is therefore not relevant to the domain of sociology? However, the rise of ideas of social capital has evolved into concerns with spiritual capital, and the subsequent openness of sociology to non-material reality. But the integration of spirituality into sociology is not proving easy, though current research suggests that more social scientists are engaging in religious practices and their spirituality (in the USA) than natural scientists (Plante 2005).

Sociology can help identify why traditional spirituality has been lost, and what social changes have brought this about (Waaijman 2002). The Enlightenment unleashed forces that changed forever the landscape of the Western world. Though no single idea was the prime mover, it was seeded by Aristotle and taken up by philosophers such as Hobbes, Locke and Descartes, whose reductionist thinking established itself as the bedrock of modern society. This created atomistic contractarianism, presenting personhood as private, individual and as the supreme thinker (Kirkpatrick 1986: 13ff). This in turn gave birth to Deism and scepticism, thus giving people permission not to believe in traditional religion. Some assert that this secularisation leads to the modern cult of self-worship. Increasingly, there are critical responses to the failure of materialism, the rise of sterile secularism and more significantly, the breakdown of community (Etzioni 1995). These processes have led Wilber (2001) and others to seek an integrated spirituality.

All of this, and more, now forms our postmodern consciousness. An increased spiritual awareness is a recognised characteristic of postmodernity, meaning that 'spirituality has unexpectedly entered the soul of sociology' (Flanagan 1999: 6). The anthology edited by Woodhead and Heelas (2000) illustrates comprehensively the conflicting discussions. Spirituality finds expression in a plethora of post-Christian spiritualities, though some argue this is not new (McCarthy 2000). We are already talking about 'spiritual society' 'learning communities' and 'learning organisations' (Baue 2002). Wexler (2000: 133ff) suggests we are moving towards a mystical society, that needs to be accompanied by a 'mystical sociology'. Lincoln and Denzin (2000: 1052) suggest that qualitative sociological inquiry for the twenty-first century will require a 'sacred epistemology'.

Sociology offers a meeting place for a variety of disciplinary research themes and methods that are tracking the rise of this phenomenon. One of the more interesting developments within the social sciences is the advent of postmodern, emancipatory and experimental theories and practices. Here the focus is on de(re)construction, multi-vocal knowledge, partial knowing, local knowledge and praxis. Theories are represented as 'tales from the field', where previously silenced groups are given voice. This tendency reflects the growth of more participatory activist oriented research where researchers are expected to declare their interests and views (Hammersley and Atkinson 1995). The search for meaning, for emancipation and for self-actualisation is all within the domain of sociological research alert to implications of spirituality. However, the jury is out on whether the current beginnings will find spirituality emerging as a disparate field of discrete research, or whether we will in time see a merging of much of this research into a new domain called the 'sociology of spirituality'.

Business and the commercial world

Business and the commercial world are getting spiritual. On the American corporate scene see Mitroff and Denton (1999) who noted most people are strongly spiritual, regardless of religion, and that where company and spiritual values coalesce, company performance improves. These movements reflect an awareness that spirituality is firmly entrenched in the marketplace (Roof 1999; Grant et al. 2004). Some are actively seeking introductions of spirituality into the marketplace (see www.globaldharma. org; Giacalone and Jurkiewiz 2002), often in an interdisciplinary way. Spirituality is being called the 'twenty-first century agenda for business' (Renesche 2000) and many thousands of books are in the marketplace capitalising on this trend. Much of this writing focuses on specific areas like business ecology (Abe et al. 1998). What is untested is whether this is merely fashion, or is it evolving into a new work ethic incorporating spirituality.

In the UK, articles in business trade magazines and a range of books on spirituality and business are now also common, as is the emphasis on ethical leadership (Covey 2001; Goleman 2002). Business spirituality is seeking a synthesis with traditional practices (Williams 2003) while it develops its own identity with a range of work-based practices from Tai Chi exercises (www.EasyTaiChi.com) before starting the day, to meditation over the lunch hour. New Age thinking has made a contribution: an office may now have crystals strategically placed around the facility or provide a library of 'spiritual' books for the benefit of staff. Senior staff will often be seen associating with spiritual values and organisations, along similar lines to movie celebrities, for example Madonna with Kabbala, Tom Cruise with Scientology and so on. Feng Shui can now accompany relocating a business. It is used to help to arrange furnishing, colours and layout. What is evident to any casual observer is that this new spirituality is not merely an extension of a Christian work ethic, but is instead a whole new cluster of spiritualities that contain a substantial range of Eastern values and ideas.

But business is perceived by many as one of the key players in plundering the earth. This opens up the conflict with the earth sciences and ecology. We have now conceded that the human contempt for our planet, at least in part, is a fruit of our 'Christian' efforts at 'subduing the earth' (Gen. 1.28) and plundering its riches without counting the cost. Since the publication of Lovelock's *Gaia* ([1979] 1987), earth ecology and its spirituality have been firmly on the map. But Lovelock and many since have pointed out that we need to love mother earth, respecting its right to exist and prosper. We have done appalling, irreversible damage already, much of it in the name of 'creating wealth'. Business and government are at the heart of this mis-behaviour. But we also urgently need a new sacred spirituality of the whole created world. Some have taken up this challenge (Ryan 1995). But opinion is divided as to whether spirituality will have the capacity within business, government or society to lead this needed reversal.

Conclusion

In this chapter, we have noted three broad shifts. First, a substantial range of definitions of spirituality has always existed in the Church, but mostly focused around a personal private 'spiritual life'. Such a spirituality can appear to contemporary people as both deadening and sterile especially for those seeking a more holistic liberating form. For this and a range of other reasons more traditional religious definitions can appear both narrow and confining. But a range of new ones is emerging from within other academic and professional disciplines that challenge traditional Christian definitions. The implications could prove far reaching.

Secondly, from this survey of spirituality in different academic disciplines, what is already becoming clear is that some domains are becoming 'spiritual' while others are resistant. A further implication of this trend is that as spirituality is increasingly perceived as a positive quality of contemporary life, it is very likely that those disciplines without a developing spirituality could be considered second rate. Along these lines John Drane (2002) has already noted that we might be seeing the emergence of a secular Church in a spiritual age.

Thirdly, some thinkers are already pushing further by noting this sporadic uneven emergence of interest in spirituality, wanting to integrate these areas under the banner of 'spirituality'. In doing so they are seeking to create a new type of domain, which although rooted within a wide range of discrete disciplines, has a common theme of 'spirituality'. It is perhaps the instinct of some academics to want to tidy matters up, and even try to regulate such an emerging field. But one can speculate that for some years to come we will not be seeing a successful integration, a single definition or a tight new field coming together called 'spirituality'. Instead we will probably see a range of academic disciplines and professional domains becoming 'spiritual', with some merging, but an ongoing trend toward a general maturing within the distinct domains themselves.

What is most likely to happen is that spirituality will continue to emerge in an increasingly disparate range of disciplines and interests, such as contemporary literature, poetry, fiction, the arts, and areas of creativity like theatre, drama, media, family, developmental psychology and community research. We will also see more emergences in areas like self, holism and personhood that focus around the question – what is it to be more fully human.

Much is already beginning to be written on the growth of spirituality, in academic disciplines and in popular culture, and in time we will be seeking discrete definitions within each field. Such ongoing developments will probably defy any attempt to arrive at one single domain definition, or even an agreed interdisciplinary approach. But with this emergence will also come the need for a whole new range of research tools. These will include methodologies for measuring spirituality and defining and calibrating what mature spirituality is. In turn, this will generate interest in what needs to be done to attain this level of spirituality? What will happen when we seek an interdisciplinary approach? Some of these tools are already being tested and recognised, but will probably prove inadequate when used across disciplines. Whatever the outcome, a vast territory worthy of further exploration has been mapped out in this chapter upon whose significance we can only touch.

Bibliography

Abe, J.M., D.A. Bassey and P.E. Dempsey (1998), *Business Ecology: Giving Your Organisation the Natural Edge*, Woburn, MA: Butterworth Heinemann.

Allender, D.B. and T. Longman (1994), *The Cry of the Soul: How Our Emotions Reveal Our Deepest Questions About God*, Colorado: NavPress.

Andresen, J. and R.K.C. Forman (2000), *Methodological Pluralism in the Study of Religion*, Bowling Green, OH: Imprint Academic.

Armirtham, S. and R.J. Pryor (1991), *The Invitation to the Feast of Life: Resources for Spiritual Formation in Theological Education*, Geneva: World Council of Churches, Programme on Theological Education.

Arweck, E. and M.D. Stringer (eds) (2002), *Theorising Faith: The Insider-Outsider Problem in the Study of Ritual*, Birmingham: University of Birmingham Press.

Ball, S. (2000), *Sociology of Education: Major Themes*, London: RoutledgeFalmer.

Ballard, P. (2003), 'The Bible and Christian Spirituality Today', *Expository Times*, 114(11): 363–6.

Baue, F.W. (2002), *The Spiritual Society: What Lurks Beyond Postmodernism*, Wheaton IL: Crossways.

Beaudoin, T. (1998), *Virtual Faith: The Irreverent Spiritual Quest of Generation X*, San Francisco: Jossey-Bass.

Bensley, R.J. (1991), 'Definition of Spiritual Health: A Review of the Literature', *Journal of Health Education*, 22(5): 287–90.

Bierman, D.J. and D. Radin (1999), 'Conscious and Anomalous Nonconscious Emotional Processes: A Reversal of the Arrow of Time?', *Toward a Science of Consciousness 3, Section 8: The Timing of Conscious Experience* (from http://cognet.mit.edu/posters/TUSCON3/BiermanRadin.html).

Bosacki, S.L. (2002), 'Spirituality and Self in Pre-Adolescents: Implications for a Connected Curriculum', *Journal of Beliefs and Values*, 23(1): 53–67.

Bowman, M. (2000), 'More of the Same? Christian, Vernacular Religion and Alternative Spirituality in Glastonbury', in S. Sutcliffe and M. Bowman (eds), *Beyond New Age: Exploring Alternative Spirituality*, Edinburgh: Edinburgh University Press, pp. 83–104.

Brewer, J.D. (2000), *Ethnography*, Buckingham: Open University Press.

Bruce, S. (2000), 'The New Age of Secularisation', in S. Sutcliffe and M. Bowman (eds), *Beyond New Age: Exploring Alternative Spirituality*, Edinburgh: Edinburgh University Press, pp. 220–36.

Burkhardt, M.A. and M.G. Nagai-Jacobson (1994), 'Reawakening Spirit in Clinical Practice', *Journal of Holistic Nursing*, 12(1): 9–21.

Burnard, P. (1987), 'Spiritual Distress and the Nursing Response', *Journal of Advanced Nursing*, 12: 377–82.

Cacioppo, J.T., D.J. Klein, G.G Berntson and E. Hatfield (1993), 'The Psychophysiology of Emotion', in M. Lewis and J.M. Haviland (eds), *Handbook of Emotions*, London: Guildford Press, pp. 119–43.

Callen, B.L. (2001), *Authentic Spirituality: Moving Beyond Mere Religion*, Carlisle: Baker Academic.

Carr, W. (2001), 'Spirituality and Religion: Chaplaincy in Context', in H. Orchard (ed.), *Spirituality in Health Care Contexts*, London: Jessica Kingsley Publishers, pp. 21–32.

Carson, V.B. (ed.) (1989), *Spiritual Dimensions of Nursing Practice*, Philadelphia: W.B. Saunders Co.

Chapman, L.S. (1987), 'Developing a Useful Perspective on Spiritual Health: Well-Being, Spiritual Potential and the Search for Meaning', *American Journal of Health Promotion*, 1(3), 31–9.

Christians, C.G. (1998), 'The Sacredness of Life', *Media Development*, 2(1–9) (retrieved 26 March 2003 from http://www.wacc.org.uk/publications/md/md1998-2/christians.html).

Covey, S.R. (2001), 'Principles Hold Key to Leadership Success', *Professional Manager*, September, 29–30.

Crick, R.D. (2002), *Transforming Visions: Managing Values in Schools: A Case Study*, London: Middlesex University Press.

Department for Education and Science (1977), *Curriculum 11–16*, London: HMSO.

Dossey, B.M. (1998), 'Body, Mind, Spirit: Attending to Holistic Care', *American Journal of Nursing*, 98(8): 35–8.

Drane, J. (2002), *Rebuilding the House of Faith: Being Spiritual, Human and Christian in Today's World* (from http://www.ctbi.org.uk/assembly/Drane.doc).

Ellison, C.W. (1983), 'Spiritual Well-Being: Conceptualisation and Measurement', *Journal of Psychology and Theology*, 11(4): 330–40.

Enquist, D.E., M. Short-DeGraff, J. Gliner and K. Oltjenbruns (1997), 'Occupational Therapists' Beliefs and Practices with Regard to Spirituality and Therapy', *American Journal of Occupational Therapy*, 51(3): 173–80.

Estep, J.R. (2002), 'Spiritual Formation as Social: Toward a Vygotskyan Developmental Perspective', *Religious Education*, 97(2): 141–64.

Etzioni, A. (1995), *The Spirit of Community: Rights, Responsibilities and the Communitarian Agenda*, London: Fontana Press.

Fairchild, L. (1978), '… As Thyself', *Journal of Religion and Health*, 17(3): 210–14.

Fenwick, T., L. English and J. Parsons (2001), 'Dimensions of Spirituality: A Framework for Adult Educators', *CASAE–ACEEA National Conference: Twentieth Anniversary Proceedings*.

Fitzpatrick, M.C. and J.J. Wellmuth ([1259]1949), *St Thomas Aquinas on Spiritual Creatures*, Marquette, WI: Marquette University Press.

Flanagan, K. (1999), 'Introduction', in K. Flanagan and P.C. Jupp (eds), *Postmodernity, Sociology and Religion*, Basingstoke: Macmillan Press, pp. 1–13.

Fox, M. (1981), *Western Spirituality: Historical Roots, Ecumenical Routes*, Santa Fe: Bear and Co.

Fullan, M. (1993), *Change Forces: Probing the Depths of Educational Reform*, London: The Falmer Press.

Fullan, M. (1999), *Change Forces: The Sequel*, Philadelphia, PA: Falmer Press.

Ganje-Fling, M.A. and P.R. McCarthy (1991), 'A Comparative Analysis of Spiritual Direction and Psychotherapy', *Journal of Psychology and Theology*, 19(1): 103–17.

Giacalone, R.A. and C.L. Jurkiewiez (2002), *The Handbook of Workplace Spirituality and Organisational Performance*, New York: M.E. Sharpe Inc.

Gilder, G. (1998), 'The Materialist Superstition' (retreived 24 November 2005 from http://www. discovery.org/scripts/viewDB/index.php?command=view&id=2053).

Glazier, S.D. (1997), *Anthropology of Religion: A Handbook*, Westport, CN/London: Greenwood Press.

Goddard, N.C. (1995), 'Spirituality as Integrative Energy: A Philosophical Analysis as Requisite Precursor to Holistic Practice', *Journal of Advanced Nursing*, 22: 808–15.

Goleman, D. (2002), *The New Leaders: Transforming the Art of Leadership into the Science of Results*, London: Little Brown.

Gorsuch, R.L. (2002), *Integrating Psychology and Spirituality*, Westport, CT: Greenwood.

Grant, D., K. O'Neil and L. Stephens (2004), 'Spirituality in the Workplace: New Empirical Directions in the Study of the Sacred', *Sociology of Religion*, 65(3): 265–83.

Green, A. (1987), 'Spirituality', in A.A. Cohen and P. Mendes-Flohr (eds), *Contemporary Jewish Religious Thought: Original Essays on Critical Concepts, Movements and Beliefs*, New York: The Free Press, pp. 903–7.

Grof, S. (1975), *Realms of the Human Unconscious*, New York: Viking.

Gushee, D.P. (2004), 'An Overview of Health and Spirituality: Spiritual Moral Choices and Health' (from http://www.cbhd.org/resources/healthcare/gushee_2004-09-01.htm).

Hall, J. (2003), 'Spirituality and Maternity Nursing', *Contact*, 140(1): 17–25.

Hammersley, M. and P. Atkinson (1995), *Ethnography: Principles in Practice* (2nd edition), London: Routledge.

Hanegraaff, W.J. (1998), *New Age Religion and Western Culture: Esotericism in the Mirror of Secular Thought*, New York: State University of New York Press.

Hannaford, R. (1998), *The Church for the Twenty-first Century: Agenda for the Church of England*, Leominster, Hereford: Gracewing Publications.

Hardy, A. (1979), *The Spiritual Nature of Man*, Oxford: Clarendon Press.

Hay, D. and K. Hunt (2000), *Understanding the Spirituality of People Who Don't Go to Church*, Nottingham: Nottingham University Press.

Heelas, P. (1996), *The New Age Movement: The Celebration of the Self and the Sacralisation of Modernity*, Oxford: Blackwell Publishing.

Heelas, P. (2000), 'Expressive Spirituality and Humanistic Expressivism: Sources of Significance Beyond Church and Chapel', in S. Sutcliffe and M. Bowman (eds), *Beyond New Age: Exploring Alternative Spirituality*, Edinburgh: Edinburgh University Press, pp. 237–58.

Heelas, P. (2002), 'The Spiritual Revolution: From Religion to Spirituality', in L. Woodhead (ed.), *Religions in the Modern World: Traditions and Transformations*, London: Routledge, pp. 357–75.

Heelas, P. (2004), *The Spiritual Revolution: Why Religion Is Giving Way to Spirituality*, Oxford: Blackwell.

Holmes, P.R. (2005), *Becoming More Human: Exploring the Interface of Spirituality, Discipleship and Therapeutic Faith Community*, Bletchley, Milton Keynes: Paternoster.

Holmes, P.R. (2006), *Trinity in Human Community: Exploring Congregational Life in the Image of the Social Trinity*, Bletchley, Milton Keynes: Paternoster.

Illich, I. (1990), *The Limits to Medicine: Medical Nemesis: The Expropriation of Health*, London: Penguin Books.

Izzard, S. (2003), 'Holding Contradictions Together: An Object Relational View of Healthy Spirituality', *Contact*, 140(1): 2–8.

James, O. (1997), *Britain on the Couch: Why We're Unhappier Compared with 1950 Despite Being Richer: A Treatment for the Low Seratonin Society*, London: Century.

Jobst, K.A., D. Shostak and P.J. Whitehouse (1999), 'Diseases of Meaning, Manifestations of Health and Metaphor', *The Journal of Alternative and Complementary Medicine*, 5(6): 495–501.

Kinerk, E. (1981), 'Toward a Method for the Study of Spirituality', *Review for Religious*, 40(1): 3–39.

Kirkpatrick, F.G. (1986), *Community: A Trinity of Models*, Washington: Georgetown University Press.

Koenig, H.G. (1999), 'Religion, Spirituality and Medicine: A Rebuttal to Skeptics', *International Journal of Psychiatry in Religion*, 29(2): 123–31.

Lerner, M. (1994), *Jewish Renewal: A Path to Healing and Transformation*, New York: Harper Perennial.

Lincoln, Y.S. and N.K. Denzin (2000), 'The Seventh Moment: Out of the Past', in N.K. Denzin and Y.S. Lincoln (eds), *Handbook of Qualitative Research* (2nd edition), Thousand Oaks: Sage Publications, pp. 1047–65.

Lindgren, K.N. and R.D. Coursey (1995), 'Spirituality and Serious Mental Illness: A Two Part Study', *Psychosocial Rehabilitation Journal*, 18(3): 93–111.

Lovelock, J.E. ([1979] 1987), *Gaia: A New Look at Life on Earth*, Oxford: Oxford University Press.

McCarthy, M. (2000), 'Spirituality in a Postmodern Era', in S. Pattison and J. Woodward (eds), *The Blackwell Reader in Pastoral and Practical Theology*, Oxford: Blackwell Publishers, pp. 192–206.

Martsolf, D.S. and J.R. Mickley (1998), 'The Concept of Spirituality in Nursing Theories: Differing World-Views and Extent of Focus', *Journal of Advanced Nursing*, 27: 294–303.

May, G.G. (1974), 'The Psychodynamics of Spirituality', *Journal of Pastoral Care*, 27(2): 84–91.

Miller, J.P. (2000), *Education and the Soul: Toward a Spiritual Curriculum*, Albany: State University of New York Press.

Miller, W.R. (1998), 'Researching the Spiritual Dimension of Alcohol and Other Drug Problems', *Addictions*, 93(7): 979–90.

Miller, W.R. (ed.) (1999), *Integrating Spirituality into Treatment: Resources for Practitioners*, Washington, DC: American Psychological Association.

Miller, W.R. and C.E. Thoresen (1999), 'Spirituality and Health', in W.R. Miller (ed.), *Integrating Spirituality into Treatment: Resources for Practitioners*, Washington, DC: American Psychological Association, pp. 3–18.

Mitroff, I.I. and E.A. Dentron (1999), *A Spiritual Audit of Corporate America: A Hard Look at Spirituality, Religion and Values in the Workplace*, San Francisco: Jossey-Bass.

Myss, C. (1996), *Anatomy of the Spirit: 7 Stages of Power and Healing*, New York: Three Rivers Press.

National Curriculum Council (1993), *Spiritual and Moral Development: A Discussion Paper*, York: National Curriculum Council.

National Forum for Values in Education and the Community (1996), *Consultation on Values in Education and the Community*, London: SCAA.

Neuman, B. (1989), *The Neuman Systems Model*, East Norwork, CT: Appleton and Lange.

O'Connor, T.J. (2002), 'Review of Quantity and Types of Spirituality Research in Three Health Care Databases (1962–99): Implications for the Health Care Ministry', *Journal of Pastoral Care and Counselling*, 56(3): 227–32.

Office for Standards in Education (2004), *Promoting and Evaluating Pupils' Spiritual, Moral, Social and Cultural Development*: OFSTED HMI 2125.

Orchard, H. (ed.) (2001), *Spirituality in Health Care Contexts*, London: Jessica Kingsley.

Pierce, J.D. and E. Hutton (1992), 'Applying the New Concepts of the Neuman Systems Model', *Nursing Forum*, 27(1): 15–18.

Plante, L. (2005), 'Science and Theology News: Spirituality Soars Among Scientists, Study Says' (retreived 24 November 2005 from http://www.stnews.org/research-1951.htm).

Prasinos, S. (1992), 'Spiritual Aspects of Psychotherapy', *Journal of Religion and Health*, 31(1): 41–52.

Puttick, E. (2000), *Personal Development: The Spiritualisation and Secularisation of the Human Potential Movement*, Edinburgh: Edinburgh University Press.

Renesche, J.E. (2000), *Getting to the Better Future: A Matter of Conscious Choosing*, San Francisco: New Business Books.

Roehlkepartain, E.C., P.E. King. L. Wagener and P.L. Benson (2005), *The Handbook of Spiritual Development in Childhood and Adolescence*, London: Sage.

Roof, W.C. (1999), *Spiritual Marketplace: Baby-Boomers and the Remaking of American Religion*, Princeton, NJ: Princeton University Press.

Ryan, W.F. (1995), *Culture Spirituality and Economic Development*, Ottawa: IDRC Books.

Schaeffer, F.A. (1972), *True Spirituality*, London: Hodder and Stoughton.

Schermer, V.L. (2003), *Spirit and Psyche: A New Paradigm for Psychology, Psychoanalysis and Psychotherapy*, London: Jessica Kingsley.

Schneiders, S.M. (1993), 'Spirituality as an Academic Discipline: Reflections from Experience', *Christian Spirituality Bulletin*, 1(2): 10–15.

Schreiter, R.J. (2001), 'Epilogue', in R. J. Schreiter (ed.), *Mission in the Third Millennium*, Maryknoll, New York: Orbis Books, pp. 149–61.

Scott, R.P. and A.E. Bergin (1997), *A Spiritual Strategy for Counselling and Psychotherapy*, Washington, DC: American Psychological Association.

Searle, J.R. (1998), 'How to Study Consciousness Scientifically', in J. Cornwell (ed.), *Consciousness and Human Identity*, Oxford: Oxford University Press, pp. 21–37.

Sheldrake, P. (1999), 'Spirituality as an Academic Discipline', in A. Thatcher (ed.), *Spirituality and the Curriculum*, London: Cassell, pp. 55–78.

Siegel, B. (1991), 'Healing of the Spirit and Curing of the Body', *Studies in Formative Spirituality*, 12: 143–7.

Spezzano, C. and G.J. Garguilo (eds) (1997), *Soul on the Couch: Spirituality, Religion and Morality in Contemporary Psychoanalysis*, Hillsdale, NJ: The Analytic Press.

Sutcliffe, S. and M. Bowman (eds) (2000), *Beyond New Age: Exploring Alternative Spirituality*, Edinburgh: Edinburgh University Press.

Suzuki, D.T. (1983), *The Essence of Buddhism*, London: The Buddhist Society.

Swinton, J. (2001), *Spirituality and Mental Health Care*, London: Jessica Kingsley.

Thompson, F. (1905), *Health and Holiness: A Study of the Relationships between Brother Ass, the Body, and His Rider, the Soul*, London: Burns and Oates.

Toynbee, A. (1948), *A Study of History*, Oxford: Oxford University Press.

Tracy, D. (2004), *The Spirituality Revolution: The Emergence of Contemporary Spirituality*, Brunner: Routledge.

Turner, E. (1994), 'A Visible Spirit Form in Zambia', in D.E. Young and J.-G. Goulet (eds), *Being Changed by Cross-Cultural Encounters*, Peterborough, Ontario: Broadview Press, pp. 71–95.

Waaijman, K.Z. (2002), *Spirituality: Forms, Foundations, Methods*, Leuven: Peeters.

Weil, A. (2003), 'Mother Nature's Little Helpers', *Time Magazine*, 17 February, 54–5.

Weiskrantz, L. (1986), *Blindsight: A Case Study and Its Implications*, Oxford: Oxford University Press.

Wexler, P. (2000), *The Mystical Society: An Emerging Social Vision*, Boulder, CO: Westview Press.

Wilber, K. (2001), *A Theory of Everything: An Integral Vision for Business, Politics, Science and Spirituality*, Boston: Shambhala.

Williams, O.F. (2003), *Business, Religion and Spirituality: A New Synthesis*, Notre Dame, IN: University of Notre Dame Press.

Woodhead, L. and P. Heelas (2000), *Religion in Modern Times: An Interpretive Anthology*, Oxford: Blackwell Publishers.

Wright, A. (1998), *Spiritual Pedagogy: A Survey, Critique and Reconstruction of Contemporary Spiritual Education in England and Wales*, Abingdon: Cullum College Institute.

Wright, H. (1999), *A More Excellent Way: 1 Corinthians 12: 31. A Teaching on the Spiritual Roots of Disease*, Thomaston, GA: Pleasant Valley Publications.

Young-Eisendrath, P. and M.E. Miller (eds) (2000a), *The Psychology of Mature Spirituality: Integrity, Wisdom, Transcendence*, London: Routledge.

Young-Eisendrath, P. and M.E. Miller (2000b), 'Beyond Enlightened Self-Interest: The Psychology of Mature Spirituality in the Twenty-first Century', in P. Young-Eisendrath and M.E. Miller (eds), *The Psychology of Mature Spirituality: Integrity, Wisdom, Transcendence*, London: Routledge, pp. 1–7.

Zohar, D. and I. Marshall (2000), *Sq: Spiritual Intelligence: The Ultimate Intelligence*, London: Bloomsbury Publishing.

Zohar, D. and I. Marshall (2004), *Spiritual Capital: Wealth We Can Live By*, London: Bloomsbury.

Chapter 2

The Spiritual Revolution:
Another False Dawn for the Sacred

David Voas and Steve Bruce[1]

From the earliest days of sociology, two ideas about religion have wrestled for supremacy. One is that the transformations of modernity cause religion to lose its grip on society and its members. The other is that while the sacred may have to adapt and evolve, faith is always with us. In *The Spiritual Revolution: Why Religion is Giving Way to Spirituality* (2005), Paul Heelas and Linda Woodhead (with Benjamin Seel, Bronislaw Szersynski and Karin Tusting) attempt to keep a foot in both camps. True, they say, secularisation is undermining conventional religion. Spirituality based on personal experience and well-being is growing in its place, however, and might overtake its older rival in just a few decades.

Their project began with a rare attempt to quantify the reach of 'New Age' practices in direct comparison with traditional churchgoing. We applaud the groundbreaking effort to assess the scale, nature and significance of what Heelas and Woodhead term the holistic milieu. Their empirical findings are woven into an extended discussion of the 'subjective turn' in religious life; the book will be a landmark in the study of alternative spirituality.

Our admiration of the work, though, is accompanied by reservations about its conclusions. It is 'perfectly clear that a spiritual revolution has not taken place' (Heelas and Woodhead 2005: 45), notwithstanding the book's title, and we see little chance that one will occur in the foreseeable future. Unconventional spirituality is a symptom of secularisation, not a durable counterforce to it. The size, projected growth, novelty and permanence of this phenomenon have been exaggerated. We are doubtful that most of the activities in this category even partake of the sacred to any great extent. The secular future of the holistic milieu may be bright; in its more spiritual form, these beliefs and practices are unlikely to do much better than those of more established religions.

In a volume on the sociology of spirituality it is important to be clear – or as clear as one can be – about the term 'spirituality'. Except where the context makes some other meaning apparent, we follow Heelas and Woodhead in applying it to

---

1   Paul Heelas and Linda Woodhead have been generous with their ideas, findings and assistance. Bronislaw Szersynski (co-investigator on the Kendal Project) helped to unearth some of the original data presented in Tables 2.1–2.3.

'subjective-life forms of the sacred, which emphasise inner sources of significance and authority and the cultivation or sacralization of unique subjective-lives'. It is thus contrasted with more conventionally religious conceptions 'which emphasise a transcendent source of significance and authority to which individuals must conform' (Heelas and Woodhead 2005: 6).

Part of our contention will be that this view of the self as sacred is not always distinguishable from a conventionally modern view of the self as precious and self-determining. The spiritual is being hollowed out; the label may be used to flatter anything from earnest introspection to beauty treatments, martial arts to support groups, complementary medicine to palm reading. It is right and proper that these activities should receive sociological attention; whether they have much to do with the sacred and hence the sociology of religion, except as a possible epiphenomenon of secularisation, is another matter.

The Method

Kendal is a town of approximately 28,000 inhabitants in the northwest of England. Its demographic and socio-economic composition is broadly typical of the country as a whole, as are the levels of churchgoing and involvement in complementary and alternative medicine (Heelas and Woodhead 2005: 52–3). Over a period of two years in 2000–02, researchers from Lancaster University investigated the scale and variety of religious and spiritual practice in Kendal and its vicinity. They examined two main types of activity – conventional churchgoing in what they call the 'congregational domain' and the alternative spirituality witnessed in the 'holistic milieu'. Within these categories they compiled an inventory of all the churches and chapels, or the groups and therapies, available in the area. They then attempted to count the number of people involved in each during a typical week. Finally, they conducted surveys of participants and also carried out case studies of selected congregations, groups and one-to-one activities.

With regard to the congregational domain, the conclusions were virtually identical to those from the English Church Attendance Survey in 1998 (Brierley 2000) – some 7.9 per cent of people were in church on any given Sunday, and this figure has been declining steadily over many years. This analysis of conventional religion is consonant with our own, and hence we focus in what follows on what Kendal is supposed to tell us about the holistic milieu. The findings here were that about 1.6 per cent of the population participate in one or more relevant activities each week, and that the trend is up. Heelas and Woodhead maintain that alternative spirituality has been growing rapidly, that this growth can be expected to continue, and that one should expect the holistic milieu to become as large as the congregational domain within the next few decades, or even to overtake it (Heelas and Woodhead 2005: 48, 149).

Three steps were important for Heelas and associates in arriving at an estimate of the number of people active in alternative spirituality in and around Kendal. First, it was necessary to arrive at an average weekly headcount for participation in each of

63 groups and a further 63 kinds of one-to-one treatment regarded by the organisers or practitioners as having a spiritual dimension. Secondly, the amount of overlap between these different activities had to be established so that a number of participants could be derived from the number of 'acts of participation'. Thirdly, the investigators sought to uncover what proportion of the participants (as opposed to the practitioners) saw their activities as spiritual.

There are criticisms to be made of the researchers' methods at each of these steps, though we confess to a certain amount of frustration in trying to examine them. Having so commendably taken a rigorously empirical approach to the study, the Kendal team seems to have abandoned its interest in quantification when it came to writing the book. The published volume contains no fewer than 17 pictures – including one of a researcher receiving a massage – but only one table (Appendix 3) and one chart (Heelas and Woodhead 2005: 91) relating to the holistic milieu. Crucial information about the counts and methods underpinning the key estimates are omitted. Some of the data have been made available on the project website – and the authors have generously assisted in uncovering other files – but gaps remain. In mitigation, it might be said that funding bodies typically allow too little time for analysis of data that have taken many months to collect.

Step 1: Counting Attendance

Participating in the holistic milieu involves either attending a group (for yoga, tai chi and so forth) or receiving one-to-one attention from a practitioner (for example of Reiki, homeopathy). The Appendix reproduced at the end of this chapter shows the full list of activities uncovered in the area (a process that involved considerable effort, not least to check whether practitioners regarded what they did as spiritually significant). Researchers from the Kendal Project observed all group activities during one particular week and obtained counts of the numbers attending. Enumerating the individual clients of therapists was more difficult; as the authors comment: 'One person might say, "up to five people a day, three days a week"; another might say, "about 20 or 30 at any one time"; another, "about 20 a month"; still others, "it's too difficult to estimate" or, "about 200–300 on my books"' (Heelas and Woodhead 2005: 39). The investigators used their knowledge and judgment to arrive at conservative estimates of the number of clients seen in a typical week by the various practitioners.

By this process a total of 840 acts of participation (not participants, some of whom were involved in multiple activities) were produced for the Kendal area. Unfortunately this figure has not been broken down into the component activities. Apparently about two-thirds of the attendances came from group activities with the balance contributed by individual treatments (Heelas and Woodhead 2005: 40). For group activities, participation was distributed as shown in Table 2.1.

For one-to-one activities, the Kendal researchers have been unable to offer a breakdown of individual client participation. The practitioners themselves were distributed as shown in Table 2.2, but the number of one-to-one activities will only follow the same pattern if all practices are equally popular, which is a very large

Table 2.1   Participation in group activities (%)

Yoga	52
Tai chi	13
Dancing, singing, art and craft	8
Therapy and counselling	3
Healing and complementary health	16
Specialised spiritual/religious groups	8

Source: Kendal Project data.

assumption. Even so, both of these tables show the predominance of activities that, notwithstanding the views of the organisers or practitioners, are not necessarily 'spiritual' – yoga, massage, and so on. By contrast there are relatively few, such as Reiki, that do seem highly spiritual, and even these are typically orientated towards healing, that is physical needs and desires. We shall return to this point shortly.

Table 2.2   One-to-one practitioners (%)

Reiki or spiritual healing	20
Massage	19
Bodily manipulation or posture	14
Zones, meridians or pressure points	13
Homeopathy	12
Psychotherapy or counselling	5
Miscellaneous	17

Source: Kendal Project data.

Step 2: Counting Participants

The second step was to estimate how many people were involved, sometimes more than once, in the 840 'acts of participation' counted for a typical week. The key problem is to work out what proportion of individuals participated in a given number of activities (one, two, three …) during the week. Questionnaires were distributed to practitioners. They were asked 'to fill one in themselves, practitioners were also asked to give the questionnaire to willing one-to-one clients and group participants or to those who came along during a particular week' (Heelas and Woodhead 2005: 153). Two questions were particularly relevant – one that listed every known activity in the Kendal holistic milieu with a tick box for 'have attended in the past seven days', and another that asked the respondent to supply the name of the group or therapy attended during the past seven days (choosing the one of greatest personal importance in the case of multiple participation).

The consistency of responses to these questions left something to be desired, as is commonly the case with surveys. Of the 252 replies, 44 had no boxes ticked for any activity during the past seven days, though most of those respondents provided (in the next question) the name of something they had done that week. Conversely 10 people ticked a box for recent participation without then specifying it subsequently. The 15 cases where people had not indicated an activity from the past seven days in either question were omitted from most analyses. A further 29 cases (in which the respondent wrote in the name of an activity but failed to tick the corresponding box in the previous question) were also excluded in estimating the distribution of multiple attendances; it would have been more consistent to impute participation in a single activity for these individuals.

The questionnaire offered no means of showing multiple attendance over the past seven days in any particular activity. As a result, if for example four tai chi sessions during the week each attracted a dozen people, there would be 48 acts of participation, but anywhere between 12 and 48 participants. There appears to be no way of knowing the actual number based on the evidence gathered, but the researchers nevertheless assume that single activities do not contribute to multiple attendance. This assumption is reasonable for many activities, but perhaps not for all of them.

Moving on from these problems, one can count the number of activities attended in the last seven days for each respondent. Of those who ticked at least one box, 60 per cent had been to one activity, 24 per cent attended two, eight per cent three, and so on. The overall ratio of attendances to attenders can be calculated at 1.74. The implication is that the 840 acts of participation would have been made by 483 individuals. The Kendal investigators believed that this ratio was too high, however, and hence the estimated number of participants was too low. If people who attended multiple activities were over-represented (since the request to do the survey would in theory have been repeated at each of the events they attended), then the ratio of attendances to attenders must be reduced. Their method of correcting for the supposed bias in favour of multiple attenders produced a new estimate of 600, nearly 25 per cent higher than the initial figure of 483. We agree that an adjustment was appropriate, but their approach seems too drastic for the following reasons.

What happens when one solicits the same person multiple times depends on the nature of the request and the interest of the individual approached. If one is asking people to help the Conservative Party, for instance, then some will consent and the remainder will refuse however many times they are asked. If one wants people to sign a birthday card for a co-worker, on the other hand, then giving them more opportunities will probably help them to get around to doing it. The Kendal researchers correctly decided that repeated requests do have some effect, but unfortunately they have gone to the opposite extreme in their correction. They suppose that the past tells us nothing (so that someone who refused to donate to the Conservative Party yesterday is just as likely to agree today as anyone else) and hence if there was a 60 per cent chance that a participant would refuse once, there was only a 36 per cent chance that he or she would refuse twice. In fact, though, an individual faced with a survey will tend to be either co-operative or resistant regardless of the number of opportunities granted; completing a 16-page form on spirituality may seem more like contributing to the Conservative Party than signing a birthday card. People have greater or lesser propensities to give to charity, talk to telemarketers, or complete long questionnaires, and giving them more chances may not change the outcome very much. The truth is likely to lie somewhere between the extreme assumptions about survey response and the numbers of attenders implied by those assumptions.

Multiple attenders may nevertheless be significantly over represented in the sample; they probably have more interest than others in alternative spirituality and hence might have been atypical in their willingness to participate. As with those prepared to help the Conservative Party, their inclination to cooperate could be more important than the fact that the form was offered to them more than once. If so, the number of participants estimated by the Kendal researchers might not be very far off, even if it was arrived at using an inappropriate method. This overrepresentation of spiritually inclined participants in the survey (discussed further below) does help to justify the substantial upwards adjustment in the estimated number of attenders, but unfortunately it undermines the reliability of the results more generally.

To recap, the basis for moving from 840 attendances to 600 attenders (or 1.6 per cent of the population of Kendal and environs) is rather insecure. The sample of participants may not have been representative. The questionnaire failed to check for multiple attendance in a single activity. Accepting that respondents had attended in the past seven days, but then not imputing an appropriate value in the key variable, seems unfortunate. The adjustment for multiple participation assumes something that may not be true, namely that how likely a person is to respond just depends on how many times he or she is offered the form. These problems may balance each other out, or they may not.

Nevertheless, the estimate reached by Heelas and Woodhead of how many people participate weekly in the holistic milieu still seems reasonably conservative; the remarks above serve mainly to emphasise that a sizeable margin of error must be allowed. In any event it is of little consequence whether the figure should be one per cent or two per cent of the population. It is more interesting to consider whether most of those involved are in fact doing something they see as spiritual, an issue to which we now turn.

Step 3: Identifying the Spiritual

In coming to the overall estimate of the size of the holistic milieu, Heelas and Woodhead counted participation in any group or one-to-one activity that the *practitioners* considered to have a spiritual dimension. It does not necessarily follow, of course, that the clients or ordinary participants viewed these activities as spiritual. Our main disagreement with Heelas and Woodhead is precisely on this issue – it seems evident to us that the attitudes of participants may have little to do with the spiritual worldviews of their therapists and activity leaders. The Salvation Army does not claim that coming to their soup kitchens amounts to religious practice, and likewise it seems misleading to assert that mere attendance at a yoga class, message therapy session or palm reader's table counts as participation in the holistic milieu.

The survey was intended to reveal how participants regarded the activities. Respondents were asked whether they had tried each practice and if so whether it had a spiritual dimension for them. In relation to the (most important) activity that they had pursued in the past seven days, they were asked to rank the reasons that originally induced them to try it and those that were most important to them now, where 'spiritual growth' was one of the options.

Given that fewer than half the acts of participation were accounted for by survey respondents, bias is a potential problem. Was this self-selected sample representative? There are good reasons to suppose that it was not. People who completed the questionnaire (which ran to 16 pages and was headed 'The Kendal Project: Patterns of the Sacred in Contemporary Society') were probably those most interested in alternative spirituality. Even in the absence of a breakdown of the 840 acts of participation, it is evident that the very 'spiritual' encounters produced a disproportionate number of respondents. For example people who participated in specialised spiritual/religious groups (Buddhism, Inter-faith, Sea of Faith, Baha'i) are over-represented in the survey while those who did yoga in the previous week are substantially under-represented, relative to the baseline information in Table 2.1. The survey results will thus be biased against secular views of the holistic milieu.

An additional reason for suspecting that the survey respondents may not be typical of participants generally is that the 95 practitioners were asked by the researchers to complete the questionnaire. They might well have been more likely to respond than lay participants – partly because they were approached directly by the project team and partly because they are unusually interested in the topic. Unless the proportion of the questionnaires coming from practitioners as opposed to ordinary clients corresponds to the proportion of those groups in the holistic milieu, the sample will be unrepresentative. By design, all the practitioners would describe their activities as spiritual, and hence the potential impact on this particular issue could be significant.

Note too that the assumption used in deriving the number of participants from the number of acts of participation implies that multiple participants are heavily over-represented (because the probability of completing the questionnaire was supposed to be a function of the number of times it was encountered). It seems very likely, though, that those most active in the holistic milieu are also the most inclined to hold spiritual views, and hence the researchers' own suppositions oblige us to believe that the survey-based estimates of participant spirituality are exaggerated.

One can in fact test the hypothesis that multiple attenders are more 'spiritual' than others. Fewer than half of those who listed a single activity from the past week identified it as having a spiritual dimension, while 71 per cent of the multiple attenders found spirituality in one or more of their activities. Similarly 45 per cent of the latter group listed 'looking for spiritual growth' as one of their top three reasons for participating, as against 34 per cent among those having done just one activity. Thus if multiple attenders are over-represented in the sample (and the Lancaster investigators believe that they are, as otherwise the estimated number of participants in the holistic milieu would have to be substantially reduced), it follows that the raw findings on the spiritual significance of these activities are too high. To the extent that those responding to the survey are more committed than average, even if involved in only a single practice, the bias may be yet greater.

Table 2.3 shows an approximate distribution of activities examined (combining the figures from Tables 2.1 and 2.2, weighted two-thirds and one-third respectively).

Table 2.3   Acts of participation in the holistic milieu (%)

Yoga and tai chi	43.3
Dancing, singing, art and craft	5.3
Massage, bodywork	15.5
Homeopathy	4.0
Counselling	3.6
Healing and complementary health groups	10.7
Reiki or spiritual healing	6.7
Specialised spiritual/religious groups	5.3
Miscellaneous one-to-one	5.6

Source: Estimated from Kendal Project data.

It is hard not be struck by how few activities listed here are clearly spiritual. Half of all involvement is in what most people would view as leisure or recreation – yoga, tai chi, dance, singing and art. Add in pampering (massage, bodywork) and one has covered nearly two-thirds. Not all the 'healing and complementary health groups' are obviously spiritual or even unconventional; CancerCare, winner of the Queen's Jubilee Award for Voluntary Service in the Community, is one of the larger ones. A fair proportion of the healing activities are based on distinctive beliefs, but even these (for example homeopathy, Reiki) seem pseudoscientific rather than necessarily spiritual. One of the main 'specialised spiritual/religious groups' is Sea of Faith, whose mission is 'to explore and promote religious faith as a human creation', namely to help preserve something of religion while jettisoning the supernatural.

Even among the 237 participants and practitioners included – a sample that for the reasons discussed above is biased in favour of 'spiritual' interpretations of these activities – only a quarter chose 'spiritual growth' as the main reason for their involvement. Fewer than half said that their participation had anything whatsoever to do with spiritual growth.

Heelas and Woodhead assert that 'the figure we have arrived at for the holistic milieu ... shows that Bruce ... is wrong when he claims that "the number of people [in Britain] who have shown any interest in alternative religions is minute"' (Heelas and Woodhead 2005: 54–5). It would be unproductive to argue over what is or is not 'minute', and we grant that in Britain as a whole the spiritually minded will number in the tens and possibly hundreds of thousands. None the less we remain struck mainly by the peculiarity of packaging a variety of imported recreational activities, miscellaneous methods of relaxation and diverse forms of alternative medicine, all practised mainly by people who do not even pretend to see them as spiritual, as the second coming of religion in the West.

Sacralisation?

Spirituality is clearly religious (in a broad sense) to the extent that it involves non-natural forces, but most activities seem to have relatively little to do with the sacred. It is hard to agree with the claim that growth in the holistic milieu represents 'sacralisation'. Much of what is called 'spirituality' seems to be merely pseudo-science (such as 'energy' circulating in the body). Indeed, Heelas and Woodhead explicitly describe 'energy', 'chi' and so forth as the 'functional equivalents' of spirituality (Heelas and Woodhead 2005: 27). Eastern medicine may indeed be holistic, but it need not be 'spiritual'. There is a distinction – not always sharp, admittedly – between alternative medicine (based on theories not widely accepted in the West) and faith healing (a kind of sacred magic).

The evidence suggests that the holistic milieu includes a hard core of spiritual enthusiasts – in particular the practitioners – and a larger group of mainly health-orientated people. Many of the latter will acknowledge a spiritual dimension in these activities, but it is not their primary concern. Only a minority were drawn into participation by a quest for spiritual growth, and spiritual training has little effect on the others – 33 per cent of survey respondents listed 'looking for spiritual growth' among their top three original reasons for participating, a figure that increased to just 41 per cent when people were asked for their current reasons.

Moreover the descriptions of spirituality given by the Kendal respondents seem to have little to do with the supernatural or even the sacred; it appears to be a code word for good feelings, the emotional rather than the material. Not even a quarter of those involved defined their core beliefs about spirituality in terms that were either vaguely esoteric ('being in touch with subtle energies') or religious ('obeying God's will'). The rest said that it was love, being a decent and caring person, or something similarly terrestrial. A proportion even described it as 'living life to the full', on which basis the London restaurateur Peter Stringfellow might qualify as a spiritual master.

Although everyone will have an opinion about whether these activities are by nature spiritual, we do not need to impose our views; respondents provided their own answers on the survey. We know, for example, that just over half of the 252 respondents have tried yoga at one time or another (making it by far the most popular activity), and almost exactly half of those see yoga as having a spiritual dimension for them. In general, the massages and exercise programmes that constitute the most popular activities are also the least likely to be seen as spiritual. Although some of the more prevalent activities (Reiki for example) are regarded by most participants as spiritual and some of the least common (such as naturopathy) are quite secular, it is evident that overall the most spiritual activities are the least practised.

One possible complication is that we may wish to argue with the actors' designations. Perhaps an imposed designation would be more revealing, if a committed

New Ager might deny that a certain activity is spiritual not because she does not believe in it but because she regards it as just good medicine or science. Fortunately that does not seem to be the case. Craniosacral therapy, for example, is seen as spiritual by 65 per cent of those involved in it.

Ten activities accounted for close to half of the total number of acts of participation recorded (for the past week or previously) – yoga, aromatherapy, massage, homeopathy, reflexology, Alexander Technique, tai chi, osteopathy, Reiki, and flower essence therapy. Collectively these ten were seen as having a spiritual dimension by 37 per cent of the people who had tried them. The next ten activities (acupuncture, counselling, foot massage, healing/spiritual healing, circle dancing, Buddhism, inter-faith group, astrology, chiropractic, shiatsu) supplied another quarter of overall participation; an average of 50 per cent of respondents considered them to have a spiritual dimension. The final quarter came from 33 different activities that received a mean rating of 54 per cent for spirituality. Because of the nature of the sample little credence should be placed in the absolute levels of these figures, but even these data make the point: the most spiritual activities are by and large the least popular and vice-versa.

The pattern is all the more striking because this self-selected sample emerges as being extraordinarily high on unconventional beliefs and low on orthodox ones. Nearly three-quarters accept the existence of subtle energy in the body, twice as many as believe in heaven. Almost as many believe in chakras as in God (55 vs. 58 per cent), and – in a revealing show of where tolerance is deployed – a mere 11 per cent do *not* believe in chakras while 29 per cent disbelieve in God. (The 'don't knows' account for the balance.) Almost one in four respondents believe in UFOs; only one in six believes in the devil. The most popular belief – in the admittedly fuzzy 'spirit or life force' – does twice as well as belief in Jesus as the Son of God (82 per cent vs. 41 per cent).

This disintegration of the Christian consensus, though, is mostly a sign of the declining significance of religion (in a broad sense) both socially and personally. Spirituality is a label for a ragbag of beliefs and practices that have slightly exotic origins, participation in which is becoming less rather than more like religious activity. The point was illustrated in a recent programme called 'Spirituality Shopper' shown on Channel 4 in Britain. The television reviewer for the *Daily Mirror* gives the flavour:

In the first of three programmes, triple-jumping Christian Jonathan Edwards performs a mystical makeover on 29-year-old Michaela Newton-Wright, whose great job in advertising leaves her feeling strangely shallow and unfulfilled. Explaining that it's not necessary for her to actually believe in any of the religions, Jonathan introduces Michaela to an array of God-bothering options for her to mix and match. She gets lessons in Buddhist meditation, cooks a meal for friends on the Jewish Sabbath, gives Sufi dancing a whirl, visits one rather surprised old lady and is even persuaded to give up her hair straighteners for an imaginary Lent. It's easy to scoff at the idea that spiritual enlightenment can be achieved in four weeks without believing in anything at all – so please don't let me stop you. ... But amazingly after one month the transformation in Michaela is astonishing – her hair really is much, much curlier. (Jane Simon, 'Today's TV', *Daily Mirror*, 6 June 2005)

The mocking tone of this and other commentators may be unjust; the three subjects of these programmes seemed to benefit from their experiences and even showed some interest in 'genuine' spirituality by the end. Nevertheless the most striking feature of the whole enterprise was its entirely secular orientation. The participants listened politely while the practitioners explained the worldview underlying each activity, but the subsequent discussion concerned what they personally might gain in stress relief, self-confidence, a sense of direction, etc. Even the blurb on the Channel 4 website asks 'but is it a spiritual journey or just a set of strategies for getting up and out of the house?'

Much in these vignettes corroborated Heelas and Woodhead's analysis of the 'subjective turn' in modern society. The young professional described above, for example, took what had been presented as temporary sacrifices for Lent (giving up hair straighteners, walking rather than riding a bus) and reinterpreted them as instructions to become more authentic or more in touch with the environment. These practices acquired a different, but in personal terms probably deeper, meaning than the one intended. The crucial point, however, is that there was nothing spiritual about her response – or if one prefers, the 'spiritual' had been utterly desacralised. Likewise Michaela's touching passage from self-consciousness to enthusiasm for Sufi twirling had nothing to do with spiritual ecstasy; her response was aesthetic and emotional, and these are 'spiritual' only in the attenuated sense of being non-material. What we see is secularisation at work, not the replacement of religion by spirituality.

Not so Revolutionary and Possibly Transient

The term 'spiritual revolution' implies two things: firstly that something new is happening, and secondly that the innovation is here to stay. There are reasons to doubt both.

There is nothing particularly new about alternative spirituality; it has been around for a long time. As J. Gordon Melton notes, the New Age should be 'seen as the latest phase in occult/metaphysical religion, a persistent tradition that has been the constant companion of Christianity through the centuries' (Melton 1991: 4). It is the descendant of past excitements over divination, Freemasonry, Swedenborgianism, mesmerism, spiritualism, New Thought, Theosophy, and so on. It resembles the supposed enthusiasm for new religions or Eastern religions of a couple of decades ago, both of which levelled out fairly quickly. Not only are the gains in alternative belief not sufficient to replace the orthodox losses, such moves away from Christian convention may mediate rather than deflect the transition from faith to secularity.

The holistic milieu is populated mainly by women from a particular generation; there is no particular sign that it will be popular among those who follow. The demographic profile is the same as that found in other studies covering alternative spirituality, for example the Scottish Social Attitudes Survey 2001 (Glendinning and Bruce 2006). Transmission to the next generation is unlikely to be easy, especially given the non-involvement of men.

If people have two children on average, then one or both must be socialised into a practice for it to survive in the long term, depending on whether one or both parents are involved. Intergenerational transmission of Christian affiliation, attendance and belief currently stands at half that level (Voas and Crockett 2005). Even if we assume that only one-eighth of the children of holistically spiritual women have fathers who are similarly involved in these practices, and even if 30 per cent of these children adopt the holistic 'faith', spirituality will likewise have a 'half life' of one generation (so that adult children are half as likely to identify, attend or believe as their parents). Thus the fact that 32 per cent of Kendal respondents with offspring said that their children were interested in the activity is not only unimpressive, *pace* Heelas and Seel (2003: 234), but shows that in this respect the holistic milieu is doing no better than the congregational domain (even assuming that 'interest' means 'participation'). Moreover there is evidence (not least from the Kendal survey; see below) that women of a spiritual disposition are more likely than average to be childless, which poses a particular threat to the New Age's hope of continuity.

Two-thirds of respondents in the Kendal survey described themselves as 'spiritual'; three-quarters as either spiritual or religious or both. People under the age of 40, however, predominantly describe themselves as neither, as the Scottish Social Attitudes Survey indicates (Voas and Crockett 2004). Only three people under the age of 30 even responded to the Kendal survey, and 83 per cent were 40 or older. The age profile differs from church congregations simply in being middle-aged rather than elderly, with perhaps even fewer young adults.

As Heelas admits, the New Age is a product of the 1960s counter-culture. The modal age group (in 2001) is 50–54; two-thirds of these people acknowledged being 'a child of the 1960s'. The five-year age groups on either side are also well represented, though interestingly only in the younger one (Heelas and Woodhead 2005: 45–9) did a majority likewise accept the designation 'child of the 1960s'. The perceived importance of that decade was higher for those who lived it as adolescents than as young adults. (It is worth noting that a third of people aged 35–44 described themselves thus, presumably because they took the statement literally – they were born during the 1960s.)

Although Heelas and Woodhead assert that spirituality is not a form of compensation for an unhappy home or work life – most members of their sample rated their lives highly in these respects – it does seem that these people have not necessarily had success (if they sought it) in conventional relationships. Of female respondents 35–49, only a third are living with husbands – as against nearly two-thirds in the general population – the rest being equally divided between unmarried partnerships, lone parenthood and living alone. (The handful of men is similarly distributed.) Only half of female respondents of childbearing age (virtually all of whom are 30–44) have children living at home, compared with three-quarters of women aged 30–44 in England generally. Notwithstanding the rising age of maternity, it seems likely that a high proportion of spiritual women will not have children at all.

There is no age group in which a majority of the female respondents were in full-time work. (The high point is reached at 45–9, with exactly half.) Certainly these women, or at any rate those aged 35–54, are working, but most are following the established feminine pattern of part-time work. A quarter of those in work are self-employed, which is remarkably high, probably reflecting the presence of practitioners in the sample. Almost all of the respondents (94 per cent) had grown up elsewhere – a revealing sign of how unusual this group is.

A large majority (71 per cent) of respondents had received a religious upbringing either at home or at church. The future of spirituality may be in doubt in the absence of forms of religious socialisation. While half of the respondents said that they were not committed Christians but supported Christian values (a rather modest vote for a relatively anodyne statement), a third described themselves as critical of or indifferent to Christianity.

Comparison with the Congregational Domain

Heelas and Woodhead maintain that comparing the 1.6 per cent of the population they find involved on a weekly basis in the holistic milieu with the 7.9 per cent found in church is valid because 'it compares like with like: namely the numbers involved in associational activities which are taken to be of spiritual or religious significance by those who organise them' (Heelas and Woodhead 2005: 46). They acknowledge that those 'involved' in the holistic milieu do not necessarily have any spiritual commitment, but claim that likewise churchgoers may be attending for personal or social reasons that are not religious. Even so, the argument that 1.6 per cent is the appropriate number to compare with the congregational value of 7.9 per cent seems unpersuasive.

It is clearly true that both churchgoers and holistic participants will fall along a continuum from the highly religious/spiritual to the wholly secular. At a service of Christmas carols one would expect to find a large number of people who were there for entertainment. No doubt a few are in church each Sunday for the same reason, or because the family and neighbours attend, or whatever. Nevertheless one supposes that the proportion of people attending in a typical week for explicitly non-religious reasons is fairly low (and survey data show that only a minute proportion of churchgoers admit to having no faith). By contrast, the proportion of people attending reflexology or even tai chi for non-spiritual reasons is clearly very high; half (and probably more in reality) of the 'holistic' participants have no sense that they are involved in anything spiritual. We disagree that Heelas and Woodhead are comparing like with like, except in the most superficial sense. Far more holistic than congregational participants are at the secular end of the scale.

Moreover a church service is defined as a religious ceremony; attendance amounts to religious participation, even if one's actual motive is different. By contrast a yoga class or an aromatherapy session need carry no public connotation of spirituality, whatever the commitment of the practitioner. There is not even the tacit acquiescence to an official view that is implicit in going to church. If its organiser determines the spiritual character of any activity then nineteenth century penitentiaries were sacred spaces because their wardens had religious goals.

Heelas and Woodhead also argue that counting participation during a single week may be less favourable to the holistic milieu (where more people may be involved sporadically or infrequently) than to the congregational domain. This claim does not really help to justify the comparison. One could likewise say that conventional belief in God is more widespread than is evidenced in weekly attendance, the familiar 'believing without belonging' argument.

The procedure seems to be at odds with the admirably conservative approach to enumeration adopted for the Kendal Project. Too much emphasis is being given to the perceptions of the providers. A teacher might see education in general as a spiritual experience, but it would be hard to justify treating all her students as part of the holistic milieu unless they recognised the activity as more than nominally spiritual themselves. Conversely, one should question the decision to exclude a hands-on healer and possibly others who denied that their activities were spiritual. Social scientists are entitled to decide what does and does not count. For many years Jehovah's Witnesses were adamant that they were not a religious group (they saw 'religion' as a satanic perversion of the Truth), which did not stop Beckford and other sociologists of religion from studying them. We are not obliged to accept the designations of groups offered by their leaders.

Projections

Heelas and Woodhead argue that the holistic milieu has grown enormously in the past few decades and that thanks to the 'subjective turn' in contemporary culture its growth is likely to continue. Though the spiritual revolution has not come yet, it may be just a matter of time before the BBC refreshes its Sunday programming with *Songs of Self-Praise*. Rapid growth is not sustainable indefinitely, however; it becomes more and more difficult to find susceptible people to recruit. If something appears to be growing exponentially, the question is when, not whether the process will hit the wall. Projecting recent growth rates forward without constraint leads to the conclusion that everyone will be simultaneously Mormon and Muslim and agnostic, as well as alternatively spiritual, in a century or two.

For predictions to be more than speculative, one needs a theory about the mechanisms at work that make the implicit mathematical model plausible. The idea that self-orientation is on the rise might imply that the holistic milieu will grow, but it does not tell us by how much over what period, and whether arithmetically, geometrically, exponentially, logistically and so forth.

What is in fact realistic? The standard population model is the logistic (or S-shaped) curve, where numbers rise slowly at first, increase rapidly, and then level out. The shape and level of the graph depend on resources (here, the supply of potential converts) and the speed with which those are processed into new members. There are limits: an environment has a certain carrying capacity for rabbits, McDonald's restaurants, and (arguably) the holistically spiritual. Being able to say where the plateau will come is not easy, but we can use experience and what we know about religious ecology and reproduction to guide us.

Heelas and Woodhead note that at present holistic spirituality has a rather narrow socio-demographic appeal, and that the relevant section of the population (educated, middle-aged women in people-orientated professions) may be approaching saturation point. The milieu 'seems to have attracted a considerable proportion of its primary "market niche" already' (Heelas and Woodhead 2005: 136). They predict that the niche will widen to make further growth possible, doubling weekly participation by the middle of this century.

This prediction assumes, of course, that New Age spirituality – now largely confined to the middle-aged – will not prove to be an artefact of the 1960s, here today, gone tomorrow, as that generation slowly disappears. Succeeding birth cohorts must replace the current participants and practitioners, something of which there is currently little sign. Heelas and Woodhead are thus doubly optimistic, believing not only that spirituality is an age-related rather than a generational phenomenon, but also that it will break out of its gender/age/class/ethnic enclave to colonise new sub-populations.

A key justification for their optimism is the argument that 'holistic spiritualities of life provide a relatively specialised or distinctive variant of the much more widespread culture of subjective well-being. This means that these spiritualities can attract those involved with the more widespread culture who are looking for activities which are in tune with what they are already familiar with *while* taking them further or "deeper"' (Heelas and Woodhead 2005: 83–4). There is at least as much evidence to suggest, though, that the wider the distribution, the weaker the spiritual dose becomes. True, clients may come to aromatherapy for the nice smells and then stay for the sermon, but is it not more likely that practitioners will do best by preaching least? Rather than the mundane being sacralised, the spiritual may become secularised.

We see the future somewhat differently. Certainly the decay of Christian orthodoxy will help to feed the growth of heterodox alternatives (as well as scepticism and indifference) as churches lose their monopoly on respectable belief and believers. The continuing unpopularity of institutional religion will lead more people to describe themselves as spiritual but not religious, at least for a time. Creators, importers and promoters of services for the mind, body and spirit will be able to sustain and possibly increase participation in the holistic milieu. Nothing in these developments, though, implies that social or even personal life is being sacralised. On the contrary, they are part and parcel of the process of secularisation. Meditation, yoga, bodywork and aromatherapy may all go mainstream but their spiritual content will be drained off. Practices like feng shui will appear, enjoy 15 minutes of fame, and then will be displaced by another fad. These activities have the same relationship with spirituality as a concert performance of the *St Matthew Passion* does with religion. Whether pleasant and diverting or beautiful and uplifting, such experiences are essentially secular.

Conclusion

Claims about the popularity of the New Age benefit from the positive connotations of being 'spiritual'. Should we be impressed that 'Eight out of ten Americans, not just "religious" people, express desire for spiritual growth' (quoting Gallup and Jones; Heelas and Woodhead 2005: 49)? One can be confident that this 'finding' did not emerge from an open-ended question (for example, 'what things do you desire?), but instead from a blunt yes/no enquiry about wanting spiritual growth. Who would say 'no – I'm spiritual enough as I am'? Likewise questions about being a spiritual person (or not) seem hopelessly loaded. Only a few of us delight in presenting ourselves as thoroughgoing materialists (though a surprisingly high proportion of young people in particular identify themselves as neither spiritual nor religious).

We are not alone in thinking that the importance of alternative spirituality has been exaggerated. The most thorough investigation into the religious and spiritual lives of American teenagers ever undertaken finds that 'the influence [of spiritual seeking] on teens has been greatly overstated. … When we came to interview questions about being "spiritual but not religious" … most teens literally did not understand what it was we were asking about' (Smith 2005: 78).

The figures from the Kendal Project are estimates and, like all such, we can argue about their basis. Nonetheless, let us grant that somewhere around 600 people in and around Kendal are involved in holistic milieu activities each week and that some 45 per cent of them, or 270 people, regard what they are doing as 'spiritual'. Is 270 a large or a small number? It is lower than attendance at virtually any professional football match; even Kendal Town FC (in the First – that is lower – Division of the UniBond Northern Premier League) generally does better.

Although Heelas and Woodhead do not make this case, others have presented the growth of alternative forms of spirituality as evidence that humankind is enduringly religious. If we are to regard holistic spirituality as compensation for the decline of the Christian churches we need to get the scale right. The church-going population of Kendal is 7.9 per cent. If we increase that to 15 per cent to give some idea of those who are at all interested in Christianity we get 85 per cent of the population or almost 32,000 people in Kendal and its environs who are not in the mainstream of religion and who are thus, in theory, available for recruitment to some alternative.

Perhaps a better way of guessing the potential market is to take the proportion of people who attended church in 1851, when England could reasonably be described as a Christian society. Horace Mann's Census of Religious Worship lists attendances in Kendal at 47.7 per cent. Because Mann's survey counted attendances rather than attenders, we have to compensate for double (and, very rarely, triple) attendance. Following Crockett's pioneering work, we might reasonably set the figure at 38 per cent. If church-going in Kendal were as popular now as it was in 1851, there would be 14,000 church-goers rather than the current 3,000. We can thus say that the current performance of the Christian churches in Kendal leaves 11,000 people un-churched, compared with the 1851 proportions. Set against that scale of decline, the 270 people involved in the holistic milieu for spiritual reasons seems very small.

Notwithstanding our reservations about the interpretation of the evidence, we agree that the trend away from religion and towards a more individualised worldview is an important phenomenon. The work of Heelas, Woodhead and their collaborators is pioneering, thorough, and engagingly sensitive to the distinctive spirit of the holistic milieu. The Kendal Project is the most innovative and impressive study to have come out of British sociology of religion in the past decade.

What is the way forward? The next step, in our view, is to try to distinguish between the different constituencies currently considered under the holistic banner. Some people are undoubtedly motivated by an attraction to metaphysical spirituality, but others are mainly interested in physical and mental methods of stress relief, or in alternative forms of healing, or in spa-type bodywork, or in opportunities for self-expression and psychological support. How the numbers break down, how much overlap there is between them, whether and when the connections reflect a shared conception of the sacred rather than simply mutual sympathy or common practice – these are the questions to address.

We do not underestimate the difficulty of drafting suitably revealing questions. Although the responsibility to design discriminating research is one that we share, ultimately the onus is on those who claim that spirituality is in the ascendant to produce convincing evidence at the societal level. There has been a tendency in the sociology of religion generally to slide from pointing out the expansion in activities and concerns that might be spiritual to claiming that therefore people are coming back to God, or finding a cosmic consciousness, or discovering a mystical power within themselves, or are otherwise becoming more rather than less faithful. Such conclusions are unwarranted. Similarly, evidence that holistic concepts are becoming part of the culture do not show that a spiritual revolution is coming, any more than the strength of the Christian heritage shows that a religious revival is just around the corner.

The individualism of the 'spiritual' is a sign that these attitudes and activities represent the consequences of secularisation rather than an alternative to it. The commonly invoked idea that 'spirituality is without the baggage' associated with religion (Heelas and Woodhead 2005: 90) is another way of saying that it is not very religious. People are unwilling to be told what to believe, when to go to church, or how they should be labelled, but they are also less willing than ever to commit *themselves* to any kind of religion or spirituality, even a spirituality of the self. If there is a revolution, we should know where to look for it: the sacred is giving way to the secular.

Bibliography

Brierley, P. (2000), *The Tide is Running Out: What the English Church Attendance Survey Reveals*, London: Christian Research.

Bruce, S. (2002), *God is Dead: Secularisation in the West*, Oxford: Blackwell.

Glendinning, T. and S. Bruce (2006), 'New Ways of Believing or Belonging: Is Religion Giving Way to Spirituality?', *The British Journal of Sociology*, 57(3): 399–414.

Heelas, P. and B. Seel (2003), 'An Ageing New Age?', in G. Davie, P. Heelas and L. Woodhead (eds), *Predicting Religion: Christian, Secular and Alternative Futures*, Aldershot: Ashgate, pp. 229–47.

Heelas, P. and L. Woodhead, (2005), *The Spiritual Revolution: Why Religion is Giving Way to Spirituality*, Oxford: Blackwell.

Melton, J.G., J. Clark and A. A. Kelly (1991), *New Age Almanac*, Detroit: Visible Ink.

Smith, C. (2005), *Soul Searching: The Religious and Spiritual Lives of American Teenagers*, New York: Oxford University Press.

Voas, D. and A. Crockett (2004), 'Spiritual, Religious or Secular: Evidence from National Surveys' (paper presented at the conference of the British Sociological Association Sociology of Religion Study Group, Bristol, March 2004).

Voas, D. and A. Crockett (2005), 'Religion in Britain: Neither Believing nor Belonging', *Sociology*, 39(1): 11–28.

Appendix: Groups and Therapies in the Kendal Holistic Milieu

Acupressure	Metamorphic technique
Acupuncture	Naturopathy
Alexander Technique	Nutritional therapy
Aromatherapy	Osteopathy
Art therapy/group	Pagan activities
Astrology	Palm readings
Buddhist group	Play therapy
CancerCare group	Psychic consultancy
Chinese College of Physical Culture	Psychotherapy
Chiropractice	Rebirthing
Circle Dancing	Reflexology
Counselling	Reiki
Cranio-sacral therapy	Relaxation therapy
Energy management workshops	Sai Baba group
Flower essences therapy	Sea of Faith group
Foot massage	Shiatsu
GreenSpirit group	Spinal touch therapy
Healing/Spiritual healing	Tai Chi/Chi Kung
Herbalism	Taizé singing group
Homeopathy	Tarot card reading

Hypnotherapy	True Vision group
Indian Head massage	Universal Peace dancing
Inter-faith group	Vision therapy
Iona Group	Wild Women group
Kinaesiology	Women's spirituality group
Massage	Yoga
Meridian therapy	

Source: Heelas and Woodhead (2005: 156–7).

Chapter 3

The Holistic Milieu and Spirituality: Reflections on Voas and Bruce

Paul Heelas

This chapter offers a response to the preceding contribution to the volume from Voas and Bruce. Their critical analysis of some of the findings of the Kendal Project is greatly appreciated. More generally, they provide a thought-provoking contribution to the study of holistic, mind–body–spirituality.

Our primary aim during the Kendal Project was to test the controversial 'spiritual revolution' claim. We sought to examine whether 'alternative spirituality' has become, or is in the process of becoming, more important than traditional Christianity in the United Kingdom. To address this claim, we embarked on a locality study of the market town and regional centre of Kendal, Cumbria. The research took place between 1 October 2000 and 30 June 2002. By taking a single relatively self-contained and relatively small locality, population 27,610 in 1999, we could be fairly confident of systematically counting the numbers involved in what most concerned us – associational forms of traditional, theistic Christianity, namely the congregational domain, and associational forms of mind–body–spirituality, namely the holistic milieu. Accordingly, we counted the numbers participating in the congregations of Kendal on a typical Sunday, and in yoga groups or spiritual homeopathic one-to-one sessions (for example) during a typical week. Many of the findings are provided in *The Spiritual Revolution* (Heelas and Woodhead 2005); more are available on the Kendal Project website (www.kendalproject.org.uk), including the holistic milieu questionnaire, the data set and graphs.[1]

---

1   In view of what Voas and Bruce have to say about the amount of quantified information provided in *The Spiritual Revolution*, it should be emphasised that the website has been specifically developed to complement the volume. It is true that a suitable breakdown of the one-to-one activities into the number of acts of participation per activity has yet to be prepared for the public domain. The tricky tasks involved (handling confidentiality and anonymity, the fact that a number of practitioners provided an overall estimate for more than one activity and so forth) will be tackled in due course. Thanks are due to Bronislaw Szerszynski for helping with some of the information provided in this chapter.

Comparing the Holistic Milieu and the Congregational Domain

Questioning the very basis of the comparison between the holistic milieu and the congregational domain which we made in the Kendal Project, Voas and Bruce provide objections which threaten to undermine – if not invalidate – much of our research. They write, 'we disagree that Heelas and Woodhead are comparing like with like, except in the most superficial sense' (Voas and Bruce 2007: 55). Their disagreement largely derives from their claim that the participants of the holistic milieu are considerably more secular than those belonging to the congregational domain. With 'half (and probably more in reality) of the "holistic" participants hav[ing] no sense that they are involved in anything spiritual' and with only 'a few' being in church each Sunday for reasons of 'entertainment' or 'because the family and neighbours attend' (Voas and Bruce 2007: 55), the argument is that the two realms of participation are too dissimilar for effective comparative purposes.

In justifying our comparison, much hangs on one of the criteria we used for comparative purposes. As formulated in *The Spiritual Revolution*, 'in order to retain comparability with the congregational domain … just as congregational activities are taken to be of sacred significance by those who lead them, so we determined we would only count those involved with activities *which were taken to be of sacred significance by those who provide them*' (Heelas and Woodhead 2005 :36–7; italics added). But why did we not compare the number of *religiously-active* people attending congregations with the number of *spiritually-active* group members and one-to-one clients in holistic, mind-body-spirituality groups and one-to-one activities? The answer is simple. Although we found out the number of participants in the holistic milieu who were engaged in activities which they took to be of spiritual significance, we did not have a comparable figure for the congregational domain. Accordingly, the only way to compare like with like was to use the 'provider's' criterion.

It might be objected that surely Voas and Bruce are justified to claim that only 'a few' go to Church each Sunday for primarily non-religious reasons – social, personal, for what Bryan Wilson (1966: 114) calls the 'matter of social respectability'; that what Chambers (2005: 161) calls 'internal secularisation' is minimal. The short answer is that convincing data is unavailable – not simply for Kendal, but also for elsewhere. True, Voas and Bruce write that 'survey data show that only a minute proportion of churchgoers admit to having no faith' (Voas and Bruce 2007: 55), but this is by no means convincing evidence. 'Secular' churchgoers are hardly likely to admit, even in a survey, that they go to church under what amounts to false pretences (Heelas and Woodhead 2005: 46–7, 162).

Although the criterion we used only concerns 'providers' (rather than church attendees or holistic milieu group members and one-to-one clients), it nevertheless remains the case that one of Voas and Bruce's objections is that 'far more holistic than congregational *participants* are at the secular end of the scale' (Voas and Bruce 2007: 55; italics added). The way this is worded makes it possible to mount another justification for the comparison we carried out. Findings from the questionnaire distributed to holistic milieu participants make it clear that respondents are by no means as secular as Voas and Bruce would have it. (Indeed, they write that questionnaire responses are 'extraordinarily high on unconventional beliefs' [Voas and Bruce 2007: 52].) 82 per cent agree that 'some sort of spirit or life force pervades all that lives'; 73 per cent express belief in 'subtle energy (or energy channels) in the body'; 91 per cent say that they are a spiritual or a religious person (with 68 per cent saying that there are the former); 81 per cent believe that there is some sort of spirit or life force or a personal God (a God which, in the context of other findings, can generally be taken to have to do with the human person); 77 per cent believe in 'special healing powers'; 71 per cent rate 'spirituality' on points six to ten on a scale from one (not at all important) to ten (very important), with 38 per cent selecting ten; and, to give two more, indicative, figures, 55 per cent meditate at home and 90 per cent are familiar with the appropriate usage of the term 'chi' (www.kendalproject.org.uk). It is true that another questionnaire finding shows that 45 per cent of respondents do not regard the holistic milieu activity (or activities) they have been involved with during the previous week as having a spiritual dimension (Heelas and Woodhead 2005: 46). But the fact remains that the great majority of respondents are 'spiritual' – quite possibly as many as are 'religious' within the congregational domain.[2]

The Numerical Significance of Kendal's Holistic Milieu in 2001

The comparison which underpins the Kendal Project might be justified. But what is to be made of Voas and Bruce's argument that the way in which we worked out that 600 people (or 1.6 per cent of the population involved) were active in the holistic milieu during a typical week of the autumn of 2001 is 'rather insecure' (Voas and Bruce 2007: 48)?

Voas and Bruce are critical of the way we handled the tricky issue of multi-participation. Before attending to what they have to say, the procedures we adopted in the project need to be briefly summarised. Earlier during the Kendal Project, we established that there were 840 acts of participation in the holistic milieu. Being aware that some participants were involved with more than one activity, we devised our questionnaire so that we could spot instances of multi-participation in different kinds of activities during a typical week. Using questionnaire results which showed the numbers of people attending once, twice, three times, etc., we worked out that 483 individuals were sustaining the 840 acts of participation. However, this did not take into account the consideration that multi-participants were more likely to return the questionnaire than those who were only involved with one activity: thereby being over represented in the questionnaire sample – the very sample which provides the key for deducing the number of participants from the number of acts of participation.

---

2   Voas and Bruce also criticise our comparison on the grounds that holistic milieu activities differ from church services in that they 'need carry no public connotation of spirituality' (Voas and Bruce 2007: 55). However, 'spirituality' is widely referred to by flyers advertising activities, verbally by practitioners (in particular), or both.

To rectify the bias, we followed a procedure, summarised by Voas and Bruce (Voas and Bruce 2007: 47), which resulted in the final figure of 600.

One possibility raised by Voas and Bruce (2007: 46–7) is that we have *underestimated* the number of multi-participants. That is to say, we have not taken into account the possibility (or likelihood) of people participating in the same activity – with the same practitioner, another or others – on a weekly basis. However, in *The Spiritual Revolution* we write that 'the rhythm of activity is of a ... weekly order' (Heelas and Woodhead 2005: 36). And a great deal of evidence – from case studies, structured questions systematically addressed to practitioners, and from interviews with group members and one-to-one clients – supports this. Thus, of the 33 activities (groups and one-to one) run from the seven 'centres', 20 are run weekly, 10 monthly, two fortnightly, with just one more frequently than weekly – a temporal distribution which is typical of the milieu as a whole. This means that it would be extremely difficult, if not impossible for an individual to attend a particular activity run by a particular practitioner during a particular week. Furthermore, we did not find a single instance of an individual going to another practitioner to take an additional session of the 'same' activity (say spiritual reflexology) during a particular week.

Another possibility raised by Voas and Bruce is that we have *overestimated* the number of multi-participants. That is to say, we have exaggerated the extent to which multi-participants (who amount to 40 per cent of questionnaire respondents) would be the most likely to return the questionnaire. Three considerations are at stake. The first is that multi-participants would be the most likely to come across the questionnaire and be asked to complete it. Given the fact that the questionnaire was distributed by practitioners, who – we know – did not always provide the questionnaire at their events, it cannot be doubted that this was the case. The second consideration is that two or more requests would serve to encourage multi-participants to return the form. Regarding this, Voas and Bruce write that our approach 'assumes something that may not be true, namely that how likely a person is to respond just depends on how many times she is offered the form' (Voas and Bruce 2007: 48). Their reason is that 'an individual faced with a survey will tend to be either co-operative *or resistant*' (Voas and Bruce 2007: 47; my emphasis). It should be noted that survey research into the usage of CAM (forms of complementary and alternative medicine which include a fair number of holistic milieu activities) typically involves reminders, 'up to three' in one study (Thomas et al. 2001: 3; see also Eisenberg et al. 1998: 1570). This resource consuming follow-up procedure is only carried out because it has been judged to be effective.

Although it could be the case that the statistical procedure we adopted in *The Spiritual Revolution* resulted in a degree of over-compensation, we did not take into account a third consideration, namely that multi-participants would be significantly more inclined to 'cooperate' (Voas and Bruce 2007: 48) than others. Thinking of the considerable number, namely 95, of spiritual practitioners who were providing the activities of the holistic milieu during the autumn of 2001, they were clearly enthusiastic and surely proud about what they were doing. Having individually received the questionnaire, having previously talked with a researcher (when the value of the questionnaire was emphasised) and – no doubt – having read articles in *The Westmoreland Gazette* (which also emphasised the significance of the research), they were surely strongly motivated to return the questionnaire. And our research shows that a considerable number of practitioners were multi-participants. Furthermore, there is little doubting the fact that other multi-participants were more interested in, or enthusiastic about, what the holistic milieu has to offer than the mono-participants.

Thinking of Voas and Bruce's analogy (Voas and Bruce 2007: 47), the question of multi-participation is best seen in terms of asking people to sign a birthday card – not providing a donation for the Conservative Party. Indeed, my reflections on the enthusiasm factor prompt me to think that the figure of 600 is somewhat on the low side. There are additional reasons for arriving at this conclusion. Together with those mentioned in *The Spiritual Revolution* (Heelas and Woodhead 2005: 161), it could well be the case that the 'environs factor' should be handled in a different way from that adopted in the volume. To explain, the 1.6 percentage is of a population of 37,150 – of Kendal itself, together with those living within a five-mile radius of the town. We included the rural environs because of the location of two holistic centres, Rainbow Cottage and Loop Cottage. However, these are relatively small – respectively housing 15 and eight activities of the 126 separate activities predominantly found in the town – and 'cater for a significant number of Kendalians' (Heelas and Woodhead 2005: 37). With the last point in mind, there is much to be said for including them within the holistic milieu of Kendal itself. With a population of 27,610, this means that the percentage participating in the milieu is *2.2 per cent* – not 1.6. Furthermore, even if the environs are included, the fact remains that we did not devote as much time as we would have liked to detailed investigation of all the rural surrounds (Heelas and Woodhead 2005: 161).[3]

Voas and Bruce write of 'the admirably conservative approach to enumeration adopted for the Kendal Project' (Voas and Bruce 2007: 56). If it were not for the fact that we were almost certainly *too* conservative, it is difficult not to agree. Indeed, in less cautious mode I am now strongly inclined to conclude that the most realistic figure is 2.2 per cent of the population of the town of Kendal *itself,* possibly slightly more.

On the 'Revolutionary' Significance of the Growth of the Holistic Milieu

According to Voas and Bruce, the argument of *The Spiritual Revolution* is that mind–body–spirituality 'might overtake its older rival ['conventional religion'] in just a few decades' (Voas and Bruce 2007: 43 and 44–5). In fact the conclusion to the volume asserts:

> We predict that in 40 or so years time the congregational domain and holistic milieu of Britain will have become much the same size' – a conclusion which is followed by the line,

---

3   Voas and Bruce (2007: 56) imply that we include the teaching of spirituality in schools within the holistic milieu – which would swell numbers. In fact we do not include activities of this variety (Heelas and Woodhead 2005: 36–7).

'as to whether a spiritual revolution will take place after that – well, predicting the future has its limits'. (Heelas and Woodhead 2005:149)[4]

Voas and Bruce do not dispute our finding that holistic milieu activities of the kind we find today have grown during recent decades.[5] What they do dispute is that it will continue to grow.

According to Voas and Bruce (2007: 54) 'as Heelas admits, the New Age is a product of the 1960s counter-culture'. Leaving aside the fact that I have nowhere made this 'admission', *if* the 1960s claim were to be true there would be a strong case for claiming that New Age spirituality is 'here today, gone tomorrow as that generation slowly disappears' (Voas and Bruce 2007: 57). It is also true that *if* the future of mind-body spirituality critically depends on transmission from participants to their children, Voas and Bruce (2007: 53–4) are correct to note that prospects do not look especially good. However, as we argue in *The Spiritual Revolution*, we do not think that the future of holistic spiritualities of inner life is going to be significantly affected by the death of the 'sixties' cohort; and neither do we attach particular importance to parental transmission (Heelas and Woodhead 2005: 132–4, 136).

In *The Spiritual Revolution,* we predict that 'the holistic milieu will continue to grow, albeit at a slower rate than in recent years, to perhaps double its size during the next 40 or 50 years' (Heelas and Woodhead 2005:149). Our reason for making this relatively cautious prediction is that at the time of our research 'the milieu caters largely to [a] relatively small market niche [primarily women, the middle aged, the better educated, and those who work (or have worked) in people-centred professions where importance is attached to subjective well-being or quality of life]'. We also noted that 'since evidence of expansion beyond this niche is not yet extensive, we remain content with the prediction [of growth to around three per cent of the population of Britain ...]' (Heelas and Woodhead 2005: 138). Information which has recently become available from a wide range of sources strongly suggests that this prediction is unduly cautious, for it seems the market niche is expanding.

---

4   Reflecting on what Voas and Bruce (2007: 1) have to say about the title of *The Spiritual Revolution*, our publisher, Blackwell, wanted a memorable title, one along the lines of Steve Bruce's *God is Dead* (also published by Blackwell) which would hopefully be effective albeit at the expense of literal truth. As we state at the beginning of the volume, we address a claim (and not one made by ourselves). Voas and Bruce also write that 'the term "spiritual revolution" implies ... that something new is happening ...There is nothing particularly new about alternative spirituality' (2007: 53). One answer to this is that 'revolutions' can be long in the making. Another is that something new is happening. Although inner-life spirituality is deeply rooted in Western culture, most importantly the Romantic Movement, the fact remains that the kind of holistic associational activities we find today have been relatively few and far between until quite recently.

5   On the growth of the holistic milieu of Kendal, see Heelas and Woodhead (2005: 42–5); on the growth of CAM, see Eisenberg et al. (1998), Heelas and Woodhead (2005: 167), Heelas 2006a), and Tovey et al. (2004).

Thus, Leo Hickman (2006: 5) reports that 'on January 1, 2005, there were 7,036,118 members of 5,486 public and private health and fitness clubs in the UK – 11.8 per cent of the population' – figures which have grown very significantly since, say, 1970, and especially recently. A considerable number of these clubs include 'self-contained' activities such as yoga and tai chi, typically run by mind–body–spirit practitioners (Heelas and Woodhead 2005: 36) (who also work in an increasing number of spas [O'Dell 2005]). Just as we included yoga at the Leisure Centre within the holistic milieu of Kendal and environs, so must these activities (run by spiritual practitioners) be included in the holistic milieu of the nation. Given the numbers which are surely involved, yoga and so forth must be appealing to more than a smallish market niche.

Another excellent illustration is provided by referrals made by mainstream health providers in England. According to Roger Dobson's report of a study, based on a postal questionnaire sent to one in eight GP partnerships, almost half (49 per cent) of the general practices which responded were providing some access to complementary or alternative medicines. GPs themselves, together with nurses and others, provided an estimated 30 per cent of the CAM activities; independent CAM practitioners worked in 12 per cent of general practices; and '27 per cent of practices made NHS referrals to external [CAM] providers' (Dobson 2003: 1250). True, many forms of CAM take a relatively 'secular', albeit holistic, 'mind–body' form. Up to a third, though, are provided by practitioners who regard their practices as spiritually significant referrals, thereby directing people straight to activities where they have the opportunity to become involved with mind-body-*spirituality*. Even when practitioners are relatively 'secular' ('mind–body'), holistic themes can sometimes prompt participation in the more comprehensively holistic.

As with health and fitness clubs, the sheer number of people involved means that referrals *cannot* be limited to the category of the middle-aged, women, the better educated and the person-centred professional.[6] But this is not all. Together with the holistic mini-cultures found within many clubs and NHS general practices, further evidence of the way in which the holistic outlook is becoming more popular and is in the process of broadening its appeal, is provided by the nursing profession within NHS hospitals. Many are increasingly likely to encounter mind–body–spirituality – perhaps during their primary university education; perhaps during their professional development courses; and most generally, by way of the cultural value the NHS has come to attach to holistic well-being, formally defined to encompass 'spirituality'. Nurses who become especially interested include those who then go part-time, or leave their jobs within the NHS, to become CAM/holistic milieu clients, group members, or practitioners (Heelas 2006a; Heelas and Woodhead 2005: 103). To mention another sphere of activity within the mainstream, Stef Aupers and Dick Houtman (2006) provide convincing evidence of the increasing appeal of holistic, 'self'-development themes, including inner-life spirituality, within business life – which no doubt prompts

---

6   In the USA, referrals almost certainly help to explain the fact that CAM is no longer 'confined to any narrow segment of society' (Eisenberg et al. 1998: 1571).

some (typically male) managers (in particular) to turn to holistic milieu activities taking place beyond the confines of the workplace. Hicks (2003: 31) indicates the significance of workplace spirituality in the USA.

A great deal more could be said about the ways in which holistic, mind–body–spirituality themes (or aspects of them) are spreading through the culture, bringing more people into contact, and thereby broadening their appeal (Heelas and Woodhead 2005: 137–8). For present purposes, the point which now needs to be made derives from the claims of Voas and Bruce 'that the wider the distribution, the weaker the spiritual dose becomes' (Voas and Bruce 2007: 57). Thinking of the predominantly 'body-mind' activities found in 'holistic' spas, which have shown considerable growth of late (Earle-Levine 2004), 'holistic' beauty salons (Black 2004: 48, 168–9) or articles in the mass media, this might well be true. The spiritual practitioner writing for the mass media, for example, is unlikely to emphasise spirituality to the same extent as he or she might in associational practice. However, our argument in *The Spiritual Revolution* in measure *depends* on this 'weakening of the dose'. For we argue that it is precisely because people often experience *just* a 'taste' of, or allusion to, what spirituality has to offer while reading holistic well-being articles in *The Daily Mail* or going to 'holistic' spas (for example) which can 'prime' them, motivate them, to go 'deeper' by signing up for a course run by for example a spiritual aromatherapist.

Neither can we neglect the related consideration that according to the Soul of Britain survey, 21 per cent of the population agree that 'there is some sort of spirit or life force' and 23 per cent that 'there is something there', with 31 per cent thinking of themselves as 'a spiritual person' (Heald 2000) – figures which have been increasing (Heelas and Woodhead 2005: 73). True, these particular findings need not imply belief in inner-life spirituality (Heelas and Woodhead 2005: 74). But they surely serve to indicate that a considerable number of people believe that spirituality is bound up with the depths of life. And this means that when they encounter a 'taste' by way of 'holistic', life-focused cultural provisions, they might be encouraged to consider mind–body–*spirituality* activities – being most obviously 'primed' when their belief is in inner spirituality, but also 'primed' when they believe that there is 'something there' in life which deserves attention (Heelas and Woodhead 2005: 134; 137).

Furthermore, we have to bear in mind recent findings reported by Eileen Barker (2004). Derived from the 1998 RAMP (Religious and Moral Pluralism) survey of 11 European countries, an arresting finding is that 29 per cent agree with the statement 'I believe that God is something within each person, rather than something out there' (the way this is worded making it unlikely that many believers in the Holy Spirit are included). In addition, 15 per cent agree with the statement 'I believe in an impersonal spirit or life force' (Barker 2004: 38). For a variety of reasons, one strongly suspects that these figures are higher for Britain. So whether it might be contact by way of GP partnerships, health and fitness clubs, nursing, 'holistic' spas, or management trainings etc., involvement with the holistic milieu is surely greatly facilitated by beliefs of this variety.[7]

Turning to younger people, the most detailed evidence is provided by Christian Smith's *Soul Searching* (2005), a survey and interview based study of the religious and spiritual lives of American teenagers. Voas and Bruce (2007: 58) cite from Smith: 'When we came to interview questions about being "spiritual but not religious" ... most teens literally did not understand what it was we were asking about'. It certainly looks as though the US market niche has not extended to incorporate teens.

However, a somewhat different picture emerges from closer inspection of *Soul Searching*. We read that 'only a minority of US teenagers are naturally absorbing by osmosis the traditional substantive content and character of the religious traditions to which they claim to belong' (Smith 2005: 171). At the same time, however, eight per cent of adolescents aged between 13 and 17 select the term 'very true' to describe the 'spiritual but not religious' questionnaire option, a further 46 per cent favouring the expression 'somewhat true' (Smith 2005: 78). With only 2 per cent selecting 'don't know' or refusing to provide an answer (Smith 2005: 78), it is pretty clear that teens have at least some understanding of the 'spiritual but not religious' formulation (see Cherry et al. [2001: 275] for slightly older people). Furthermore, and considerably more specifically to do with inner spirituality than this pretty indeterminate formulation (Heelas and Woodhead 2005: 74), '14 percent take a more New Age approach to God as an impersonal, cosmic life force' (Smith 2005: 41) –a figure which would almost certainly be higher if the expression 'not personal' had not been used in the question. And '4 per cent of American teens not affiliated with an Asian religion – such as Buddhism, Hinduism, or Zen – try to include spiritual practices from such religions in their own spirituality' (Smith 2005: 82). (On 'spirituality' among young people, see also Clark [2003: 9, 14]; Gallup and Bezilla's report that 11 per cent of teens have 'a great deal or some interest' in 'New Age' [1992: 79]; and Smith [2002].)

Most significantly of all, though, 'for many US teenagers, God is treated as something like a cosmic therapist' (Smith 2005: 148). 'What we hardly ever heard from teens', writes Smith, 'was that religion is about significantly transforming people into, not what they feel like being, but what they are supposed to be' (Smith 2005: 148–9). Rather than 'life-as' religion and spirituality (to use a term from *The Spiritual Revolution*) teens 'seek out religious and spiritual practices, feelings and experiences that satisfy their own subjectively defined needs and wants', not least

---

7   While not providing conclusive evidence, the role played by prior 'beliefs' in explaining appeal is indicated by the facts that around 80 per cent of respondents to our holistic milieu questionnaire hold spiritual 'beliefs', 33.3 per cent indicating that 'looking for spiritual growth' was one of their top three reasons for originally participating, and 41 per cent provide this reason for current participation. The 'conversion' rate is just 8 per cent. With this low increase, to 41 per cent, the implication is that the 80 per cent figure is at least partly due to people already having a 'pre-existing orientation towards spirituality' (as Hasselle-Newcombe 2005: 312) puts it in her study of Iyengar Yoga – a study which provides similar percentages).

'personal realisation and happiness' or well-being (Smith 2005: 175. See also Clark 2003: 190, 231–2; cf. Wolfe 2005.)

Smith in fact provides a powerful illustration of what we call the 'subjectivisation thesis' in action (Heelas and Woodhead 2005: 78–82). The massive subjective turn of modern culture – taking the form of what Smith calls 'therapeutic individualism' (Smith 2005: 172–9) – serves to fuel interest in the 'cosmic therapist' rather than the conformism and disciplines of life-as tradition. Accordingly, it is perfectly reasonable to argue that large numbers of teenagers are close to inner-life spirituality, with some already holding 'New Age' beliefs or practising. There is evidence that significant numbers might build on the 'platform' provided by what has taken place within Christian quarters to pursue the path within.

According to Marler and Hadaway, 22.6 per cent of Protestant 'baby busters' (those in their twenties and thirties, with many presumably brought up with the notion of the 'cosmic therapist') say they are 'spiritual only', this term being 'linked exclusively to non-traditional beliefs and practices (like New Age or Eastern beliefs …)' (Marler and Hadaway 2002: 293, 294). Significantly, the 'spiritual only' figure is highest for baby busters, progressively declining as one moves to the oldest people surveyed, a picture which also applies to Europe (Barker 2004: 37). Furthermore, according to a Harris poll 25.2 per cent of the 15 million practising yoga in the USA are aged between 25 and 34 (Heelas and Woodhead 2005: 137). At least in the USA, the claim of Voas and Bruce that 'the holistic milieu is populated mainly by women from a particular generation; there is no particular sign that it will be popular among those who follow' (Voas and Bruce 2007: 53, 57) does not appear to be secure.[8]

To return to Britain, the absence of data of the kind provided by Smith means that the picture remains unclear. What we can say, though, is that Ofsted (the English government schools inspection agency) officially formulates spirituality in an inner-life (and inclusivistic) manner. To illustrate from a representative document:

> Spiritual development relates to that aspect of inner life through which pupils acquire insights into their personal experience which are of enduring worth. It is characterised by reflection, the attribution of meaning to experience, valuing a non-material dimension to life and intimations of an enduring reality. 'Spiritual' is not synonymous with 'religious'. (Ofsted 1994: 86)

---

8   For more on younger people and inner life spirituality, in the USA and elsewhere, see Heelas and Woodhead (2005: 137–8), Petre (2004) and Simpson and Rowman (2000). Useful references are provided by Smith (2005) and Clark (2003). According to a recent survey carried out by BBC 100 FACES research, '44 per cent of Mind, Body and Spirit books are bought by young people (vs. 22 per cent of all books)'. There is growing evidence that 'younger age groups' are 'disproportionately represented' (Barnett 2001: 13) in CAM circles. Hollinger's International Student Survey finds that 'c. 50 per cent reported use of alternative medicine a few times or more frequently', with '20–25 per cent of respondents [having] tried out oriental spiritual methods or massage techniques' (Hollinger 2004: 295).

Bearing in mind that Ofsted again appointed inspectors to assess spiritual development, it is reasonable to suppose that numbers of younger people (especially those at primary school) encounter and become familiar with the themes – and perhaps experiences – of inner-life spirituality.

To close this discussion of the 'revolutionary' significance of the growth of the holistic milieu, it remains to discuss the point of Voas and Bruce that 'for predictions to be more than speculative, one needs a theory about the mechanisms at work' (Voas and Bruce 2007: 56). Leaving to one side the (to my mind) unfortunate use of the word 'mechanisms' to describe human affairs and motivations, and leaving aside the fact that well-established trends themselves are by no means devoid of significance for the future, the predictions we make in *The Spiritual Revolution* (Heelas and Woodhead 2005) are explicitly underpinned by the subjectivisation thesis (see especially 78–82). We explain why we think the 'massive subjective turn of modern culture' has taken place and is highly likely to continue (see, for example, Heelas and Woodhead 2005: 130–32); and we go into considerable detail whilst exploring the operation of the various processes – including the roles played by the growth of subjective well-being culture – which help to explain much of the growth of the holistic milieu (see Heelas and Woodhead 2005: 82–94 for the subjectivisation thesis formulated in terms of subjective well-being culture).[9]

Voas and Bruce suggest that 'projecting *recent* growth rates forward *without constraint* leads to the conclusion that everyone will be simultaneously Mormon and Muslim and agnostic, as well as alternatively spiritual, in a century or two' (Voas and Bruce 2007: 56; italics added). In our study, it will be recalled that we predict that the holistic milieu of the nation will continue to grow – 'albeit at a slower rate than in recent years'. It is not as though we project 'recent growth rates forward'. And it is not as though we neglect constraints. This is far from the case. The reason we argue that growth will slow is precisely because of the constraint imposed by the relatively small market niche. As for an argument in this chapter, namely that the appeal is becoming more extensive, constraints are undoubtedly at work, including those to do with time and monetary factors, cultural stereotyping, theistic beliefs, and indifference or apathy.[10]

---

9 Thinking of the point of Voas and Bruce that 'evidence that holistic concepts are becoming part of the culture do not *show* that a spiritual revolution is coming' (Voas and Bruce 2007: 59; italics added), my response is that what matters is showing the ways in which holistic themes can encourage people to turn to mind–body–spirituality activities – something we endeavour to do in *The Spiritual Revolution*.

10 We reckon that the 'mathematical' considerations made by Voas and Bruce (2007: 56) are precisely imprecise (or inappropriate).

But What is Growing?

According to Voas and Bruce, 'unconventional spirituality is a symptom of secularisation, not a durable counterforce to it. ... We are doubtful that most of the activities in this category even partake of the sacred to any great extent' (Voas and Bruce 2007: 43). In *The Spiritual Revolution*, we did not dwell on the extent to which holistic milieu activities are secular, or whether the growth of holistic milieu activities is bound up with increasing secularisation. As should be apparent, our concern very much had to do with measuring the number of participants by using the criterion of activities run by practitioners who accord spiritual significance to what they do.

A great virtue of the chapter by Voas and Bruce in this collection is that it directs attention to the important matter of the extent to which the holistic milieu is secular. One of their arguments in this regard is that 'it is hard not to be struck by how few activities listed here [in Table 2.3] are clearly spiritual. Half of all involvement is in what *most people* would view as leisure or recreation: yoga, tai chi, dance, singing, art' (Voas and Bruce 2007: 50, italics added). In response, these activities – together with all the others mentioned by Voas and Bruce (including specific CancerCare provisions) as well as the reminder of those we included in the holistic milieu – were carefully scrutinised to ensure that they met our criterion of being run by holistic, inner-life spirituality practitioners. Within reason (and perhaps beyond it!), while pretty well any activity can be put to the service of cultivating mind–body–spirituality, what matters is how practitioners understand their activities – not 'most people'.

Another of Voas and Bruce's arguments is that we have over-estimated the number of participants (at 55 per cent) who accord spiritual significance to their current activities. Whilst this stands for respondents to the questionnaire, Voas and Bruce provide good reasons for supposing that these respondents are not representative of the milieu as a whole. For as they argue, 'spiritual' respondents to the questionnaire are over-represented (Voas and Bruce 2007: 49). Accordingly, it is fair to say that we were unduly precipitous to apply the 55 per cent figure to the milieu *per se*. This said, though, the fact remains that spirituality is considerably more in evidence among the questionnaire respondents than is suggested by the 55 per cent figure to do with spiritual understanding of practices. To illustrate this point, recall the figures presented earlier in this essay, including the 82 per cent who agree that 'some sort of spirit or life force pervades all that lives'; and consider the fact that the mean response to the question 'how important is spirituality in your life?' is 7.3 (with point one on the scale being 'not at all important', point 10 being 'very important').[11]

11　The response rate of our holistic milieu questionnaire is 42 per cent; that achieved by Thomas et al. (2001: 2), in their study of complementary medicine, is virtually 60 per cent. To improve on response rates in the future, thereby handling representativeness issues, various resource-demanding strategies are called for. These include devising more effective ways of distributing questionnaires; providing reminders; and, possibly, providing financial incentives (see Eisenberg et al. 1998: 1570 on the last). A particular issue to handle concerns the fact that to retain comparability with the congregational domain, the holistic milieu questionnaire

A third argument provided by Voas and Bruce (2007: 51–2) helps to confirm a claim made by Bruce in an earlier publication, namely that 'the most popular products [of the 'New Age'] are those which are the most secular' (Bruce 1996: 273). Assuming that the associational activities of the holistic milieu continue to grow, the points made by Voas and Bruce strongly suggest that the number involved with 'the most secular' activities will indeed grow the fastest. However, this does not rule out the fact that the number of participants whose practices enable them to engage with what they take to be the spirituality of life will also almost certainly increase.[12] Furthermore, there is nothing to indicate that the high percentage of participants believing in life-spirituality has diminished to date, the expectation instead being that it will continue to increase - for much the same reasons as it has grown in the past.

Finally, Voas and Bruce raise the objection that 'the descriptions of spirituality given by the Kendal respondents seem to have little to do with the supernatural or even the sacred' (Voas and Bruce 2007: 51). Since academics cannot establish whether or not spirituality really exists, since it cannot be studied 'in itself', if it does exist, we report and interpret on the basis of what participants have to say. We rarely encountered the term 'supernatural' (or, for that matter, 'sacred') – but this should not serve to distract from the frequency that we encountered the language of 'spirituality-cum-life', 'spirituality-cum-energy', 'spirituality-cum-healing', and so on.

Using the language of Voas and Bruce, *relative to* traditional religion, mind-body-spirituality might well appear to be 'hollowed out' (Voas and Bruce 2007: 44) or 'without the baggage' (Voas and Bruce 2007: 59). But holistic spirituality must be understood *in its own terms*. Taking into account the consideration that mind–body spirituality is very much to do with experience – and thus is far from easy to formulate in words – it is nevertheless apparent that the spirituality found in much of the milieu is by no means devoid of *substance*. One might think of the widespread 'belief' in 'special healing powers' or 'subtle energy (or energy channels) in the body'. One might think of the regularity with which we encountered participants who spoke of spirituality flowing through, and thereby integrating, aspects of themselves. One might think of the importance attached to getting in touch with one's authentic or natural self, being true to oneself, healing oneself, expressing love and care, living life to the full: all in the context of 'spirituality' (see Graph 9 of the holistic milieu questionnaire, www.kendalproject.org.uk). One might think of the ways in which 'how to' advice is provided for practice, advice having ethical significance as well

---

was distributed during a particular week (commencing on Monday the 12 November, 2001) – but as we have seen, a fair number of group members and one-to-one clients participate on a monthly basis.

12 The reasons why this number will almost certainly increase have already been introduced. The fact that the most popular activities (and therefore the ones which have grown the fastest) tend to have the highest proportions of 'secular' participants by no means rules out the growth of the number of those people who are spiritually-involved, can be illustrated by a key Kendal Project finding. Yoga groups are currently the most popular activity; around half of the questionnaire respondents report a spiritual dimension; in 1970 there were no yoga groups in Kendal – and therefore, of course, no one to report spiritual involvement.

as suggesting experiential possibilities. One might think of the 'tools' which are offered, tools which operate according to experientially grounded 'basic principles'. One might think of the fact that practitioners sometimes provide 'that is the way it is' statements – about the nature of the chakra system, for example. Thinking now of inner-life spirituality within the mainstream institutional order, one can also think of those nurses who become involved (especially those engaged with palliative care). For their concern lies with the 'substantive' experiences which they want to encourage – improving the quality of life of their patients; calming them; alleviating their sense of isolation; trying to enable them to be hopeful and confident; trying to facilitate peacefulness, acceptance and a sense of 'completion'.[13]

Voas and Bruce might treat much of this as 'pseudo-science' (Voas and Bruce 2007: 51) – as well as 'non-natural' (Voas and Bruce 2007: 51). But very few spiritually aware participants think in terms of the scientific frame of reference (legitimating their 'spirituality' by reference to 'science', for example). Talk of the 'deep inner self and inner knowing', or statements like 'the more you get in touch with your true nature, the more peace and love you have', do not belong to the language of science, even 'pseudo-science' (Heelas and Woodhead 2005: 26–7; see also Taylor 1989). 'Creative intelligence', 'the wisdom of the child within', and other renderings of how the inner-life provides knowledge and ethicality, do not belong to the scientific register. The vitalism experienced at the heart of life – variously known as chi, ki, yin and yang, prana, the 'vital energy' concentrated in the chakras, or, most generally, the life force and inner spirituality – is not considered to be the same as what scientists are able to find, thus being 'metaphysical' (Coulter 2004: 113, cf. 103). Generally speaking, although the chakra system (for example) is thought of as 'natural' (in the sense of belonging to human nature), it is explicitly distinguished from physicality. Many, including nurses, turn to CAM (including mind–body spirituality activities)

---

13   Voas and Bruce do not help their case by comparing those going along to Salvation Army soup kitchens with those attending yoga classes and so forth (Voas and Bruce 2007: 48). Run by members of the congregational domain, but not belonging to this territory, soup kitchens should be compared with similar activities run by holistic milieu participants. Since Voas and Bruce do not do this, and since there are too many other differences between soup kitchen and yoga attendees (to do with life-issues, values, beliefs, expectations, etc., and therefore salience), their comparison is not illuminating. Neither do they help their case by introducing Peter Stringfellow (Voas and Bruce 2007: 51) and Channel 4's 'Spirituality Shopper' (Voas and Bruce 2007: 52–3). The former example is probably not relevant; the Channel 4 example concerns a programme which is too contrived, artificial and misleading to be of illustrative value. It is much more useful to reflect on the extent to which holistic milieu activities are informed by experiential teachings, practices and outcomes by talking with spiritual practitioners, groups members or one-to-one clients; or by dwelling on primary literature (for instance Richard Ellis's *Empower Your Life with Reiki* [2000]) and works by academics (for instance Sarah Strauss's *Positioning Yoga* [2005]). For more on the 'substantive' issue, which is attracting increasing attention from academics, see also Aupers and Houtman (2006), Besecke (2005), Hammer (2001) and Heelas (2006b). See also the growing literature on nursing and spirituality, for example Partridge (2005) and Heelas 2006a.

precisely when the limitations of scientific medicine call for *another* or an *additional* approach. In sum, it follows that rather than thinking in terms of the scientific frame of reference, spiritually aware participants would find favour with the interpretative term *supernatural*. This is a term which is very much in the spirit of the Romantics, with their 'natural supernaturalism' as Abrams (1980) typifies it, where spirituality is ultimately taken to belong to what the fundamental nature of life in the here-and-now has to offer.

Conclusion

As we write in *The Spiritual Revolution*, 'in Britain ... the growth of the holistic milieu has not compensated for the decline of the congregational domain' (Heelas and Woodhead 2005: 127). Remaining with associational activities, our conclusion is the same as Voas and Bruce as they close their essay, 'the sacred is giving way to the secular' (Voas and Bruce 2007: 59). But is it possible to agree with the claim of Voas and Bruce that 'in Britain as a whole the spiritually minded [of the holistic milieu] will number in the tens and *possibly* hundreds of thousands (Voas and Bruce 2007: 50; italics added)? In *The Spiritual Revolution* we concluded that somewhat over 900,000 of the inhabitants of Great Britain were active in the holistic milieu on a weekly basis during the autumn of 2001 (Heelas and Woodhead 2005: 53). Two of the key findings from the Kendal Project are that some 80 per cent maintain that some sort of spirit or life force pervades all that lives and that over 70 per cent maintain that subtle energy flows through the body. Together with other evidence, a considerable number of these participants are in fact 'spiritually-minded'. Rather than the figure being 'possibly hundreds of thousands', a conservative estimate would thus be in excess of half a million – quite possibly considerably in excess of this mark.[14]

Voas and Bruce assert that: 'The secular future of the holistic milieu may be bright; in its more spiritual form, these beliefs and practices are unlikely to do much better than those of more established religions' (Voas and Bruce 2007: 43). This statement does not take into account the consideration that the number of those who understand their holistic milieu activities in a spiritual way has grown since 1970, and very much looks set to continue growing. Neither does it take into account the fact that the great majority of participants in the holistic milieu believe in inner-life-spirituality – the key belief, which has developed with the growth of the holistic milieu and which is also set to continue growing. And briefly, to mention an additional point, the culture

---

14 For comparative purposes, it is surely more useful to compare the number participating in the holistic milieu with similar (or overlapping) participatory activities, rather than the spectator sport football (see Voas and Bruce 2007: 58 on the latter). Compare, for example, the 11.8 per cent of the population who (we have seen) are active in health and fitness clubs with the 1.6 per cent holistic milieu figure. Or compare the 'about 110,000 therapists' reported by Bunting (1998) with the 146,000 spiritual practitioners we estimate for Great Britain (Heelas and Woodhead 2005: 53).

and organisation of the holistic milieu is by no means as 'precarious' as Bruce (2002: 79) has argued (see Heelas (2006b) for a criticism of this point). Whether or not a spiritual revolution takes place with regard to congregational and holistic associational activities in the predictable future, the fact remains that the holistic milieu (including its spirituality) has a 'much better' future than the congregational domain. For whereas the holistic milieu will continue to grow, it is highly likely that the congregational domain as a whole will continue to decline – probably bottoming out at some time in the future but not, so far as one can tell, turning to growth.

Rather than being a secularised 'fag end' of Christianity (as implied by Voas and Bruce (2007: 59; see also Marler and Hadaway 2002: 297), the provisions of the holistic milieu are of a relatively substantial order. And just as the ethic of humanity (for example) has been fuelled by deep-rooted dynamics within modernity rather than merely being an attenuated form of Christianity, so the holistic milieu (as well as the internalisation of the sacred in popular belief) has been fuelled by deep-seated developments within modernity: in particular the turn to subjective-life – the desire to *be* oneself, only better, the quest for subjective-well-being, quality of life and overall health, the goal of finding 'ultimate' significance 'within' one's life, the search for that inner truth, wisdom, expressiveness and vitality which can enable one to be oneself *with* others.

Bibliography

Abrams, M.H. (1980), *Natural Supernaturalism*, New York: W.W. Norton.

Aupers, S. and D. Houtman (2006), 'Beyond the Spiritual Supermarket: The Social and Public Significance of New Age Spirituality', *Journal of Contemporary Religion*, 21(2): 201–22.

Barker, E. (2004), 'The Church Without and the God Within: Religiosity and/or Spirituality?', in D.M. Jerolimov, S. Zrinscak and I. Borowik (eds), *Religion and Patterns of Social Transformation*, Zagreb: Institute for Social Research, pp. 23–47.

Barnett, M. (2001), 'Overview of Complementary Therapies in Cancer Care', in J. Barraclough (ed.), *Integrated Cancer Care. Holistic, Complementary and Creative Approaches*, Oxford: Oxford University Press, pp. 3–19.

Besecke, K. (2005), 'Seeing Invisible Religion. Religion as a Societal Conversation about Transcendent Meaning', *Sociological Theory*, 23: 179–96.

Black, P. (2004), *The Beauty Industry*, London: Routledge.

Bruce, S. (1996), 'Religion in Britain at the Close of the Twentieth Century: A Challenge to the Silver Lining Approach', *Journal of Contemporary Religion*, 11(3): 261–75.

Bruce, S. (2002), *God is Dead*, Oxford: Blackwell.

Bunting, M. (1998), 'Holy Ghosts', *The Guardian*, 8 April: 4–5.

Chambers, P. (2005), *Religion, Secularisation and Social Change in Wales*, Cardiff: University of Wales Press.

Cherry, C., B.A. Deberg and A. Porterfield (2001), *Religion on Campus*, London: University of North Carolina Press.

Clark, L.S. (2003), *From Angels to Aliens. Teenagers, the Media, and the Supernatural*, Oxford: Oxford University Press.

Coulter, I. (2004), 'Integration and Paradigm Clash: The Practical Difficulties of Integrative Medicine', in P. Tovey, G. Easthope and J. Adams (eds), *The Mainstreaming of Complementary and Alternative Medicine*, London: Routledge, pp. 103–22.

Dobson, R. (2003), 'Half of General Practitioners offer Patients Complementary Medicine', *British Medical Journal*, 29 November, 327: 1250.

Earle-Levine, J. (2004), 'Glorious, Luxurious Mud', *Financial Times*, 22–23 May: W10.

Eisenberg, D.M., M.D. Rogers, B. Davis, S.L. Ettner, S. Appel, S. Wilkey, M. Van Rompay and R.C. Kessler (1998), 'Trends in Alternative Medicine use in the United States, 1990–97', *Journal of the American Medical Association*, 280(18): 1569–76.

Ellis, R. (2000), *Empower Your Life with Reiki*, London: Hodder and Stoughton.

Gallup, G.H. and R. Bezilla (1992), *The Religious Life of Young Americans*, Princeton: The George H. Gallup International Institute.

Hammer, O. (2001), *Claiming Knowledge. Strategies of Epistemology from Theosophy to the New Age*, Leiden: Brill.

Hasselle-Newcombe, S. (2005), 'Spirituality and "Mystical Religion" in Contemporary Society: A Case Study of British Practitioners of the Iyengar Method of Yoga', *Journal of Contemporary Religion*, 20(3): 305–21.

Heald, G. (2000), *Soul of Britain*, London: The Opinion Research Business.

Heelas, P. (2006a), 'Nursing Spirituality', *Spirituality and Health International*, 7: 8–23.

Heelas, P. (2006b), 'The Infirmity Debate: On the Viability of New Age Spiritualities of Life', *Journal of Contemporary Religion*, 21(2): 223–40.

Heelas, P. and L. Woodhead (2005), *The Spiritual Revolution. Why Religion is Giving Way to Spirituality*, Oxford: Blackwell.

Hickman, L. (2006), 'Health and Fitness', *The Guardian* (G2), 9 January: 4–5.

Hicks, D.H. (2003), *Religion and the Workplace. Pluralism, Spirituality, Leadership*, Cambridge: Cambridge University Press.

Hollinger, F. (2004), 'Does the Counter-Cultural Character of New Age Persist?', *Journal of Contemporary Religion*, 19(3): 289–309.

Marler, P.L. and C.K. Hadaway (2002), '"Being Religious" or "Being Spiritual" in America: A Zero-Sum Proposition?', *Journal for the Scientific Study of Religion*, 41(2): 289–300.

O'Dell, T. (2005). 'Meditation, Magic and Spiritual Regeneration. Spas and the Mass Production of Serenity', in O. Lofgren and R. Willim (eds), *Magic, Culture and the New Economy*, Oxford: Berg, pp. 19–36.

Ofsetd (1994), *Handbook for the Inspection of Schools. Part 4. Inspection Schedule Guidance. Consolidated Edition*, London: HMSO.

Partridge, C. (2005), *The Re-Enchantment of the West*, vol. II, London: T. and T. Clark.

Petre, J. (2004), 'The Young put their Faith in Mysticism', *The Times*, 18 September: 5.

Simpson, N. and K. Roman (2000), 'Complementary Medicine Use in Children: Extent and Reasons. A Population-based Survey', *British Journal of General Practice*, 51: 914–16.

Smith, C. (2002), 'Mapping American Adolescent Religious Participation', *Journal for the Scientific Study of Religion*, 41(4): 597–612.

Smith, C. (2005), *Soul Searching. The Religious and Spiritual Lives of American Teenagers*, Oxford: Oxford University Press.

Strauss, S. (2005), *Positioning Yoga*, Oxford: Berg.

Taylor, C. (1989), *Sources of the Self: The Making of Modern Identity*, Cambridge: Cambridge University Press.

Thomas, K.J., J.P. Nicholl and P. Coleman (2001), 'Use and Expenditure on Complementary Medicine in England: A Population Based Survey', *Complementary Therapies in Medicine*, 9: 2–11.

Tovey, P., G. Easthope and J. Adams (eds) (2004), *The Mainstreaming of Complementary and Alternative Medicine*, London: Routledge.

Voas, D. and S. Bruce (2007) 'The Spiritual Revolution: Another False Dawn for the Sacred', in K. Flanagan and P.C. Jupp (eds), *A Sociology of Spirituality*, Aldershot: Ashgate, pp. 43–63.

Wilson, B.R. (1966), *Religion in Secular Society*, London: Watts.

Wolfe, A. (2005), *The Transformation of Religion*, Chicago: University of Chicago Press.

Chapter 4

Beyond Secularisation versus Sacralisation: Lessons from a Study of the Dutch Case

André Droogers

The current debate about religion in Western Europe focuses on at least two questions. The first question is: is secularisation here to stay and to win (shorthand: the 'secularist' stance), or is it more and more complemented – or even undone – by a new sacralisation and a transformation of worldviews (the 'sacralist' position)? The second question relates to methodological issues generated by the first question. Is it to be studied by either quantitative or qualitative methods – or both? As shown in a research programme on the Dutch situation, the combined discussion of these two questions opens out a real possibility of going beyond the present stalemate between secularists and sacralists.

Going beyond its original meaning as the confiscation of church property by secular authorities, secularisation may refer to de-churching, to people leaving the churches, but also more generally to religion losing influence in society. This can be expressed as the exile of religion from sectors of civil society (as distinguished from state and market). It may also refer to the privatisation and individualisation of religion (Casanova 1994: 211). Correspondingly sacralisation, although not as often used as secularisation, presents different connotations. Returning church property to the church would not be a very common meaning of the term, but desecularisation may occur in various forms: 'churching' and church growth; religion gaining influence in society; the boundaries of the religious sector in society eroding; religion returning to civil society from its exile; or religion moving from the private to the public sphere. Views centring on the term 'spirituality' have gained considerable attention (for example Heelas and Woodhead 2005). The term is defined in contrast with religion, being understood as based on the authority of the unique subject, and thereby differing from institutionalised religion that accepts an external transcendental authority. The 'spiritual revolution' that Heelas and Woodhead predict means that more people will participate in the realm of spirituality than in that of religion – as they define these terms. Sacralisation then takes the form of the growth of spirituality.

This growth presents a number of methodological options and these can be expressed as a preference either for correct sampling and statistical generalisation, or for narrative plausibility, a form that requires an eye for complex detail. Each approach, whether as secularists or as sacralists, exhibits methodological preferences, the former tending to utilise hard statistical facts, whereas the latter find part of their inspiration in qualitative work, albeit sometimes requiring quantitative confirmation. In its most extreme expression, secularists accuse sacralists of being unable to generalise and thus not to have a case, while the sacralists reproach the secularists with being blind to the obvious, only because they are unable to measure it. As an undercurrent in the debate, difference in views on the mission and demands of science in general may play a role, some forms of (neo-) positivism being opposed to a modality of constructivism.

This chapter explores the findings of a research programme, based at the Department of Social and Cultural Anthropology of the Vrije Universiteit (Amsterdam). Funded by the Vrije Universiteit with about half a million € and employing five full-time researchers, the programme has for the last five years studied the problem of secularisation and sacralisation in the Dutch context. Appropriately the programme was called 'Between Secularisation and Sacralisation' (abbreviated hereafter as BSS). The spectrum between secularisation and sacralisation, including the grey zone of 'believing without belonging' (Davie 1994), was explored, mainly – though not exclusively – using qualitative methods. From the start the programme had a methodological component, since it was meant to complement quantitative studies, relatively abundant in The Netherlands, qualitative work having been done more rarely. The team was fascinated and puzzled by the co-occurrence of secularisation – The Netherlands being among the most secularised countries in the world – and sacralisation, as visible in new forms outside but also inside the churches.

In this chapter, the characteristics of the Dutch situation in regard to religion will be explored. This leads on to a discussion of the merits and deficiencies of using quantitative and qualitative methodologies to research on such a topic. In the following section the design of the BSS project will be sketched, leading to a summary of the results of the five projects. The conclusion reflects on some of the lessons to be learnt from this research programme.

The Dutch Case

The Dutch situation has gained some fame where secularisation is concerned. Not only do statistics show a high rate of secularisation, the fact that churches have lost so many members is in strong contrast with the dominant role those churches, especially the Calvinist oriented, have for centuries played in Dutch society – and beyond. Although the pillarisation system was instrumental in postponing secularisation – in all senses mentioned in the introduction – it was unable to turn the tide, thereby adding to the contrast between a predominantly religious and a deeply secularised society. Despite all the statistical evidence, in Holland too the question is whether religion is disappearing or is returning – or continuing – in different guise.

Quantifying studies have been done in The Netherlands since the middle of the last century, not only by government offices such as the Centraal Bureau voor de Statistiek (CBS, Central Office for Statistics) and the Sociaal en Cultureel Planbureau

(SCP, Social and Cultural Planning Office) but also in academia. Especially in the last decade SCP has published a number of quantifying studies (Becker and Vink 1994; Becker et al. 1997; Becker and De Wit 2000; Phalet 2004). In addition, since the 1960s, sociologists of religion have on three occasions organised a survey, entitled 'God in The Netherlands', each time using the same questionnaire (Zeegers et al. 1967; Goddijn et al. 1979; Dekker et al. 1997). At the Catholic University of Nijmegen (now Radboud University), the SOCON programme (Sociaal-culturele Ontwikkelingen in Nederland [Social-cultural developments in The Netherlands]) has regularly produced statistical data and analyses on worldviews in The Netherlands, including doctoral theses (for example Te Grotenhuis 1999). The country was of course also included in the European Values Study (EVS), and several studies, again including doctoral theses (such as at Tilburg University, Verweij 1998), have provided analyses of data on religion and secularisation taken from this data bank.

In a recent summary of the relevant publications, Felling (2004: 24–7) has shown the changes that occurred in The Netherlands. Church membership, at 58 per cent in 1979, was down to 38 per cent in 2000. Between 1979 and 2000 weekly church attendance had halved from 26 to 13 per cent. Since 1995, the percentage of people who no longer identify with the religious context in which they were brought up has stabilised at around 40 per cent, having increased from 25 per cent in 1979. The number of respondents explicitly subscribed to the traditional Christian faith (for the purpose of the survey, defined as belief in a God who cares for every person and who has to do with the meaning of life and death, of good and evil), at 38 per cent in 1979, was reduced to 19 per cent in 2000. Not all changes are strictly linear, the period between 1990 and 1995 showing a remarkable stabilisation. Until 1995 belief in a life after death was common among half of the Dutch people, but only 40 per cent so believed in 2000. Another development shown in the studies that Felling summarises is the increase in the number of people with what he calls an 'inner worldview', one constructed by the person (Felling 2004: 25). That person may use traditional ideas regarding the afterlife, an external God or transcendence, but may also construct this inner view without these. In 1985 the percentage of people having such an inner worldview was 80 per cent and this increased to 87 per cent in 2000. People with an inner worldview but rejecting any reference to transcendence numbered 73 per cent of the population in 2000. Those who rejected both traditional Christian faith and an inner worldview constituted eight per cent in 2000.

Quantitative studies providing a prognosis, forecast a continuing trend in these figures, or, at the most, stabilisation at the current level in some sectors of institutionalised religion. The rise of Islam and of alternative forms of religiosity are said not to produce a change in these trends. A slight increase was considered possible in the number of people, including young people, accepting certain religious and moral convictions (Becker and De Wit 2000: 73–4, 79–80). The question remains, however, whether secularisation, in the sense of de-churching, is accompanied by secularisation as denoting the disappearance of religious beliefs. Part of the problem is methodological and concerns how to translate a concept such as transcendence into survey questions for the average public. Moreover, some of the figures seem contradictory.

In analysing these data and trends, the usual references to general macro-social processes such as modernisation, individualisation, urbanisation and detraditionalisation are used, though adapted to the Dutch case and depending on the author's theoretical, paradigmatic and methodological preferences. The role of pillarisation and subsequent de-pillarisation processes has been mentioned already. The latter contributed especially to a lesser role for institutional religion, and to a diminished importance of religion in public life. Interestingly Islam has contributed to a certain re-pillarisation, strategically using the legal remnants of the pillar system in education and broadcasting. These remnants are still considerable. For example, they are visible in the political party system where Christian parties play an active role.

As a motor of secularisation, individualisation may appear in these explanations in two ways: as a cause of the marginalisation of religious institutions in public and private life, but also as a cause of existential insecurity that results in the adherence to some old or new form of religiosity, possibly even in an institutionalised form such as in evangelical groups (Van Harskamp 2000). This way of looking at religious change pays much attention to experience as the heart of individualised worldview. The double role of individualisation is most helpful in explaining the simultaneous occurrence of secularisation *and* sacralisation, thereby putting the debate between secularists and sacralists in another light (cf. Heelas and Woodhead 2005: 9). A paradoxical outcome of individualisation, as a secularising *and* a sacralising factor emerges from the Calvinist Reformation – of religion, apparently digging its own grave, yet preparing for its eventual resuscitation.

Religious differentiation has marked Dutch history since Reformation. Calvinism stimulated an anti-papist attitude, which led to conflicts with and discrimination against Catholics, as during the Iconoclastic Fury (1566) and the Eighty Years' War (1568–1648) and afterwards. This produced a regional differentiation, Catholics being a majority in the southern provinces of Brabant and Limburg whereas a Bible belt of orthodox Calvinism stretches to this day from the southwest to the northeast of the country. Differentiation also occurred through theological quarrels resulting in recurring fission of Protestant churches. Efforts to heal these breaches, as in the case of disputes between the followers of the Leyden professors Gomarus and Arminius (settled at the synod of Dordrecht in 1618 and 1619) led to the formulation of an orthodox version of Protestant faith that to this day serves as a measuring-rod for Calvinist orthodoxy. These struggles were part of the creation of a Dutch national and political identity, even though this did not lead to a state church – with the possible exception of a short period in the nineteenth century. From the sixteenth century onwards the Orange dynasty, part of the Dutch holy trinity of 'God, The Netherlands, and Orange', served to sustain the national identity. In the nineteenth century the privileged position of The Netherlands Reformed Church and its theology, enjoying the support of the Orange monarchy and the state, was contested. This ultimately led to the foundation of the Reformed Churches in The Netherlands, mainly attracting lower class people. In due time the process of fission also affected these latter churches, leading in 1892, 1926 and 1944 to the foundation of other Reformed churches.

The unique twentieth century pillar system, so distinctive in Holland, was formed as a means of translating religious and ideological differentiation into democratic politics and of guaranteeing some form of social cohesion. Besides Protestant and Catholic pillars, a socialist pillar and a conservative pillar were part of the system. It was a way of living apart together, each pillar having its own political party, trade union, broadcasting system and economic mainstays. Democracy introduced new values that affected church organisations. Most of the Protestant churches followed in principle the democratic Presbyterian system (practice could be different). This climate of democratic expectation shaped Roman Catholicism into seeking to develop its own Dutch brand, especially after World War II and even more so after Vatican II. This also led to strife and differentiation within the Catholic Church.

Migration and globalisation have added to the religious diversity of The Netherlands. The colonial past contributed to this, bringing in Indonesians, Surinamese and Antilleans as migrants. In addition, the migration of workers from Mediterranean and North African countries aided in the introduction and expansion of Islam in The Netherlands. The arrival of asylum seekers, as another form of migration, has added to the diversity, including African Christians, Ghanaians being best known to the public. Globalisation and the mass media brought the electronic church to the Dutch population, used in an individual form and adding to the growing idiosyncrasy. The commodification of religion played its own role, from bestsellers to 'reli-pop', from expensive training courses to fairs on the paranormal.

Modernisation, and all the processes that came in its wake, introduced new repertoires forcing out issues of choice. Were people to settle for the adoption of existing repertoires, or were they to change these? Similarly it can be asked whether pluralism necessarily leads to relativism and thus to secularisation, or does it reinforce a conscious and possibly exclusive choice of one particular alternative? After all, the seemingly unavoidable consequences of modernity do not appear to be as necessary as might be expected (Davie 2000: 27). This nuance has made the debate on the two questions mentioned in the introduction even more interesting. Repertoires have the characteristic that not all of their elements are activated and may even be forgotten by almost all. This latency complicates the prognoses made with regard to the future of religion.

In closing this section, one aspect should be mentioned that has received less attention: the changes *within* the churches (cf. Davie 2001). Whereas the secularisation thesis stimulated research of the processes by which the churches were losing members, those who decided to remain in the churches have received much less attention in sociology. The exodus has deeply marked many of the churches, leading to change and adaptation, even to the assimilation of new forms of religiosity. New forms of religiosity, such as those of the New Age, that emerged as a reaction to the churches, have found their way into these without being identified as such, gaining an influence that seems to surpass their rather modest explicit presence outside these (Mak and Sondorp 2003).

The faithful who remained faithful did not escape change and were sufficiently integrated into society to undergo the same influences as those who left the churches. Liberal theology has been developed in dialogue with the modern context, adopting scientific insights regarding evolution or literary criticism. Yet, ironically the more conservative sectors seemed to stand a better chance of survival (Davie 2000: 26). Despite their anti-modern position, Dutch conservative Protestants managed to maintain their influence through a high degree of organisation, one that sustains a Reformed orthodox mini-pillar in times of depillarisation. This is also stimulated by strong social control, doctrinal discipline, media presence, and a highly developed educational system, including schools at all levels. The adaptations in the more liberal-progressive churches may have been a reason for church members not to leave their church. Individualist influences may make it even possible that people remain active in their church, finding there enough space, experiences and ideas to construct their idiosyncratic individual worldview, perhaps without necessarily being influenced by that same church or its theology. In this adapted manner the institution may stand a chance to survive de-institutionalisation.

Method

When the BSS programme was designed, the issue of the merits and shortcomings of quantitative and qualitative methods became relevant, especially as research was to be undertaken on religious behaviour that was becoming increasingly idiosyncratic.

To find some degree of regularity and therefore a basis of generalisation is an obvious goal in much scientific work. Generalising statements are often based on causality chains of causes and consequences – or at least on a correlation of factors – under certain conditions and evident in a considerable number of cases. This laboratory model is – consciously or unconsciously – applied in studying the factors that play a role in a causal chain. When one such factor – for example pressure, temperature, adding a chemical substance – is altered, measuring the changes, preferably including repeating the experiment, shows causal regularity. The scientist should do everything to avoid being one of the factors himself or herself. Though the variables in research that measures religious change are quite different ones, the basic view on science is often the same. A change of gender, education or age – or of any contextual factor related to modernisation – is supposed to cause a change in another area, as in the case of religious practice or beliefs. Correspondingly trends can be predicted, once a factor is supposed to bring change in the near future. Thus, to give an example from recent Dutch literature, if more young Muslims turn away from their home and social context, there is an increasing chance that they will turn away from Islam (Becker and De Wit, 2000: 78). This method of measuring changes through the control of variables, where the researcher is not a factor in the situation under study, is often presented as the normal scientific method. When it is said that 'research has shown that …' or that 'there is evidence that …' this usually means that quantified research has been done.

In social science research the adoption of a method that stems from the natural sciences, including the corresponding view on science as a way of measuring, has been facilitated by the classic presupposition that under the same conditions people will develop similar and consistent behaviour. People in society thus appear to obey the laboratory model. In that case as well, causality of factors can be shown. Much of the secularisation debate starts from the presupposition that persons being subjected to modernisation processes will differ from others and thus will show changed behaviour, for example *in religiosis*. These changes can be measured. As long as the context under study shows some homogeneity and continuity, social or cultural, allowing for the identification of factors, the reasoning seems valid. This made the secularisation thesis possible. Undeniably, important insights have been gained in this way, also in the field of sociology of religion.

What then is the role of qualitative work and what characteristic of human beings does it specifically address? Can all be said and done with quantifying methods? But does part of the field then remain uncovered? Since the BSS programme was conceived in an anthropology department, though from the start taking sociology of religion into account, other methodological options were available, such as participant observation, or open interviews and life histories. In short, narratives were considered instead of statistics. The perspective that comes with such work is different. The application of the laboratory model to the study of social and cultural situations has to be reconsidered and this includes the researcher's role. The rule-driven nature of human reality is not necessarily accepted as obvious. Thus, it can be argued that 'much of what social scientists try to explain is the consequence of inner existential choices made by people' (Kirk and Miller 1986: 10). In qualitative studies human beings are shown not to conform directly to the notions of mechanistic causality proper to nature and to the physics laboratory. In my view part of the criticism against the secularisation theory stems from this insight.

What complicates social science work is that human beings study human beings and therefore explicitly have to find a way to deal with subjectivity. In the laboratory, the object of research does not talk back; in social science research he or she does. Meaning-making researchers do the study of meaning making, most obviously in research on religion and the construction of worldviews. As a result, objectivity is not easily presupposed. It is difficult to realise, even in 'objective' quantitative research. The construction of meaning depends on the demands of the context and is an inter-subjective process. At a particular moment and in a specific context, the researched and the researchers create insights into the construction of complex constellations of meaning and the repertoires from which actors borrow relevant meanings. From the practice of qualitative research, it is clear that human beings have the capacity to disobey trends and rules and to think no while saying yes (for example in a survey), to talk in politically correct ways (such as in an interview) but to speak differently elsewhere. To a certain degree these problems for survey research can technically be solved, but always at the cost of nuance.

It is precisely the distance required in guaranteeing objectivity and the need to make general statements that may be the reason why significant data are overlooked.

Even in quantitative evidence, objectivity is not without problems. Researchers make variables: 'We defined them into being' (Deutscher 1987: 18). Or again: 'Numbers do not protect against bias ... All statistical data are based on someone's definition of what to measure and how to measure it' (Patton 1987: 166). Quantitative work, despite its high status, especially among policy makers who depend on it, does not cover all social or cultural – or religious – reality, especially when people deviate from the rule.

To this it must be added that in view of the idiosyncrasy of modern individualised worldview, deviation and authenticity having become the rule ('be an original!'), regularity has in our days become even more doubtful. Quantitative methods may have their value in discovering general trends and characteristics that are common to a considerable number of people, but people have less and less in common. For the more complex details, the smaller categories and the deviations from the rule, the need for qualitative methods is indicated. Thus the – undeniable – perspective of rule-directed behaviour of conditioned social beings must be complemented by a view of strategically operating human beings who follow interests and emotions and in doing so may show inconsistent behaviour and deviations from the average. Their behaviour is not easily predicted, especially when, as in our days, individualisation is rampant. Concretely they may find difficulty in recognising their conviction among the pre-printed answers to a multiple-choice question.

Figures must be put into perspective and be complemented by narratives – just as constructivism has complemented positivist and post-positivist perspectives on science's mission and on the nature of human beings (cf. Guba 1990). The qualitative researcher's expert use of his or her own subjectivity, turning a seeming disadvantage into an asset, opens up avenues to new insights, from within and through close contact with the person approached. In short, qualitative methods are very useful in studying the subjective turn and its fragmented and diverse manifestations. They serve to show the 'uniqueness of individual subjects and instances' that can disappear within statistics (Brink 1995: 464).

The trench war between secularists and sacralists could be brought to an armistice if the selection of methods that both factions prefer to use is taken into account. In an armistice in the more general methodological trench war, qualitative and quantitative methods have been given a complementary role in the empirical cycle, qualitative work suggesting hypotheses through explorative work that can be tested in quantitative work (Newman and Benz 1998, Tashakkori and Teddlie 1998). As it is recognised that each method uncovers different aspects of human behaviour, a division of scholarly labour is becoming possible. Consequently, if the exclusive claims of each method are abandoned, the debate on the religious trends in Western Europe can be taken further, beyond the current stalemate between secularists and sacralists, and so allowing for combined eclectic approaches. The appropriate questions can then be combined with the right methods to answer them.

The pitfall to be avoided is to pretend to produce through qualitative work the same type of data that quantitative studies had put forward: generalised statements and predictions. These are meant to be complementary, but qualitative studies need not repeat what quantitative researchers do and have done. Qualitative methods have a quality of their own that need not be defined as 'not quantitative' (Kirk and Miller 1986: 10), just as quantitative methods are never defined as 'not qualitative'. Yet, just as is the case with quantitative work, reliability and validity can be demanded from qualitative studies, though with the criteria that are proper to the – usually rather constructivist – setting to which they belong. The results should be plausible, even though they may not obey the criteria that (neo-) positivist quantitative research designers adhere to from the perspective of the laboratory model. As Kirk and Miller (1986: 20) put it: 'Objectivity is the simultaneous realisation of *as much* reliability and validity *as possible*. Reliability is *the degree* to which the finding is independent of accidental circumstances of the research, and validity is *the degree* to which the finding is interpreted in a correct way' (italics added). These criteria are perfectly applicable to qualitative and to constructivist work (see also Seale 1999). Though having different roots – or exactly for that reason – the proponents of the two methodological paradigms can complement each other and should bury their disagreements and engage in a dialogue.

The BSS Research Programme

The view developed in the preceding section was *in statu nascendi* when from 1999 onwards the BSS programme was developed. Quantifying sociologists of religion had done most of the work on religious change in The Netherlands. Anthropologists had hesitantly begun to study Dutch society, having traditionally focused on Third World cultures and on their development. In wanting to study the Dutch religious scene, they were newcomers to a field that had always been dominated by sociologists. Apart from the focus on culture, instead of society (and thus on religion as a cultural phenomenon) and a more holistic view on cultural phenomena such as religion (drawing attention to the relationships between religious, social, economic, political and so forth aspects), anthropologists came to the field with expectations that qualitative methods 'worked'. These would make it possible to provide a complement to the statistical data that had been collected so far by the sociologists. The stories behind the numbers, the processes behind the trends, and the concrete persons behind the general categories could be discovered. The diffuse complexity and individuality of the new forms of religiosity, such as spirituality), which fell through the statistician's sieve, could be shown. Besides, some of the views from the non-empirical studies could be further explored.

Accordingly we opted for a case study approach in the anthropological tradition, and selected five locations at the micro-level. Since we were also interested in changes within the churches, the feedback from what happened outside to within the churches, some of the projects dealt with the situations of the established churches. Moreover, we combined the five locations with five themes that in our understanding more or less covered the different aspects of the changing Dutch religious field: identity, experience, ritual, morals and language. PhD students were to do three of the five projects. Two were the responsibility of students who had just obtained their doctorate. The programme suffered a dramatic setback when, in this initial phase, one of the team's PhD students, Ronald Schouten (see Schouten 2003), died from cancer at the age of 32. Later on his project – on ritual – was finished by one of the post-doctoral students. After the programme had started, other PhD students joined the team, finding in it a platform for the discussion of common interests.

Though each of the five initial researchers had his or her individual project, the researchers worked as much as possible as a team. Especially in the first years, much time was invested in developing a common theoretical and methodological approach. To this end, the method of 'relay writing' was introduced. One team member started writing a short paper on a particular concept or topic – for example identity, or worldview. The team discussed this paper. For the next meeting, another team member would write a second paper on the same topic, without repeating what had already been said. This second paper was discussed, and so on – until the issues that were relevant had all been considered and the map of the debate had been sufficiently drawn. Then a new theme was selected and the cycle began anew. Besides the team meetings, bi-monthly study meetings were organised in which other scholars and researchers from within or outside the university were welcome to participate. From the start there was also a supervising group of senior scholars, formally the applicants for the funding of the programme. This committee has only functioned for some time in the beginning of the programme. Two members were always present at the team meetings, though, and another senior researcher joined the team at a later stage.

Part of the preparation for the programme was the application to a dozen people of the questionnaire used since the 1960s in the 'God in The Netherlands' surveys, with the purpose of asking them, after they had answered the questions in the survey, why they had answered as they did.[1] Interestingly, we discovered that people giving the same answers could have contrary opinions, whereas it also occurred that interviewees giving different answers did not differ in opinion, once they were asked for their motives. This small study showed that nuances remained hidden behind the pre-printed answers, thus underscoring the necessity and complementary nature of the programme we were designing. Some of the authors working with the questionnaire had readily admitted that the survey had its shortcomings, mentioning points such as that comparability was limited, as the phrasing, as formulated in the 1960s, came to carry different meanings in the 1990s (Dekker, De Hart and Peters 1997: 126). This was a symptom of the growing openness among sociologists of religion to admit the relative value of quantitative research and to discover the importance of qualitative studies. In fact, on two occasions the BSS team was invited to present its work to the Dutch Study Group of Sociologists of Religion.

The five projects that from the start were part of the programme can be briefly described. The projects of the PhD students, who later on joined the team, will also be mentioned. In the final section an indication will be given of some of the results.

---

1   Barbara Boudewijnse executed this project.

The *identity* project, run by Els Jacobs, was initially meant to be the synthesising project of the programme. In the application a drawing was included of a square with diagonals between the corners. The identity project was at the crossing of the diagonals, whereas the other four projects – experience, ritual, morals and language – each occupied one of the corners of the square. In practice, the identity concept was not relevant for all the team members, even though it was one of the concepts that were extensively discussed in the first years. The location selected for the identity project, in Leiden, was in a way unique in that it combined Catholic and Protestant church members in one parish, attending the same Sunday church service or mass. The parish had been founded in the 1970s, in a newly built neighbourhood where all people had been making a fresh start and at a time when such ecumenical contacts did not yet meet with the bishop's veto. We presupposed that in such a setting identity was an important issue. Besides, it was expected that the ecumenical contacts would influence the members' construction of a Christian identity.

The second project, on *experience*, the responsibility of Peter Versteeg, was included because of the emphasis that studies of new religious forms put on experience. The locations selected for the study of this theme were three centres in Amsterdam, run by Catholic orders, which offered courses and trainings that often carried the word spirituality in their name. In fact, these orders had a long history of practising spirituality. They had responded to the growing demand for spirituality, the term being acceptable when 'religion' was considered incorrect or outmoded. The interesting characteristic of these spirituality centres was that they were run by an important and official sector of the Catholic Church, which did not prevent them from attracting, apart from Catholics, people who considered themselves part of the exodus that had taken place from that church. Also other people, who had become marginal to institutional Christianity, took part in the activities of these centres. Versteeg reports on this project in the next chapter.

Initially, the third project, on *ritual*, was a PhD project. Until he died, it was the responsibility of Ronald Schouten. Afterwards, Versteeg continued his work. The location selected was a town near Utrecht, Houten, that was being transformed from a village into a suburb of greater Utrecht, adding one new neighbourhood after the other, to house an increasing population, many of whom commute to Utrecht. The local churches had to adapt to the new situation and some did so with great enthusiasm, introducing important changes to parish life. Thus one of the more orthodox Calvinist churches was rapidly adopting evangelical practices and beliefs, introducing Alpha courses to The Netherlands and thereby serving as a model parish to many other churches in the country.

PhD candidate Kim Knibbe undertook the project on *morals*. She did her fieldwork in the border area with Belgium, in the south of Limburg province. A Catholic context was considered most appropriate for a project on morals, since an increasing distance had developed in moral matters between the official doctrine and the actual practices and beliefs of the average member. Once it had started, the project concentrated on three dimensions of religious change in the region. One concerned members' stories of their experiences in the local parish, especially after a conservative priest had succeeded a progressive one. Another sub-location was a convent in the region where courses, usually from a progressive liberal theological stance, were given to lay people from the surrounding parishes. The third dimension represented spiritualist societies and paranormal fairs in the region, whose importance became evident during fieldwork.

Rhea Hummel, also preparing her PhD, has undertaken the fifth project. Coming from literary science, her topic was *language*. Initially the idea was that reading clubs represented excellent locations for the study of changes in worldview language. Once the fieldwork had started this rarely proved to be the case. Having met an artist when visiting a reading club, Rhea discovered that it was worthwhile to study how artists and writers speak about their worldview and to make an inventory of themes and vocabularies. Artists and writers are very outspoken and in the habit of reflection. Besides, they appear to be the model manifestation of the individualised modern subject and often serve as a role model.

Then there are the additional PhD projects. They have not been part of the application, but these researchers joined the team once the programme had started. Marten van der Meulen studied the role of the churches in civil society, doing his fieldwork in a new town, built to the west of Utrecht, Leidsche Rijn. His concern was with the question of how churches marked presence? Another project, executed by Johan Roeland and, like the ritual project, located in Houten, revolves around the question of how youngsters create their religious identity within evangelical youth groups. How is faith transmitted in a secularised society? The third project is on similar questions in Islam. Through his fieldwork in a mosque in Gouda, Martijn de Koning studies the transmission of Islam to young people. As some young Dutch Muslims have become radicalised, this project gained topicality. In the last years, two other PhD projects have started, as part of another programme that I coordinate, on 'Conversion careers and culture politics in Pentecostal churches: An intercontinental comparison'. Two of the five projects in that programme, both at the PhD level, include fieldwork in The Netherlands. One is on migrant churches (Regien Smit) and the other is a comparison of an evangelical and a Pentecostal community (Miranda Klaver). Though operating in another programme, these two researchers are in the same department and share their experiences with the BSS researchers, one of whom (Versteeg) acts as a supervisor. Another PhD researcher, Hanneke Minkjan, who started in the summer of 2005, focuses on Dutch neo-paganism. Her project is the most recent addition to the BSS programme. Finally, a promising MA thesis, by Daniëlle Koning, on the views of Muslim students in Amsterdam on religion and science, has led to an application for funding of a PhD thesis on the same topic.

In sum, there are 11– hopefully soon 12 – projects, nine at the PhD level, two being done by post-doctoral fellows. Eight projects deal with locations within or at the margin of the churches; one project is on Islam; one on neo-paganism, and one, on language, does not have a particular religious context. Of the researchers, the late Ronald Schouten included, five had been trained in anthropology, five in theology with relevant majors, and one in literary science.

Provisional Results

Since each of the five researchers will elsewhere report in detail about his or her project, only a general summary will be given here, despite the fact that the real richness of the results would only become visible through a detailed description of each. As expected, these qualitative studies are strong on detail and idiosyncrasy. The complexity of the field between secularisation and sacralisation was made visible. At the moment of writing, most of the researchers are still producing their reports (articles and PhD theses), so this summary is inevitably provisional. Yet, some conclusions can be formulated and discussed, keeping in mind the two questions the chapter started with.

Secularisation, as loss of institutional religious influence on members and on society, has become visible in all five projects. This happens in most of the locations studied, and not only outside the churches, the Leiden ecumenical parish being a special case from the start because of its inbuilt revolt against church authority, thus ignoring the differences between Catholics and Protestants that were maintained and defended by church authorities. The Leidsche Rijn case has shown the failure of mainstream institutional religion to occupy a relevant position in this new town, while a group of evangelicals, with an emphasis on experience, has proved relatively more successful.

The reduced influence of the churches also applies to the church members who remained in the church, but who nevertheless subjected themselves much less to its control. The emphasis that respondents put on experience as the legitimating source of their religion contributes to the loss of influence by the institution. Consequently these members also tap sources outside the institution, including a selection from all kinds of alternative therapy, thus feeding ideas and practices back into their church. The need for an authentic experience becomes a criterion for the members' appreciation of the ritual services for which the institution is still deemed necessary. Though identity had been chosen as the synthesising concept of the programme, experience would have served as well, with identity as its result. In Dutch society, experience has become an important ingredient of certain massive public reactions, as shown recently when national celebrities died (for example singer André Hazes) or were murdered (such as politician Pim Fortuyn).

Though always a companion of doctrine, in the Calvinist tradition, experience is an important marker of a church's and a member's identity and identification with the institution; and it has recently gained much more importance as the basis for conviction. The church's truth has accordingly been redefined as *my* truth. Strategic negotiation with the clergy is replaced by self-defined responsibility. In the Catholic context under study, it is accompanied by anger when a representative of the clergy does not respect people's self-proclaimed responsibility. Responsibility is no longer a quality imposed by the institution's discipline, but rests in the certainty (and sometimes uncertainty) of the self, even in cases where the concrete behaviour proves to be very similar to that in the days of old. Soul-searching has become more important than truth finding. Even experiencing the absence of the sacred is sometimes perceived as more authentic than feeling its presence. Thus blind surrender to the sacred offers consolation to the tired modern subject who normally has to be in control of life. The boundary between the transcendent and the immanent is blurred. Terms from the old time religion, such as salvation and trust, may obtain fresh meanings, depending on one's authentic experience.

At the same time as members enjoy more liberty within the church; they also introduce elements that came from alternative sources of religiosity or spirituality. Despite the commodified nature of many of these sources, people do not behave as passive consumers, but make their own selection from what is on supply. Consequently the church may be treated in a similar consumptive way, as one of several sources, even though the local clergy may act as if nothing has changed – as if they were the last to know that they are in fact operating and competing on a market where their mode of Christianity is treated as one of the options.

In the locations we studied, the contrast between religion and spirituality – and thereby the predicted substitution of (institutional) religion by (subjective) spirituality – as suggested by Heelas and Woodhead (2005), is not as strong as the latter propose. Interestingly Catholic orders are among the main providers of spirituality training in Amsterdam. Christianity is one of the sources, as happened in a course on St Francis and the charkas.

But even within the churches, the loss of authority of the institution has created a space that cannot adequately be described in either/or terms as religion or spirituality. More and more people use the church in the same way as they would use the ANWB, the Dutch equivalent of the British Automobile Association – as a service institute that should be available when they need it, just as the supermarket around the corner. Interestingly the new merged Dutch Protestant church (PKN: Protestant Church in The Netherlands) recently put an advertisement of one page in one of the biggest newspapers, using the supermarket style. The slogan was 'All our branches open every Sunday!' and there were additional texts such as 'Free shopping for the whole family', the word 'boodschappen' in Dutch meaning both shopping *and* messages.

The nature of identification with the institution has changed, with the possible exception of the more evangelical parishes, though even there this change may be encountered. The new criterion for appreciating the quality of a church service or a 'reli-pop' festival is experience: 'what did it do for me?' The increase in freedom of experience, also stimulated by the Alpha courses, changes the nature of the religious institutions that come to obtain a more virtual or imaginary status. In the Leiden case the metaphor switched in the course of time from the parish as a home, to a garden, to an inn. That parish shows a large degree of self-consciousness, the parish council reflecting explicitly on the identity and the mission of the community. In the Catholic context of South Limburg the younger generation tends to use the church as a supplier of ritual services that are indispensable in the context of the extended family, honouring the elder generation's preferences. Simultaneously the church, through the local convent, also facilitates people's individual search for meaning, offering an open atmosphere in which, on principle, only what counts is personally fitting and acceptable. Meanwhile, the neo-conservative leadership of the diocese has manoeuvred itself into an isolated position, thus reducing even more the church's limited institutional outreach.

Though Heelas and Woodhead refer to the possibility that the subjective turn occurs in what they call 'the congregational domain' (Heelas and Woodhead 2005: 60–68), they conclude on the basis of evidence from both sides of the Atlantic that 'subjectivisation' is not strong enough in the domain to warrant such a conclusion (Heelas and Woodhead 2005: 67). They add however that they looked especially at the 'supply-side' of the congregational domain and therefore allow for the possibility that on the demand side, subjects participate in the subjective turn, despite being regularly discouraged. In my view it is most probable that in the Dutch context, even before secularisation had its impact and became a theme, people traditionally cherished a certain degree of independence, especially when church authority was strong and conflicts were common. This independence is now stronger than ever.

Looking for the roots of '... the unique experiences of my self-in-relation' (Heelas and Woodhead 2005: 3), the Reformation – in The Netherlands in its Calvinist version – and Enlightenment have contributed to a reflective attitude and to individual responsibility. The importance of personal choices and individual conversion was regularly emphasised. The Reformed Churches in The Netherlands for example put much emphasis on the training of young members, not just to socialise them into the right faith, but also to demand a studious attitude and conscious reflection on faith and salvation. This attitude became the motive force of many conflicts and fissions. Orthodox consensus and strict discipline had to compete with personal conviction and freedom of choice. In Dutch Reformed Protestantism, the relation of the individual with the sacred cannot be adequately expressed in terms of the contrast between the subject's experience as internal authority and the transcendental as external authority. In fact the constant struggle was to reconcile the doctrine of sovereign divine grace with personal experiences of the sacred as the ultimate proof of salvation. Current individualisation in The Netherlands has one of its roots in centuries of Reformed Protestantism.

In the church locations we studied, the common believers were the main group of informants, even though leaders were interviewed as well. Lay members construed their own repertoires. This might even mean that as a reaction to the continuous rhetoric of the self in modern culture, the 'we' was gaining popularity, especially under the impact of the radicalisation of Islam as felt in Dutch society since 9/11. In fact, a presupposed linear and irreversible process of change from religion to spirituality (or for that matter from religion to secular views) does not reflect the degree of unpredictability in individualised unique subjects. It runs the risk of serving as a matrix in which reality does not fit or is misrepresented. Subjects may at one time put large parts of their more traditional repertoire to rest, and yet activate them again when the situation seems to demand their renewed application. They may leave the church institution, rejecting its control, and yet eventually come to participate in an alternative non-Christian setting that is equally institutionalised and marked by control. Strikingly, training courses are a nice synthesis between an organised framework and complete liberty, having their own time span, with a beginning and an end. In the case of the spiritualist societies it is possible that participants, despite the subjective turn, treat 'the other side' as a new authority over the subject, establishing objective truths that may even be given a scientific status. The commonly adopted importance of self-centered reflection as the motor for the construction of a new personal repertoire need not be permanent. Establishing responsible relationships with other persons and with nature may be the result. All in all, the current way of moving on the worldview market is motivated by the newly conquered freedom and certainty of the individualisation process at its best, but also by the simultaneous insecurity of the new responsibility – individualisation at its worrying worst.

The language project, being the only project without a clear location and involving people, who in the majority of cases did not identify with the churches, represents the whole spectrum of possibilities, as mirrored in the respondents' vocabulary. Though church language was radically done away with by some and substituted by the language of the positive sciences, in most of the cases it was used in some way, though always transformed in its meanings. It kept its influence, even when people never went to church or used its language to create their own vocabulary, sometimes arriving at the opposite of what the church defended.

In sum, what emerges inside and outside the institutions can best be understood and studied as the formation of individual repertoires. These repertoires are not necessarily filled or used in a systemic or consistent manner. They do not obey the distinction between religion and spirituality. People play with their possibilities and thus adapt to the demands of the contexts they find themselves in at a particular moment or place – an interview being one of these occasions. Contradictions can then be accommodated without much trouble, simply because a repertoire is never activated in its totality. Depending on the context for which it is used, people activate parts of it, often in a routine and unreflective manner. They easily add to this repertoire, not worrying about impossible combinations (resurrection and reincarnation being one striking example). People may do away with parts that are not helpful in a particular situation, yet activating it within days when necessary. Parts of these repertoires are supra-individual and can be shared at will with other people, just as they are often socially constructed, even when being transformed into idiosyncrasies and sources of fashionable authenticity.[2]

Because these worldview repertoires remain hidden in responses to surveys, qualitative methods provide a necessary complement to these. The consistency presupposed in the respondent – often subjected to a hidden test as part of the survey – is more the exception than the rule. Respondents comply with this implicit consistency, constructing a temporal regularity, a momentary system to serve the occasion. Not everything can be measured, and numbers are not always the measure of validity. Surveys are useful to discover general trends, but because of their generalising

---

2   It may well be that paradoxes and inconsistencies in theological discourse are the result of this basic characteristic of human meaning-making, for example the human and divine nature of Jesus, the idea of Trinity, positive and negative theology and so on.

goals, they can miss the relevant details of human inconsistency that only patient qualitative work can uncover.

Secularisation and sacralisation are therefore mutually connected reflections of human duality. People change opinions depending on the context – the interviewer's visit being one particular and one very specific context. Trends are therefore not as linear as one might think, also taking into account that – as a rule – subjects, being unique subjects, do not comply necessarily with the rule. The repertoire approach seems more promising, especially when accompanied by a rehabilitation of qualitative methods. The pioneer efforts of the BSS researchers, though provisional and representing 'only' five+ locations, have tested and confirmed the importance of this approach.

Conclusion

This chapter started with two questions that are central to the current debate on worldviews. The first asked: is secularisation here to stay and to win, or is it more and more complemented – or even undone – by a new sacralisation and a transformation of worldviews? The second question asked what are the best methods to study the situation addressed by the first question – either quantitative or qualitative, or both?

With regard to the first question, our research on the Dutch situation shows that a double movement is occurring. On the one hand secularisation is taking place, mainly in the sense that religious institutions are losing influence in society and in the lives of individuals. New forms of religiosity emerge that are added to the repertoires of those who leave the Church but continue constructing their own inner worldview. On the other hand these developments outside the institutions make themselves felt within the institutions, rescuing to a certain degree their loss of influence in the life of their members. Within the churches individualising members turn into active worldview consumers seeking relevant experiences to combat their insecurity. The institutions they visit are more and more driven into the role of attending to the needs of these members and may thus attract outsiders, including those who once were insiders but opted for the exodus. In other words – secularisation and sacralisation are co-occurring in a seemingly paradoxical way, undermining institutional religion but at the same time reinforcing experienced religiosity. This must not be understood as a confirmation of the distinction Heelas and Woodhead (2005) make between religion and spirituality, even though there are similarities with the trends they suggest are happening. But the situation is more complex and contradictory. One reason is that the feedback into the religious institutions of what is happening with the people who chose to leave them makes the contrast between religion and spirituality less plausible. The congregational domain is affected by what happened outside it, because the faithful are influenced by it. Ironically this adaptation increases the chances of institutions to survive secularisation. Besides, developments are not necessarily linear, people having developed a rather liberal, contextualised and therefore inconsistent way of using available repertoires, from both inside and outside the institutionalised religion.

Turning to the second question, the lesson that can be drawn from the Dutch research programme 'Between Secularisation and Sacralisation' and its case studies is that the nature of the current worldview situation in The Netherlands demands that qualitative methods should be applied to attend to the diversity and the complexity of what is happening. This does not exclude the use of quantitative methods. Just as secularisation and sacralisation occur in a complementary tied up way, quantitative and qualitative methods should be combined, the first to show the rule-driven nature of human behaviour that is subject to structural conditioning and the second to uncover the deviating and complex way of individually managing current repertoires that are also part of human nature and that include forms of resistance against impositions and power mechanisms. When these two methods are taken into account, then mechanistic and subjectivist tendencies can both receive due attention. In terms of paradigms for responsible scholarly behaviour, this eclectic approach means that inspiration can be found in both (neo-) positivist and constructivist models.

In sum, the sharp and polemic characteristics of the debate on secularisation could be softened and polished if the coincidence of theoretical and methodological viewpoints is addressed. In an eclectic way the strong qualities of both factions can be put to work, with the purpose of increasing insight in worldview developments, its regularities and its complexities. Thus the trench war that has been waged can be transformed into a constructive approach in which both secularists and sacralists have their role to play.

Bibliography

Becker, J.W. and R. Vink (1994), *Secularisatie in Nederland, 1966–91*, Den Haag: SCP.

Becker, J.W., J. De Hart, and J. Mens (1997), *Secularisatie en alternatieve zingeving in Nederland*, Den Haag: SCP.

Becker, J.W. and J.S.J. De Wit, (2000), *Secularisatie in de jaren negentig: Kerklidmaatschap, veranderingen in opvattingen en een prognose*, Den Haag: SCP.

Brink, T. L. (1995), 'Qualitative and/or qualitative methods in the scientific study of religion', *Zygon*, 461-75.

Casanova, J. (1994), *Public Religions in the Modern World*, Chicago: University of Chicago Press.

Davie, G. (1994), *Religion in Britain Since 1945: Believing Without Belonging*, Oxford: Blackwell.

Davie, G. (2000), *Religion in Modern Europe: A Memory Mutates*, Oxford: Oxford University Press.

Davie, G. (2001), 'The Persistence of Institutional Religion in Modern Europe', in L. Woodhead, P. Heelas and D. Martin (eds), *Peter Berger and the Study of Religion*, London and New York: Routledge, pp. 101–11.

Dekker, G.J, J. De Hart, and J. Peters (1997) *God in Nederland 1966–96*, Amsterdam: Anthos.

Deutscher, I. (1970), 'Words and deeds: social science and social policy', in W. J. Filstead (ed), *Qualitative Methodology: Firsthand involvement with the social world*, Chicago: Markham.

Guba, E.G. (1990), 'The Alternative Paradigm Dialog', in E.G. Guba (ed.), *The Paradigm Dialog*, Newbury Park: SAGE, pp. 17–27.

Felling, A.J.A. (2004), *Het proces van individualisering in Nederland: een kwarteeuw sociaal-culturele ontwikkeling*, Nijmegen: Katholieke Universiteit.

Goddjin, W., H. Smets and G. van Tillo (1979), *Opnieuw: God in Nederland*, Amsterdam: De Tijd.

Heelas, P. and L. Woodhead (2005), *The Spiritual Revolution: Why Religion is Giving Way to Spirituality*, Oxford: Blackwell.

Kirk, J. and M.L. Miller (1986), *Reliability and Validity in Quantitative Research*, Newbury Park: SAGE.

Mak, A. and O. Sondorp (eds) (2003), *In 's hemelsnaam: Dialoog tussen oud en nieuw geloof*, Zoetermeer: Meinema.

Newman, I. and C.R. Benz (1998), *Qualitative–Quantitative Research Methodology: Exploring the Interactive Continuum*, Carbondale and Edwardsville: Southern Illinois University Press.

Patton, M. Q (1987), *How to use qualitative methods*, NewburyPark: SAGE.

Phalet, K. (ed.) (2004), *Moslim in Nederland*, Den Haag: SCP.

Schouten, R. (2003), '"Rituals of Renewal": The Toronto Blessing as a Ritual Change of Contemporary Christianity', *Journal of Ritual Studies*, 17(2): 25–34.

Seale, C. (1999), *The Quality of Qualitative Research*, London: Sage.

Tashakkori, A. and C. Teddlie (1998), *Mixed Methodology: Combining Qualitative and Quantitative Approaches*, Thousand Oaks: Sage.

Te Grotenhuis, M. (1998), *Ontkerkelijking: oorzaken en gevolgen*, Nijmegen: SOCON.

Van Harskamp, A. (2000), *Het nieuw-religieuze verlangen*, Kampen: Kok.

Verweij, J. (1998), *Secularisering tussen Feit en Fictie: Een internationaal vergelijkend onderzoek naar determinanten van religieuze betrokkenheid*, Tilburg: Tilburg University Press.

Zeegers, G.H.L., G. Dekker and J.W.M. Peeters (1967), *God in Nederland*, Amsterdam: Van Ditmar.

Chapter 5

Spirituality on the Margin of the Church: Christian Spiritual Centres in The Netherlands

Peter Versteeg

One of the most remarkable developments within Dutch Christianity in the last 10 to 20 years is the increasing interest in what is called spirituality (Aalders 1969; Beumer 1989; Bouwman and Bras 2001; cf. Nouwen 1992; Waaijman 2002). This can be seen in the popularity of such diverse phenomena as monastic retreats, silent celebrations, Taizé celebrations and the study of the Gnostic gospels. Although being described by the same umbrella term, Christian spirituality represents in fact a variety of spiritualities. With the emergence of Christian spirituality outside the churches, the picture has become even more complex. Christian spiritual centres, in particular, are successful in attracting a distinct audience of modern seekers and spiritual pilgrims, offering a wide range of worldviews and practices, which in some respects overlap with what is offered on alternative spiritual circuits. This makes the place of Christian spiritual centres within the religious landscape interesting, as they may be placed somewhere in between Christian faith communities and alternative spirituality. A crucial issue arises over how the significance of marginal spirituality is to be understood within a secularised context.

Marginal spirituality should not be understood in a quantitative sense but in a qualitative sense, which means that it represents a set of ideas and practices that are peripheral to the doctrinal agreements that form the basis of the orthodox Christian tradition. Moreover, marginal Christian spirituality often has a distant relationship to Church authorities. The margin refers also to liminality, understood here as a space where people start questioning the given and sometimes create something new out of it (Turner 1991: 128).

In this chapter, the first concern is with how Christian spirituality can be understood within the context of the current interest in spirituality, including alternative spirituality. Secondly, we consider how Christian spiritual centres act as providers of Christian spirituality in The Netherlands, their place within the religious market, and their customers. Thirdly, a further investigation of the spiritual beliefs and practices in Christian centres is undertaken through a case study of a course in 'basic spirituality'. The Franciscan spiritual centre La Verna, which offers this course, serves throughout the chapter as a case example. The spirituality of Christian spiritual centres needs to be understood in terms of religious representations and practices and how these relate to other forms of spirituality.

Although sociological studies of religious change in The Netherlands and Western Europe can neatly map religious behaviour and representations at a certain moment in time, understanding the religiousness of people requires the use of qualitative methods. Dutch statistics show a rapid decline in the number of people expressing traditional Christian beliefs, yet the percentage of atheists uncovered does not increase. This means that the amount of people having all sorts of religious belief grows. Within the context of Christian spirituality this issue is pressing, because it is a field which is related to the congregational domain but which moves both beyond it and the belief system it embodies. We assume that a certain kind of Christianity is practised here, but we have to find out what its nature is.

In order to do so, the author participated for twelve months in various Christian spiritual settings, mainly in retreat centres. Fieldwork included participation in meditation groups, retreat weekends and spiritual training, as well as topical and biographical interviews with 22 persons, both participants and leaders. Most of the time the researcher was only allowed the role of a participant, which meant that he had to share with other participants and reflect on his spiritual process. In interview situations with fellow participants this gave the opportunity for a dialogical and comparative perspective, which formed a valuable basis for interpretation. A small part of the research was quantitative. It served to provide a more accurate picture of the average visitor to these spiritual centres and covered matters of gender, church affiliation and worldview. In cooperation with La Verna spiritual centre in Amsterdam, a short survey was undertaken administered to participants on most of the La Verna courses in the second half of 2003. The respondents were informed that the material was to be used for research and for internal evaluation purposes of La Verna. A total of 332 questionnaires were handed out, of which 188 were returned, which was a response of 57 per cent.

Christian Spirituality

What is Christian spirituality? One can answer this question by turning to one's informants first to try to understand what they mean by it. This approach is valuable in the sense that it can map the various uses of the word and thus the way in which people have appropriated it to describe a certain belief and practice. Obviously, this 'emic' approach will not automatically lead to a more general level of conceptualisation, but it can show how the term 'spirituality' might be reduced to a limited number of options. In this case, a distinction between theistic and holistic spirituality became clear. On the one hand, there was a spirituality that stressed relationships to an external sacred, and on the other hand, a version emerged that marked a quest for connectedness to a sacred whole. Examined more closely, the difference between the two spiritualities appeared to be quite fundamental. What Heelas and Woodhead write about the distinction between religion and spirituality is very similar. They note that the use of the term 'spirituality' within Christianity often refers to devotion to the sacred as an external authority, whilst their academic construction of spirituality refers to a worldview that finds fulfilment in the sacredness of life itself. They therefore classify most Christian spirituality as 'religion', which means that it involves a commitment to a higher truth that is 'out there', rather than a discovery of a truth that is intrinsic to the individual self and the world. Even though many new forms of Christianity are very much focused on self and subjective experience, their orientation to an external moral authority places them outside what Heelas and Woodhead (2005: 5–6) call 'subjective-life spirituality'.

Clearly, many of the spiritual practices that are now on offer in Dutch mainline churches would fall within the category of 'religion', being strongly focused on subjective experience and personal fulfilment, yet placed within a framework in which deference to the external authority of God, Scripture or tradition is a necessary condition of practice and affiliation. However, the distinction between 'religion' and 'spirituality' may look clearer when describing them as ideological and institutional options, as Heelas and Woodhead do, but this is much less the case when these are assessed from the angle of individual experience. Thus, for example, Taizé and Iona singing may be categorised as subjective-life spirituality (Heelas and Woodhead 2005: 157), whereas many people in Dutch mainline churches see Taizé and Iona as belonging to an experiential liturgical repertoire that has more in common with influences from the charismatic renewal. The point is that what is called 'holistic' in an institutional sense, can be experienced as continuous with traditional Christian devotion. But in Christian spiritual centres the opposite is also true, for example, when a traditional religious vocabulary is lifted from its original parameters and is made to mean something quite different. The conceptualisation of 'religion' and 'spirituality' works well, taking into account that these categories do not always fit the individual and practical level. People involved in religious activities simply do not use the same classifications as academic researchers and may feel that the variety of different, and perhaps, in the eyes of the outsider, inconsistent, representations and practices may belong to the same field.

It could be said that the adjective 'Christian' in Christian spirituality poses a similar problem. In Christian spiritual centres, spirituality is often just identified as that, without referring explicitly to Christian belief. Although it is clear to the visitors that the context of the spiritual centre is related to Christianity, what the centre supplies is treated with a great deal of pragmatism. While not everybody may be open to spiritual resources from non-Christian traditions, in the end it is all 'spirituality', its value being first of all the possibility of providing well-being to the individual participant. This suggests that to the clients of Christian spiritual centres, the distinction between Christian and alternative or holistic spirituality is not always either meaningful or helpful. Spirituality is foremost evaluated through practical and experiential criteria, and not by using formal labels. At the same time, the centres themselves explicitly maintain reference to their respective traditions wishing to show their Christian inspiration and their place in Christian history. In the next section we will take a closer look at the meaning of spirituality from the perspective of Christian spiritual centres and their position within the wider spiritual field.

Christian Spiritual Centres and their Visitors

Christian spiritual centres offer spiritual activities often in the form of a short-term training or course. The centres have a more or less distant relationship to church authorities and church institutions, but present themselves as having their own spiritual identity rooted in the Christian tradition. What strikes us first is that most centres have a Catholic background, and, to be more precise, most are aligned to an order or a congregation.[1] The prominent role of orders and congregations within the Dutch spiritual field is partly the result of the transformation of mission and ministry since the 1960s (cf. Coleman 1978; Goddijn 1975). Religious vocations decreased, membership declined and the religious life itself seemed to be in crisis. In a more positive sense, the Second Vatican Council inspired orders to bring their traditions up to date. A period of reinterpretation and experimentation followed, in which the generation that did not leave played a prominent role. A reformulation of the religious life meant that orders, the Jesuits and the Franciscans for example, became more sensitive to democratic and emancipatory ideas. Orders clearly saw a role for themselves in the democratisation of the church and the emancipation of its believers. This new role enabled them, at the same time, to transmit their traditions to new generations. What are now called spiritual centres developed out of this democratic and liberating vision of Faith and the Church. Some alternative spiritual centres have developed from these new forms of Catholic religious work.

Many of these Christian spiritual centres should be placed on the liberal and ecumenical side of the Catholic spectrum. They usually sympathise with progressive movements within the Church, which struggle for all kinds of reform of authority and liturgy. Spirituality and a progressive interpretation of Christian faith have some things in common, as both strive to liberate people from oppressive structures. The popularity of these new forms of Christian spirituality corresponds with the demise of the progressive and horizontal oriented theology at the end of the 1980s. The inward turn of faith and theology has been favourable to the emergence of experiential religion, a need these Christian spiritual centres are geared to fulfil. Societal and political involvement are still important in goals of these centres where it is enshrined that healthy spirituality will lead to feelings of responsibility for the world. On the programmes themselves, these do not seem to have a high priority.

Spiritual centres operate with a definite market-orientation, seeing their clientele in terms of individual seekers, who are looking for a way to freely explore their spiritual preferences and who are willing to pay for it. La Verna, which started as a spiritual centre in 1998, explicitly describes its target groups as both seekers without

---

1   There is one Protestant ecumenical retreat centre with a clear orientation on Taizé. This centre also attracts church members with an evangelical leaning.

a religious background but also as people who want to look for a different approach to their religious background. Different from the churches, spiritual centres show a greater awareness of the dominance of religious individualism and the fragmentation of religious needs. Despite this stress on interested individuals, these centres have aspirations to establish a network of more or less committed visitors, even one that might evolve into an alternative community of faith. Sometimes these different perceptions clash, in particular when leaders expect more commitment than visitors are willing to give.

The market-orientation of Christian centres brings them close to the alternative spiritual field. For example, a number of Christian spiritual centres advertise on the monthly agenda of the alternative magazine *Koörddanser*. However, the share of Christian spiritual centres on this market is relatively small – approximately 20 centres of varying size. Some centres draw relatively large numbers of people. Thus, the Ignatiushuis, affiliated with the Dutch Jesuits and located in the centre of Amsterdam, has organised more than 900 courses since 1993, with more than 4,400 people subscribing to these activities. There can be some overlap on the supply side of Christian and alternative spiritual centres. On both circuits meditation and bodywork are the most popular practices, although differences are also obvious, for example, in courses about the Bible or Christian art. The presence of Christian spiritual centres in the alternative spiritual circuit shows that they expect their potential customers to have a wide spiritual interest. Indeed, it is not uncommon to meet visitors who discovered Christian spirituality after being involved in neo-shamanism or Buddhist meditation. Similarly, regular clients of Christian centres may on occasion also visit alternative centres. What sort of people visits these Christian spiritual centres?

Doing fieldwork as well as reading studies about the Dutch New Age population (Aupers and Van Otterloo 2000) conveys a strong impression of the average participant of these centres – female, higher education and past middle age. The small survey of La Verna participants showed that this impression was not far from the truth. Women comprised 75 per cent of the visitors to the centre. Most participants were between 50 and 70 years of age and in the next largest group were aged between 40 and 50. Many had received higher vocational school or university education. In the survey, people were asked about their church affiliation, and whether they thought of themselves as having a worldview. Subsequently, they were asked to describe this worldview in one or two sentences. Nearly two-thirds of the participants identified with a church, Catholics forming the largest group (34 per cent) of these. One-third of the participants were non-denominational. Most interestingly, three quarters of the participants who responded claimed to have a worldview. Oddly, a number of the denominational respondents indicated they had *no* worldview and these were all Catholics. This response probably has to do with the fact that they are not familiar with the term 'worldview'. The term 'worldview' (*levensbeschouwing*) was not specified in the survey questions.

Some typical examples of how people described their worldview were – 'Christian with a pinch of Zen', 'connected to and in service of God (via Christianity and Hinduism)', and 'inspired by the contemplative/mystical core of all traditions'. Striking was the similarity between denominational and non-denominational respondents in describing their worldview, although the former referred more often to Christianity. In interviews with Catholic visitors of La Verna and other Christian spiritual centres, it became clear that they saw spiritual practices of various origins as a part of their way of being Catholic (Versteeg 2006b).

The objective of spiritual centres is to enable people to develop a personal spirituality, one that gives Christian spirituality an individual focus. Spirituality is seen as a personal quest, a path that leads to meaning and ultimate values in life. It is formed around the personal questions and preferences of the individual. Christian spiritual centres have in fact a rather positive idea of individualism. With the decline of traditional authority, the sources of inspiration are now open to all people who now may choose their own path freely. In this sense, spirituality is presented as having no fixed boundaries and as being open to other traditions than Christianity. Here again we see a liberating characteristic of Christian spirituality: what is meaningful cannot be prescribed by the Church or by tradition, but is to be discovered by paying attention to what is inside the individual person. Looking more closely to the Franciscan centre La Verna, we read in an internal note that spirituality should start with 'the self-experience of people', asking 'how can we experience the depths that we may call God, which concern the self, the relationship with God, the relationship with the other, our own roots [and] ancestors?'

According to this view, self-experience is the starting point of a process of spiritual learning, although the issue of a particular worldview is not mentioned. In this respect, La Verna's open view on spirituality is not that different from the expectations of its visitors. Yet, the affinity of the centre with the Franciscan heritage and the whole of Catholic tradition is outspoken, although it never becomes self-evident, since the centre knows that their open attitude to other spiritual traditions is not endorsed by every Catholic. In the words of the director of La Verna, the Catholic tradition is like a huge house, where there is room for many kinds of religious expressions. Sometimes one will find some useful things in the basement, although others may prefer to keep the doors to other rooms closed. This means that La Verna is selective in the things it wants to offer to people, for the criterion it operates with is that it should help people to develop their own spirituality. Set against this expectation, Catholic tradition is treated as a resource and an inspirational source, rather than a doctrinal body to which one has to submit. But the selectivity of La Verna also concerns what is on offer on the alternative market.

Interestingly, esoteric influences are viewed critically for what is seen as their strict blueprinted worldviews, which do not fit the idea that people should find their spiritual quality within themselves and their life world. In a similar vein, La Verna stresses that spirituality should address the reality of suffering and poverty. Here they explicitly refer to the example of St Francis, whose spiritual life was marked by pain and brokenness. The centre will not easily endorse spiritual methods that do not take this reality into account. In this sense, La Verna's approach to spirituality is close to the practice of pastoral care and social action, in which they follow the Franciscan spirit of being close to people in need.

A recent development is that La Verna is becoming more focused on offering people 'a spiritual path'. It was felt that the structure of the programme made it too easy to just 'shop for spirituality', leaving visitors too much to cope with their own choice. The La Verna board suggested that the centre had a greater responsibility to supply something more definite that would enable people to follow a spiritual path. This led to the development of a more integrated programme, one geared to serving both beginners and advanced participants.

Techniques of Self-experience

The programmes of Christian spiritual centres can be divided according to several themes. La Verna, for example, offers activities around the themes of meditation, art, reading and story telling, and retreats and pilgrimages. From a few years ago, La Verna also organises a 'Basic course spirituality' established to introduce people to certain spiritual forms. In this course, which lasts four evenings, several spiritual techniques are practised in order to help people to 'track down' their spirituality. Here spirituality is presented as related to finding a personal 'direction' and 'a way of life'.

After every meeting the participants were asked to do certain exercises, which were meant to structure spirituality according to a certain place and time during the day. In the first three meetings, a different spiritual form was central and the last meeting was meant to share what participants had learnt and how they had progressed. The forms were presented as the means to discover personal spirituality but they were also viewed as techniques to experiment with in order to find a form that would fit the needs and aspirations of the participant. The techniques that were introduced during the course were mandala drawing, meditation forms and the writing/drawing of a spiritual autobiography. Although these forms are quite different, they all had a very similar outcome, namely the sharing of experiences within the group. Reflexivity within a group was considered very important because it provided a means of representation of spiritual growth. By being reflexive, participants disclosed the spiritual process they were undergoing while at the same time they could display their command of the spiritual discourse.

Although the following examples are not entirely representative they give a good impression of the kinds of practices and spiritual forms that can be encountered in Christian spiritual centres. They also give an idea of the (religious) focus of the courses and what people encounter and experience in these.

Example 1: Mandala Drawing

Presented as the mirror of the soul, mandala drawing serves as a kind of soul mining. Here the spiritual focus is on the inner life of the participants. In some ways this suggests that the question of whether something is religious, psychological or spiritual is not very relevant. A notion of transcendence was important to the participants, although the issue of its nature of this transcendence was not significant. As has been observed by researchers of alternative spirituality, what is religious often takes on psychological properties, a development which has been identified as the legacy of Carl Jung (Main 2002). Within the Christian field the work of the Benedictine monk Anselm Grün should be mentioned. He promoted a so-called 'spirituality from below', in which emotion and God seemed nearly identical (Grün 1998; 1999; 2001). This notion of spirituality seems better than holistic spirituality to describe the form used in these Christian spiritual centres. It is a spiritual method that looks to the inner self and helps it to come to terms with difficulties, to surmount them and to realise the potential of the self. The language used to describe these individual processes refers to notions of 'light', 'warmth', 'energy' or 'growth'. It serves to enhance a certain 'psychologising' of religion or the 'religionising' of psychology.

Example 2: Meditation

Meditation is the central technique of experience in Christian spirituality, but its purpose is rarely explained. In this technique, the concepts of 'silence', 'here and now' and 'attention' appear and these can be described as the content of meditation. Although meditation is strongly associated with the religious life of orders, in spiritual courses it rarely has a straightforward religious focus. The focus of these techniques of meditation seems related to notions of practice. This relates to walking, a visualisation, mantra singing or sitting in silence.

In a particular meeting the course leader explains what he calls 'the four rules of meditation':

- accepting what appears to you, no matter what it is;
- observation of what appears to you;
- transformation – what appears to you has a message that can change you; and
- even if these three things do not happen, they still happen.

These rules show that transformation through meditation is expected but that the outcome is left open. Similarly, the nature of the meditation experiences is not circumscribed. It can be a feeling, a memory, a physical sensation or an image in the mind. In guided meditations, the purpose is to experience what is visualised, for example, walking through a forest and touching the trees or feeling rooted while imagining that one is a tree. Identifying an experience, as coming from the 'other side', from a transcendent source, other than the individual self, is a possibility that meditation leaders mention explicitly. The leader of this course explained that 'in biblical language' the 'other side' is called God.

Example 3: Writing and Drawing a Spiritual Autobiography

The participants draw a timeline of their life and mark this with colours, symbols and words. In this way the personal spiritual process in the timeline is discovered. Participants explain to the group what they have drawn. The training leaders then interview the participant in order to structure uncertain interpretations or to make meanings more clear. While they explain their work, people tell a story of their life. They may suddenly become moved by something they are sharing. In this sense, the drawing and the narrative accompanying it, work as a kind of free association, which gives the suggestion that they reveal something significant about the person (for a similar spiritual autobiographical method see Wakefield 1990).

What is striking about the diversity of forms in this 'basic spirituality' training is that in the end they lead to the sharing of a narrative. Spiritual forms can be seen as hermeneutic spaces in which symbols are used, invented and eventually adopted as personal symbols to be expressed in a public narrative (Versteeg 2006a). Within the hermeneutic space there is a clear sense of personal revelation; symbols are there for the individual who is free to attach his or her meaning to them. The structure of the training leads people to the point where they can express this revelation. This is a crucial moment, because here the participant has the opportunity to display his or her personal spiritual process. Interestingly, Christian spirituality has little explicit ideological input but it has a strong expectation that people actually become transformed through spiritual practices. Thus, in order to be 'successful', participants have to prove a certain kind of spiritual and emotional literacy, what can be called a discursive reflexivity. This idea was developed after the author observed repeatedly during course sessions how he was not always successful in giving a satisfying account of his own spiritual growth.[2] The ability to express oneself emotionally, thereby making use of a spiritual vocabulary, is taken as a sign of personal health and progress in the context of the spiritual course. In this sense, the hermeneutic space always involves a negotiation between the individual, his or her sensations and memories, and the discursive boundaries of the spiritual group.

An Interpretation of Christian Spirituality

The above examples show some important characteristics of Christian spirituality. First, it demonstrates an inclusive attitude toward meaning and enables many personal experiences to be articulated, simply because these forms of Christian spirituality seem to have very little ideological input. It is almost as if the spiritual forms provide an empty framework for meaning. Secondly, there is a certain logic of experience in Christian spirituality. Experience becomes an interpretive schema through which fragments from different cultural repertoires become individually integrated. Thus, the Zen Buddhist principles of 'here and now', of non-judgment and of acceptance lead to the recognition or discovery of similar principles within the rule of St Francis or other traditional sources. In this way Christian tradition no longer monitors religious experience. Rather, religious experience uses tradition as a personal resource for meaning. Thirdly, Christian spirituality has a therapeutic quality, one that becomes

---

2   This is of course an interesting aspect of qualitative research – getting information as a result of failing to be an insider.

visible in a psychological narrative and that requires a certain emotional-spiritual 'literacy' on behalf of the participants to understand the testimonies given. Personal growth is a strong value that has to be expressed through a reflexive account in which symbols are appropriated as personal tools. Sometimes, this spirituality appears to be almost self-made.

The meaning of Christian spirituality seems complex, exactly because it shows a great variety of forms and practices. However, as my interpretation of the examples suggests, there is certainly a cultural idiom and ethos underlying it. Christian spirituality is a type of religion that responds to and corresponds with a self-ethos that is itself a product of a radically individualised and secularised culture. This ethos is foremost focused on the self as both an object and an individual trajectory. A religion that addresses this ethos will have a high view of the self: both the self as a 'sacred self' (Heelas 1996) waiting to become enlightened; and the self as the highest moral authority. In both cases, subjective experience is seen as the only valid method to prove its basis. This 'religion of and for the self', as the Dutch social theorist Van Harskamp (2000) calls it, looks to both therapy and religion as repertoires that enhance this self. Religious traditions still have their value, but only as resources for the individual. Christian spirituality shows that detraditionalisation is not so much the destruction of tradition but rather its deconstruction and subsequent reconstruction. Here again, experience is crucial in the way elements from tradition are selected or neglected.

The examples also show how this form of Christian spirituality has a this-worldly focus in which life itself is a locus of the sacred. In other words, it can be categorised as a 'subjective-life spirituality', rather than a traditional Christian form of devotion. The search for the balanced and healthy self, discovering the real core of the self and expressing it through a personal spirituality are essentially secular interpretations of redemption and salvation (cf. Hervieu-Leger 1993: 147). It is not so much an instrumentalisation of religious language for the benefit of individual experience, as can be seen in some neo-charismatic Christian movements, but is rather a shift from a traditional theistic discourse to a self- and experience-focused discourse.

In 1933 Romano Guardini, one of the popular Roman Catholic theologians of the twentieth century wrote a book about spiritual exercises called *Wille und Wahrheit* (*Will and Truth*). In this book, he compared the 'dark will' of the unconscious to the believer's reality of 'Christ in us'. According to Guardini, there is an unconscious will in spiritual life, just as in natural life. Whenever the believer reaches silence and receives a divine word in meditation, the 'dark will' of faith will take over. Although Guardini speaks the language of surrender, of letting go and of opening up, a language that is familiar to the visitor to Christian spiritual centres, there is a great difference between their two worlds. Whereas Guardini compares natural and spiritual as two distinct phenomena, the contemporary spiritual adherent will see them as one and the same. In the contemporary context of Christian spirituality, spiritual progress has become a process of attending to one's emotional life and 'becoming what you are within the life-span' (1933: 30). Paradoxically, this is a development which indicates secularising and sacralising tendencies occurring at the same time, that transform

Christian notions into worldly concerns, yet within a framework which, to most spiritual adherents, is still of a religious nature.

Conclusion

What is called spirituality nowadays is more and more becoming identified with a certain inclusive religious approach, one based on individual experience. The spirituality of Christian spiritual centres is no exception to this process. Different from other kinds of Christian spirituality, what is offered cannot be called theistic. Although God may be mentioned, there is no explicit commitment to God as an external transcendent authority. Instead, there is a commitment to the self as something that can be explored through spiritual practices. Following Heelas and Woodhead, the spirituality of Christian spiritual centres can be categorised as a subjective-life form. In that sense, Christian spiritual centres are a part of the alternative spiritual market. Within that market they occupy a small niche with their own orientation, although in many ways overlapping with the world of alternative spirituality.

The focus on the self and the disappearance of an external form of the sacred both show a change of Christian faith and practice. It is one where no faith is required. The shift to immanence in these forms of Christian spirituality also means that the representations are multivocal and vague. By valuing inductive experience as a ground for truth, the qualification 'religious' has become redundant and meaning has become a therapeutic insight. The vagueness and fuzziness of this type of spiritual discourse is telling and may point to the absence of God, as Graham Ward (2003: 119) suggests, although from a certain theological viewpoint it can be regarded as a sign of God. Yet, the vagueness of the sacred that appears here has a certain cultural meaning. It points to the growing number of people who feel that traditional notions of religious commitment *vis-à-vis* an external transcendent truth have little to do with their everyday lives. To say that one believes in 'something' is a quite common statement in The Netherlands nowadays, which is meant to show that one is not religious but not entirely without belief.

What we see in these Christian spiritual centres is in part an affirmative form of 'somethingism'. Clearly, the conceptual fuzziness, the emphasis on silence, bodily sensations, personal symbols, even the idea of a sacred self, all point to the fact that people express devotion without being entirely sure what its object is. The case of Christian spiritual centres shows that this is not only the case with ex-Catholics but with Catholics too. People who still identify themselves as Catholics, who search for a more individualised and experiential belief and practice, are open to what spiritual centres have to offer, and what they see as a reinterpretation of or an alternative to the religious praxis in which they were raised. To a number of older Catholic visitors, spirituality means a liberated, personal and experiential religion, with openness toward other religious and cultural repertoires. What Christian spiritual centres offer in their practices is exactly this openness, a space that is surrounded by a clear discursive tendency in which a certain kind of expressiveness is required. It affirms religion as a personal preference and an individualised trajectory and in this sense it is secularising as well as sacralising.

This also suggests why Christian spiritual centres are a predominantly Catholic phenomenon, since a positive view on human nature does not sit comfortably with Protestantism. Against the background of a rapidly secularising society an individualised spirituality such as offered by La Verna is a logical option. However, the average age of the visitors is high and this group will decline in the not so distant future, which means that Christian spiritual centres are likely to decline as well, unless they succeed in reaching younger target groups.

Bibliography

Aalders, C. (1969), *Spiritualiteit: over geestelijk leven vroeger en nu*, The Hague: Boekencentrum.

Aupers, S. and A. Van Otterloo (2000), *New age: een godsdiensthistorische en sociologische benadering*, Kampen: Kok.

Beumer, J. (1989), *Als de hemel de aarde raakt: Spiritualiteit en mystiek*, Kampen: Kok.

Bouwman, K. and K. Bras (eds) (2001), *Werken met spiritualiteit*, Baarn: Ten Have.

Coleman, J.A. (1978), *The Evolution of Dutch Catholicism, 1958–74*, Berkeley: University of California Press.

Goddijn, W. (1975), *The Deferred Revolution: A Social Experiment in Church Innovation in Holland, 1960–70*, Amsterdam: Elsevier.

Grün, A. and M. Dufner (1998), *Spiritualiteit van beneden*, Kok/Carmelitana: Kampen/Gent.

Grün, A. (1999), *Heaven Begins Within You: Wisdom from the Desert Fathers*, New York: Crossroad.

Grün, A. (2001), *God ervaren*, Tielt: Lannoo.

Guardini, R. (1933), *Wille und Wahrheit: Geistliche Übungen*, Mainz: Matthias-Grünewald-Verlag.

Heelas, P. (1996), *The New Age Movement: The Celebration of the Self and the Sacralisation of Modernity*, Oxford: Blackwell.

Heelas, P. and L. Woodhead (2005), *The Spiritual Revolution: Why Religion is Giving Way to Spirituality*, Oxford: Blackwell.

Hervieu-Léger, D. (1993), 'Present-Day Emotional Renewals: The End of Secularization or the End of Religion?', in W.H. Swatos Jr (ed.), *A Future for Religion? New Paradigms for Social Analysis*, Newbury Park: Sage, pp. 129–48.

La Verna, Franciscan Centre for Spiritual Development, http://www.laverna.nl/ (accessed: 30 August 2005).

Main, Roderick (2002), 'Religion, Science and the New Age', in J. Pearson (ed.) *Belief Beyond Boundaries: Wicca, Celtic Spirituality and the New Age, Milton Keynes?*, Aldershot: Open University/Ashgate, pp. 173-222

Nouwen, H. (1992), *The Return of the Prodigal Son: A Story of Homecoming*, New York: Doubleday.

Turner, V. (1991), *The Ritual Process: Structure and Anti-Structure*, Ithaca, NY: Cornell University Press.

Van Harskamp, A. (2000), *Het nieuw-religieuze verlangen*, Kampen: Kok.

Versteeg, P. (2006a), 'Marginal Christian Spirituality: An Example from a Meditation Group', *Journal of Contemporary Religion*, 21(1): 83–97.
Versteeg, P. (2006b), 'Meditation and Subjective Signification: Meditation as a Ritual Form in New Christian Spirituality', *Worship*, 8(2), 121–39.
Waaijman, C. (2002), *Spirituality: Forms, Foundations*, Methods, Leuven: Peeters.
Wakefield, D. (1990), *The Story of Your Life: Writing a Spiritual Autobiography*, Boston: Beacon Press.
Ward, G. (2003), *True Religion*, Oxford: Blackwell.

Other Bibliographical Sources

Aupers, S. (2004), *In de ban van de moderniteit: De sacralisering van het zelf en computer-technologie*, Amsterdam: Aksant.
Blommestijn, H. (2003), *Spiritualiteit voor beginners*, Zoetermeer: Boekencentrum.
Bowman, M. (2000), 'More of the Same? Christianity, Vernacular Religion and Alternative Spirituality in Glastonbury', in S. Sutcliffe and M. Bowman (eds), *Beyond New Age: Exploring Alternative Spirituality*, Edinburgh: Edinburgh University Press, pp. 83–104.
Corrywright, D. (2003), *Theoretical and Empirical Investigations into New Age Spiritualities*, Oxford: Peter Lang.
Davie, G., P. Heelas and L. Woodhead (eds) (2003), *Predicting Religion: Christian, Secular and Alternative Futures*, Aldershot: Ashgate.
Dreyer E. and M. Burrows (eds) (2005), *Minding the Spirit: The Study of Christian Spirituality*, Baltimore and London: The Johns Hopkins University Press.
Forman, R.K.C. (2004), *Grassroots Spirituality: What Is It, Why It Is Here, Where It Is Going*, Exeter: Imprint Academic.
Fuller, R. (2001), *Spiritual but not Religious: Understanding Unchurched America*, Oxford: Oxford University Press.
Goulding, G. (2000), *On the Edge of Mystery: Towards a Spiritual Hermeneutics of the Urban Margins*, Oxford: Peter Lang.
Houtman, D. and P. Mascini (2002), 'Why Do Churches Become Empty, While New Age Grows? Secularisation and Religious Change in the Netherlands', *Journal for the Scientific Study of Religion*, 41(3): 455–73.
Lyon, D. (2000), *Jesus in Disneyland: Religion in Postmodern Times*, Cambridge: Polity.
Meek, D. (2002), 'The Faith of the Fringe: Perspectives and Issues in "Celtic Christianity"', in J. Pearson (ed.), *Belief Beyond Boundaries: Wicca, Celtic Spirituality and the New Age*, Milton Keynes/Aldershot: Open University/Ashgate, pp. 251–7.
Murray, S. (2004), *Church after Christendom*, Bletchley/Waynesboro: Paternoster Press.
Ostwalt, C. (2003), *Secular Steeples: Popular Culture and the Religious Imagination*, Harrisburg, PA: Trinity Press International.
Partridge, C. (2005), *The Re-Enchantment of the West: Alternative Spiritualities, Sacralisation, Popular Culture and Occulture*, London and New York: T. and T. Clark.
Possamai, A. (2003), 'Alternative Spiritualities and the Cultural Logic of Late Capitalism', *Culture and Religion*, 4(1): 31–45.
Rose, S. (2001), 'Is the Term "Spirituality" a Word that Everyone Uses, But Nobody Knows What Anyone Means by It?', *Journal of Contemporary Religion*, 16(2): 193–207.
Sheldrake, P. (2005), *The New SCW Dictionary of Christian Spirituality*, London: SCM Press.

Stark, R., E. Hamberg and A.S. Miller (2005), 'Exploring Spirituality and Unchurched Religions in America, Sweden and Japan', *Journal of Contemporary Religion*, 20(1): 3–23.

Sutcliffe, S. (2003), *Children of New Age: A History of Spiritual Practices*, London: Routledge.

Tracy, D. (2004), *The Spirituality Revolution: The Emergence of Contemporary Spirituality*, New York: Brunner Routledge.

Wink, P., M. Dillon and K. Fay (2005), 'Spiritual Seeking, Narcissism, and Psychotherapy: How Are They Related?', *Journal for the Scientific Study of Religion*, 44(2): 143–58.

Woodhead, L. and P. Heelas (2000), *Religion in Modern Times: An Interpretive Anthology*, Oxford: Blackwell.

Chapter 6

Why so Many Women in Holistic Spirituality? A Puzzle Revisited

Linda Woodhead

Post-traditional women are more likely than post-traditional men to be haunted by the questions of meaning and identity that are evoked by detraditionalisation and that stimulate late-modern individuals to explore the depths of their souls – 'what is it that I really want?'. 'Is this the sort of life I want to live?' 'What sort of person, am I really?'

Dick Houtman and Stef Aupers (2008)

I hope I will find out who I am ... The children are my life.

Participant in the holistic milieu, Kendal

One of the most striking findings of the research carried out in Kendal between 2000 and 2002 by a small team of us from Lancaster University was that 80 per cent of those active in holistic spirituality – both practitioners and clients/group members – were female. This was a finding which we struggled to explain, and though we made some progress in doing so in Chapter 4 of *The Spiritual Revolution* (Heelas and Woodhead 2005: 94–107), we felt rather like explorers taking slow and tentative steps into relatively uncharted territory.

In retrospect it has become clearer to me that our difficulties were mainly due to the gender-blindness of the theoretical frameworks we were employing to explain our main findings in Kendal (above all, the finding that 'religion is giving way to spirituality', as the subtitle of the book puts it). This was a classic case of empirical evidence exposing the limitations of the theoretical framework which should have been able to illuminate it. But rather than discard the theory which informs our approach in *The Spiritual Revolution* as a result of this limitation, it may be more helpful to consider what happens when we view it as limited by its refusal to acknowledge the gender differences that structure social and symbolic worlds. The theory may be perfectly adequate as an account of male experience, but limited by its failure to acknowledge that such experience cannot be assumed to be universal human experience. In what follows I will sketch out what the theory might look like if we take more account of differences between the sexes, particularly with regard to the differentiation of labour, and the roles and identities related to such difference.[1]

If this experiment is successful, it should have the effect of enhancing the theory's explanatory power. The proof of the pudding will lie in its ability to make greater sense of the preponderance of women in holistic spirituality; rather than generate a puzzle, it should point us towards some solutions.

Gender Bias in the Foundational Narrative of the Sociology of Religion

We explain our main finding from Kendal – that spirituality is faring much better than religion – by appealing to a massive subjective turn within western culture since the 1960s. In drawing attention to such a turn we draw on the work of theorists and sociologists such as Peter Berger, Charles Taylor and Ronald Inglehart, all of whom note a cultural transformation in late industrial societies, one marked by reaction against established orders of outer authority and deference, but also one that is attracted towards more inward forms of authority rooted in the inner life of the individual. It is this general subjective turn, we suggest, which can help explain the more particular shift within the sphere of the sacred which has seen forms of religion which appeal to the higher authority of a transcendent God decline relative to forms of spirituality which offer to put people in touch with the spiritual dimension of their own unique lives. Thus we view the growth of holistic spirituality since the 1960s as the sacralisation of the wider cultural turn to subjective life.

The origins of this theoretical framework can be traced back to the narrative of modernisation which constitutes the foundational story of the discipline of sociology itself – and hence of the sociology of religion as well. The story of a subjective turn represents a continuation of, or sequel to, the main story, and carries over the latter's gender bias. Elsewhere we have referred to the main narrative as 'the German story' (Heelas and Woodhead 2002), since it owes so much to Marx, Weber, Tonnies and Simmel. It tells the story of an inexorable and tragic march from the enchanted world of pre-modern societies to the iron cage of industrial society. Modernisation involves a disenchantment and de-mystification of the world, as industrialisation wrenches men and women from the humanly-meaningful bonds and beliefs of rural society into the vast, anonymous and rationalised worlds of urban-industrial society where human need and dignity is subordinated to the impersonal demands of capitalist production.

---

1   In what follows I use 'sex' and 'gender' interchangeably. I do not assume that men and women are different from one another in any significant way, other than with respect to reproductive biology (and even that can be read and represented very differently). I am convinced by the many studies which suggest that differences, which go beyond this basic biological difference, are rooted in the sexual division of labour which characterises most human societies, and in which most men occupy positions of greater power, status and reward than most women. For a good survey of such studies see Kimmel (2000).

Despite its obvious interpretive power, the German story tells only half of the story – what Hochschild (2003: 11) refers to as *his* story of modernisation rather than *her* story. While industrialisation removed men from the domestic into the public sphere, for women it had the opposite effect. It excluded them from the public world of paid work and tied them to the unpaid or lowly paid work of care in the domestic sphere – as housewives and/or domestic servants. Thus women assumed the status of what Hochschild (2003: 254) calls 'urban peasants', keeping alive some of the traditions and securities of pre-modern society – including religion – and thereby helping to ease men's transition into urban-industrial society. As many recent works in nineteenth-century women's history have revealed, the role of wife and mother was given fresh weight and significance in industrial society, with benevolence and self-sacrifice being identified with female nature itself (Cott 1977; Ginzberg 1990; Laqueur 1992). Thus, women found themselves trapped in a very different iron cage from men – the iron cage of domestic duty rather than the iron cage of capitalist production.

Gender Bias in Accounts of the Subjective Turn

As a sequel to this story, the account of a subjective turn in late industrial societies dwells upon the ways in which men struggle against the inhuman constraints of the iron cage and find meaning elsewhere. For Peter Berger et al. (1974), Christopher Lasch (1977) and Charles Taylor (1989; 1991) the 'homeless mind' of late modernity seeks significance in private and/or domestic worlds of subjective meaningfulness. Metaphorically speaking, men work in the iron cage by day but throw off its restrictions and demands in the evening when they put on their slippers, close the door on the world, and sink into the satisfactions of private, personal experience. It is to this sequel that we appeal in *The Spiritual Revolution*, drawing upon its insights to present holistic spirituality as one of the possible ports of call for those in search of subjective satisfaction.

Yet the sequel, like the story from which it grows, treats male experience as a universal experience, and fails to consider the situation of women. If the latter experience an 'iron cage' within the context of industrial society, it will be the iron cage of the home and the unpaid – and hence under-valued – work of care that must be performed within it (care for home, husband, children and other relatives). Although some women rebelled against the restrictions of this iron cage from the late nineteenth century onwards, they gained only very limited access to the public world as a result of their efforts. It was not until the 1960s that the situation changed in a more fundamental way, as women gained greater equality of access to higher education, the professions, and the world of paid work in general (Walby 1990; Wharton 2005). Women might now try to escape their iron cage of imposed roles, the home, in order to enter a world of work in which their labour would be more highly rewarded, and, perhaps, more suited to the development of unique aptitudes and abilities.

If women sought to find subjective satisfaction in the world of work, however, they were destined for disappointment. If the iron cage had proved an inadequate container for the aspirations of men's fulfilment, it was even less likely to prove adequate for female fulfilment – for at least two reasons. First, equality of opportunity and reward has still not been achieved by women in any society, with horizontal and vertical sex segregation resulting in a situation in which men continue to dominate the most powerful positions in the public sphere and to be more highly rewarded for their work (Walby 1990; Wharton 2005). Secondly, the gender revolution which began in the 1960s and which sought to eliminate sex differentiation in the labour market has become a stalled revolution, not only because women failed to achieve equality with men in the workplace, but because men have not taken on an equal share of domestic work. Hochschild averaging estimates from the major studies of time use in the USA in the 1960s and 1970s, found that on average women worked roughly 15 hours longer each week than men, and over a year worked an extra month of 24 hour days (Hochschild 2003: 4). Although there is some evidence that this gender gap narrowed in the 1980s, the latest research shows the gap opening up again in the 1990s (Hochschild 2003: xxviii). The fact that women work a 'second shift' is, of course, a major factor in their failure to achieve equality with men in the workplace. The outcome is that most women are unable to give the same commitment to their work as most men.

The result is that men are still significantly more likely than women to give the majority of their time and energy to their paid work, and to derive their primary sense of identity from this work.[2] If they find their work life insufficient to realise their full subjective potential or provide adequate fulfilment, they will normally try to supplement their paid labour with other roles and activities rather than abandon the iron cage altogether. One option is for them to give more time and significance to a domestic role by sharing a greater proportion of the unpaid labour of care with their wives or partners. Another is for them to give more time to a hobby or leisure pursuit, particularly one with significant experiential 'pay off'. For men there are a wide range of sports and other leisure pursuits readily available; some have their own 'lifestyle' attached, and many play a significant role in masculine identity-formation (Jackson et al. 1999; McKay et al. 2000). What is more, such a wide variety of activities are available and are culturally legitimate that it is usually possible to choose one to suit whatever form of subjective satisfaction is being sought, from calmness of mind and meditative states (angling, archery, for example), to intense excitement (extreme sports).

For women the situation is likely to be different. Unless they make a conscious decision to be a 'career woman', their role of care is still likely to constitute their primary identity. Career women can escape from domestic labour to much the same extent as men only by choosing not to have a family or by paying others to take care of the domestic labour for them (or, in rare instances, by having a husband who cuts back on his own career advancement in order to share duties of care). Other women, both married and single, are more likely to make their primary commitment of time to

---

2   Here and throughout the chapter I am assuming – in Marxist vein – that identity is constituted more by what people do than by what they say and believe. Time use is therefore a key indicator of identity.

the work of care, and their primary identity is likely to follow from this commitment. Whether by choice or necessity, commitment to paid work will come second, with the welfare of the organisation (and self) being seen as a lesser priority than the welfare of family and friends. Since it is impossible to be successful in a demanding occupation whilst being sole carer for a family, women are therefore likely to be torn between tasks, roles and identities to a much greater extent than men. The tension is exacerbated by the often incompatible nature of the different roles they must occupy, with competitive dedication being rewarded in the workplace but emotional and material care required in the intimate sphere being disregarded (Kanter 1977; 1998; Gilligan 2002). As for leisure occupations or hobbies, the dual demands of work and home leave women with far less, if any, time for such pursuits – at least as long as their children are still at home.[3] There are correspondingly far fewer, and far less well-developed, leisure and sports activities for women. Those that do exist have far less cultural legitimacy and far less potential to sustain a lifestyle or identity. Expressing this diagrammatically, one might contrast the typical situation of men and women in late industrial societies as follows:

Men (and career women without children)	**Women (with children)**
Work – primary identity	Family – primary identity
Family – secondary identity	Work – secondary identity
Leisure pursuit/hobby – competing secondary identity	Leisure pursuit/hobby – no spare time (in first half of life)

Having established these gender differences, it is possible to see more clearly the different forms that the subjective turn is likely to take for men and for women. A 'subjectivised' or 'post-traditional' man is likely to retain an identity based around paid work as primary identity, but to choose his work according to his subjectivised priorities, and perhaps to supplement it with additional activities and roles which offer more by way of subjective satisfaction, whether in relation to leisure pursuits or friends and family. Post-traditional women, by contrast, have to struggle against the constrictions not only of a work role but, more importantly, of the traditional women's roles – as dutiful wife and mother – which are likely to leave even less scope for subjective expression and fulfilment. Thus, women have both less and more freedom than men – less freedom to cut themselves loose from traditional roles, less freedom

---

3   Thus Hochschild's (2003) intensive study of working couples finds that although many men make time in evenings and weekends for 'life-enhancing' activities from carpentry to novel-writing, sport to reading, their wives spend little or no time on such activities or on 'themselves'.

to choose and dedicate themselves to occupations which give them strong subjective satisfaction, and less freedom to pursue fulfilling leisure pursuits; but more freedom (and necessity) to forge new forms of identity which try to reconcile conflicting demands of individual assertion and relational care.

Explaining Women's Preponderance in Holistic Spirituality

Having developed a more adequate account of the subjective turn by revising it in order to take account of gender differences, it is easier to identify some of the reasons why women who participate in this cultural shift are more likely to be attracted to holistic spirituality than men. Like men they become dissatisfied with the 'iron cage', finding the traditional roles to which they are expected to conform incompatible with the free exploration and expression of their desires, aptitudes and life-potential. For women, however, the roles which constrict them are as likely to be those of domestic duty as of workplace routine. Many of those who are unable to find satisfaction either at home or in work will have no time to explore other avenues of fulfilment – at least so long as they are tied to their domestic roles. For working-class women this may prevent post-traditional exploration altogether, for middle-class women it may prevent it until their children leave home.

Now for those women who are able to explore post-traditional identities, the exploration is likely to be more far-reaching than it will be for men. While they rarely abandon their primary – work-based – identity, post-traditional women are often drawn to explore 'who I really am' apart from the roles they have occupied. Lacking the occupational identity which tends to support a sense of personal identity, worth and entitlement, women who become dissatisfied with the roles of wife, mother and nurturer may embark upon 'deep' quests of self-exploration. If some element of primary identity survives the quest it is more likely to be an identity which has some relation to the work of care than with a workplace role.

As well as these differences on the 'demand side' of the subjective turn, there are differences for men and women on the 'supply side'. Women who seek greater subjective satisfaction than their current roles can offer are likely to find that the outlets for subjective fulfilment which are open to men are closed or uncongenial to women. Most of the culturally dominant leisure and sports activities tend to be shaped around male interests and identities. Whereas spending more time with the family may be an attractive option for men wishing to supplement their work lives with more personally and emotionally meaningful activities, for women, who are struggling to avoid submerging their identity within traditional roles of care, this option is closed as well. Consequently women engaged in a quest for greater personal fulfilment are likely to find and forge avenues of exploration within the spheres traditionally open to them – healthcare, the beauty industry, and religious activities – as well as the female social networks centred around kinship, friendship and parenting.

Women's pursuit of subjective fulfilment within the beauty industry has been noted by Gimlin (2002), who notes how women used the hairdressing salon, for example, as a safe space to talk about subjective concerns. A commercial emphasis on the potential of beauty-treatment as a means of fostering a sense of self-worth and subjective fulfilment has become very evident in recent years. Slogans affirming 'because you're worth it', are used to sell beauty products. Increasingly, beauty treatments advertise the fact that they produce 'holistic' fulfilment. The beauty industry meets the leisure industry in the growing number of spas that cater for women's total subjective well-being. Equally notable is the explosive growth of complementary and alternative forms of healthcare (CAM) that enable women to take healthcare out of the sole control of male healthcare specialists and back into closer relation with their own lives and concerns (Stacey 1997).

In the sphere of religion as well, women take greater control of a realm which they have always occupied, but which has previously been under male control. Much of traditional Christianity proves an inhospitable context for women pursuing subjective exploration because it tends to sacralise the family and women's roles of care and self-sacrifice (Woodhead 2005). Rather than abandon religion altogether, some post-traditional women participate in the growing female-dominated sphere of 'spirituality' where issues of beauty, health and self-identity often come into connection with one another, but where the body is used as a means of gaining access to the 'deeper' realms of psyche and soul. This participation helps to tip the balance, so that this sphere of spirituality becomes increasingly female-dominated.

Our research in Kendal provided significant evidence to support the view that holistic spirituality is being used and shaped by women to explore forms of identity which move beyond what are perceived to be the more damaging aspects of traditional domestic identities. The comment that spiritual practices are being engaged in order to 'find out who I really am' was made many times in the course of interviews and conversations. Similarly, the observation that spirituality enables one to 'go deeper' than is normally the case with forms of CAM and beauty treatment was made a number of times (even though holistic practices often start with the body and/or meditative techniques for stilling the mind). Most telling of all is the way in which the language of 'spirit', 'energy', 'chi', 'soul' and 'core self' is used frequently and interchangeably within the holistic milieu in Kendal in ways in which no clear line is drawn between spiritual exploration and self exploration. The central place which this family of concepts occupies in the holistic milieu signals the centrality of post-traditional identity-exploration. As a hynotherapist puts it – 'We are here for a soul purpose, one major issue that we have to "get" in this life'. As a Shiatsu client comments – 'When you're getting to the essence of yourself as a person and seeing yourself in those moments, it becomes spiritual'.

Although there is some exploration of issues surrounding work and career in the holistic milieu in Kendal, this is not a primary concern. Despite the fact that the instrumentalisation of subjective-life spirituality to enhance effectiveness in the workplace has been common since the 1970s – often within workplace trainings – we found little trace of such activity. In keeping with the fact that this is a realm run largely for and by women, we found much greater emphasis being given to difficulties relating to roles of care and responsibility for others. Above all, women were trying to cope with difficulties relating to roles of care and responsibility for others and not least the difficulty of being 'over-powered' by others at the expense of their own self-development. Thus, in a class on 'Energy Management' exploring 'personal development and boundary issues', its facilitator warned the members of her class that 'the most common area in which we allow damage to our energy field is when we are too invested in wanting to "help"' and 'end up sacrificing our own life force for the other person'. The goal is 'to find your own truth' by 'feeling what's right for *you*'. Similarly, an aromatherapist told us that many of their clients are dealing with 'issues of self-esteem and self-confidence', and a Reiki practitioner revealed that, 'I get a lot of abuse clients – a large percentage were abused in some way as children'.

To a greater extent than had been anticipated, our data reveal that holistic spirituality was often being used as a safe space in which women (and some men) were able to recognise and deal with a sense of worthlessness and low self-esteem related to the subordination of their own needs to those of others, and to the use and abuse of the self by (male) others. To cite examples from different interviews, holistic participants told us that – 'I had a lot of guilt and my self-worth was crap. I wept my way through the course'; '[I had to learn] to know myself. That was important because I wasn't a full person. I couldn't separate from other people and felt like everyone else was leaning on me and pushing me down. I tried to solve everyone's problems'; 'I still have my life journey around relationships with men'; 'I sacrificed myself and sacrificed my truth for the sake of relationships'.

What this evidence suggests is that holistic spirituality was often being used, not merely as a means of enhancing and developing an existing sense of self-identity, but also for developing a new and stronger sense of self achieved by getting in touch with one's emotions and desires and thus with a 'core self' which lies beyond conventional roles and performances. Many of the holistic practices we witnessed had to do with basic identity construction. These were realised by listing one's core desires, or by reflecting upon one's emotional state and 'blockages', or by learning how to meditate, or by getting in touch with feelings and sensations by way of bodily exercises or healings. For those whose traditional role required them to pay more attention to others than to themselves, the very act of taking time for oneself in the holistic milieu was an act of self-assertion and identity-construction. 'A lot of it', said one participant, referring to holistic spirituality, 'is having the time out where no one can make demands on you. It's total "you" time'. Similarly, a member of the 'True Vision' group, reflecting within the group on her personal growth over the last week commented, 'I have grown in the last week by refusing to take too much responsibility for other people'.

Many of those we interviewed also speak of the rewards of spiritual practice in terms of gaining greater awareness of, and control over, emotions, identity, and life. This, in turn, leads to greater feelings of confidence, self-esteem and agency. As a male nurse explains, for him the process has been 'about understanding and letting go of some of the feelings I've been carrying around … to do with self-worth ultimately'. In some cases 'unhealthy' relationships may be abandoned or their emotional legacy left behind, but generally the outcome – or desired outcome – seems to be not the total rejection of activities of care, but their placement on a new, more subjective, footing – 'as something I want to do as part of my "soul work", rather than as a duty imposed on me'. You have to learn to 'hold your own power in the relationship', says one practitioner, whilst a group member speaks of learning to 'create relationships that reflect where I am'.

If many of those who enter the holistic milieu as 'clients' are seeking a way of reconciling their primary – caring – roles with their own personal feelings, needs and desires, the growing numbers who go on to take up the role of full-or part-time paid practitioner or group leader find an even more direct way of solving typically female conflicts of identity. What the latter are doing, in effect, is to take women's traditional role of care for the material and emotional well-being of others, and turn it into a career in which they have considerable autonomy, self-direction, and some economic reward. In Kendal some of those who pursue this path spoke to us of their growing dissatisfaction with the ways in which their work was previously under-valued, whether in the domestic sphere or in a caring profession like nursing. For them, transformation of identity is effected by withdrawing their labour from contexts in which it was undervalued to contexts in which they can own that identity and develop it in directions of their own choosing, but continue to base it upon relational work of care.

Conclusion

By gendering theory from the outset, that which appears puzzling is rendered more explicable. We see that one result of the nature of the changes and continuity in the gendered division of labour since the 1950s is that women in late modernity are more likely to suffer from more complex and far-reaching conflicts of role and identity than men. The continuing pressure on women to do more of the work of care in society than men still shapes women's primary identity, but the social invisibility of such work, its low status and reward, its incompatibility with self-assertion and self-development, and its often routine and exhausting nature means that those who seek subjective satisfaction are likely to look beyond these traditional roles or seek to place them on a new footing.

Driven by the widespread cultural imperative to develop one's full potential and to seek satisfying personal experience, significant numbers of women, therefore, turn to spheres and activities which enable them to escape from constricting roles and expectations and explore deeper satisfactions and alternative forms of identity. Whereas men are likely to look to the readily available spheres of family and leisure/sports in order to supplement their primary, work-based identities, women may embark on a deeper and more open-ended quest for identity, and are more likely to pursue this within the traditionally female (albeit male-controlled) spheres of beauty, healthcare and religion. In doing so they shape each of these spheres in new ways, with beauty care flowing into well-being practices, healthcare into CAM activities, and religion into holistic spirituality.

Thus women are attracted into the holistic milieu in much greater numbers than men because it makes use of resources traditionally drawn upon by women – religion and the nurturing care of other women – in order to move beyond traditional activities and the roles they entailed. The holistic milieu offers supportive and easily accessed spaces in which the conflicts of identity facing post-traditional women in late modernity can be negotiated. Precisely because this sphere is women-dominated, it is also inhospitable to the many forms of male identity based upon negation of the female. The way in which both academic and popular discourses often dismiss such spirituality as 'pseudoscientific', 'pampering', 'trivial', 'diverting', 'irrational', 'psychobabble' – often without any experience of this milieu – is a sign of this unease.

With hindsight it is clear that our struggle over the 'puzzle' of women's disproportionate involvement in the holistic milieu in Kendal was generated by the failure of the sociological theory on which we depended to take issues of gender seriously. The gendering of such theory attempted here leads one to address not only cultural issues of meaning and identity, but deeper underlying issues concerning the sexual division of labour and unequal distributions of power in society. There are encouraging signs that the 'sociology of spirituality' is beginning to pay more attention to such issues. As it does so, it is less likely to find itself as puzzled by its empirical findings as we were.

Bibliography

Berger, P., B. Berger and H. Kellner (1974), *The Homeless Mind. Modernisation and Consciousness*, Harmondsworth: Penguin.

Cott, N.F. (1977), *The Bonds of Womanhood*, New Haven: Yale University Press.

Gilligan, C. (2002), *The Birth of Pleasure*, New York: Vintage.

Gimlin, D.L. (2002), *Body Work. Beauty and Self-Image in American Culture*, Berkeley, CA: University of California Press.

Ginzberg, L.D. (1990), *Women and the Work of Benevolence. Morality, Politics and Class in the Nineteenth-Century United States*, New Haven and London: Harvard University Press.

Heelas, P. and L. Woodhead (2002), 'Homeless Minds Today?', in Linda Woodhead (ed.), *Peter Berger and the Study of Religion*, London: Routledge, pp. 43–72.

Heelas, P. and L. Woodhead (2005), *The Spiritual Revolution. Why Religion is Giving Way to Spirituality*, Oxford: Blackwell.

Hochschild, A.R. (2003), *The Commercialisation of Intimate Life: Notes from Home and Work*, Berkeley, CA: University of California Press.

Houtman, D. and S. Aupers (2008), 'The Spiritual Revolution and the New Age Gender Puzzle: the Sacralisation of the Self in Late Modernity (1980–2000)', in G. Vincent, S. Sharma and K. Aune (eds), *Women and Religion in the West: Challenging Secularization*, Aldershot: Ashgate, 2008.

Inglehart, R. (1977), *The Silent Revolution. Changing Values and Political Styles Among Western Publics*, Princeton, NJ: Princeton University Press.

Inglehart, R. (1997), *Modernisation and Postmodernisation. Cultural, Economic and Political Change in 43 Societies*, Princeton, NJ: Princeton University Press.

Jackson, P., N. Stevenson, and K. Brooks (1999), 'Making Sense of Men's Lifestyle Magazines. *Environment and Planning D: Society and Space*, 17: 353–68.

Kanter, R.M. (1977), *Men and Women of the Corporation*, New York: Basic Books.

Kanter, R.M. (1998), 'The Impact of Hierarchical Structures on the Work Behaviour of Women and Men', in K.A. Myers, C.D. Anderson and B.J. Risman (eds), *Feminist Foundations: Towards Transforming Sociology*, Thousand Oaks, London and New Delhi: Sage, pp. 259–77.

Kimmel, M.S. (2000), *The Gendered Society*, New York and Oxford: Oxford University Press.

Laqueur, T. (1992), *Making Sex: Body and Gender from the Greeks to Freud*, Cambridge, MA and London, England: Harvard University Press.

Lasch, C. (1977), *Haven in a Heartless World: The Family Besieged*, New York, Basic Books.

McKay, J., M.A. Messner and D. Sabo (eds) (2000), *Masculinities, Gender Relations and Sport*, Thousand Oaks, CA: Sage.

Stacey, J. (1997), *Teratologies: A Cultural Study of Cancer*, London and New York: Routledge.

Taylor, C. (1989), *Sources of the Self: The Making of Modern Identity*, Cambridge: Cambridge University Press.

Taylor, C. (1991), *The Ethics of Authenticity*, London: Harvard University Press.

Walby, S. (1990), *Theorising Patriarchy*, Oxford: Blackwell.

Wharton, A.S. (2005), *The Sociology of Gender: An Introduction to Theory and Research*, Oxford: Blackwell.

Woodhead, L. (ed.) (2005), 'Gendering Secularisation Theory', *Kvinder, Køn og Forskning*, 1: 24–35.

Chapter 7

Contentious Headscarves: Spirituality and the State in the Twenty-First Century

Paul Chambers

This chapter argues that spirituality is a complex phenomenon that cannot always be easily reduced to the realm of private religiosity, even within ostensibly secularised societies. Modern liberal democracies are ideologically underpinned by the centrality of the state. It affirms the notion that the appropriate place for religion is within the private sphere. In theory, this private-public dichotomy necessitates the adoption of a principle of religious neutrality by the state. In practice, however, states need to define religion in order to determine its acceptable limits within the public sphere (Martin 1994: 2–3).

These limits have recently been tested in France, where, from 2003–2006, a lively public debate arose over the right of students to wear visible religious symbols, notably the Islamic headscarf (*foulard*), in public schools. Two major parliamentary enquiries produced reports on the matter (totalling over a thousand pages) and this was followed by 25 hours of parliamentary debate with 140 speakers (Gemie 2004). This debate culminated in legislation (September 2004) that outlawed all 'ostentatious' forms of embodied spirituality in schools, a measure that gained widespread support among the French public, including the majority of French Muslims (Gemie 2006). Gemie notes, however, that these measures have drawn widespread criticism from within the Muslim world and without.[1]

In attempting to legislate against certain outward expressions of religiosity, states are open to the accusation of being guilty of religious discrimination, but also the denial of fundamental human rights. Moreover, in seeking to regulate religion in these ways, states are in effect promoting what Casanova (1994) has termed the 'deprivatisation' of religion. This arises in terms of the politicisation of religious issues over the past decade as certain faith groups seek to defend religious freedoms. This not only represents a limited return of religion to the public sphere but also raises important questions about the relationship between the public-private dichotomy, the legitimate place of religious populations and ideologies within formally secular states and arguably, in the final instance, about secularisation and the secularisation thesis.

---

1 Including among others, Human Rights Watch, Rowan Williams (the Archbishop of Canterbury), Jürgen Habermas and Christine Delphy.

This chapter will first consider the spiritual, sociological and anthropological dimensions of the headscarf and its relation to the politics of culture. This leads on to a discussion of the recent controversy surrounding the *affaire du foulard* and related cultural and political issues that have been played out within a wider European context. These generate questions about the impact of the return of culture and religion to the public sphere but also the impact of state regulation on minority spiritualities. It will be argued that, contrary to the expectations generated by the secularisation thesis, spirituality has a public dimension, one that raises doubts about the utility of private/ public dichotomies in discussions of European religion or indeed the claim that the social significance of religion inevitably declines in modern societies.

Contentious Headscarves

The wearing of headscarf or veil for religious reasons is not a uniquely Islamic convention. The notion of embodied spirituality its use generates, in various times and contexts, has been a key element in Jewish, Christian and Muslim belief systems (Gemie 2004: 388–9). Embodied spirituality has gained increasing sociological attention in recent years (Mellor and Schilling 1997). In terms of the current debate in France surrounding the veil, Gemie highlights the paucity of references to veiling in the *Qu'ran*, noting that there are only two obvious references. One explicitly refers to the need for women to cover their chests and the other refers to the separation of men and women in worship by means of a veil or curtain. The majority of prescriptions on dress are to be found in supplementary Islamic sources (*Hadith* and *Sira*). Thus, Gemie (2004: 388) suggests that 'the status of the veil in Islamic thinking is less clear than non-Muslims might think'. For example, he cites the liberal Marseilles cleric Bencheikh (1998: 145) who argued that the practice of the veiling of women pre-dates Islam. He concluded that the veil cannot be a religious signifier specific to Islam and went on to argue that Islam, by its very nature, 'refuses all signifiers'.

Nevertheless, in practice it is clear that the emotional and religious significance of the veil for many Muslims cannot be lightly discounted. Islam differs from most modern expressions of Judaism and Christianity in that it continues to place particular stress on modesty in dress as a central aspect of religious faith and practice, although how this highly embodied approach to religious practice is interpreted within the context of modern Western societies differs widely (Hussain 1984; Hussain and O'Brien 2001). Discourses surrounding Islamic *hijab* (religious dress) and the wearing of the headscarf have been a recurring theme in the public sphere since the 1980s. They throw into sharp relief the tension between 'private' and 'public' religion while also raising issues regarding the rights of religious minorities in modern secular societies. These issues take on an increased importance with the greater visibility of Muslims in Europe (Davie 2000: 154–5). The adoption of a distinctive item of dress, such as the headscarf, might be said not only to advertise the visible presence of Muslims in European societies, but also to represent a decisive move away from a passive invisibility (and marginalisation) to an active engagement with the meta-narrative of multiculturalism. In terms of visibility in European life, it arguably represents one aspect of the 'evolution of Islam from the private to the public sphere' (Cesari 2005: 1018).

The cultural practice of wearing the headscarf is a relatively modern phenomenon, with no specific historical precedents, although in general terms, it conforms to prescriptions for female modesty as laid down in the *Qur'an* (Ahmed 1992). It is not a compulsory item of dress for Muslim women and its adoption is, in theory, a voluntary act. As with all cultural practices that draw on a living 'tradition', there is some tension between the principles of voluntarism and compulsion. Consequently, it has been seen variously as an expression of personal spirituality, as a symbolic marker of cultural identity, as a duty incumbent on Muslim women, as a signifier of intolerance, as an expression of patriarchal control, and as a cultural refusal to integrate into the democratic values of secular societies (Ruthven 1997: 108–11).

This marked lack of agreement as to the cultural significance of the headscarf has made for a lively debate within the European Muslim community. Sa'id (2003) represents one strand of Muslim opinion in that he argues that Islam itself is undermined by the insistence of some of its adherents on reducing faith to superficial questions of form and outward appearance. He suggests instead that Muslim spirituality is essentially a private and intimate phenomenon. This reflects the related secularist contention that the proper place of religion lies in its practice within the private sphere. Thus, for Sa'id, the adoption of the headscarf is merely one more public expression of the refusal of Muslims to properly integrate into their host societies. For Maqsood (2003) matters are not so clear-cut. Islam requires modesty from its adherents and this principle is given visible expression through dress and public behaviour. However, he also notes that Muslim women do not all interpret the *hijab* in the same way. The crucial element here is free-will where choice is related to levels of faith and personal spirituality. Maqsood suggests that:

> There is no stipulation in the *Qur'an* or *Hadith* that any particular styles of garment are in any way compulsory, and any male trying to force a woman in matters of religion is breaking the Islamic injunction against coercion in religion, and going completely and ironically against the true spirit of Islam. (Maqsood 2003: 235)

Laudable as these sentiments are, it is also clear that the options for choice in this matter are limited for many Muslim women living in Europe. Familial pressure on young women to adopt the *hijab* is common within some communities and it would be foolish to deny that these practices exist (Knott 1994; Hashmi 2000).

However, Islam is not a monolithic entity and Muslim practice is informed by many variations in patterns of social and cultural understandings. Ahmed Andrews (1994) cautions against stereotypical readings of Islam, noting that variations in religious observance and social practice are often related to the diverse theological understandings and approaches to religious law (*fikh*) that underpin the broad unity of Islam. These understandings in turn are informed by the inherited cultural and social traditions that migrant ethnic groups bring from their various territorial points of origin as well as broader characteristics such as class and economics (Lewis 1994). Moreover, these traditions are not static and consequently their custodians must take account of these traditions and their interaction with the dominant cultural and religious understandings of their host societies. As Knott (1992a) emphasises, the majority of these interactions are likely to take place in the 'unofficial' context of banal everyday life and that this can be highly subversive of 'official' understandings of the dilemmas of religious practice in a highly secularised environment. It is within this secular context, however, that an increasing number of young women are voluntarily adopting various forms of the *hijab* worn in order to demonstrate their religious commitment visibly (Idleman Smith 2004: 219). There are a number of sociological reasons why this should be so.

One line of argument, with a long tradition in sociological thought, focuses on identity, whereby second and third generations of migrant families might 'rediscover' religion as a means of reconnecting with inherited religious and cultural traditions (Herberg 1960). When we consider this argument within the context of the well-documented patterns of social exclusion and the resultant sense of alienation that many young Muslims experience in Britain and Europe (Weller et al. 2001; Solomos 1993; Vertovic and Peach 1997) then it contains a certain plausibility. Knott (1992b) suggests that voluntarist arguments such as these cannot easily be ignored. Many migrant families consciously choose the path of assimilation into the host society. Quite often, the decision by young women to adopt the headscarf can attract some parental disapproval. Clearly, familial coercion is not a factor here. Moreover, even when families are supportive of traditional practices, their children are often acutely aware of the difference between cultural traditions as understood by their parents and broader religious prescriptions (Knott 1994: 220). Özdalga in her discussion of Islamist women students makes a very similar point, albeit within the Turkish context (1997).

These comparative understandings have led some young Muslims to question the relevance of the *hijab* to their personal spirituality while others continue to see it as an essential component of their identity as a practising Muslim. Those who choose to make a visible affirmation of faith often perceive the adoption of the headscarf as a symbolic marker of the transition from a normative religious affiliation to a conscious spirituality grounded in personal experience. This type of spirituality is defined in Islam as *Taqwa* (literally 'God consciousness') and it is derived from the process leading up to *ihsan*, the moment when the individual realises their personal spirituality within the context of Islam (Maqsood 2003: 1). Maqsood compares this event to being 'born anew' and while caution should be exercised when comparing religious systems, there are clearly striking similarities here with the collective and individual experience of some Christian groups who define themselves as having been 'born again'.

Within both these developmental models of religious identification, the key principle is the acquisition of some sense of God that leads to profound changes in an individual's life and which defines the believer in terms of separation from the world and identification with the community of faith. In both religious systems this can be an event, or a moment of illumination or a process that eventually leads to personal enlightenment. Thus, for Muslim women, the decision to adopt the *hijab* serves both as a symbolic marker of faith in God and also acts as a means of identification with the community of believers. However, individual motivations for visible identification with a discrete religious community through the adoption of the *hijab* can only constitute a partial explanation of this phenomenon.

While it is clear that many young women in Europe are voluntarily taking up the veil, what is less clear is how this social movement is informed by the social, cultural and economic characteristics of modern societies. Theissen (1978) suggests that in pluralistic societies where a dominant cosmopolitan culture is in tension with traditional ethno-religious cultures, the latter may attempt to resolve these tensions in two ways: either through a stricter interpretation of religious traditions *or* their relaxation. Focussing on the historical example of Judaism within the Roman Empire, he argues that Judaism's increasingly trans-national character led to an internal crisis of identity and an intensification of customary norms reflected in both inter-cultural segregation and intra-cultural differentiation. This led to schisms within Judaism and the crisis was only resolved towards the end of the first century AD when those norms were relaxed and Judaism emerged as a universal religion. Interestingly, this transformation was primarily the result of internal discourses within Judaism. In a suggestive parallel with contemporary experience of Muslims in Europe (notably, Islamophobia) Theissen notes that where special privileges were extended by the state to Jewish communities within the empire, this often led to an increase in anti-semitism and religious discrimination (1978).

No discussion of embodied spiritualities can ignore the work of Mary Douglas (1984, 1996). Douglas has famously argued that the body is symbolic and figurative of both social cohesion and social differentiation and central to her argument is the use of the 'grid/group' classificatory schema. Here, collective ideas about and orientations towards the body are classified in terms of 'grid' and the power of communities to enforce these norms is expressed in terms of 'group'. Within this schema, Islam would be classified in cosmological terms as 'high grid' although the capacity of religious leaders to enforce normative compliance will differ within different national societies and could be anywhere along a continuum of 'high' to 'low' group.

For Douglas (1996), minority group concerns about the maintenance of appropriate boundaries based upon bodily purity (analogous in this argument with the *hijab* and personal modesty) are often to be found with religious groups operating within societies that are rapidly becoming religiously pluralised or secularised (analogous to a slackening of group and grid at the societal level) and where these groups occupy a marginal position. The physical body (and by extension, any form of embodied spirituality) becomes constrained by the social body which encompasses those social meanings and symbolic representations that are the shared property of communities, in this case, those of Islam. The ways in which factors such as social exclusion, economic hardship and cultural difference have an impact upon minorities such as Muslims can significantly influence the way in which the physical body is both perceived and, in some cases, harnessed as a means of boundary maintenance, symbolically distinguishing a minority from the dominant culture it inhabits. Moreover, Douglas suggests that it is often women who are called upon to represent these boundaries symbolically and that this is usually exemplified through types of restriction on their activities or person. Simply, the experiences of marginalisation that arise from the interaction between minority and majority cultures and religious and secular cultures (and where the former perceives itself as under threat from the latter) come to be expressed and reflected in the creation of symbolic boundaries, in this case relating to dress, the easiest available form of symbolic body modification. The Durkheimian parallels with the 'sacred' and 'profane' are fairly straightforward at this point.

The approach of Douglas to these issues centred on the experiences of newly arrived rural Irish Catholics in 1960s England. These have come to encapsulate many of the dilemmas facing migrant ethno-religious groups. Faced with discrimination and exclusion, and feeling de-valued within a host society that was at best ambiguous about their presence, many Irish people rejected assimilation into the prevailing secular society and retreated into a revisionist Catholic practice that both emphasised their rural Irish identity and also cultural allegiances. The issue here was about identity and the Friday fast, but as Douglas also argues in the context of Jewish dietary restrictions, the practice of distinctive dietary rules both sets Jews apart from other groups and forms the basis for a distinctive identity (Douglas 1996: 37–8). Clearly there are parallels here with Islamic strictures on diet and, arguably, with strictures on dress. Douglas suggested that the strength of these symbols as markers of group allegiance is enhanced by their lack of meaning for other cultures and this is an important observation given the well-documented ignorance of European populations about Islam and the generally dismissive tenor of much of the discourse surrounding the headscarf. Four decades later ethno-religious groups are as likely to originate from the Punjab or Bengal as from Ireland but the parallels with their collective experience as migrants remain. Moreover, in terms of Islam in Europe, it is women who are seen as the main agents for the transmission of traditional values (Herbert 2003: 187) and the upholders of recognised standards of embodied modesty.

Mellor and Shilling have developed Douglas' argument within the context of what they term 'frontier bodies', suggesting that in societies under strain, where the dominant *conscience collective* is no longer able to constitute a framework for whole societies, symbolic boundaries have been reconstituted at the level of sectional interest groups (Douglas 1996: 190–92). They suggest that marginalised, oppressed and exploited groups (defined by Mellor and Schilling as 'outsiders') are increasingly '*visibly* not prepared to recognise the established 'rules of the game as valid' (Douglas 1996: 190). Conversely, where dominant identities, and those groups who traditionally control them, feel under threat from both competing (minority) symbolic systems and the erosion of customary 'national' boundaries by global processes, then concerns with the maintenance and purity of embodied boundaries are likely to be amplified generally throughout societies. Thus we see how it is that the embodied cultural practices of one minority group, Islam, might come to be seen as an affront to the normative values of the majority general population. In this sense the headscarf comes simultaneously to embody notions of both 'purity' (from the Islamic viewpoint) and (from the viewpoint of the secular societies) 'danger' (Douglas 1984).

Clearly, 'frontier bodies' whether they be those of asylum seekers, economic migrants or visible ethno-religious groups are increasingly coming to be seen as a problem for European states, not least because in a globalised world where religions and cultures are progressively becoming disembedded from their customary territories, it is no longer clear where symbolic 'frontiers' begin and end (Haynes 2002). Moreover, the increasing transnationalism of religion generally and the progressive relocation of Islam in Europe, has led to a situation where societies, once assumed to be progressively secularising, now have to come to terms with migrant and diasporic ethno-religious minorities in their midst. In turn these raise questions relating to both boundary maintenance and its erosion and even the possibility of the emergence of hybrid identities (Brubaker 2005).

One response to these uncertainties has been to seek the marginalisation of religious groups either indirectly, through social and cultural exclusion, or directly, through secularist public policies promoted by the state. Although, as Martin notes, the tendency of European states to want to control the expression, and even the content, of spiritualities is nothing new (Martin 1994: 2). Douglas suggests that one response of groups so marginalised in this way is an increasing propensity 'to adopt approaches to the body which correspond to their social location' (cited in Shilling 1993: 73). 'Frontier bodies' are of necessity bounded bodies and under conditions of globalisation these cultural boundaries (or borders) to some extent compensate for the increasing porosity and irrelevance of physical borders and the collective fears that this new openness inspires.

Seen in this way, 'frontier bodies' are highly implicated in the project of cultural politics, both from above and below. In part, this sense that 'the personal is political' goes some way to explaining why the headscarf has become so contentious. Clearly, as Douglas suggests, minority ritual (and related) practices can and do cause offence to majority populations, particularly where they appear to have no utility in the general schema of social, economic and cultural life. Particular difficulties emerge when educational or employment opportunities might be restricted by a refusal to conform to public norms that seek the abandonment of the headscarf. On the other hand, as Douglas argues, practices such as the adoption of the headscarf should be approached analytically in terms of their internal functions. The creation of symbolic boundaries is a way of bringing order into experience. Thus, these symbols 'are capable of creating a structure of meanings in which individuals can relate to one another and realise their own ultimate purposes' (Douglas 1996: 50).

The last point directs attention to the spiritual dimension behind veiling. But herein lies the problem for Muslims (and French Muslims in particular). Increasingly, the right to express individual spirituality through embodied practices appears to be progressively under threat from the public sphere. This raises interesting questions relating to the customary private-public dichotomy that has informed religious practice in modern societies (and by extension, raises questions about the continuing utility of a key element of the secularisation thesis.) Moreover, in terms of cultural politics, the increasing popularity of the headscarf among young Muslim women and growing state ambivalence to this expression of embodied religion offer one example of the political anxieties surrounding the twin notions of 'accommodation' and 'assimilation' of newly arrived ethno-religious groups in European societies.

Muslims do not practise their religion in a political or social vacuum, and clearly, any discussion of embodied spiritualities must incorporate some recognition of contemporary policy issues and their impact on Muslims in Europe. Conversely, as Taylor (2003) argues, religion, simultaneously and increasingly has an impact on the political sphere. It is to these cultural politics and related issues such as the public limits of religion, the changing nature of the public–private dichotomy (deprivatisation), and the ethics of state management of religions that we now turn.

The State and Spirituality

The increasing visibility of Muslims in European societies and concerns regarding the compatibility of Islamic belief and practices with liberal secular conceptions of society have fuelled much public debate about the nature of 'rights' and 'duties' of ethno-religious minorities and other minority faith groups in modern democracies. Significant questions arising from this discourse include both the ways and means in which the needs of religious minorities might be accommodated by society but also the need for those minorities to recognise and to accept liberal constitutionalism and the respect for individual rights it enshrines (Malik 2003). To strengthen and re-define the nature of 'citizenship' and also to secure the 'integration' of minorities, states have had to move towards legislating or considering legislation on a number of publicly contentious issues associated with religion. These include the public display of personal religious affiliations (France and Belgium), tightening immigration rules for Muslim clerics (Denmark, the United Kingdom), regulating or banning ritual slaughter of animals (United Kingdom), denying faith groups the right to opt out of religious education in schools (Germany) and the right to set up confessional schools (The Netherlands). Islam has not been the only focus of putative state regulation. New religious movements have also encountered significant problems of state acceptance in Italy, Germany and Greece. Clearly, this raises uncomfortable issues for those scholars (notably Steve Bruce) who would seek to diminish or even to deny the significance of religion in European public life.

At the same time, it is generally agreed by observers that there has been a significant growth in Islamophobia and anti-Semitism among European populations (Allen 2004). The so-called 'war against terrorism' and the activities of the Israeli state in the Palestinian territories have had a distinct impact on minorities living in Europe. In considering these, it is realised that ethnicity, as a related issue, is not easily separated from religion (Martin 1978). Certainly, it could be argued that the recent banning of the *foulard* in France and discriminatory legislation elsewhere on the European mainland is as much about governments attempting cynically to negate the growing electoral influence of far-right political parties and to co-opt potential supporters for the next round of elections. However, the debate goes deeper than this.

Successive waves of Muslim immigration into Europe from 1945 onwards, and the growing recognition that this harbours a continuing phenomenon have resulted in a lively debate surrounding the various merits and problems associated with models of 'integration' proposed by various European governments (Heckmann and Schnapper 2003). At one end of the spectrum, France has opted for a culturally unifying universal model that subsumes all differences under the ideal notion of the republic, whereas at the other end, the United Kingdom and The Netherlands have opted for a multicultural approach implying official support and recognition of ethnic minorities and their cultural practices, although in the case of The Netherlands, this liberal approach has progressively come under some strain in recent years (Shadid and van Koningsveld 1996; Howley and Hein 1999; Doomernik 2005).

In terms of the French state's fairly rigid stance towards its Muslim population, Gemie's (2004) analysis of the Debré and Stasi reports (2001 and 2003) and the media discourse that surrounded them is illuminating. Debré argued that in line with the French principle of *laïcité* there should be a ban on *all* visible symbols of religious allegiance in French schools while Stasi merely suggested a ban on overt symbols such as the headscarf, leaving open the possibility that students might wear 'discreet' symbols of religious identity, such as crosses, Stars of David and so forth. Lawyers advised the French government that a ban on all visible symbols would be in contravention of Article 10 of the European Declaration of Human Rights, so the decision was made to accept Stasi's recommendations. Despite a highly polarised debate in the French media, where the Roman Catholic Church came out strongly in defence of the rights of Muslims, both the *Chambre des Deputes* and the Senate approved these measures and the new law came into effect in September 2004. Gemie notes that on the face of it, this legislation is akin to cracking a nut with a sledgehammer, given that the statistical incidence of students wanting to adopt the *foulard* is tiny. Therefore, he suggests that any analysis should focus on the wider issues of *Islamophobia* and points to the sense of threat to the French way of life and the constant references to religious 'extremism' that characterised many of the parliamentary speeches. Gemie further suggests that what is also notable in this affair is the marginalisation of moderate Islamic opinion both within the parliamentary debate and large sections of the media and the implied assumption that the Muslim religion is inimical to democracy. A notion has emerged that Muslims are incapable of voluntary social and cultural integration into a modern liberal democracy.

As indicated above, similar strains are becoming increasingly apparent in The Netherlands (Alptekin 2005). Despite a long history of religious toleration realised through the principle of pillarisation (the vertical separation of religious groups and groups of no religion) (Davie 2000: 18) and a strong commitment to multiculturalism in a society based on the collective recognition of the principle of 'differences' rather than any artificial principle of 'commonness' (Doomernik 2003: 170–71), Muslims and Islam are coming to be seen as increasingly problematic. Recent developments in the public domain have seen a renewed emphasis on citizenship, exemplified by the 1998 introduction of the *Wet Inburgering Niewkomers* (Law on the Integration of Newcomers). This provides for compulsory citizenship classes and has been recently extended to include all visiting imams. The election, on a nationalist platform, of a conservative government in 2002 can be linked to subsequent debates within Dutch society about the nature and desirability of multiculturalism (Doomernik 2005).[2] More recently, and controversially, the employment rights and access to social security benefits of Muslim women who choose to wear the *burkha* (but not the headscarf) have been severely curtailed. Indeed, the Dutch Immigration Minister, Rita Verdonk, has called for the banning of the *burkha* in some public places. These issues are not merely restricted to European countries. In Turkey there has been an ongoing debate about the Turkish Government's exclusion of all religious symbols from state institutions generally and from the public education system in particular (Gruen 1999; Özdalga 1998) The European Court of Human Rights has recently ruled in favour of the ban.

The long-term picture in the United Kingdom appears somewhat brighter in terms of civil liberties but remains rather muddled in terms of policy towards religious groups. Arguably, this confusion reflects wider issues related in part to the factors outlined above in the discussion of Muslims in France, but it also encompasses a more nuanced and developed public discourse surrounding religious identity, much of it emanating from moderate Muslim sources. Therefore it is worth examining the British experience in some detail, not least because the United Kingdom has sought (*contra* France) to accommodate ethno-religious minorities in a relatively tolerant and even-handed manner.

Commencing with the Race Relations Act 1976 and culminating with the Race Relations (Amendment) Act 2000, successive British governments have introduced strong anti-discriminatory legislation relating to 'race' onto the statute books and this has been fairly rigorously enforced. However religious pressure groups such as the Muslim Association of Britain and the Muslim Association of Lawyers have consistently highlighted the fact that legislation of this type has favoured Muslims rather less than Jews or Sikhs. This is primarily because the latter are legally defined as ethnic groups while Muslims are not. As a result, Muslims have not been fully protected against religious discrimination in areas such as employment rights (Malik 2003). Commenting on this situation in 1999, the Deputy Chair of the Association of Muslim Lawyers suggested that, despite this limited protection, there were many anomalies remaining. Muslims

> have yet to receive the recognition, protection and status that the various branches of Judaism and Christianity already take for granted … at present British justice does not extend to protecting people from religious discrimination or to providing any legal recourse … if direct loss is suffered as a result of such discrimination. (Thomson 1999: 2)

2　Informed in part by the murder of the Dutch filmmaker Theo van Gogh who had recently made a film critical of Islam.

This unsatisfactory situation has now been partially resolved with the introduction of the Employment Equality (Religion or Belief) Regulations 2003. This represents the British Government's response to the EU Council Directive 2000/78/EC of November 2000 that seeks to establish a common European framework for equal treatment in employment and occupation. This legislation outlaws direct and indirect religious discrimination, harassment and victimisation in the workplace and requires employers to consider factors such as provision for prayer facilities, religious holidays, and respect for dress and customary practices. Welcome as these changes are in terms of recognising the religious factor in individual and group human rights, their terms of reference remain limited to employment. Legal protections in other fields of social and cultural life remain elusive. This has led some religious groups to call for a Commission for Religious Freedoms to be established to address the wider picture of religious discrimination.

At present, there seem to be a number of contradictions in the ways that European states seek to relate to religious minorities. On the one hand there are moves to protect their general rights within a common European framework while at the same time many individual states are seeking to place restrictions on some religious groups. Viewed from elsewhere, some European governments can appear discriminatory in religious matters. Concerns about politically generated religious discrimination were first voiced by members of the United States Commission on Security and Co-operation in Europe that met in Washington in 1997. Muslims, Jews, Evangelical Christians and members of New Religious Movements were all found to have suffered group and individual religious discrimination at the hands of certain European governments. Five years later, at a briefing session at the American Embassy in London to publicise the work of the US State Department's *Annual Report on International Freedom*, John Hanford, the Ambassador-at-Large for Religious Freedom, voiced further concerns about those European states that negatively discriminated against religious minorities. In a similar vein, Abdelfattah Amor, the Special Rapporteur on Religious Intolerance at the UN Commission on Human Rights, has noted that while Western Europe has had in many ways an exemplary record on these matters, present practice is unsatisfactory in many countries (Dasi 2001).

Much of this censure might appear rather strong when we compare religious discrimination in Europe with other less developed parts of the world. Moreover, the fact that so many of these criticisms emanate from the United States government is perhaps less a reflection of matters on the ground in Europe and more a reflection of the fact that American society has historically been more hospitable to religion in general and that government has had to take account of this (Asad 2005). Nevertheless, part of the current problem with ethno-religious minorities lies in the ways that European states have sought to address the question of their human rights. The states have appeared to be more concerned with questions relating to ethnicity and racial discrimination than with matters of religious discrimination (Parekh 2000; Weller et al. 2001; Chambers 2003).

In terms of European rights legislation and policy making, the emphasis has predominantly been on racial rather than religious equality, although as noted above, this is now changing. Some states, notably the United Kingdom, have moved towards creating some protections for religious groups and there is now a growing body of supra-national legislation relating to religious discrimination, which European states, in theory, must take into account. Many states, however, are ill prepared for this development. For example, while France is subject to the terms of the Treaty of Amsterdam, by virtue of its membership of the European Union, French law has no specific provisions regarding religious discrimination. Indeed, this problematic state of affairs in France reflects a broader and deeper antipathy towards any manifestation of religion within the public sphere (Gemie 2004).

So, while individual states are subject to supra-national constraints, it would appear that they still retain considerable latitude in the ways that they frame rights legislation and, by extension, the ways in which they relate to religious minorities in their midst. In the case of the longstanding Europe-wide discourse surrounding the wearing of the headscarf in public it is clear that, despite attempts by the EU to harmonise national approaches to human rights, national law and even regional or local policy continue to be the prevailing reference points in practice in most countries.

This reluctance to engage with the presence of religion in public life needs some further explanation. In broad terms, Stefano Allievi (2003) suggests that we are now witnessing the return of culture and religion to the public sphere throughout Europe and that this is the unintended consequence of the global migration of so many migrants from a wide variety of cultural and religious backgrounds. As Gemie notes, the *affaire du foulard* exposes the 'fundamental inability' of the French media and the state to adapt to the resurgence of visible religiosity within the public sphere – and by extension, the complex cultural politics associated with globalisation, migration and Diaspora (2004: 395). Moreover, as Talal Asad (2003) argues more generally, modern nation states are often uncomfortable with religion and religious matters. This discomfort is strongly related to the ideology of secularism that has underpinned the development of European nation states. In a similar vein, Delacoura is also critical of the ideology of secularism and the ways in which it underpins notions of human rights in Western societies. She suggests that, at the very least, secular states need to consider and reaffirm the principle of official neutrality towards the religious choices that their citizens make and that it is unhelpful to marginalise and stigmatise Muslims on the basis of negative cultural stereotypes (Delacoura 2003). Indeed, in terms of Islam and the current controversy over headscarves, and as the work of Douglas suggests, the official stigmatisation of religious practices through legislation is likely to have the unintended consequence of reinforcing rather than undermining contentious symbolic boundaries.

Spirituality, Secularisation and the State

Despite the apparent secularisation of European societies and the partial loss of the social significance of religion within the public sphere, recent controversies surrounding the Islamic headscarf suggest that spirituality cannot easily be reduced to the realm of 'privatised religion'. Throughout most of the twentieth century it was generally assumed by many social scientists that religion would continue to decrease in social and political significance in modern societies. This particular narrative suggested that European societies have progressively taken on a secular character and one of the key markers of this transformation has been the increasing separation of state and religion, the progressive marginalisation of religious institutions and the parallel emergence of 'privatised' religion. This influential evolutionary thesis has (rightly or wrongly) also provided the ideological backdrop for much European policy making as it relates to religious matters and, more generally, has informed related discourses surrounding the desirable public limits of religion. However, it has also become apparent that elsewhere in the world, religion continues to be a vehicle for political expression and social change in ways that undermine the idea that secularisation automatically accompanies modernisation. Even in terms of a secular Europe, migration, Diaspora and the increasingly trans-national nature of religion, and related public policy issues have all progressively undermined the public-private dichotomy that has customarily subsumed religion to the margins of public life. As the evidence above suggests, not everyone is happy with the resurgence of religion in the public sphere.

Nevertheless, as Rex (1981) has argued, pluralistic societies are invariably shaped not by consensus and models of 'integration' but by diversity, conflicts between values and ideologies and challenges from below, and that this is healthy for societies. Casanova (1994) makes a very similar point when he suggests that religion has a part to play in the public sphere, not least in its ability to challenge the ideological claims of individualism and secularism. These challenges can take many forms – including the headscarf – and as Taylor (2003) has argued, such challenges raise questions about the utility of private/public and sacred/secular dichotomies.

From a sociological standpoint and viewed in an anthropological spirit, it is readily apparent that the Islamic headscarf represents a legitimate form of embodied spirituality. While its meaning is polysemic and its status as a religious signifier has been contested by some liberal Muslim commentators, it is also clear that it retains emotional and symbolic significance for many European Muslims. Moreover, *qua* Douglas, embodied spirituality arguably represents the social body, its collective concerns and fears, and its strategies for bringing meaningful order into experience. As such, the concept of 'frontier bodies' is a useful metaphor, both in terms of the way that it highlights the shifting porous nature of national and symbolic boundaries (and the ways in which these have customarily reinforced dominant forms of 'national' consciousnesses) but also the renewed importance of religiously inspired cultural politics in ostensibly secular societies.

In terms of those elements of the secularisation thesis that pertain to differentiation and the public-private dichotomy, it is clear from the evidence outlined above that the publicly visible profile of religion (both as a focus for public discourse *and* increasing state regulation) is currently expanding not contracting. Whether this is a long-term structural trend or a more short-term development remains as yet unclear, but whatever the case, as Davie succinctly notes 'the Islamic presence in Europe is here to stay' (Davie 1994: 61).

The *affaire du foulard* and the fact that these events are being played out in what is arguably the most politically secular of European states provides us with a particularly compelling example of an important trend. These ongoing tensions suggest that in political, cultural and social terms, religion in Europe is not as marginalised an institution, as some proponents of the secularisation thesis would suggest. In this respect, the headscarf controversy is informative. On the one hand, as Gemie notes, the banning of the headscarf from French schools represents something of an over-reaction to the actions of a small minority of religious schoolgirls who are hardly in a position to bring down the French state. On the other hand, the largely negative discourse surrounding this visible manifestation of spirituality represents a Europe-wide amplification of collective fears surrounding visible religious minorities within a broader secularised milieu. The crucial question here is whether this is merely a short-term return of religion to the public agenda, that is something that may be nothing more than a blip on the progressive secularisation of European societies. A combination of the continued presence of large numbers of Muslims in Europe and continuing geo-political factors (notably the 'war on terror' and its continued fallout) are likely to keep religion in the public eye (and therefore the public sphere) for some time yet.

Bibliography

Ahmed, L. (1992), *Women and Gender in Islam: Historical Roots of Modern Debate*, New Haven, CT: Yale University Press.

Allievi, S. (2003), 'Multiculturalism in Europe', transcript of unpublished paper presented at the 'Understanding and Responding to the Islamic World after 9/11' conference, St Anthony's College, Oxford, 25–26 April.

Allen, C. (2004), 'Endemically European or a European Epidemic/Islamaphobia in a post 9/11 Europe', in R. Geaves, T. Gabriel, Y. Haddad and J. Idleman-Smith (eds), *Islam and the West post 9/11*, Aldershot: Ashgate, pp. 130–45.

Alptekin, E. 'The Dutch Myth of Tolerance', in *Humanity in Action: 2005 Newsletter* (available online at http://www.humanity in action.org/index.php?option=content&task=view&id=214).

Andrews, A. (1994), 'Muslim Women in a Western European Society: Gujarati Muslim Women in Leicester', in J. Fulton, and P. Gee (eds), *Religion in Contemporary Europe*, Lampeter: Edwin Mellen, pp. 78–92.

Asad, T. (2003), *Formations of the Secular: Christianity, Islam, Modernity*, Stanford, CA: Stanford University Press,

Asad, T. (2005), 'Reflections on Laïcité and the Public Sphere', *Social Science Research Council: Items and Issues*, 5(3): 1–3 (available online at http://www.ssrc.org/publications/items/v5n3/).

Bencheikh, S. (1998), *Marianne et le Prophete: l'Islam dans la France Laicite*, Paris: Grasset.

Brubaker, R. (2005), 'The "Diaspora" Diaspora', *Ethnic and Racial Studies*, 28(1): 1–19.

Casanova, J. (1994), *Public Religions in the Modern World*, Chicago: University of Chicago Press.

Cesari, J. (2005), 'Mosque Conflicts in European Cities', *Journal of Ethnic and Migration Studies*, 31(6): 1015–24.

Chambers, P. (2003), 'Religious Diversity in Wales', in C. Williams, N. Evans and P. O'Leary (eds), *A Tolerant Nation? Exploring Ethnic Diversity in Wales*, Cardiff: University of Wales Press, pp. 125–38.

Dasi, M. (2001), 'Religious Freedom and New Religious Movements in Europe', *ISKCON Communications Journal*, 8(2): 65–77.

Davie, G. (1994), 'Unity in Diversity: Religion and Modernity in Western Europe', in J. Fulton and P. Gee (eds), *Religion in Contemporary Europe*, Lampeter: Edwin Mellen, pp. 52–65.

Davie, G. (2000), *Religion in Modern Europe: A Memory Mutates*, Oxford: Oxford University Press.

Debré, J.L. (2003), *Rapport fait au nom de la mission d'information sur la question du port des signes religieux a l'ecole*, No. 1275: tome 1 and 2, Paris: Assemblée Nationale (available online at www.assemblee-nationale.fr).

Delacoura, K. (2003), *Islam, Liberalism and Human Rights*, London: Taurus.

Doomernik, J. (2003), 'Integration Policies towards Immigrants and their Descendants in The Netherlands', in F. Heckmann, and D. Schnapper (eds), *The Integration of Immigrants in European Societies National Differences and Trends of Convergence*, Stuttgart: Lucius and Lucius, pp. 165–83.

Doomernik, J. (2005), 'The State of Multiculturalism in The Netherlands,' *Diversitié Canadienne*, 4(1): 32–5.

Douglas, M. (1984), *Purity and Danger: An Analysis of the Concepts of Purity and Taboo*, London: Ark.

Douglas, M. (1996), *Natural Symbols: Explorations in Cosmology with a New Introduction*, London: Routledge.

Gemie, S. (2004), 'Stasi's Republic: The School and the "Veil"', December 2003–March 2004', *Modern and Contemporary France*, 12(3): 387–97.

Gemie, S. (2006), 'The Trial of Fatima: Anarchists, Muslims and the *Monde Libertaire*, 2003–05', *Anarchist Studies*, 14(1), pp. 9–19.

Gruen, G.E (1999), 'Defining Limits on Religious Expression in Public Institutions: The Turkish Crisis over Headscarves', *Jerusalem Viewpoints*, 399, 1 February, 1–12 (available online at http://www.jcpa.org/jl/vp399.htm).

Hashmi, N. (2000), 'Gender and Discrimination: Muslim Women Living in Europe', conference paper presented at the 'European Political-Economy Infrastructure Consortium (EPIC): Ionian Conference', Corfu (available online at http://www.epic.ac.uk/documents/ICHashmi.pdf).

Haynes, J. (2002), 'Religion', in L. Gearon (ed.), *Human Rights and Religion*, Brighton: Sussex Academic Press, pp. 17–30.

Heckmann, F. and D. Schnapper (eds) (2003), *The Integration of Immigrants in European Societies National Differences and Trends of Convergence*, Stuttgart: Lucius and Lucius.

Herberg, W. (1960), *Protestant, Catholic, Jew*, New York: Doubleday.

Herbert, D. (2003), *Religion and Civil Society: Rethinking Public Religion in the Contemporary World*, Aldershot: Ashgate.

Howley, L. and D. Hein (1999), *Ethnic Minorities in Dutch Politics: Improving through Mutual Understanding*, New York: Humanity in Action Report (available online at http://humanityinaction.org/publications/1999/8.html).

Hussain, F. (1984), *Muslim Women*, New York: St Martin's Press.

Hussain, F. and M. O'Brien (2001), 'South Asian Muslims in Britain: Faith, Family and Community', in C.D.H. Harvey (ed.), *Maintaining Our Differences: Minority Families in Multicultural Societies*, Aldershot: Ashgate, pp. 15–28.

Idleman Smith, J. (2004), 'Conclusion', in R.Geaves, T. Gabriel, Y. Haddad and J. Idleman Smith (eds), *Islam and the West Post 9/11*, Aldershot: Ashgate, pp. 210–19.

Knott, K. (1992a), 'Points of View: Transforming Inter-Faith Relations', in H. Willmer (ed.), *20/20 Visions: The Futures of Christianity in Britain*, London: SPCK, pp. 82–101.

Knott, K. (1992b), 'The Changing Character of the Religions of Ethnic Minorities of Asian Origin in Britain: Final Report of a Leverhulme Project', in *Community Religions Project Research Papers*, New Series 11, Leeds: University of Leeds, Department of Theology and Religious Studies.

Knott, K. (1994), 'Women and Religion in Post-War Britain', in G. Parsons (ed.), *The Growth of Religious Diversity: Britain From 1945*, vol. II, London: Routledge, pp. 199–230.

Lewis, P. (1994), *Islamic Britain: Religion, Politics and Identity Among British Muslims*. London: Taurus.

Malik, M. (2003), 'Discrimination and Legislation', transcript of unpublished paper presented at the 'Understanding and Responding to the Islamic World after 9/11' Conference, St Anthony's College Oxford 25–26 April (available online at http://www.ox.ac.uk/princeton/pap_malik.shtml).

Martin, D.A. (1978), *A General Theory of Secularsation*, Oxford: Basil Blackwell.

Martin, D.A. (1994), 'Religion in Contemporary Europe', in J. Fulton and P. Gee (eds), *Religion in Contemporary Europe*, Lampeter: Edwin Mellen, pp. 109–24.

Maqsood, R.W. (2003), *Islam*, London: Hodder and Stoughton.

Mellor, P.A. and C. Shilling (1997), *Re-forming the Body: Religion, Community and Modernity*, London: Sage.

Özdalga, E. (1997), 'Civil Society and Its Enemies: Reflections on a Debate in the Light of Recent Developments within the Islamic Student Movement in Turkey', in E. Özdalga and S. Persson (eds), *Civil Society and Democracy in the Muslim World*, Istanbul: Swedish Research Institute, 1997, pp. 73–84.

Özdalga, E. (1998), *The Veiling Issue: Official Secularism and Popular Islam in Modern Turkey*, Richmond: Curzon.

Parekh, B. (2000), *The Parekh Report: The Future of Multi-Ethnic Britain*, London: The Runnymede Trust.

Rex, J. (1981), *Social Conflict*, London: Longman.

Ruthven, M. (1997), *Islam: A Very Short Introduction*, Oxford: Oxford University Press.

Sa'id, A.A. (2003), 'Pulling a Veil over Reason Itself', in *Index on Censorship* 4/03 (available on line at http://.indexonline.org/en/news/articles/2003/4/pulling-a-veil-over-reason-itself.shtml).

Shadid, W. and S. van Koningsveld (eds) (1996), 'Dutch Political Views on the Multi-cultural Society', in W. Shadid and S. van Koningsveld (eds), *Muslim in the Margin. Political Responses to the Presence of Islam in Western Europe*, Kampen: Kok Pharos, pp. 93–113.

Shilling, C. (1993), *The Body and Social Theory*, London: Sage.

Solomos, J. (1993), *Race and Racism in Britain*, Basingstoke: Macmillan.

Stasi, B. (2003), *Commission de reflexion sur l'application du principe de laïcite dand le republique; rapport au Président de la République,* Paris: Présidence de la République (available online at www.elysee.fr).

Taylor, J. (2003), 'After Secularism: British Government and the Inner Cities', in G. Davie, P. Heelas and L. Woodhead (eds), *Predicting Religion: Christian, Secular and Alternative Futures*, Aldershot: Ashgate, pp. 120–32.

Theissen, G. (1978), *A Sociology of Early Palestinian Christianity*, Philadelphia: Fortress.

Thomson, A. (1999), 'Religious Discrimination and the Human Rights Act 1998', Information Sheet prepared for the Minority Lawyers Conference, London, High Wycombe: Association of Muslim Lawyers.

Vertovic, S. and C. Peach (1997), 'Introduction: Islam in Europe and the Politics of Religion and Community', in S. Vertovic and C. Peach (eds), *Islam in Europe: the Politics of Religion and Community*, Basingstoke: Macmillan, pp. 3–47.

Weller, P., A. Feldman and K. Purdham (2001), *Religious Discrimination in England and Wales*, Research Study 220, London: Home Office.

Chapter 8

Georg Simmel: Religion and Spirituality

Ivan Varga

Much has been written on the rise of spirituality and the decline of churched religion, at least in the Western world and, in particular, in Europe. There are as many diverse efforts to elucidate this phenomenon as there are different explanations of what constitutes spirituality. In my understanding spirituality means a belief that there are forces or there is a God or there are gods beyond the experienced reality of the individual. It is therefore a rather diffuse sentiment or belief in transcendent forces that may or may not directly influence the individual's life. Similarly, spirituality may or may not be linked to the sacred (and the sociological understanding of what constitutes the sacred also varies). While churched religions may include spiritual elements, spirituality is therefore highly individual and does not depend on church-related dogmas or canons.

The (re)discovery of spirituality re-presents the individual's effort to make conscious his or her 'inner life', that is, his or her personality and moral ideas. Contemporary spirituality therefore expresses several features of postmodern conditions, especially the possibility offered to the individual to shape his or her view of the world.[1] It also makes possible for someone to join a spiritual or religious group that is rooted in a different culture to one's own. Thus, one can join a Hare Krishna community or practice yoga or join a Taoist tai-chi group or become a follower of a so-called nature religion (shamanism, Wikka). In addition, beliefs in faith healing are increasing. The spread of so-called 'do-it-yourself religions' and 'diffuse religions' involves choosing elements from different religions irrespective of dogmatic positions. The beliefs vaguely formulated (usually connected to beliefs in a God or gods, in an afterlife, as well as to ideas of good and evil) need not be accompanied by formal adherence to a church or regular attendance at its rituals.

Aspects of everyday life that previously had no connection with the sacred have become sacralised and have had spiritual significance attributed to them. Heelas and Woodhead analyse this process in their book *The Spiritual Revolution* (2005). The

---

1   This often proves to be an illusion only because the mass media, the educational system or the group to which the individual belongs, shape and influence his or her worldview. Nevertheless, the existence of different and competing worldviews immensely broadens the scope of choice, including the choice to join a spiritual group.

Kendal Project examined the emergence of various forms of spirituality and sought to understand the different motivations for turning to non church-related spiritual experiences. These emerge as important, and eventually central moving forces in the lives of people. This movement reflects a point of Beaudoin that for Generation X, spirituality based on their personal experience has become of importance to those who do not have faith in churches (cf. Chapter 4: 'Institutions are suspect', Beaudoin 1998: 51–72). Hunt concludes her essay 'Understanding the Spirituality of People who Do Not Go to Church' by remarking that the 'traditional religion of this country [Britain] appears to be in terminal decline and it seems highly unlikely that this trend will change' but warns that 'without a shared language, spirituality will continue to be privatised' (Hunt 2003: 168).

Why does spirituality occupy an increasingly important place in people's lives, whether they belong or not to a church? In my view, this is mainly because in modernity or postmodernity the individual is increasingly de-rooted, that is, deprived of the traditional cultural significants; the individual is – to paraphrase Sartre – 'thrown into choice', and collective memory is becoming ever more fragmented. In order better to understand these developments, in particular the emergence of new forms of spirituality, Simmel's ideas on the distinction between religion and religiosity are of paramount importance. His views on the role religion plays in society and in the life of the individual were shaped by his social theory.

Georg Simmel (1858–1918) has a prime place in the classics of sociology and was one of the first sociologists of religion. His academic career suffered from his Jewish origin (even though he grew up as a Protestant), and in spite of his brilliant teaching record, he never got an appointment to a full professorship either in Berlin or in Heidelberg. He received this title only in 1914 at the University of Strasbourg (which at that time belonged to Germany). A contemporary of Weber, Durkheim and Tönnies, Simmel developed his own theory of society, one whose importance in sociology cannot be underrated.

In Simmel's time sociology still had to establish itself as a distinct discipline, with its own methodology and specific concepts of society.[2] During his university years Simmel studied history, *Völkerpsychologie* (a discipline comprising the study of culture, language and social forms), history and philosophy with outstanding teachers of these disciplines. This shaped his conception of society, the individual, culture, art and religion. His complex approach that emphasised dialectical tensions between, as well as the complementary nature of, the individual and society, objective and subjective factors, form and content, reason and emotions led some to think of him rather as a philosopher than a sociologist. Despite his growing importance in the history of sociological theory, his contributions to the formulation of the sociology of

---

2   Frisby gives a detailed description of the various disciplines that were engaged in the study of society as well as the different ways the classics of sociology developed for delineating the discipline's boundaries in relation to psychology, history, economics and so forth (Frisby 1992: 5–19).

religion have been oddly neglected, if not undervalued.[3] Lately, however, particularly because of the growing interest in spirituality, his contribution to sociology of religion is gaining greater recognition.

Simmel's Concept of the Social: Form and Content, Individual and Society

Simmel was not a system-builder. He saw sociology 'as a study of individuals within groups and subgroups and within a network of social interaction' (Coser 1965: 2). His basic idea of society – contrary to organicist conceptions, such as those of Comte and Spencer, that were built on the claim to discover laws of society's development as well as to the idealist school that considered society as something different from the aggregate of individuals – was 'an intricate web of multiple relations established among individuals in constant interaction with one another' (Coser 1965: 5). This approach to sociology permeates his considerations concerning religion. Thus, religious groups create specific affiliations but their members cannot be identified solely by these; they are also involved in other groups, and this complexity defines their place in societal relations. As Simmel notes

> Society exists where a number of individuals enter into interaction. This interaction always arises on the basis of certain drives or for the sake of certain purposes. Erotic, religious, or merely associative impulses; and purposes of defence, attack, play, gain, aid, or instruction – these and countless others cause men to live with other men, to act for them, with them, against them, and thus correlate his condition with theirs. In brief, he influences and is influenced by them. (Simmel 1971: 23)

In Simmel's view there is a tension between the individual and the social. Sociation (*Vergesellschaftung*)[4] is the process through which an individual becomes a member of society. In this process the individual recognises the other and through the other his or her self. Sociation as a process includes individuation. But it also involves a tension between association and dissociation whereby the individual, who belongs to a group or to several groups, asserts his or her individuality thus counteracting the tendency towards homogenisation. Simmel admits that there are a few exceptions to this process, such as monks in a monastery. For him, society was neither an entity in itself nor a sum total of individuals. Rather, he viewed it as specific interactions of individuals who create the forms in which they constitute the groups that make up society. Thus society is a dynamic process involving individuals in their interactions within and amongst groups.

---

3   Even Jean Séguy, the noted French sociologist of religion, in his presentation of Simmel's essay, *Die Religion*, whilst acknowledging that Simmel's work is 'one of the first attempts to study the religious phenomenon as social one' (Séguy 1964: 10), remarks that he represents a point of view that is 'in our opinion antiquated' (Séguy 1964: 5).
4   The German term is usually translated as 'sociation' but some translations use the word 'sociality' or 'association'.

In Simmel's writings, the term 'individual', 'self', 'Ego'[5] are pivotal concepts for understanding the nature of society. The superiority of the individual over the mass is emphasised (cf. Wolff 1950: 31–3). For the sociology of religion, however, this raises the problem whether individual religiosity, deeply held beliefs, is superior to practising religion in a group. New Religious Movements, evangelical communities as well as those of Judaism maintain religious, and often social, identities through group adherence.[6] Yet, as it will be later analysed, for Simmel individual religiosity takes precedence over institutionalised religion.

Simmel saw a dialectical relationship between the affective and the rational elements, not only in cognition but also in social relationships. There are no social bonds without an affective base. In stating this, he developed a view of rationality that was different from Weber's conception, and this influenced Simmel's approach to religiosity.

Central to Simmel's sociology was the notion of the dialectic of form and content. Broadly speaking, forms are abstractions, mental constructs studying various areas of nature (for example geometry) or activities of the mind (such as linguistics) or knowledge (logic, epistemology). Sociology studies the various contents of social life and of cultural creations (economy, law, fashion, sexual behaviour, religion, art and so forth). This does not mean that the contents of social forms are abstractions; they influence the forms of social interactions. Economy's forms are different from, say, forms of religion. However, contents do change the forms, for example the transition to a capitalist economy changes the forms of economic interactions. Simmel made only cursory reference to religion in his major work *Soziologie: Untersuchungen über die Vergesellschaftung* (Sociology: Investigations into the Forms of Sociation (1992 [1908])). Nevertheless, in chapter II, '*Die quantitative Bestimmtheit der Gruppe*' ('The quantitative determination of the group') he does mention that the number of individuals determines the forms of collective religious life.

He refers to early Christians amongst whom the subjective experience of a direct relation to Jesus was the bond holding together the community. He also mentions that there are church-like groups that in their sociological structure do not require a large number of members. Examples of this point would be the sects such as the Mennonites, the Waldenses, etc.[7] This inhibition of numbers served to distinguish themselves from the surrounding larger groups, it being felt that an increase in membership would destroy the bonds within the religious communities. The expansion

---

5   The translation of the German word '*Ich*' as 'Ego' does not correspond to the Freudian concept nor to the 'I' as G.H. Mead understood it but rather refers to the uniqueness of the individual.

6   Simmel, unlike Weber and Durkheim, did not analyse non-Western religions. Therefore Islam, with its strong group affiliation and strict rules, as well as non-Western religions in general received only cursory mentions. Simmel's focus of interest was modernity and social relationships unfolding in modern times.

7   One could question the correctness of this statement because contemporary sects could be large communities although still smaller than established churches.

of Christianity to the whole of the state (*Gesamtstaat*) compelled Christianity 'to thoroughly change its sociological character as well as its spiritual content' (Simmel 1992 [1908]: 66). Likewise, the Reformation changed the form of religious institutions. The 'mass crusades' of evangelical Christians and the so-called 'televangelism' have also brought about a change in the 'sociological character' and 'spiritual content' of Christianity. They make the individual either just a number in a mass or a passive viewer-listener but not a member of a group. The recent emergence (mostly in the USA) of the 'mega-churches' that cater also for non-spiritual needs of their members and provide support for various aspects of their everyday life is also an expression of that change. (It is telling that some heads of the mega-churches call themselves 'pastorpreneurs'). And, as has already been mentioned, contemporary spirituality is changing the forms of belief.

Religion and Sociation: The Difference between Religion and Religiosity

Between 1898 and 1918 Simmel published 16 works on religion (cf. Schwerdtfeger 1999: 62) and in many other writings made passing remarks on religion. According to Simmel, religion – together with art, morals (*das Sitliche*), science, and play – serves as form in which humans order the world. Helle suggests that he treats religion 'not as a finite province of reality' but rather 'as an *attitude* or a *perspective* – a way of looking at the world as a whole' (Helle 1997: xii). In other words, religion is not 'a particular segment of social reality juxtaposed to other segments but rather a form of the whole life that in reality exists side by side with other – artistic, scientific and so forth – forms that in their own language express the totality of life' (Willaime 2001: 119). Religion is also viewed by Simmel as a link, a 'bridge' between the realm of the objective and of the subjective. It is indicative of Simmel's outlook that he gave the title *Brücke und Tür* (Bridge and Door) to one of the defining essays on his philosophy of life (*Lebesphilosophie*) (1957).

This collection of essays contains ideas concerning the Simmelian concept of the individual as well as contributions to his theory of religion. The essay on 'Individualism' explores the nature of the individual and individuality in its dialectical contradiction. On the one hand, what we call individuality – whether it appears as being, as feeling or yearning – goes back to a behaviour that cannot be deduced from any other cause or from an original drive. It has a relation to the world, be it ideal or practical, whether it rejects or affirms the world, dominates it or is subordinated to it, indifferent or passionate towards it, the individual is a world for itself (*für sich*), centred on itself, in a way closed in itself and is self-sufficient.

Thus the individual 'is at the same time part of one or several wholes, it is in relation to a totality which is outside and beyond it. The individual is always limb and body, part and whole, complete (*Vollkommenes*) and in need of completion' (Simmel 1957: 252). Thus: 'We call individuality the form in which this dual meaning of human existence could or seeks to unify itself' (Simmel 1957: 252). The analysis of the dialectical and contradictory nature of the individual is reflected in Simmel's conception of religion in general and also in the distinction he made between religion and religiosity.

While Simmel considered religiosity as a subjective, 'irreducible and fundamental disposition' of human beings, he knew that religions institutionalise it. None the less 'the religious man as much as the artistic or practical man does not exist merely as such in reality because the concrete man[8] is at the same time an artistic, practical, religious individual in greatly varied degrees and combinations' (Willaime 2001: 120). The religious form, however, is an 'a priori category', a special one because everything can be seen from a religious point of view as well as from an artistic point of view. This is why Simmel makes strong connections between religion and art, as in his essays on 'Christianity and Art' (Simmel 1997a [1907]) and 'Rembrandt's Religious Art' (Simmel 1997e [1914]).

Simmel's analysis of religion is a complex one. It combines philosophical, psychological, historical and sociological approaches. Of his many writings on religion, the essay, *Die Religion* (1906, revised and enlarged in 1912, English translation 1997) stands out as a quasi synthesis of these elements. It connects the emergence of religious feelings with the human condition so implying that human beings are inherently religious beings. It also analyses the individual as well as the group-forming aspects of religion.

For Simmel, religion is a 'form of being' (*Seinsform*). In a shorter essay, titled 'The Problem of Religion Today' (*Das Problem der religiösen Lage*) he refers to the 'religious person' in the most perfect sense.[9] In this sense, such a person not only *has* religion as a possession or an ability. His very *being* is religious; he functions in a religious way, so to speak, just as the human body functions organically' (Simmel 1997c [1911]: 10). Religion is a more encompassing form than other – intellectual, practical or artistic – forms because it

> penetrates the contents of life [...] and draws them up into the transcendent sphere in their new form. Thus religiosity as an inner quality of life or a unique kind of existence acquires its substance only when it pervades the material diversity of the world [...]. (Simmel 1997d [1912]: 144)

It is therefore the individual who (under conditions that are objective, that is, outside of his or her inner life) creates and sustains religion. Thus one can say that 'Just as cognition does not create causality, but instead causality creates cognition, so religion does not create religiosity, but religiosity creates religion' (Simmel 1997d [1912]: 150). This indicates that in Simmel's view there is a dialectical relationship between the subject and his or her objectified creation, namely, it is the subjective energy that creates and maintains the religious forms. He views religion and its emergence from 'the relationships of human beings to the human world' as involving

---

8 Most of the translations of Simmel's writing use the word 'man' to denote both men and women. The German word '*Mensch*' refers to human beings irrespective of their gender.

9 This is close to the 'ideal type' as Max Weber understood it.

processes whereby 'energies and sources of meanings take effect, on which religious significance has not been imposed externally from some existing source'. Rather, 'they carry it within them as a disposition of the individuals in question, so that [...] religion develops from them as a mental-objective pattern' (Simmel 1997d [1912]: 151).

One of Simmel's theses, that has a particular relevance for the understanding of contemporary spirituality, is 'that religiosity is a particular *being*, a functional quality of humanity [...] which entirely determines some individuals and exists only in rudimentary form in others and that a religious person is always religious, whether or not he believes in God' (Simmel 1997b [1909]: 5). He explains this seemingly paradoxical statement by saying that a person is religious

> In the particular way in which he reacts to life in all its aspects, how he perceives a certain kind of unity in all the theoretical and practical details of life – just as the artist gives *his* own particular response to existence as a whole and fashions *his* own world from it, and the philosopher does likewise in his own way. (Simmel 1997b [1909]: 5)

Therefore religiousness is 'a form according to which the human soul experiences life and comprehends its existence' (Simmel 1997b [1909]: 5), thus it is less (or not at all) dependent on the content of given beliefs because it is the believing that creates its object. Spirituality, viewed in this light, is an individual's outlook on the world – the physical one and beyond – according to his or her beliefs without necessarily believing in a Supreme Being. Undoubtedly, this has a deep influence on the person's moral views and practical activities. Religiosity, whether formalised in adhering to a church or religious community or else, expressed as individual belief or spirituality, creates an object for itself that follows its own logic. This is because religion is the expression of the human soul.

Simmel also investigates the role of religion in establishing and shaping social relationships. He indicates that there is a

> Remarkable analogy between the individual's behaviour toward the deity and his behaviour towards society. [...] The individual feels bound to some general, higher principle from which he originates and to which he ultimately returns, to which he dedicates himself but from which he expects elevation and redemption, from which he is distinct and to which he is yet identical. (Simmel 1997d [1912]: 156–7)

He went on to add that:

> The interaction between the human being and his God [...] encompasses the whole range of possible relationships,[10] both sequentially and simultaneously. In doing so it unmistakably reiterates the behavioural patterns that exist between the individual and his social group (Simmel 1997d [1912]: 156–7).

---

10 Simmel refers to 'love alienation, humility and pleasure, delight and regret, despair and trust'.

Analysing different social groups and their relationship to religion, Simmel remarks that the 'original religious community was the tribe', and in the ancient world 'the god and his people formed a community within which the relationships of the faithful among themselves found the same expression as their relationship toward their deity' (Simmel 1997d [1912]: 158). In tribal societies and in the ancient world 'serving the gods is an element of life in the political or family community and is just as much a part of such communities as language' (Simmel 1997d [1912]: 158). With the increasing complexity of society and it being marked by individualising relationships, this intertwining of religion and community is weakened. As a result, the individual enters into an ever-growing personal relation with God or the supernatural. In Christianity the process of individuation reached its high point. Thus Simmel argues: '[T]he *Christian God is the God of the individual* because the line that extends from the individual to God does not first pass through the intermediate stage of the group' (Simmel 1997d [1912]: 203 italics added).

An important insight of Simmel's was his concern with the relationship between religion and sociation (thus not between religion and society). This distinction is important for several reasons. First of all, it points to the role of the individual in creating religion. Krech suggests that 'in Simmel's perspective the process of socialisation is "religion-like"; it represents a "religious half-product". In itself it is not yet religion but could be an *empirical point of departure* for constructing religious meanings' (Krech 1998: 262). Thus in the individual – society relationship religion forms personal identity and brings the individual's life into a meaningful and consistent context. Further, religion does not remain in the private sphere because the individual is an actor in economic, political and other spheres of life. Finally, religion shapes an individual's ethical stand in setting goals and in actions. However, as Simmel and Weber both indicated, religion has the potential to create conflicts as well. This is barely noticed by the French school of the sociology of religion – that began with Comte and culminated in Durkheim – which placed the emphasis on the integrative function of religion in a society.

There are two aspects of the above-mentioned difference. One is that, even in a religiously rather homogenous society, conflicts can arise amongst groups who interpret differently the tenets of their religion. The history of Christianity provides ample examples, from the Eastern–Western split, through the Albigenses to the Reformation, just to mention two. While one could argue that religious wars had underlying non-religious motives as well, the participants believed that they were fighting for their own religion. Of course, other religions also experience splits arising from dogmatic differences that are condemned by religious authorities as heresies. One could also mention splits and animosities amongst different branches of Islam. These strengthen group cohesion (and Simmel explored the mechanisms of group formation and maintenance) but in large-scale societies, they do not contribute to the cohesion of society as a whole. In the second place, the concept of sociation in the Simmelian sense presumes the active role of the individual. He did not think society subsumes the individual but rather conceptualised a dialectical relationship between them, that is the individual is part of society but is not dissolved in it. Thus 'religion in a sociological perspective is part of society and at the same time transcends it' (Krech 1998: 266).

In a somewhat different context Simmel analysed religion as a factor of multiple group affiliation. He wrote:

> Religious affiliation is the most important and at the same time the most characteristic example [of individualisation] ever since religion has been emancipated from racial, national, or local ties, a world-historical fact of immeasurable significance. Either the religious community embraces the civic community in terms of its other essential or comprehensive interests, or the religious community is entirely free of all solidarity with whatever is *not* religion. (Simmel 1955: 157)[11]

Another important distinction Simmel made was to differentiate between *faith* and *belief*. Beliefs are akin to knowing something. The existence of God can be believed as plausible, like believing in the atomic structure of matter. Faith, however, is not simply a belief in God but also 'implies a spiritual relationship to Him, an emotional dedication, an orientation of life toward Him.' (Simmel 1995: 166) This indicates that Simmel links spirituality to belief in a personal God. Moreover, he considers faith – and spirituality – the source of the theoretical belief in God's existence. Theologians would certainly agree with this reasoning albeit contemporary spirituality does not necessarily refer to God, at least not to an anthropomorphic God and does not always accept the canons of a religion. Nevertheless, by this distinction Simmel, again, suggests that religiosity expressed in faith is the individual's approach to the transcendent. Thus he suggests: 'Religion stands juxtaposed to religiosity which in itself is a *state* or a spiritual rhythm lacking any object' (Simmel 1955:165).This idea helps to understand the modern phenomenon of 'diffused religion'.

---

11   The quotation is from the English translation of the segment 'Die Kreuzung sozialer Kreise' (Intersection of Social Circles) of the book Soziologie. Untersuchungen über die Formen der Vergesellschaftung. (Sociology: Studies into the Forms of Sociation). The translator, Reinhard Bendix, explains the reasons for changing the wording, in particular, for the substitution of the term 'group' for 'circle'. He wrote: 'The title of this chapter, "Die Kreuzung sozialer Kreise" has not been translated. A literal translation of this phrase, "intersection of social circles" is almost meaningless. What Simmel had in mind was that each individual was unique in the sense that his pattern of group-affiliations is never exactly the same as that of any other individual. [...] And because the same individual belongs to many groups, Simmel refers to him as "standing at the intersection of social circles." [...] In using the word "circle" as a synonym for "group", Simmel often plays with geometrical analogies; [...] He speaks [...] of women as a social circle or group, not only when they "form" a group or are "affiliated" with one, but also when they perform a given social role in society' (Simmel 1955 [1922]: 125).

Religion and Postmodernity

Simmel is *par excellence* a philosopher and sociologist of modernity. He was preoccupied with the culture in modernity and the place and role of religion in it. In his essays 'The Conflict in Modern Culture' (*Der Konflict der modernen Kultur*, 1918 [1968b]) and 'On the Concept and the Tragedy of Culture' (*Der Begriff und die Tragödie der Kultur*, 1911 [1968a]), 'The Metropolis and Mental Life' (*Die Grosstadt und das Geistesleben*, 1903) as well as in his monumental work *The Philosophy of Money* (*Philosophie des Geldes*, Second edn, 1907 [1990]) and in numerous other essays and lectures on contemporary art and artists, Simmel developed a critical outlook on modern culture.

Central to his concept of modern culture is the conflict between the subjective and the objective culture. Culture is what distinguishes humans from nature; it is the creation of human spirit or soul (*Seele*) but the forms these creations acquire are objectified. In conditions where they are mediated through money, the creations of the subject turn to be independent of their creators. Moreover, as Habermas mentions in the introduction to Simmel's collection of essays, *Philosophische Kultur* (Philosophical Culture), 'science and technique, art and moral create material relations [...] to which the knowing, the creative and practically judging and acting subject has to submit himself' (Habermas 1986: 11).

Modernity destroys the old and creates new forms of interactions, not only broadly speaking in society and in culture but also in the religious field as well. Simmel exemplifies this in the turn towards mysticism amongst 'quite a few intellectually advanced intellectuals' as a means of satisfying their religious needs. He sees the reason for this turn in the dissatisfaction with the dogmas of existing churches and states that 'the forms which objectify and direct religious feeling are felt to be inadequate for contemporary life'. Indeed, it may be the case that 'life's longing may be frustrated by objective forms in themselves, that the religious impulse must search for different goals and ways' (Simmel 1968 b [1918]: 22–3). The reason for that inadequacy and search for new forms of religiosity is that

> Until recently, changes of religious culture have always proceeded in the following way: a certain form of religious life, originally fully adequate in its strengths and essential characteristics, gradually rigidifies in superficialities and narrow specialisation. It is displaced by a new rising form in which religious impulses can flow, dynamically and without impediment. In other words, a new religious form, a new series of beliefs took the place of the outmoded one. (Simmel 1968b [1918]: 23)

These thoughts are instrumental in understanding and explaining the contemporary changes in the religious landscape: the decline of the mainstream Protestant churches,[12]

---

12 In Canada, for example, the membership in the Anglican Church has diminished since 1960 by 60 per cent. The United Church has lost nearly half of its members, Presbyterians 39 per cent while Lutherans have lost only 4 per cent and Baptists 7 per cent. In contrast, membership

the growth of Pentecostal churches in Latin America and Africa, but also in North America as well as the expansion of non-churched religiosity and spirituality. As Simmel explains, for 'a relatively large number of people today, the supernatural objects of religious belief have been radically excised; their religious impulse, however, has not thereby been eliminated'. While previously 'the development of a more adequate dogmatic content' of religions was effective, in modernity religious belief 'can no longer express itself through the polarity of a believing subject and a believed object' (Simmel 1968b [1918]: 23). Simmel, however, does not anticipate the disappearance of religious beliefs in modernity; instead, he assumes that 'religion would function as a medium for the direct expression of life' (Simmel 1968b [1918]: 23).

In the same essay he explains the persistence of religion, however, in changed form and expresses it in this way:

> Life wishes to express itself directly as religion, not through a language with a lexicon and prescribed syntax. One could use an apparently paradoxical expression and say: The soul can find faith only by losing it. To preserve the integrity of religious feeling, it must shake off all determined and predetermined religious forms (Simmel 1968b [1918]: 24)

Simmel's distinction between 'pious meditation' and 'intellectual reflection' is also relevant for understanding contemporary spirituality. Namely, 'pious meditation' takes the form of piety and is characteristic to faith. 'Intellectual reflection', that is, the form of rational analysis whose object is God, would not qualify for religion in the sense of faith; it is rather characteristic of belief. This returns again to Simmel's distinction between 'religion' and 'religiosity', the latter being subjective and referring to what fills the individual's soul and life.

This raises the question whether in postmodernity 'intellectual reflection' cannot grasp divinity and pursue a religious life. 'Intellectual reflection' on the transcendent can lead to a religious life, although not necessarily concentrating the individual's whole life around faith. 'Pious meditation' can be found in both churched religion and non-churched spirituality. However, a number of New Religious Movements as well as charismatic, evangelical or 'strong' religious communities (for example, Pentecostals) tend towards 'pious meditation'.

The distinction between religion and religiosity implies the acknowledgement of the dual nature of religion. Religion is oriented towards the transcendent, towards the other world – salvation, eternal life or reincarnation – and this is its main reference point but, it exists in society, incarnated in churches, sects, movements or institutions. Simmel noticed the paradoxical nature of religion. He thought that on the one hand, religion is the counterpart of the experienced life inasmuch as it is beyond and above the lived life. On the other hand, it is also part and parcel of everyday life because it shapes the relationships of the individual and groups. Thus

---

in Pentecostal churches grew by 38 per cent. Similar phenomena can be observed in other advanced Western societies.

As a result a remarkable involution occurs. *The disavowal of all social ties, which is evidence of a deep religiosity*, allows the individual and his religious group to come in contact with any number of other groups with whose members they do not share any common interests. And the relationships again serve to distinguish and to determine the individuals concerned as well as the religious groups. (Simmel 1955 [1922]:158; italics added)

In order to illustrate this point, Simmel refers to historical events, for instance when the Huguenots supported the French king against the Spanish one but then switched their allegiance when they were persecuted in France. In another example he mentions the Jewish workers of Manchester who organised themselves in one organisation, irrespective of their trades while in Germany Catholic workers had their own union based on the division of labour but within the general Catholic organisations. Thus the workers did not affiliate with non-Catholics in the same trade. Simmel makes reference to the priesthood as a special case of group formation where the 'relationship between believers and priests involves representation and leadership, control and cooperation, veneration and provision of material sustenance' (Simmel 1955 [1922]: 161). Either as individuals or taken together as a group belonging to a national as well as to a denominational association, priests represent overlapping group affiliations.

Reflecting on these statements one ought to ask whether in postmodernity 'deep religiosity' or spirituality is coupled with the 'disavowal of all social ties'. It is reasonable to assume that people who hold deep religious beliefs still maintain manifold social ties, such as belonging to different organisations, groups, even to political parties, and actively participating in their activities. There are political parties in several countries that were established on religious principles, such as various Christian Democratic or Christian Socialist parties, the Hindu religious party in India or religious Jewish parties in Israel. They have their religious and moral-ethical agenda (even if many Christian parties are today rather right-of-centre ones, not too different, if at all, from the secular ones, and are Christian only in their names. The same applies to Christian trade unions established in some European countries after World War II. By now most of them have even dropped the adjective 'Christian' from their name).

Churches or religious organisations increasingly take a stand on social (and not infrequently political) issues. Often, these are congruent with the moral aspects of their teachings, such as opposing abortion, sexual mores and practices, or civil marriage in Israel, and the list could be continued. The 'social ties', even through the religious groups to which they belong, affect people who might be regarded as having 'deep religious beliefs'. Evangelical churches or movements that advocate spirituality based on biblical teachings regulate those ties and impose moral and behavioural norms on their members but also want to impose their values on society. At the same time they are bound to norms and laws of their society.

The conflict between subjective and objective culture that Simmel considered the 'tragedy of culture' is deepened in postmodernity.[13] His concept of culture is a

---

13 For the sake of brevity, my understanding of the character of postmodernity is that it is the excess of modernity and at the same time the expression of its crisis.

dynamic one – it is a process that flows between the 'soul' and its 'forms'. Culture for Simmel is the objectivation of the products of the subject in which life stemming from the subjectivity is exteriorised (the objective spirit) and, conversely, the formation of a soul that develops from nature to culture (the subjective spirit). In modernity the physical and mental creations of the subject become independent of their creators and dominate them. Science and technology create objects that dominate modern people's lives, but their spiritual and cultural life could not keep up with them. Also, in *The Philosophy of Money* Simmel analyses the mental and cultural consequences as well as the alienating effects of the monetary economy.

In his writings on modern culture (around the turn of the nineteenth and twentieth centuries) he also examines the consequences of these developments for religion. In his assessment of modern culture, Simmel points out that there is an overarching struggle between life and form and says that one 'can find the same tendency in contemporary religion'. He refers to the already mentioned turn towards mysticism. The reason for this is twofold. On the one hand, 'it can be assumed that these people were socialised into the ideologies of one or another existing churches' but 'the forms which objectify and direct religious feeling are felt to be inadequate for contemporary life'. On the other hand, 'these mystical tendencies suggest that life's longing may be frustrated by objective forms in themselves' (Simmel 1968b [1918]: 22–3). For Simmel

> Mysticism aspires toward a deity which transcends every personal and particular form; it seeks an undetermined expanse of religious feeling which does not conflict with any dogmatic barrier, a deepening into formless infinity, a mode of expression based only on the powerful longing of the soul. (Simmel 1968b [1918]: 23)

If one substitutes 'spirituality' for 'mysticism', one can find a plausible explanation for the spread of contemporary spirituality and for the decline of churched religion. It also helps us to understand the increased interest in the mystical aspects of religions (transcendental meditation, Taoist tai-chi, cabalism and so forth). Simmel explains this change by saying that traditional religions are gradually rigidified, and there is an emergent need for a religious feeling that is not constrained by declared dogmas, tenets and teachings of established religions. He postulated that this change would revitalise religion as a direct expression of life which would permeate the increasingly secularised societal life and even that of the believing individual. This is happening because religiosity (or faith) 'does not require an object which prescribes for it a certain form – just as an expressionist painter does not satisfy his artistic needs by clinging to an exterior subject'[14] (Simmel 1968b [1918]: 24).

Simmel thus envisages a kind of spirituality that is diffuse ('does not require an object') but for those who embrace it, would effect their lives deeper than by adhering

---

14 It is interesting to note that Wassily Kandinsky, the great expressionist painter published in 1911 a treatise entitled *Über das Geistige in der Kunst* (Concerning the Spiritual in Art). In it, he stated that art had to depart from the objective world and to discover a new subject matter based on the artist's 'inner need'. See the 'Introduction' in Kandinsky (1977:1–5).

to an organised religious group – churches – with its credos, dogmas or tenets. He sees the conflict between form and content, objective and subjective culture, individual and society, 'to have religion' and 'to be religious' or 'religion' and 'religiosity'. He writes that in regard to 'the deepest inner difficulties of numerous modern people … it is impossible to further protect the religions of church tradition while at the same time the religious drives continue to persist in spite of all "enlightenment"' (Simmel 1968b [1918]: 24). This approach to religion and religiosity is close to the phenomenological one, even though Simmel cannot be regarded as a phenomenologist. However, the German tradition of *Relgionswissenschaft* (science of religion or scientific study of religion) influenced his thoughts.

In his essay 'Some Second Thoughts on Substantive versus Functional Definitions of Religion' (1974: 125–33) Berger makes reference to Rudolf Otto who considered religion from the point of view of the meaning given to it by religious consciousness. Religious experience is thus different from other experiences, particularly those of everyday life. However, spheres of life, as for example art or music, which in themselves are not necessarily religious[15] still infuse a spiritual aspect into everyday life. Simmel's thoughts on religious aspects of art amply illustrate this point. Similarly, his aforementioned analysis of the religion-based trade unions provides an insight into the possible combination of group affiliations based on everyday life experience (associating for defence of jobs, wages and so forth) and on shared religion.

As mentioned before, Simmel anticipates not only the changes in the dynamic of religion but also of the human condition in postmodernity. The spirit or 'soul' of modern culture, with its open-endedness and *at the same time* restrictive nature, places a burden on the individual who must navigate between the Scylla of rapid technological and social changes and the Charybdis of finding a meaning of life amongst the competing worldviews. Simmel's emphasis on spirituality and quest of an overarching meaning also explains the stubbornness of religiosity in a world that is secularised in its institutions.

The *Zeitgeist* of the postmodern culture fosters the individual's striving for 'self-realisation', but it is discordant with the constraints created by the irreconcilable conflict of objective and subjective culture. Simmel, however, acknowledges that this polarity is an essential element of the progress of culture. His analysis of the possibilities of the individual's potential within the asymmetry of the objective and subjective culture helps us to understand the role of spirituality and its relation to church-oriented religion.

Bibliography

Beaudoin, T. (1998), *Virtual Faith: The Irreverent Spiritual Quest of Generation X*, San Francisco: Josey-Bass.

---

15 Of course, this does not imply that there is no expressed religiously motivated art or music, even in modern times.

Berger, P.L. (1974), 'Some Second Thoughts on Substantive versus Functional Definitions of Religion', *Journal for the Scientific Study of Religion*, 13(2): 125–33.

Coser, L.A. (ed.) (1965), *Georg Simmel*, Englewood Cliffs, NJ: Prentice-Hall.

Frisby, D. (1992), *Simmel and Since: Essays on Georg Simmel's Social Theory*, London and New York: Routledge.

Habermas, J. (1986), 'Simmel als Zeitdiagnostiker' ('Simmel as Diagnostician of His Times'), in Georg Simmel, *Philosophische Kultur* (*Philosophical Culture*), Berlin: Wagenbach, pp. 7–17.

Heelas, P. and L. Woodhead (2005), *The Spiritual Revolution*, Oxford: Blackwell.

Helle, S. J. (1997), 'Introduction', in G. Simmel, *Essays on Religion* (trans. and ed. H.J. Helle with L. Nieder), New Haven: Yale University Press, pp. xi–xx.

Hunt, K. (2003), 'Understanding the Spirituality of People Who Do Not Go to Church', in G. Davie, P. Heelas and L. Woodhead (eds), *Predicting Religion: Christian, Secular and Alternative Views*, Aldershot: Ashgate, pp. 159–69.

Kandinsky, Wassily (1977 [1911]), *Concerning the Spiritual in Art* (trans. M.T.H. Sadler), New York: Dover Publications.

Krech, V. (1998), *Georg Simmels Religionstheorie* (*Georg Simmel's Theory of Religion*), Tübingen: Mohr Siebeck.

Schwerdtfeger, J. (1999), *Die Individualitätskonzept Georg Simmels* (*Georg Simmel's Concept of the Individual*), Heidelberg: FEST.

Séguy, J. (1964), 'Aux enfances de la sociologie des religions: Georg Simmel' ('At the Beginning of the Sociology of Religions: Georg Simmel'), *Archives de sociologie des religions*, (17): 5–11.

Simmel, G. (1950) [1903], 'The Metropolis and Mental Life', in G. Simmel, *The Sociology of Georg Simmel*, trans. and ed. K. Wolff, New York: Free Press, 1950, pp. 409–24.

Simmel, G. (1955) [1922], 'The Web of Group Affiliation' ('Die Kreuzung Sozialer Kreise') (trans. R. Bendix), in *Georg Simmel. Conflict and The Web of Group Affiliations*. New York: The Free Press, pp. 125–95.

Simmel, G. (1957), 'Individualismus' (Individualism), in *Brücke und Tür* (*Bridge and Door*), ed. M. Landmann, Stuttgart: Koehler, pp. 251–9.

Simmel, G. (1968a) [1911], 'On the Concept and Tragedy of Culture' in *Georg Simmel. The Conflict in Modern Culture and Other Essays* (trans. and ed. P. Etzkorn), New York: Teachers College Press, pp. 27–46.

Simmel, G. (1968b) [1918], 'The Conflict in Modern Culture' (trans. and ed. P. Etzkorn), *The Conflict in Modern Culture and Other Essays*, New York: Teachers College Press, pp. 11–26.

Simmel, G. (1971) [1908], 'The Problem of Sociology' (trans. K. Wolff), in Donald N. Levine, *Georg Simmel On Individuality and Social Forms*, Chicago: The University of Chicago Press, pp. 23–35.

Simmel, G. (1990) [1907], *The Philosophy of Money* (trans. T. Bottomore and D. Frisby), London: Routledge.

Simmel, G. (1992), *Soziologie: Untersuchungen über die Vergesellschaftung*, vol.11, ed. Ottheim Rammstedt, Frankfurt am Main, Suhrkamp Verlag. ..

Simmel, G. (1997a) [1907], 'Christianity and Art', in G. Simmel, *Essays on Religion* (trans. and ed. H.J. Helle with L. Nieder), New Haven, CT: Yale University Press, pp. 65–77.

Simmel, G. (1997b) [1909], 'Fundamental Religious Ideas and Modern Science: An Inquiry', in G. Simmel, *Essays on Religion* (trans. and ed. H. J. Helle with L Nieder) New Haven: Yale University Press, pp. 3–6.

Simmel, G. (1997c) [1911], 'The Problem of Religion Today', in G. Simmel, *Essays on Religion* (trans. and ed. H.J. Helle with L. Nieder), New Haven, CT: Yale University Press, pp. 7–19.

Simmel, G. (1997d) [1912], 'Religion', in G. Simmel, *Essays on Religion* (trans. and ed. H.J. Helle with L. Nieder), New Haven, CT: Yale University Press, pp. 137–214.

Simmel, G. (1997e [1914]), 'Rembrandt's Religious Art', in G. Simmel, *Essays on Religion* (trans. and ed. H.J. Helle with L. Nieder), New Haven, CT: Yale University Press, 78–97.

Willaime, J.-P. (2001), 'Georg Simmel (1858–1918). Permanence et fluidité de la religiosité' ('Permanence and Fluidity of Religiosity'), in D. Hervieu-Léger and J.-P. Willaime, *Sociologies et religion: Approches classiques* (*Sociologies and Religion: Classical Approaches*), Paris: Presses Universitaires de France, pp. 111–46.

Wolff, K. (1950), *The Sociology of Georg Simmel*, New York: The Free Press.

Chapter 9

Spirituality: From a Religious Concept to a Sociological Theory

Giuseppe Giordan

The theory of secularisation, especially the 'radical' early 1960s version, seemed clearly and unquestionably to resolve the relationship between religion and modernity – the advancement of the modernisation process was to have been accompanied by the progressive and inexorable disappearance of religion, at least as far as public displays of it were concerned (Acquaviva 1961; Berger 1969). Things, however, were different by the 1970s and 1980s and expectations regarding the loss of public relevance of religion were not met. Not only did religion not disappear, but also its presence in the public sphere has become excessive, sometimes cumbersome and, more recently, problematic.

Religious phenomena, long since marginal and residual, now grasp the attention of scholars thanks to their vivaciousness, their 'new' aspect. In just over 30 years, we have gone from the theological theory of the 'death of God' (Cox 1965), to the ascertainment of His 'return' and even His 'victory' (Stark and Introvigne 2003; Kepel 1991).[1] This 'return of God', which has fitted into the centre of the new religious landscape, is difficult to compare to traditional contexts. In recent decades, and with growing intensity from the 1970s onwards, the relationship with the sacred has been party to a complex process of decomposition and re-composition, at both an individual and collective level. The transition from the traditional world to its modern and postmodern counterpart has redrawn the arrangement of religion. It often comprises the juxtaposition of a certain number of heterogeneous elements that range from new religious movements both, pertaining to and foreign to traditional churches, to the establishment of sects and esoteric and magic groups.

The relevance of religion to the heart of contemporary society is open to multiple interpretations. These include those which aim to explain the individualisation of religious sentiment and the subjectivism of belief and also those focusing on the challenge represented by fundamentalist movements and the use of religion as a key to identity and ethnicity. Pluralism is the most relevant aspect which specifically denotes the socio-religious situation of the contemporary world as it forces us to re-examine

---

1   The theory of secularisation, as in Cox's (1965) book, has provoked a heated debate both at the heart of theology and the sociological ambit. Some time ago, Greeley (1972) observed that the ideas of scholars differed greatly from wider and common forms of belief.

and rewrite the relationship between all the various religions as well as the beliefs, rites and moral convictions at the centre of traditional religions.

The concept of spirituality emerges into the sociological ambit of religion from this context of contemporary pluralism. This 'new' perspective points to an increasingly important role for the believer in which the believer is covered by the comparison with religious institutions. Establishing individual freedom and creativity of faith signifies the possibility of marrying the sacred to relatively new themes such as the search for well-being and personal realisation, the understanding of personal feelings and the search for health and the meaning of life (Bégot 2004; Dericquebourg 2004). An interesting element to underline in the 'sociological' use of the term 'spirituality' is that its origins are linked to a different context, that of theology where it had, and still does have a precise and clearly-defined meaning. Marty almost 40 years ago observed that the term 'spirituality' was progressively disappearing from the theological debate only to be replaced by terminology which more adequately described the expansion of various churches after the Second World War (1967). Along with academic discussions focusing on the 'death of God', religious institutions had concentrated on topics such as the social and political character of the Vietnam War and the fight against poverty and discrimination.

Marty also pointed out at the same time that the disappearance of the term 'spirituality' was accompanied by a growing interest in 'spiritual matters' and the search for a 'spiritual lifestyle'; this research was however conducted on the very borders of or completely outside traditional religious institutions (1967). Although the term 'spirituality' disappeared in the 1960s, it began to make a rather shy reappearance in the 1980s and became more commonly used in the 1990s, so much so that it became a 'new' category to describe and interpret the relationship with the sacred of the contemporary era (Roof 1993; 1999; 2003; Flory and Miller 2000; Heelas 2002; Heelas and Woodhead 2005). It is rather curious that a term that can trace its origins back to historical traditional religion, where it has now become almost obsolete, should make an increasingly visible reappearance in the sociological ambit, but with a modified significance. Somehow, 'spirituality' has moved from the shadowy realms of theology to become a 'fashionable' sociological concept. This gives rise to a number of pressing questions.

How can the relationship between the sacred and contemporary society really be understood? Why is the term 'religion' no longer enough to adequately describe this relationship? What does the concept of 'spirituality' possess in order to render it fitting to describe these profound dynamics? What has changed in the last 40 years to render the term 'religion' so difficult to use and on the contrary what has happened to so exalt an old word, 'spirituality', to modify its meaning? What makes a concept 'new' when, in reality, it is anything but so? How is 'spiritual language' different from 'religious language'?

The appearance of the term 'spirituality' in the contemporary sociological debate is thus part of the complex web which characterises the transition from the traditional world to the modern and postmodern: the shift in interest from religion to spirituality and the 'recycling' of the same 'theological' concept of spirituality in the sociological ambit all of which make up an enormous mosaic of many tessera. In this chapter, the aim is to examine only some of these. The chapter will discuss why the term 'religion' has suffered and what are the facts which have questioned the plausibility of redrawing the reference of the sacred with the modern Western world. Then we will focus on the theological significance of the concept of spirituality and will highlight how many aspects in the past indicated a certain 'reserve' regarding autonomy and creativity with reference to official religious institutions, both on the part of individuals and on the part of groups or communities. Finally, attention will be paid to the progressive appearance of the concept of spirituality in the sociology of religion and to Italian sociologists of religion who, without explicit reference, highlight the hidden dynamics which explain the 'particular case' of religion in Italy.[2]

Religion: The 'Crisis' of a Concept

The 'crisis' of the concept of religion is part of the wider process of redefinition and re-understanding of terminology which define the various ambits of social life and also the ever faster and evermore profound changes which characterise modern society. Thanks to the strong pressure of social changes, words, which were once to indicate specific realities, are becoming less useable in an unequivocal manner. This is because the realities themselves are changing and thus are less easy to describe with precise concepts: perfect examples are the concept of 'family' or 'nature'. We find ourselves confronted with 'old' words, which are inadequate to describe new situations and contemporarily; we are faced with new situations which we are, as yet, unable to clearly define.

Religion, in its transition from traditional society to modern and postmodern societies, has undergone profound changes. The debate regarding the usefulness of the term religion has always been rather heated at the heart of the sociology of religion (Hervieu-Léger 1993) and in recent years, especially as a result of the terrorism of the fundamentalist matrix, the ambiguity of the term religion has been further highlighted. The events of 9/11 made it painfully obvious how religion responds to dynamics of a political nature and to subjects regarding identity and recognition.

---

2   Diotallevi (2001) has indicated that available sociological theories are not able to explain adequately the 'headache' of the socio-religious situation in Italy. From the point of view of the paradigm of secularisation, the modernisation process has marginalised, fragmented and destroyed religion; in Italy there is 'too much' religion, specifically church religion, for a modernised country. According to 'rational choice theory', religion will only succumb to the modernisation process if does not modernise itself: if religion matches advanced modernisation with an adequately differentiated offer, the consumption of this good will increase not decrease. The crisis of religion in Europe, for economists of religion, will be a 'crisis of monopolies', specifically a crisis of church religions which have always held the monopoly or are at the heart of protected markets: yet this theory is unable to explain the Italian case which demonstrates too much participation to be considered a religious monopoly. Diotallevi (2001; 2002) states that this 'anomaly' is the result of the vast internal differentiation present in Italian Catholicism.

In spite of the continued cries for peace from all religious leaders, the concept of religion is linked, both individually and collectively, to conflict and violence. As Enzo Pace (2004) noted, the question which is always asked with reference to acts of violence, done in the name of God or any particular faith, is 'why does religion end in war?' In other words, why do politicians so often arm their speeches with religious symbolism in order to make their message more effective and also to mobilise their people into fighting and suppressing 'the enemy'? Reflecting on violent conflicts which contrast systems of religious belief in various parts of the world, Pace underlines the new way in which these conflicts are publicly presented. Thus he suggests that 'religion gets to places where politics does not; rhetoric is not enough to send people into war. It is often religious rhetoric which gives politics the last chance to make killing seem like a right' (Pace 2004: ix).[3]

What is important is not really the safeguarding of the purity and integrity of the truth of the faith but rather the establishment of a collective ethnic identity which is endangered by another, different, one. Thus religion in this way becomes a fundamental symbolic resource which legitimises the public language of the politics of identity. The relevant presence of religion in the public sphere (Casanova 1994) is easily linked to the realisation of political objectives such as the establishment of a national identity, the suppression of diverse ethnic groups, the strategic alliance with certain political parties and the construction of barriers which clearly distinguish the difference between 'them' and 'us'.

The large-scale presence of religion in the public arena on the one hand forces the re-calibration of various versions of the secularisation theory and on the other creates great problems for the use of the term itself. If religion is so frequently used in politics and for the fight for identity, what word can be used to denote the reference to the sacred which the contemporary world seems to have claimed and fitted with a multitude of unexpected aspects? How can we plausibly denote the transcendent, the mystery, the meaning of existence without passing through the bottlenecks imposed by the constraints placed on this term by religion?

The traditional understanding of the concept of religion is debated alongside the dynamics of globalisation and pluralism which characterise the modern world. If every single religion perceives itself as the exclusive and unique path to truth and salvation, the establishment of the democratic mentality and the freedom of choice has led to the relativism of all religious monopolies and capital. This has resulted in the fact that different beliefs must relate to others and sometimes compete, thus setting off a process of 'contamination' and hybridisation.

The shifting of the axis of the legitimisation of significance from the authority of the institution to the freedom of the individual has not been free of consequences for the relationship between believers, tradition and religious institutions. The relationship with the sacred is no longer regulated by moral laws and the beliefs of churches, but rather by individual creativity and expression. The processes of globalisation and

---

3   For questions pertaining to fundamentalism, specifically the Islamic matrix, see Vrcan (1994), Pace and Guolo (1998) and Guolo (2004).

individualisation do not signify the sunset or disappearance of religion, but rather its profound change: belief will not disappear but will be reformulated in terms of relativity and its relational nature (Michel 1994; Gauchet 1998; Giordan 2003).

In this light, Willaime (1996) has highlighted how the secularisation process has, alongside various effects of decomposition, led to the re-composition of the religious universe. Functional differentiation, the transfer of various social activities (for example education, health and social work) from the religious sphere to secular institutions, purifies religion of all activities that were not exactly completely religious. In other words, this process gives religion back to the religious sphere, through spiritualisation. Thus, Willaime would argue that 'in a very secular society, the social question of the religious insists on spiritualization and assumes mystic aspects. Functional differentiation is therefore an element of the secularisation process which contemporarily contributes to the re-spiritualisation of the religious' (Willaime 1996: 109).

From Spiritual Theology ...

It is interesting to note that the 're-spiritualisation of the religious' constitutes one of the needs which has been ever-present in the history of traditional religions, and this is particularly true of Christianity. Over the centuries, at the very heart of Christianity itself, the term 'spirituality' has acquired meanings which all point in the direction of the recovery of the 'true origins' of belief. In doing so, there is the desire to overcome all historical incrustations which have slowly made ever less believable the reference to the transcendent.

In pre-modern society, the terms 'religion' and 'spirituality' were sometimes interchangeable and institutions, which regulated the limits and the possibilities of the aforesaid, legitimised spirituality or at least different forms of it. It was therefore at the horizons of authority that the individual, or more frequently, religious communities, were able to experiment with 'original' pathways for relating to the sacred. In spite of this, the relationship with institutions was never taken for granted and through detailed analysis of various spiritual traditions, some examples of the Catholic faith such as Benedictine, Franciscan, Dominican and so forth, one notes that relations with authority underwent moments of tension and solutions were found after not always easy bargaining.

Still within Catholicism, other very relevant examples are the reforms of the Carmelite order that involved such figures as St Theresa of Avila (1515–82) and St John of the Cross (1542–91). The highest manifestations of Spanish mysticism propounded a radical form of spirituality, one founded on mystical asceticism and on the rigorous exploration of the soul. At the beginning, their proposition was misunderstood and often hindered by the Catholic Church that sternly controlled their thought and their behaviour through the Inquisition. It is interesting to note that Theresa of Avila in her autobiography reports her conversion after living nearly 20 years in the Avila nunnery. Reading St Augustine's *Confessions*, she searched for a deeper and more significant relationship with God, even through experiences of corporal mystical asceticism. Although she was free in her spiritual research, she was constantly controlled and often severely rebuked by her superiors and her confessors. John of the Cross, one of the greatest mystics of Christianity, during his activity in the spiritual reform suffered great accusations and even eight months of severe imprisonment. Nevertheless the reforms of both of them were acknowledged by the ecclesiastic institution that later proposed them through their canonisation as models to be imitated.

As observed by Špidlík (1978), the term 'spirituality' is so familiar that no-one has ever really worried about defining it: however, behind this apparent simplicity there are hidden nuances and strong changes of meaning, which range from in the extreme, heresy, to a more gentle form of secularisation. According to the Bible, the spirit is the breath of life and is a dynamism full of energy and is always moving, something which could be taken as the vital force of God. For Greek philosophers, the spirit was 'a way of being' and 'a way of knowing' and this term was used in opposition to all that was material and corporal (Borriello 2003).

In the New Testament, the term 'spirituality' is not to be found,[4] but the apostle Paul regularly used the adjective 'spiritual', which has a meaning that is precisely the opposite to 'carnal' and 'physical'.[5] According to Paul, the spiritual man is a man free from physical passion and is animated by the spirit of God: a spiritual life is thus the growth of the 'inner man' up to the point of the complete and definitive attainment of personal identity. The word spirituality began to be commonly used in the theological ambit from the seventeenth century and was used to indicate the teachings referring to the actions of the Spirit in the life of man. The concept of spirituality as described above, superimposes the 'mystic' concept and is used to indicate two very different meanings – on one hand, the term was applied to so-called 'normal' Christians and on the other, to 'contemplative' Christians. It is interesting to note that when used to indicate 'contemplative' Christians this term was used with certain diffidence and often negativity, as it referred to illusion, trickery and sometimes even heresy. In the epoch of Quietism, the 'spirituals' were always treated with suspicion as a result of their interpretation of the actions and inspiration of the Spirit with reference to the borders of reason and 'natural' morals.

The sociologically relevant aspect of the theological debate in the seventeenth century regarding the concept of spirituality is that the French term *spiritualité* began to indicate man's relationship with God and particularly highlighted the personal,

---

4   The abstract use of the term 'spirituality' was, until the middle of the last century, considered a neologism for the Italian language. It is interesting to note that this word, which is now commonly used, was not part of classical theological encyclopaedias until the end of the 1800s and the beginning of the 1900s. The first tome, *Dictionnaire de Spiritualité*, was not published until 1937.

5   Analysis of the history of spirituality points to 'spiritual practices'. These often consisted of very strict ascetical exercises such as fasts and vigils and also 'corporal mortification', which was consequently judged as excessive and later banned by the church. For further information refer to Downey (2003).

intimate and subjective aspects of this relationship. The modern trend which underlines the importance of experience has developed along these very lines and focuses on the dimension of affectivity and emotions which are the concrete environment for the realisation of the Spirit's actions.[6] The importance of underlining the role of the individual in the spiritual life, along with the contrary view that highlighted only the role of Divine Grace has been gaining increased importance since 1700 and 1800.

Toffanello states that Christian spirituality can be significant today if it matches individual needs and is committed to improving the quality of life. It must therefore surpass the mentality of corporal mortification and be able to change and meet the needs of different situations and be able to marry simplicity with the essence of faith and thus be open to the dimension of universality. In other words, this means the 'discovery of common aspects of all types of spirituality and the discovery of that which distinguishes true spirituality from slavery, the search for power, money and success. Religious or human spirituality can help us discover what it really is to be "human"' (Toffanello 2000: 22).

Secondin (2000) is of the same opinion and underlines the urgent need for Christian spirituality, specifically Catholic, to elaborate new paradigms which can interpret experience and match this to old dualistic contradictions such as interiority and exteriority, earth and heaven, nature and the supernatural, grace and sin, male and female, reason and emotion, body and soul, institution and prophecy, past and future. This new theory of spiritual theology requires the abandonment of the strictly confessional theological approach in order to become open to more complex dimensions such as multi-disciplinarism, ecumenism, multi-culturalism, holistic and inclusive theories (Schneiders 1990).

Throughout the history of the Christian churches,[7] the 'return' to spirituality has been the antidote to the corruption of ecclesiastical institutions. Spiritual revivals have also been antidotes against those who wanted to defend the privilege and property of the church. The example of St Francis of Assisi is pertinent: on one hand his intuition to reform the ecclesiastical institution was genuinely radical, especially if we compare it to the power of the papacy of Innocent III; on the other hand, this reform was not entirely foreign to the Church but was, as 'spirituality', part of and developed within the Church. The aspiration to poverty, simplicity and humility that characterised the young 'anti-conformist' of Assisi embodied qualities far removed from the church model which dominated between the twelfth and thirteenth centuries. It was the political

---

6   Dogmatic theology has studied in depth these two versions of belief – the subjective version of the believer and the objective version which refers to the contents of faith, the deposit of revealed truth and the moral laws which believers should conform to throughout their lives. These two dimensions are often designated with the Latin expressions *fides qua creditur* and *fides quae creditur* – the first indicates the attitude towards faith of the believer; and the second refers to the objective content of belief composed of various doctrines and reference to the Bible and tradition.

7   I refer to Moioli (2003), Secondin (1997), Bernard (1989), Congar (1965) and Küng (1997) for the principal traits of spirituality in Christian churches.

intelligence of Pope Innocent that precluded Francis's movement from joining one of the many heretical sects of the time. The complete prohibition on possessing money like that of building great churches or asking any favour from the Roman curia was completely different from the 'court' mentality of the official Church. The same can be said for humility as total renouncement of any type of power and for the simplicity that allowed Francis to discover a new relationship with nature, animals and plants. It is important to point out that these 'revolutionary' intuitions were not in contrast and conflict with the hierarchy – Francis asked and obtained approval from ecclesiastical authority and thus avoided charges of heresy. This struggle between institution and charisma was resolved in just a few decades – the Franciscan order was completely integrated into the ecclesiastical institution, even if it continued to support the ideals and criticisms of its founder. Proof of this very fact is that, for more than a century, heated debates took place in the same Franciscan order between the 'strict' and the 'lax' regarding the interpretation of poverty.

The same dynamics of the regulation of power at the heart of a sacred area and the return to 'spirituality' as a bargaining point between personal or community freedom and institutions may be found when analysing the debate of various late Medieval mystical elements where women played a fundamental role. Not only did mysticism represent a reaction against the worldliness of the church, the 'rational' theory of theology and also the excessive exteriorisation of various forms of piety but, more radically, it aimed at providing a new theological model and church organisation. The fascination of many mystics and the resulting suspicion of ecclesiastical institution focused on the trend of interiorising, spiritualising and simplifying both the message and the practice of the Christian life – all of which was conducted with great interior liberty removed from institutional rules and distanced from every form of exteriority and authority.

It is interesting to note, especially with reference to the reinterpretation of the term 'spirituality' in the sociological ambit, that the common trait of all mystic movements is the search for the salvation of one's own innermost self, where one can experiment with profound and immediate unity with all that is absolute. These moments of ecstasy were the zenith of many ascetic practices that secured the concentration of will, often by using physical and psychic expedients and the free contemplation of the Mystery. The seeking of mystic experience was not immune to pathological deviations (Bell 1985; Lupton 1996; Vandereycken 1994). It also led to sentiments of unity with ourselves, with nature, with the cosmos and with the fundamental absolute of being, thus surpassing the dualistic subject–object division.

This brief analysis clearly shows us how the Church has always feared losing the monopoly of the administration of the Word and Sacrament and also the control of the consciences of believers. This explains why the history of mysticism has always been accompanied by suspicion, repression, excommunication, inquisitions and sometimes even burnings at the stake. On the side there was normativeness and on the other the impossibility of the complete recognition of obedience to formal and exterior laws.

Even 'pietism', as diffused by the reforms in all Catholic Europe between the seventeenth and eighteenth centuries, repeats the steps as outlined above: the heart of which is personal religiousness, alive and interior, the cardinal point being the experience of re-birth. The heart of the matter is therefore no more the doctrine of justification or the Bible and Sacraments but the profound transformation of man – this refers to an existential rather than dogmatic turning-point in which the necessity for a 'religiousness of heart' is reaffirmed and experienced in social commitment. This programme of reform, charged with individualism and 'spiritualism', recalls the original church and primitive Christianity. The itinerary of re-birth required the intensification of Bible study, the renovation of the ministry of all believers versus the hierarchical ministry and finally the verification of the authenticity of dogmatic content with reference to daily matters.

Examining different eras in the history of spirituality with reference to the relationship between institution and liberty, both in individual and community terms, we can catch a glimpse of the establishment of various concepts of the body and sexuality. Regarding sexuality, examples are the frequent dualistic theory and the renunciation of 'pleasures of the flesh'. In the case of food, examples are fasts and abstinence and in relation to sleep there are the various prayers to be said during the night or in particular moments of the liturgical year. Another point relates to the birth and development of specific vocabularies that aim at describing the diverse possibilities of the spirituality experience.

A brief analysis of technical terms shows the measures of distance-discontinuity as well as of the proximity-continuity with reference to the contemporary sociological debate regarding spirituality and the spiritual experience of past centuries. In the monastic tradition, spiritual exercise is fundamental in enabling man to overcome temptation and to win in his fight against sin. These techniques which encompass the physical, intellectual and the psychological are known as 'asceticism'. There is also 'abnegation' which consists of the renunciation of all that is material, intellectual and anything that creates obstacles to the achievement of an authentic interior life. Another example is 'corporal mortification' which may be included under the umbrella term of renunciation but has a specific connotation with regard to the detachment from the 'pleasures of the flesh'; more moderate is 'temperance' which signifies 'self-control'.

Another historical theme of spirituality is that of 'escape from all that is worldly'. It reflects the assumption that those who genuinely loved God could not be part of earthly matters. In the effort to achieve purification, it is not easy to distinguish between the borders of a simply moral interior detachment or a genuine physical escape. Whatever the case, this attitude of refusal of the world is part of a profoundly dualistic mentality – the past and present world, the visible and invisible world, public and solitary life, sin and virtue, body and soul and truth and false opinions. The characteristic trait of this dislocated vision of existence, containing a rigid dualism, stipulates the necessity for a spiritual fight that is as constant in life as temptation. In this fight, the most unlikely ways are found to test those who aim to reach intimacy with God. 'Wicked thoughts' are at the centre of this invisible battle as they have the ability to slither into the most hidden depths of the heart. All the previously mentioned practices risk excesses and not unusually the Church itself has condemned these. The prime objective of this theme of spirituality, however, is that of obtaining freedom from human conditioning in order to allow one to communicate directly with God.

What has been previously stated is sufficient to highlight the fact that the term spirituality as part of the theological ambit enjoys a wide range of meanings. Focussing on this evolution from past centuries to the present day, one notes the shift in meaning from the rigid reference to institution, to the return of tradition and the Bible as interpreted by believers, and finally to a more attentive formulation regarding individual needs with reference to emotional and relationship needs. One can thus state that various dynamics which are used in the sociological debate on spirituality emerge from recent spiritual theology.

The transition from traditional to modern and postmodern society, and this is true also of theology, shows the re-definition of the relationship between religion and society in which the dialectic tension between institution of belief and individual freedom of choice is ever more visible. The debate regarding the Protestant Reformation and the consequent Catholic Counter-Reformation as well as the accentuations of Pietism and religious Romanticism, may be re-interpreted from this perspective.

... to the Sociology of Spirituality

Having briefly shown that the term 'spirituality' is historically linked to the theological ambit, we return to the issue raised earlier. Why has the term become used by and reformulated for the sociological ambit? What is sociologically speaking 'new' about this concept which in fact is anything but new? As already stated, in the last few decades, the sociology of religion has manifested a shift in the parameters of belief: there has been the move from a 'strong' institutional legitimisation to the recognition of 'weak' belief on the part of the individual. The concept of spirituality in the sociological ambit not only focuses on the relationship between institution and personal experience, but also places these two aspects in hierarchical form thus legitimising the relationship with the sacred, no longer from the point of view of obedience to external authority but instead centralising the freedom of the individual.[8] If religion refers to a normative universe to which we must adapt, spirituality makes the sacred open to the individual to build and find the meaning for his or her own life (Berger 1967; 1969; 1992).

This change in perspective, 'from the institution to the individual', an established theme in sociological studies of the 1960s and throughout the 1970s and 1980s, has never been explicitly theorised in the dyad of 'religion' and 'spirituality'. As noted by Hervieu-Léger (1993), the autonomy of the subject, the rationalisation of social life and that of the institution have sanctioned the end of the 'society of memory'. The collective memory of modern society is one made up of fragments. Lacking in

---

8   In addition to the cited works of Roof, Heelas and Heelas and Woodhead, consult also the contributions of Demerath (2000), Seidlitz et al. (2002), Wuthnow (1998; 2001), Yip (2003) and Zinnbauer et al. (1997).

coherence, the principle is sanctioned of allowing each person to find his or her own way in life. This principle, which has been somewhat adapted by religion, has led to a 'religion without memory' which has set off the dynamism of the 'exit from religion' and, simultaneously, the process of religious re-socialisation which is based on the 'elective' dimension.

This figure of 'elective fraternity' as noted by Hervieu-Léger (1993) observes the tension between the freedom of the subject, its feelings and needs, and the institution of belief, with its dogmatic and normative reference marks. At the heart of traditional religion, 'elective fraternity' represents the attempt to place together the modern culture of the individual, with his or her realisation of needs in regulated form of faith and religious practice that conforms to tradition. At the very fulcrum of this process of 'deregulation of authorised memories' the concept of religion is being redefined and reassembled, thus placing all the symbolic patronage of historical religious traditions at the disposition of the individual. This fact is part of the logic of 'do it yourself' or 'bricolage' (Trombetta 2004). As so effectively expressed by Poulat, 'once upon a time everything was according to the grace of God, nowadays everything is the result of man's freedom, within the limits of possibility and the only control or prohibition of rules are defined by society' (Poulat 1996: 9).

The transformation in the way we perceive the relationship between power and authority has been decisive. Since the three recent revolutions (English, American and French), power no longer derives 'from the other and from on high', either in political and religious terms, but is now at 'man's level' (Gauchet 1998). The 'democratic' management of power seems to sanction this new situation where the human condition is no longer defined according to man's relationship with religion, yet, currently, it is religion which is reassembled in order to safeguard the needs of the individual.

Although the term 'spirituality' is not always used, it is clear that the concept of religion does not adequately express the new democratic mentality which safeguards the freedom of the individual, also with respect to religious aspects. This process of the 'democratisation of the sacred' has resulted in the radical individualisation of ways of believing: the principle consequence of this is that the individual in his or her search for meaning no longer accepts pre-packaged external norms. Contemporary beliefs are not functional regarding religious identity, which was created according to the criteria of stability. Instead, they focus on experience rather than on dogma, on subjective personal authenticity rather than on objective truth; this perspective legitimises change as normal rather than exceptional (Michel 1994).

In the sociological debate regarding religion in Italy, the concept of spirituality has made an explicit appearance only recently (Garelli 2003; Giordan 2004),[9] although the use of the 'religion' category for several years has been problematic. Even in the 1980s, some elements that are now classed as 'spirituality' were part of the terminology of religion at a conceptual level and utilised for empirical research.

---

9   The term 'spirituality' appears in the work of other Italian writers, but it is often used as a synonym for 'religion'; Berzano (1994), Marchisio (2000) and Lucà Trombetta (2004), however, make explicit reference to the 'need for spirituality' and to 'mystical spirituality'.

Nesti (1985) speaks of the category of 'implicit religiousness', which emerges from various (at the time) little researched spheres of Italian religiousness. Examples of this are: 'Christianity without faith'; 'Christianity without church'; scepticism as a way to deal with the transience of the present; agnosticism as pre-eminence of the 'inexpressible'; and 'atheism as metaphor'. Nesti meets the challenge posed to the official institution of belief (the Catholic Church) as a result of the acceleration of the processes of democratisation and 'transignificance'.

Nesti (1985) states that the category of 'implicit religiousness' serves to uncover the religious connotations which are beyond official and codified images of religion; it is also useful for unveiling the symbolic system, the states of the soul, the strong motivation and the formulation of ideas regarding existence that are constructed by social players. Thus, religion may be experienced in a personal and autonomous manner rather than in terms set by official institutions and accountable in a confessional form. Through his analysis of various religious terminologies, Nesti also attributes great importance to silence as a characteristic of the mystical experience.

Participating in religious rites, one can understand how silence constitutes the search for a special relationship with God. Silence is the best way for man to experience his relationship with the Divinity in terms of a total sense of abandon. In addition to representing the stupor and emotion one feels when confronted by mystery, silence can also indicate to those who are in search for a state of 'interior research' something which may be conducted within but is yet at the borders of and outside historical religious traditions. Half way between the official institution of belief and personal religion that is separated from every institutional reference mark lies popular religion. According to Nesti (1985), it manifests conformity to traditional rites, those often interpreted as providing a sense of integration in society, as something that is independent from belief and the adhesion to the symbolic system and the norms of the Church.

In order to specify the particular Italian relationship with religion, Garelli (1986) uses the concept of 'scenario religion'. This indicates the blunting of the concept of religion, thus reflecting the lack of an unequivocal meaning for this term – the result of which is the loss of relevance for all its symbolic capital. However, Italians refer to the Church for important moments in their lives that require the celebration of sacraments. They also attach special importance to the religious education of their children. Garelli (1986) refers to the 'weakness of faith', which may be interpreted as a loss of basic conviction and the scarcity of moral tension. This phenomenon is attributable to 'excessive Catholicism' as present in Italian society and is characterised by the difficulty in understanding the authenticity of the evangelical message and in conforming to the all-too-visible demands of the clergy and other religious groups in the public sphere.

According to Garelli (1986), Italy was establishing 'scenario religion': in spite of interpreting the stage of life, using a profane script, social players, as an ultimate pointer, referred to 'a light from on high which illuminates the stage that is human life', in other words, religion. This author also underlines the importance of the autonomy of individual decisions that interpret systems of belief based on personal choice. In this regard, the Catholic Church cannot possibly be considered as the only body able to guarantee social integration.

Cipriani's questioning (1988) focuses on the persistence of Catholicism in modernised and secularised Italy, not only at a cultural level, but also more recently in the complex web which exists between religion and politics. This category introduced by Cipriani is that of 'diffused religion' and this is placed between traditionally rigid religiousness, such as that linked to 'church-oriented religion' (as visible in the public sphere), and that which Thomas Luckmann defines as 'invisible religion', something which is more private and individual.

Via numerous interviews conducted in Italy and specifically in certain quarters of Rome – the centre of Catholicism and sacred city *par excellence* – Cipriani states that 'diffused religion' is not only rooted in history and geography but is more deeply connected to the dimensions of values and culture. With respect to the aforesaid, religion is 'diffused' because 'vast parts of the population cross over the pure limits of church religion and this is in open contrast to motivation of a religious nature, such as the dissent at the centre of Catholicism regarding the divorce and abortion referenda' (Cipriani 1988: 31). There are, however, other reasons for defining Italian religiousness 'diffused', principally because religion represents the historical and cultural result of the two thousand year presence of the Catholic Church in Italy and its functions of legitimisation and socialisation. Another reason is Italy's openness to other various religious experiences, both individual and collective.

Cesareo's introduction to research carried out in the mid-1990s focused on the religiousness of Italians. It established that the modality of belief that emerged from the data specified two particularly diffused modern traits. These were: 'subjectivity which makes self-fulfilment the goal of life, and uncertainty, which on an existential plain, may be translated into the trend of the temporariness of choices' (Cesareo 1995: 7). It is evident that these two dimensions collide with Catholic tradition on different levels. If the culture of narcissism results in radical individualism, this closure has consequences for the capacity to recognise a superior being and also for belonging to the Church established as a mediation instrument between man and God. Uncertainty, focused solely on the present, leads to a culture of the 'here and now' which leaves little space for past traditions and future eschatology.

Diotallevi (2001; 2002) confronts the subject of pluralism and proposes a special interpretation for the Italian religious reality which has not experienced strong external pluralist competition outside of Catholicism but presents instead what are internally elevated regimes of competition. He claims that there are two elements that help the understanding of this diversification. First there is the relatively scarce success of new religious movements and sects in Italy, as scarcity is matched by the variety and vivacity of Catholic-inspired groups. Second, there is the sometimes excessive competition between different Catholic groups which has led ecclesiastical authority to produce numerous (rarely applied) official documents regarding the different quality of the experience and involvement of the laity. Italian Catholicism is subject to strong internal competition and this explains the still high recruitment levels of the clergy and the highest European participation in liturgical rites. This openness to flexibility and to internal complexity has enabled Italian Catholicism to face the challenge of modernity but not to foresee the results of this process.

Abbruzzese has noted the difficulty of the relationship between faith and culture in the Italian social and religious context. He states that the recovery of interest in the religious dimension no longer focuses on the traditional functions of legitimisation and reassurance regarding significant life events, but says that: 'If religion no longer provides protection and reassurance against tragedy, it is legitimate to ask exactly what is religion now and how does it match up to modernity and its subjective expectations' (Abbruzzese 2000: 415). He also affirms that new Italian religiousness requires theoretical and methodological clarification; new approaches and categories are necessary for an adequate survey of the presence of the sacred in contemporary society.

As has been schematically illustrated, over the last 20 years in Italy there has been much discussion regarding the 'religion' category. However all this discussion has come to nothing with regard to the creation of a new concept, one able to exceed the narrow-mindedness of this term. As we have pointed out earlier, the 'spirituality' category has not been used, even if some authors discerned the (to a greater or lesser extent) veiled characteristics of this concept. Garelli (2003) catapulted the 'spirituality' category into the sociological debate on religion in Italy. Through his analysis of data regarding Italy as part of research on moral and religious pluralism in different areas of Europe, he developed a typology which connects the categories of 'religion' and 'spirituality'.

Table 9.1   Awareness of being a religious person and the perception of having a spiritual life

	%
• Atheist/agnostics (*neither religious nor spiritual*)	12.3
• ethno-cultural.religiousness (*medium/high religiousness, low or absent spirituality*)	17.3
• critical spirituality (*low or absent religiousness, medium/high spirituality*)	8.8
• weak believer (*mid religiousness and mid spirituality*)	23.0
• more religious than spiritual (*high religiousness, mid spirituality*)	10.3
• more spiritual than religious (*high spirituality, mid religiousness*)	9.5
• the faithful (*high religiousness and high spirituality*)	18.8

As reported in Table 9.1, the percentages of the different combinations between the spiritual dimension and the religious dimension in Italy prove that even in a context strongly characterized by Catholicism it is possible to trace the presence of both the objective element ('religion model') and the subjective element ('spirituality model') of creed. Analysing the different profiles of religiousness, the age variable (especially for the young) was particularly important for the critical spirituality category. This was similar in the atheist–agnostic group, but older subjects tended to belong to the 'integrated' model of religiousness. With regard to the gender variable, more males were part of the atheist–agnostic and critical spirituality group, while women were predominantly part of the 'integrated' model of religiousness. Via analysis of education levels, it is clear that the more educated focused on the 'spirituality' dimension rather than on 'religion', while the less educated tend to identify more with the 'faithful', who attributed great importance to *both* spirituality and religiousness.

It is particularly important to note that Garelli's conclusions (2003) point out the limits and difficulties of the use of the 'spirituality' category. The term 'religiousness' may be applied to many more Italians than the term 'spiritual' – almost four-fifths of people consider themselves mid-high religious, while only two-thirds consider themselves to have an element of mid-high spiritual tension. Garelli notes that self-definition in terms of one being more spiritual than religious is 'more ideal than realistic, more an intent than actual practice, more theoretical than object of experience' (Garelli 2003: 90). Observing carefully, one notes that the level of religious expression with reference to spirituality is verifiable in the atheist–agnostic group. Garelli also affirms that the majority of the population knows the meaning of and is able to distinguish the difference between 'religion' and 'spirituality' and is also able to define clearly the level of personal involvement in these two dimensions: it is thus important to refine the heuristic significance of the concept of 'spirituality', without using it as an alternative to 'religion'. These two dimensions will be investigated with a more detailed model of analysis capable of highlighting the complex web that connects the freedom of choice of the individual and what religious institutions can provide.

Conclusion

The first question that emerges from reflections in this chapter relates to matters of epistemological character. Changes in the contemporary world are so fast and deep that they render scientific reflection difficult. In other words, one can say that not only are 'things' in day to day life changing but also the meanings of the terms which we use to describe them. Concepts and theories are instruments that the social scientist has at his disposal to describe the world around him, but, if this world changes excessively fast, research requires new conceptual instruments to illustrate and to interpret that which remains as well as that which is transformed. Thus it is necessary to find 'new words' to help us to understand 'new situations' which are created in the transition from traditional society to modern and postmodern society.

If this consideration is true for sociology in general, it is even more so for that which is verifiable in the sociology of religion. Not only do external ways of believing change, but so also are there profound changes attributed by individuals to their relationships with the sacred and to concepts of practice and belonging. Secularisation and belief need to be revised and reinterpreted as part of the heart of the new landscape of pluralism and globalisation. As Allievi (2003) points out, the complexity of the religious sphere poses 'conceptually intriguing' questions that underline the need to find new interpretative categories. The conceptual tools that in the last decades seemed to describe the religious changes effectively, nowadays seem unable to grasp the new situations that are emerging in the contemporary religious sphere. The sociologist is thus required to invent new, more sophisticated and sensitive tools to record changes which may be in turn microscopic or imperceptible (such as changes in belief or values or the use of concepts) but no less important as a result of this.

A second consideration, which is closely linked to the aforesaid, concerns the return to the term 'spirituality' in the postmodern sociological ambit – this bears witness to the 'reinvention' of the meaning of a concept which had a specific content in traditional theology – one which is partially, if not completely, different from that of its contemporary usage. This traditional term traces its roots back to the first centuries of Christianity, but is today almost entirely obsolete in the ambit of its conception and is re-born to describe the new situation of contemporary belief. This is a typical example of 'postmodern reinvention', which looks to the past as a source for meanings and then contextualises the term in a changed profile. As previously stated, the theological concept of spirituality has always pointed to the borders between the individual and institution, between the freedom to believe on one hand and the legitimate control of belief on the other. However, this complex and often painful bargaining process always took place in the space and within the limits of institution: what happened outside of these confines was deemed dangerous, deviant, heretic and wicked. History is not devoid of these marginal experiences, but they rarely were strong enough to outlive the memories of those involved.

If, on one hand, Christian spirituality distinguishes the subjective and objective elements of belief, on the other the hierarchical disposition of the two dimensions is unquestionable: the certainty and solidity of the objectivity of tradition and the rules of institution stabilised the possibility of the practice of the freedom of the individual. The use of the term 'spirituality' in the sociology of religion is placed in continuity with its theological origins and recovers the polarisation between the individual and institution, but it also sanctions a radical discontinuity with the past, thus completely capsizing the process of legitimisation. The sacred is no longer the realm only of traditional church prescriptions, but may be accessed by the individuals' freedom of choice, their need to search for meaning and their hopes for self-realisation and the need to express creatively the relationship with the transcendent. In addition, as previously stated, the concepts of religion and spirituality are also used to indicate two different and non-overlapping dimensions of belief, so much so that Heelas and Woodhead (2005) state these are polar opposites.

A third conclusion relates to the relationship between 'religion' and 'spirituality'. Without a doubt they appear to be two different paths that lead the subject to the sacred, one is based on obedience to institutional and traditional churches and the other focuses on the free choice of the individual. However, this must not lead one to make a quick, simplified dichotomies which do not adequately consider the complex web which connects the moral and religious cosmos of the individual and his social and cultural background. In other terms and with particular reference to Italian religiousness, it seems that within the (sometimes rather vague) institutional framework, there is the functioning of criteria regarding the legitimisation of liberty, even if this, for cultural rather than strictly religious reasons, is expressed via typical forms of church religion. If one considers sexual morality, some individuals pay no attention to Catholic morals; however, important events are no better celebrated than with traditional liturgy; other individuals build a relationship with God through the selective choice of resources provided by traditional religion. Most probably, unlike what is maintained by Heelas and Woodhead (2005) analysing the English situation, religion and spirituality are not mutually exclusive and therefore should not be used as alternatives: between total exclusion and total inclusion, for there is a vast range of possibilities for different types of relationship regarding faith between individuals and institution. It is thus opportune to welcome the suggestion to study further the 'spirituality' category, which, in my opinion, has a heuristic range of undoubted value (Giordan 2004; Roof 2003; Zinnbauer et al. 1997).

A final observation focuses on the institution of belief, specifically in relation to traditional religious institution. Various sociologists have questioned the role of the aforesaid in a pluralist and globalised world. Several scholars and some theologians have arrived at the point of questioning whether churches are destined to become an ever-more residual phenomenon until they eventually disappear altogether. There is absolutely no doubt that the new criteria of the legitimisation of the sacred as highlighted by the term 'spirituality' have not only changed the 'belief' of individuals, but have also re-formulated the 'ways of making us believe' on the part of religious institutions. The 'silent spiritual revolution' that has transversally concerned all historical churches in recent years is forcing the aforesaid to re-comprehend their presence in society correctly in terms of the requirements which seem to place them in check. Thus, historical churches must take into consideration individuals' freedom of choice and their ability to seek independently their own meaning of life.

Complex dynamics exist between institution and individuals and these result in ways whose implications are difficult to quantify. It would be naïve to think that traditional churches are unable to change and accept the challenges presented to them by the social and cultural context.

The theme of institutional change and in religious institutions in particular, needs to be examined without the examiners being dazzled by the 'excessive brightness' produced by the social recognition attributed to personal freedom – this of course is an indispensable starting point for every argument focusing on current changes in the modern era, but it must be considered in relation to the 'updated' offer of institution. The question at this point raises another. Just how far are religious institutions prepared to go with regard to their secular patrimony, in terms of symbolism and belief, rites and moral laws, in order to meet the needs of the contemporary era? To what extent is this 'restoration' possible without risking external credibility and internal cohesion? How can the eternity of principle and monopolistic claim of the truth be matched by temporariness and relativity (which does not always signify 'relativism')? As observed by Guizzardi (2003), what is required is an articulated negotiation process involving the different social players of the religious scene. But these negotiations need to be alert to the ability of religious institutions to mask this change, as this very process could weaken the façade of 'immutability' which characterises the bodies who must defend 'ultimate values' and 'unquestionable principles'. It thus remains to be seen if these processes of change will be credible and coherent with the heritage of tradition and with the requests for the control of power that inevitably characterise all hierarchical institutions.

Bibliography

Abbruzzese, S. (2000), 'Il posto del sacro', in R. Gubert (a cura di), *La via italiana alla postmodernità. Verso una nuova architettura dei valori*, Milano: FrancoAngeli, pp. 397–455.

Acquaviva, S.S. (1961), *L'eclissi del sacro nella civiltà industriale: dissacrazione e secolarizzazione nella società industriale e post-industriale*, Milano: Edizioni di Comunità. (English translation, 1979, *The Decline of the Sacred in Industrial Society*, Oxford: Basil Blackwell.)

Allievi, S. (2003), 'Il pluralismo introvabile: i problemi della ricerca comparativa', in F. Garelli, G. Guizzardi and E. Pace (eds), *Un singolare pluralismo. Indagine sul pluralismo religioso degli italiani*, Bologna: Il Mulino, pp. 249–95.

Bégot, A.-C. (2004), 'Il ruolo della spiritualità nella cura dell'HIV/AIDS', *Quaderni di Sociologia*, 35: 131–9.

Bell, R.M. (1985), *Holy Anorexia*, Chicago: Chicago University Press.

Berger, P.L. (1967), *The Sacred Canopy*, Garden City, NY: Doubleday Anchor.

Berger, P.L. (1969), *A Rumour of Angels: Modern Society and the Rediscovery of the Supernatural*, Garden City, NY: Doubleday Anchor.

Berger, P.L. (1992), *A Far Glory: The Quest for Faith in an Age of Credulity*, New York: Free Press.

Bernard, Ch-A. (1989), *Teologia spirituale*, Cinisello Balsamo: Paoline.

Berzano, L. (1994), *Religiosità del nuovo aeropago. Credenze e forme religiose nell'epoca postsecolare*, Milano: FrancoAngeli.

Borriello, L. (2003), 'Presentazione', in M. Downey (ed.), *Nuovo Dizionario di Spiritualità*, Città del Vaticano: Libreria Editrice Vaticana, pp. 5–36.

Casanova, J. (1994), *Public Religions in the Modern World*, Chicago: Chicago University Press.

Cesareo, V. (1995), 'Introduzione', in V. Cesareo, R. Cipriani, F. Garelli, C. Lanzetti and G. Rovati, *La religiosità in Italia*, Milano: Mondadori, pp. 4–17.

Cipriani, R. (1988), *La religione diffusa*, Roma: Borla.

Congar, Y. (1965), *Le vie del Dio vivo*, Brescia: Morcelliana.

Cox, H.G. (1965), *The Secular City: Secularisation and Urbanisation in Theological Perspective*, New York: Macmillan.

Demerath, N.J. (2000), 'The Varieties of Sacred Experience: Finding the Sacred in a Secular Grove', *Journal for the Scientific Study of Religion*, 39(3): 1–11.

Dericquebourg, R. (2004), 'Le cure spirituali: terapie sociologiche?', *Quaderni di Sociologia*, 35: 119–29.

Diotallevi, L. (2001), *Il rompicapo della secolarizzazione italiana: Caso italiano, teorie americane e revisione del paradigma della secolarizzazione*, Soveria Mannelli: Rubbettino.

Diotallevi, L. (2002), 'Internal Competition in a National Religious Monopoly. The Catholic Effect and the Italian Case', *Sociology of Religion*, 63(2): 137–55.

Downey, M. (ed.) (2003), *Nuovo Dizionario di Spiritualità*, Città del Vaticano: Libreria Editrice Vaticana.

Flory, R.W. and D.E. Miller (ed.) (2000), *GenX Religion*, New York: Routledge.

Garelli, F. (1986), *La religione dello scenario. La persistenza della religione tra i lavoratori*, Bologna: Il Mulino.

Garelli, F. (2003), 'L'esperienza e il sentimento religioso', in F. Garelli, G. Guizzardi, and E. Pace (eds), *Un singolare pluralismo. Indagine sul pluralismo morale e religioso degli italiani*, Bologna: Il Mulino, pp. 74–114.

Gauchet, M. (1998), *La religion dans la démocratie. Parcours de la laïcité*, Paris: Gallimard.

Giordan, G. (2003), *Dall'uno al molteplice. Dispositivi di legittimazione nell'epoca del pluralismo*, Torino: Stampatori.

Giordan, G. (2004), 'Dalla religione alla spiritualità: una nuova legittimazione del sacro?', *Quaderni di Sociologia*, 35: 105–17.

Greeley, A.M. (1972), *Unsecular Man: The Persistence of Religion*, New York: Schocken Books.

Guizzardi, G. (2003), 'La pluralità dei pluralismi', in F. Garelli, G. Guizzardi and E. Pace (eds), *Un singolare pluralismo. Indagine sul pluralismo morale e religioso degli italiani*, Bologna: Il Mulino, pp. 13–47.

Guolo, R. (2004), *L'Islam è compatibile con la democrazia?*, Roma–Bari: Laterza.

Heelas, P. (2002), 'The Spiritual Revolution: from "Religion" to "Spirituality"', in L. Woodhead, P. Fletcher, H. Kawanami and D. Smith (eds), *Religions in the Modern World*, London, Routledge, pp. 357–77.

Heelas, P. and L. Woodhead, (2005), *The Spiritual Revolution. Why Religion is Giving Way to Spirituality*, Oxford: Blackwell.

Hervieu-Léger, D. (1993), *La religion pour mémoire*, Paris: Cerf.

Kepel, G. (1991), *La revanche de Dieu*, Paris: Seuil.

Küng, H. (1997), *Cristianesimo. Essenza e storia*, Milano: Rizzoli.

Lupton, D. (1996), *Food, the Body and the Self*, London: Sage.

Marchisio, R. (2000), 'Forme di spiritualità mistiche e contesto culturale contemporaneo', *Credere Oggi*, 117(3): 77–89.

Marty, E.M. (1967), 'The Spirit's Holy Errand: The Search for a Spiritual Style in Secular America', *Daedalus*, 96(1): 99–115.

Michel, P. (1994), *Politique et religion: La grande mutation*, Paris: Albin Michel.

Moioli, G. (2003), *L'esperienza spirituale: Lezioni introduttive*, Milano: Glossa.

Nesti, A. (1985), *Il religioso implicito*, Roma: Ianua.

Pace, E. (2004), *Perché le religioni scendono in Guerra?*, Roma–Bari: Laterza.

Pace, E. and R. Guolo (1998), *I fondamentalismi*, Roma–Bari: Laterza.

Poulat, E. (1996), *L'era post-cristiana: Un mondo uscito da Dio*, Torino: Società Editrice Internazionale.

Roof, W.C. (1993), *A Generation of Seekers: The Spiritual Journeys of the Baby Boom Generation*, San Francisco: HarperCollins.

Roof, W.C. (1999), *Spiritual Marketplace: Baby Boomers and the Remaking of American Religion*, Princeton, NJ: Princeton University Press.

Roof, W.C. (2003), 'Religion and Spirituality: Toward an Integrated Analysis', in M. Dillon (ed.), *Handbook of the Sociology of Religion*, Cambridge: Cambridge University Press, pp. 137–48.

Schneiders, S. (1990), 'Spirituality in the Academy', in B. Hanson (ed.), *Modern Christian Spirituality: Methodological and Historical Essays*, Atlanta, GA: Scholar Press.

Secondin, B. (1997), *Spiritualità in dialogo. Nuovi scenari dell'esperienza spirituale*, Milano: Paoline.

Secondin, B. (2000), 'Possibilità e compiti della spiritualità nell'epoca moderna', *Credere Oggi*, 117(3): 91–104.

Seidlitz, L., A.D. Abernethy, P.R. Duberstein, J.S. Evinger, T.H. Chang and B.L. Lewis (2002), 'Development of the Spiritual Transcendence Index', *Journal for the Scientific Study of Religion*, 41(3): 439–53.

Špidlík, T. (1978), *La spiritualité de l'Orient chrétien. Manuel systématique*, Roma: Orientalia Christiana.

Stark, R. and M. Introvigne (2003), *Dio è tornato. Indagine sulla rivincita delle religioni in Occidente*, Casale Monferrato: Piemme.

Toffanello, G. (2000), 'La spiritualità in questione: il postmoderno alla ricerca di sé', *Credere Oggi*, 117(3): 7–24.

Trombetta, L. (2004), *Il bricolage religioso: Sincretismo e nuova religiosità*, Bari: Edizioni Dedalo.

Vandereycken, W. (1994), *From Fasting Saints to Anorexic Girls: The History of Self-Starvation*, New York: New York University Press.

Vrcan, S. (1994), 'Una guerra di religione nell'Europa contemporanea', *Religioni e società*, 18: 16–26.

Willaime, J.-P. (1996), *Sociologia delle religioni*, Bologna: Il Mulino.

Wuthnow, R. (1998), *After Heaven: Spirituality in America Since the 1950s*, Berkeley: University of California Press.

Wuthnow, R. (2001), *Creative Spirituality: The Way of the Artist*, Berkeley: University of California Press.

Yip, A.K.T. (2003), 'The Self as the Basis of Religious Faith: Spirituality of Gay, Lesbian and Bisexual Christians', in G. Davie, P. Heelas and L. Woodhead (eds), *Predicting Religion: Christian, Secular and Alternative Futures*, Aldershot: Ashgate, pp. 135–46.

Zinnbauer, B.J., K.I. Pargament, B.C. Cole, M.S. Rye, E.M. Butter, T.G. Belavich, K.M. Hipp, A.B. Scott and J.L. Kadar, (1997), 'Religion and Spirituality: Unfuzzying the Fuzzy', *Journal for the Scientific Study of Religion*, 36(4): 549–64.

Chapter 10

In Search of Spiritual Capital: The Spiritual as a Cultural Resource

Mathew Guest

Definitions of spirituality are notoriously slippery. However, understandings have in recent times achieved some clarity and consensus among scholars. The spiritual is associated with the personal, the intimate, the interior and the experiential, contrasted with 'religion', which is associated with the official, the external and the institutional, often picking up negative connotations of the hierarchical and patriarchal along the way (Heelas 2002). Acknowledging the word's many connotations, Wade Clark Roof isolates four as being most important, focusing on spirituality as 'a source of values and meaning beyond oneself, a way of understanding, inner awareness, and personal integration' (Roof 1999: 35).

'Spirituality' has been invoked in this way to articulate dissatisfaction with mainstream religious traditions and to signal an attempt to move beyond their limitations. This is the rhetoric used within discussions of the 'New Age' movement, focussed on inner-transformation and the holistic, spiritual healing of the self. However, this language also lends itself to descriptions of mysticism, and of the more experiential dimensions of mainstream religion. While located within various contexts, spirituality is increasingly associated with aspects of religiosity focused on the experiential, the interior, and generally the subjective dimensions of personal identity.

Within the contemporary context, it is sometimes argued that the spiritual is replacing the religious, as a more meaningful expression of identity for many people living within advanced post-industrial societies. In support of this, recent research has revealed that a focus on the subjective is not restricted to alternative or New Age enclaves; many mainstream churches in the UK and USA are placing a fresh emphasis upon connecting with the inner lives of members, upon affirming their subjective lives rather than stressing a need for conformity to an externalised body of truth (Heelas and Woodhead 2005; Miller 1997). Hence the popularity of charismatic mega churches, inner-city Pentecostalism, Christian retreat centres and the kabala branch of Jewish mysticism. All place a premium on personal experience and the spiritual dimensions of the inner life. The argument here is that as contemporary western society places an increasing emphasis upon the cultivation of the subjective self – on catering to the emotional, intuitive, interior dimensions of identity – so religious traditions are evolving so as to meet these needs. On this understanding, late modernity is the age of the spiritual, rather than the religious.

Studies that highlight the importance of subjective spirituality draw our attention to some important dimensions of the contemporary religious landscape. They move the analysis beyond church and chapel, shifting our focus to the boundaries of the religious mainstream and beyond. However, they often highlight the individualistic aspects of spirituality at the expense of the social, the subjective at the expense of the inter-subjective. Existing treatments have been driven largely by what Steven Tipton (1982) calls 'expressive individualism', that is, a model that conceives religious identity as shaped by the subjective experiences of individuals. Indeed, this is a fair description of many post-1960s religious movements, such as charismatic renewal, the Jesus Army, and the 'soft' capitalism of courses such as *est*. However, while 'expressive individualism' captures the fact that subjective experience feeds a sense of spiritual identity, it does not account for the complex exchange of resources that underlies this process.

Charismatic Christians do not simply draw from their experience as raw data in forging a sense of meaning out of life; their experience is filtered, interpreted, expressed, re-expressed, and negotiated in dialogue with a received set of traditions alongside conventions of authority and acceptability. Their 'spirituality' is shaped by an interactive process, set within a complex network of relationships. It draws on cultural resources which are deployed and negotiated, not merely absorbed. In sum, spirituality is not the preserve of autonomous individuals; it is subject to a broader social distribution of power.

In support of this argument, we recall Beckford's insightful comment that religion is not being eclipsed by the forces of contemporary society, as the hard-line secularisation theorists would have us believe. Rather, religion has undergone a change in form – it has ceased to function primarily as a social institution, and is now better conceived as a 'cultural resource'. As Beckford suggests:

> Religion has come adrift from its former points of anchorage but is no less potentially powerful as a result. It remains a potent cultural resource or form which may act as the vehicle of change, challenge or conservation. Consequently, religion has become less predictable. The capacity to mobilize people and material resources remains strong, but it is likely to be mobilized in unexpected places and in ways which may be in tension with 'establishment' practices and public policy. (Beckford 1989: 170)

Lyon (2000) endorses Beckford's analysis, arguing that in late modernity, religion has become 'deregulated', free to take on new forms and occupy novel spaces in ways that demand a fresh approach to the sociology of contemporary religious phenomena. Such an approach would do well to take account of the transition of religion into spirituality – that is, into more subjectivised forms, but it would also need to account for the ways in which this spirituality functions as a cultural resource.

This chapter seeks to explore the possibilities of analysing spirituality in these terms, through the notion of 'spiritual capital', that is, as a cultural resource to be acquired and exchanged. The introduction of 'spiritual capital' as a theoretical tool in the sociology of religion is contentious, not least because the use of the word 'spiritual' is suggestive of theological discourse. This implies, for some, a quasi-confessional approach lacking in sociological rigour. Furthermore, to approach religion in terms of capital is to venture into relatively unchartered waters. Much of the literature takes as its central theoretical focus the institution or the individual, and by comparison 'capital' appears somewhat elusive and ambiguous to say the least. However, it is our strong conviction that to approach religious phenomena in terms of 'spiritual capital' carries important advantages. Most clearly, it allows us to shed new light on the nature of religion as a cultural resource in late modernity, and in so doing facilitates a more accurate sociological analysis of spirituality, and of spiritual identity.

Some authors have already attempted to conceptualise 'religious' or 'spiritual capital'. In so doing, they build on a long tradition within which 'capital' has been deployed as a metaphor for mobilisable resources. Consequently, an examination of the theoretical possibilities of spiritual capital demands a consideration of this tradition, and this will proceed in the following section. This will be followed by a discussion and development of religious and spiritual capital, drawing particularly from the work of Pierre Bourdieu. The final section will explore and develop the proposed theory of spiritual capital by addressing its application within the context of a specific research project, exploring the process of value transmission among the families of Anglican clergymen.

The Development of 'Capital' as a Theoretical Tool

While it has an earlier history, most contemporary understandings of 'capital' owe their greatest conceptual debt to Karl Marx, who published his monumental critique of political economy, *Capital*, in three volumes between 1867 and 1894 (Marx 1970). Seeking to identify the processes at the heart of capitalist economics, Marx uses capital as a dynamic metaphor for the fluid entity that, by virtue of its circulation, accrues material value. He distinguishes between 'fixed capital' – that which is tied up in plant and equipment – and 'circulating capital', which turns over more rapidly in production, such as wages or the value of raw materials (Foley 1986: 45). However, capital is not merely defined by the material in which it is embodied (for example money or commodities); rather, it has value by virtue of the fact 'that it is involved in a particular process, the process of producing surplus value' (Brewer 1984: 35). Moreover, while inextricably linked to – and generated by – capitalist society, Marx insisted that capital be seen not as a concrete entity, but as a socio-economic relation. It is this, more abstract, dimension, together with its metaphorical connotations of exchange and circulation, which has shaped the multiple development of 'capital' as a social scientific reference to *mobilisable resources*. Indeed, it has acquired a variety of qualifying prefixes throughout the twentieth century[1] – we speak of academics

---

1   There is evidence to suggest that a more general, multi-referential use of 'capital' was a part of social scientific discourse at least as early as the first decades of the twentieth century. For example, in his discussion of the nature of 'social categories' within the Introduction to

deploying 'intellectual capital'; the aristocracy benefiting from their 'cultural capital'; and government ministers trading 'political capital' for reasons of personal advancement or as leverage in policy debates. In this sense 'capital' has in some ways fallen foul of the same indiscriminate deployment as 'spirituality', and risks losing all force as a conceptual tool. However, its development has not been entirely capricious, and it is possible to trace a coherent and rich conceptual history by appealing to the work of several key authors.

One of the first major embellishments emerged as 'human capital' in the 1960s. Economist and latterly Nobel Prize winner Gary Becker (1964) used this term to develop a theory that explained the relationship between education and family upbringing and a person's capacity to excel in the job market. In this sense, 'human capital' refers to resources that reside in human beings, rather than in plant or machinery. Becker retained Marx's concern for resources that can be traded for economic gain, but broadened the possibilities of capital by acknowledging the integral role that learnt behaviour can play in generating material advantages and disadvantages. Human capital has continued to be used in this sense, remaining particularly popular in the discipline of economics.

Putnam claims the term 'social capital'[2] was coined independently at least six times during the twentieth century. Put to theoretical use in such varied fields as education and economics, it has always referred to 'the ways in which our lives are made more productive by social ties' (Putnam 2000: 19). Pierre Bourdieu, whose work reflects the dominant understanding, first developed the term within the sociology of education during the 1970s (Bourdieu and Passeron 1977; Bourdieu 1980; 1985). Bourdieu (1985: 248) refers to the resources linked to a 'durable network' of relationships, thus defining social capital – as Becker had with 'human capital' – in functional terms, as a means to an end, this end often expressed as material or economic gain (see also Loury 1981).

James Coleman (1990; 2000) continued in this vein, speaking of social capital as a resource generated between individuals. His work carries us further, however, setting social capital within a sophisticated theoretical framework for understanding human action more generally. Coleman argues that whereas sociologists have traditionally tended to see human behaviour as moulded by rules and norms, structures in which individuals are embedded, economists have presented humans as autonomous agents who construct their own opportunities and forge their own values. For Coleman, social capital serves as a meso-level concept that captures the constraining and yet at the same time empowering capacity of social relationships. In this way he echoes Bourdieu, who operationalises 'capital' as a dynamic motif intended to overcome the dichotomy between objectivism – the tendency to explain human action purely in

---

The Elementary Forms of Religion, first published in 1912, Emile Durkheim makes reference to 'intellectual' and 'material' capital without feeling the need to offer any further explanation or definition of terms (Durkheim 1995: 18).

2   For a detailed account of the theoretical history of social capital within the social sciences, see Woolcock 1998.

terms of social structures – and subjectivism – the tendency to account for behaviour in terms of human agency alone (Jenkins 1992: 74). In this way, both Bourdieu and Coleman use social capital to advance and refine wider debates in social theory.

Robert Putnam is the name which is now most readily associated with social capital. His monumental study *Bowling Alone* (2000) charts the decline of community participation across US culture during the latter half of the twentieth century. Putnam's emphasis upon social capital as the 'connective tissue' which holds society together, conjoined with his pessimistic prognoses, have lent his work something of a political edge, and have secured it for a broad audience, from academic scholars to government policy makers. His work is not as theoretically ambitious as that of Coleman or Bourdieu, but he has done more than anyone to popularise the term and set it within the context of broader questions pertinent to late modern society. Most clearly, he has established the sense that social capital – connections among individuals – is a social good, a potent commodity within an age of hyper-individualism and consumer culture. He emphasises human relationships as potential reservoirs of power and the key to social improvement, and associates social capital with norms of reciprocity and trustworthiness, arguing that it is closely related to what many have called 'civic virtue'. This is 'most powerful when embedded in a dense network of reciprocal social relations' (Putnam 2000: 19).

Putnam's theoretical innovation is his distinction between *bridging* and *bonding* forms of social capital. Bonding social capital builds up connections between members of a group, and hence strengthens social cohesion. Bridging social capital links individuals within different social groups, thus generating wider networks of reciprocity. The former is what undergirds the collective identities of marginalised groups, while the latter is what may enable the members of those groups to overcome their marginalised status (Putnam 2000: 22–4). Though the relationship between these two types is complex, Putnam's distinction highlights some moral issues raised by the social capital debate, some of which he deals with in a chapter on the 'dark side of social capital'. For example, while bonding social capital may lie at the heart of the black protest against apartheid, the same kinds of social forces drove the passion of the Ku Klux Klan.

We must return to Pierre Bourdieu in outlining the meaning of 'cultural capital', which he has developed alongside economic, social and symbolic capital as elements in the wider social field. To expand, in Bourdieu's framework for understanding society, a social field is a structured system of positions. These positions, and the relationships that pertain between them, are determined by the distribution of various resources, or forms of capital. Bourdieu distinguishes between economic capital (material resources and wealth), social capital (significant relationships between individuals), symbolic capital (accumulated prestige or honour), and cultural capital which features heavily in Bourdieu's work, particularly in discussions of the generation and maintenance of power in society. In its simple usage it refers to skills and knowledge, acquired through education, which can be used to acquire jobs, money and status. However, Bourdieu deploys 'cultural capital' in a more complex fashion, to capture the ways in which the very minutiae that make up the social identities of the social elite are recognised as indicative of value and currency, so that the dominant social classes are able to sustain their dominant status.

This is most eloquently expressed in Bourdieu's essay on the transmission of social values, 'Cultural Reproduction and Social Reproduction'. Here he takes the example of the French education system to demonstrate how conventions of assessment and the discernment of academic ability work to the advantage of particular social groups. Bourdieu expands, commenting that only particular social classes generally acquire the cultural dispositions required to excel in the academic world, because of the process of the reproduction of cultural capital, advanced by 'familiarisation, that is imperceptible apprenticeships from the family upbringing, which is the mode of acquisition of the instruments of appropriation of the dominant culture of which the dominant classes hold the monopoly' (Bourdieu 1977a: 495). Moreover, by concealing these mechanisms, the education system legitimates them, and ensures their future success (Bourdieu 1977a: 496).

For Bourdieu then, cultural capital is an acquired set of resources – knowledge and skills, but also the behavioural and stylistic conventions attached to them – which serve as a means to achieving, or maintaining, social status. His Marxist leanings are evident in his argument that cultural capital is essentially used by the elite strata of society to maintain their position and, by implication, to constrain others from usurping them from it. In this sense, 'capital' is appropriated and developed in a manner that carries moral, as well as political, implications, built on an analysis of social power and its associated inequalities. For our present discussion, Bourdieu's work is also important in so far as it highlights the ways in which certain forms of capital may be converted into others – education (cultural capital) into employment (economic capital), association with other elites (social capital) into prestige and status (symbolic capital). He maps out a theoretical scheme that draws attention to the complex processes of interaction and exchange that shape the distribution of power in society. Moreover, he demonstrates how experiences at one point in a person's life-course can have a shaping influence upon their advancement at later stages, in very different social spheres. In this respect, he lays the theoretical foundations for an analysis of 'spiritual careers', shaped by the variety and availability of a range of resources drawn upon in the ongoing process of identity formation.

'Capital' has enjoyed a rich history of development that has bequeathed to the social sciences a wealth of theoretical insight. In reaction to Marxian economics, human capital has been presented as a broad concept, intended to capture the non-material aspect of the production process. It incorporates all kinds of human skills and experience that may be theorised as resources likely to confer benefits upon the individual who holds them. These benefits are often presented as economic rewards. Social and cultural capital, while variously conceived, refer to specific sub-species of human capital, and their particular definition makes for more nuanced analyses of human action and opportunity. Furthermore, theoretical subtlety has been accompanied by moral critique, with scholars like Bourdieu and Putnam using 'capital' not only to trace patterns of human empowerment, but also to highlight social inequalities and developments perceived as detrimental to the social good. From this theoretical canvas, in recent years, notions of religious and spiritual capital have emerged.

From 'Religious' to 'Spiritual' Capital

While some studies have sought to shed light on religious behaviour by using an existing 'capital' framework – for example by using Becker's notion of 'human capital' to shed light on issues relating to religious participation (Iannaccone, 1990; Neuman, 1986) – others have responded to the specific challenges of religion by proposing a fresh theory of 'religious' or 'spiritual' capital. In these cases, it is assumed, religion presents such a novel construction and distribution of power that it demands its own nomenclature, namely that it is impossible truly to capture its distinctiveness using the existing concepts of human, social or cultural capital. Again, Pierre Bourdieu is the theorist who has done most to initiate a discussion of a distinctive 'religious capital'.

Throughout his vast corpus of publications, Bourdieu repeatedly conceptualises resources as 'capital' – whether economic, social, cultural or symbolic – as a way of expressing how they function as objects of struggle. 'Capital' is valued because it is comparatively scarce, and individuals and groups compete for it as part of their broader quest for power and legitimation within the social fields in which they find themselves. Bourdieu concerns himself with religion in only a handful of articles (for example Bourdieu 1987; 1991). He is heavily indebted to Max Weber in these articles, particularly in adopting an essentially economic model in understanding religion (Weber 1978). Consequently, he goes to some lengths in describing the 'resources' at stake in the 'religious field'. These are 'the legitimation of the social order, the sanction of wealth and power, and the sense of meaning that religion brings to people's lives' (Rey 2004: 337). In associating such wide-ranging themes with religious capital, Bourdieu is expressing his argument that networks of power often occupy overlapping social fields, so that a position of dominance in the world of finance, for example, may draw, in part, from the symbolic capital accumulated in the fields of culture or religion. An example may be the historical complicity of the Church of England with the institutions of the British state, or the close relationship between Roman Catholicism and political elites in the South American nations. Both reflect cases of religion achieving dominance through strategic political affiliations, and of political hegemonies using the symbols and language of religious tradition as a means of sustaining legitimacy and respectability. Indeed, one of Bourdieu's key claims about religious capital is that religious specialists – and the elites aligned with them – use religion to veil the arbitrary nature of the unjust social order that they represent. By associating themselves with religious institutions, the ruling classes create the illusion that they are themselves religious and moral, and therefore are deserving of their power (Bourdieu 1977b: 183). In this way, the existing social order is religiously sanctioned and those who occupy positions of dominance maintain their privileged status.

This is Bourdieu at his most Marxist, and his argument is in this sense hardly novel, the association of religion with ruling class interests being well known and well rehearsed. However, Bourdieu takes his argument further, identifying what he sees as distinctive about a specifically 'religious' form of capital. This is partly to do with the esoteric or secret knowledge he sees as the preserve of the official priesthood. It is access to this knowledge that distinguishes those who have a monopoly on religious capital from those who are subject to the power that this monopoly realises. Bourdieu expands on the structure of this power in his distinction between 'practical mastery' and 'knowledgeable mastery'. 'Practical mastery' amounts to schemes of thinking and action acquired by familiarisation – namely through experience rather than explicit teaching. It is therefore common to all members of a group, who apply this mastery in the pre-reflexive mode. 'Knowledgeable mastery' is a body of knowledge, systematised and taught through a specialist institution, such as, in the Christian context, a theological training college. These institutions are mandated to produce and reproduce religious capital as a knowledge and competence that sustains the distinction between priest and laity (Bourdieu 1991: 10). Consequently, while Bourdieu allows for some complexity in the distribution of religious power – in his acknowledgement of the broader availability of 'practical mastery' – his analysis is still predominantly shaped by a sharp distinction between religious specialists and those they purport to serve.

The distinctive aspect of this dimension of 'religious capital' relates to how this coveted knowledge is linked to what Bourdieu calls the 'goods of salvation'. For Bourdieu (1987: 132f.;1991b: 15f.), the goods of salvation are most obviously the sacraments, but they may also refer to a form of recognised membership of a church. Broadly speaking, they are *the resources deemed by a religious tradition to be requisite to salvation*. The nature of these 'goods', according to Bourdieu, is controlled by religious specialists, and articulated fully only in the esoteric preserve of knowledgeable mastery. In this respect, religious capital is distinctive in expressing the means for making life meaningful in ultimate terms; it is for this reason, also, that it is so precious and so coveted by ruling powers.

Bourdieu's understanding of religious capital is not without its problems. Not least, it is shaped by a particular appropriation of French Roman Catholicism, specifically in its conceptual organisation around the priest/laity distinction. His treatment is therefore limited, not least as it advances a conceptual scheme that is only applicable to a narrow range of contexts. An uncritical application of Bourdieu's model to non-Christian or indeed non-Roman Catholic contexts would risk serious misrepresentation of the phenomena under study.[3] The argument for the complicity of ruling powers with the religious elite is difficult to sustain in heavily secularised cultures, such as those of late modern Western Europe. His focus on networks of power also means

---

3   In her innovative sociological analysis of contemporary religion, Danièle Hervieu-Léger makes a similar point about the Durkheimian distinction between the sacred and the profane which, she suggests, distorts the Christian distinction between the temporal and the spiritual into a universal aspect of all religious phenomena (Hervieu-Léger 2000: 48–51).

that Bourdieu's analysis, while illuminating on the broader – perhaps global – canvas, is of limited utility when addressing bounded communities like denominations or congregations (Rey 2004: 340). However, the most serious criticisms, which may be levelled at Bourdieu's framework, relate to its inability to cope with the complexities of the contemporary religious landscape, including the expansion of religion into a more detraditionalised spirituality.

Bourdieu presents religious power in essentially dualistic terms, as a struggle between priesthood and laity, thus making little room for a more complex distribution of resources. As Lyon argues, our contemporary age leaves the religious realm increasingly deregulated, so that processes of identity formation are less constrained by older organisations and individuals are able to 'seek their own meaning routes through the postmodern maze' (Lyon 2000: 42). This context of deregulation has generated numerous fresh configurations of religious meaning, so that traditional groups and organisations are increasingly open to or at least available for re-appropriation and reinvention in accordance with the subjective predilections of individuals. The reclamation of Celtic traditions by New Agers, and the growth in syncretistic new religious movements are just two examples. Traditional Christian ideas are also being reinterpreted and reconfigured in light of changing cultures and the changing perceptions of those within them. For instance, in the UK, the USA and Australasia, networks emerging from the margins of the evangelical tradition have explored new forms of community organisation and corporate identity – as they put it, new ways of 'being church' – that reflect their equally experimental approach to prayer, ritual and collective worship (Guest and Taylor 2006). Within such a context, the sources of spiritual significance are not restricted by the boundaries of traditional religious hierarchies, but are more freely available within a complex matrix of exchange. As Verter comments on Bourdieu's approach:

> This model treats religion as an institution but not as a disposition, as an intricate system of coercion but not as a liquid species of capital. In short, it employs categories that are too rigid to account for the fluidities of today's spiritual marketplace. (Verter 2003: 151)

As a consequence of his emphasis upon the dominant position of the priesthood, Bourdieu also leaves little room for the empowered lay religious agent. The religious identity of the individual is always constrained by the fact that religious capital is controlled by religious institutions and by those who represent them. Recent studies of religion in the contemporary West have increasingly used the language of consumerism, with individuals presented as religious consumers, empowered to construct reflexively their own identities within a detraditionalised context. We might go further, and speak of 'spiritual entrepreneurs', those innovators engaged in the creation of fresh religious forms, and we only need think of the explosion of religion on the world wide web to appreciate the opportunities in this field, both reactionary and subversive. Finally, the power that Bourdieu invests in the hegemonies of the church depends in large part on their control of religious capital in the form of esoteric knowledge. Given the deregulated exchange of information and cultural resources in late modernity – bolstered by accelerated globalisation – it is difficult to sustain such a notion. The knowledge that was once the preserve of elites is now widely available, at least throughout the advanced economies of the West. Power has become more complex, and can no longer be conceived as purely grounded in ownership and control of esoteric knowledge. The empowerment of the late modern individual simply precludes this notion, traditionally conceived.

It is important to stress that these criticisms do not seek to advocate a radical subjectivisation thesis, that presents the individual reflexively constructing his or her own spiritual identity free from any external constraint (Giddens 1991). Religious or spiritual capital is best presented as subject to collective boundaries, but if an abstract collective metaphor is appropriate, then it is not the congregation, organisation, denomination or church, so much as the network. Indeed, in late modernity, the relationship between religion and locality is contentious at the very least. In a context characterised by social uprootedness, selective and temporary community allegiance, and 'glocalisation', religious identities are more likely to be sustained by discrete networks, forged throughout the life course in accordance with individual tastes and lifestyles (Hirst 2003). Indeed, Putnam's 'bonding' and 'bridging' forms of social capital may provide one way into this problem, highlighting as they do the complex ways in which reciprocal relations both reinforce collective boundaries and generate fresh interactive networks, both of which provide a context of exchange for emerging forms of 'spiritual capital'.

This more open conception of religious resources, allowing for a more deregulated exchange and the empowerment of individuals, may go some way towards overcoming the shortcomings of Bourdieu's presentation of religious capital. In reflection on the recent popularity of endeavours into things 'spiritual', a few authors have already begun to use the term 'spiritual capital',[4] although they differ in what they mean by this. For example, it is used within two of the most well-known and influential recent discussions of religious life in the contemporary USA – Wade Clark Roof's *Spiritual Marketplace* (1999) and Nancy Ammerman's *Congregation and Community* (1997), although in both books, 'spiritual capital' is not defined, nor is it even mentioned outside of the titles of concluding sections. This reflects the ambiguous utility of the term 'spirituality' – it is a useful category in a context that shies away from pinning down religious phenomena with clear-cut definitions.[5]

---

4   While achieving popular appeal in recent years, the use of the term 'spiritual capital' to refer to a source of positive social energy can be traced back at least as far as the nineteenth century. Woolcock points to the case of German social critic Adam Muller, whose opposition to Adam Smith's materialist economics included a conviction that a community's stock of 'spiritual capital' was instrumental in determining levels of economic prosperity. Muller's understanding of spiritual capital appears to have been broad-based, incorporating cultural values and the 'organic unity of society and state' (quoted in Woolcock 1998: 199). His opposition to free trade suggests a conception that focuses on church and society as an integrated force for moral restraint, necessary in an equitable and just economic system.

5   An alternative take on spiritual capital is offered by Robert Wuthnow, who identifies it as a sub-specie of social capital. For Wuthnow, spiritual capital characterises 'activities that

A more fruitful way forward may be found in a theoretically sophisticated discussion of 'spiritual capital', published by US-based sociologist, Bradford Verter. He acknowledges the problems that were earlier identified in Bourdieu's model of religious capital, but he finds enough in Bourdieu's later writings that allow a refinement of this model into a more subtle and multi-dimensional theory, which he calls 'spiritual capital'. Verter's starting point is to acknowledge the deregulated religious marketplace and the fluid nature that religion takes on as it functions as a cultural resource within this context:

> Thus, if religious capital is conceived à la Bourdieu as something that is produced and accumulated within a hierocratic institutional framework, spiritual capital may be regarded as a more widely diffused commodity, governed by more complex patterns of production, distribution, exchange, and consumption. (Verter 2003: 158)

Seeking to distance himself from the work of Stark and Finke (2000), which relies heavily on rational choice theory, Verter does not wish to imply that spiritual capital operates within a 'free market'. As he comments, there is no fixed scale in the cultural field, 'competitors do not enjoy equal advantages' (Verter 2003:158). Rather, in keeping with his theoretical indebtedness to Bourdieu, Verter acknowledges that individuals occupy positions of relative strength or weakness, depending on the capital one possesses, and on one's relationship to the processes that shape the distribution of that capital. In other words, spiritual capital is not simply accumulated in proportion to individual effort; its relative distribution is influenced by existing structures of power (Swartz 1996: 78).

Drawing from Bourdieu's classification of cultural capital, Verter distinguishes between three different forms of spiritual capital: the embodied state, the objectified state and the institutionalised state (Bourdieu 1985). The *embodied* state refers to the personal disposition made up of a collection of knowledge, tastes, and other resources an individual amasses throughout their experience, inculcated through education or a process of unconscious socialisation. It is a form of spiritual capital embodied in what Bourdieu calls 'habitus', that is 'the socially structured mode of apprehending and acting in the world' (Verter 2003: 159). In the *objectified* state, spiritual capital appears as material and symbolic commodities, including theological knowledge and ideology. If the embodied state refers to embodied processes of consumption, the objectified state refers to what is consumed. The two are intimately related, not least because it is often necessary to possess certain knowledge before one knows how to properly consume or appropriate spiritual capital. An example would be the act of taking Eucharist in an Anglican Church, which involves an intricate range of learnt behaviours as well as responses to liturgy, and an acquired body of knowledge

---

have a specific religious emphasis or that are explicitly concerned with relating people to the sacred or divine ...' (Wuthnow 2000: 128). Most, but not all, of the examples Wuthnow cites are collective activities, such as discussing religious texts, group prayer or group study, and all are interpreted as a means of generating spiritual capital.

drawn upon in interpreting and affirming the significance of the event. Finally, spiritual capital exists in an *institutionalised* state in the power religious organisations possess in determining the meaning of and access to the 'goods of salvation'. It is in its institutionalised state that spiritual capital is most clearly visible and demarcated.

Verter's understanding of 'spiritual capital' retains Bourdieu's sensitivity to power relations as well as his Weberian tendency always to seek out the complex relationships between religious phenomena and the non-religious forces that infuse them. However, he adapts Bourdieu's work to the late modern context, re-conceiving spiritual capital as a fluid, multi-faceted phenomenon, emerging from a variety of sources and taking on a variety of forms as it is actively negotiated within the lives of individuals, and among the networks in which they are active. His distinction between the embodied, objectified and institutional states illustrates how spiritual capital takes on numerous forms and suggests some arguments for how it may lend itself to being converted into other forms of capital. For example, spiritual capital may be vested in a position of institutional advantage – that of a senior cleric or religious official, perhaps – which is used to acquire symbolic capital or prestige. Or it may be identified in objectified religious knowledge, perhaps acquired through specialised training, which is later mobilised in a broader arena as cultural capital. In this Verter offers a sophisticated scheme that is rich in theoretical insight and multifaceted in its scope.

Following this extended theoretical discussion, it is now possible to explore some of the heuristic advantages of this concept of 'spiritual capital' by putting it to use within a particular case study. The research addressed below is appropriate to the purposes of this chapter, as it highlights both the fluidity of spiritual resources and their propensity to be converted into other forms of capital under certain conditions. The research is into the children of senior Anglican clergymen, and presents spiritual capital as a powerful but ambiguous entity, diffusing outwards from the central hierarchies of the church, through the families of its leaders and into the wider world. In this sense it becomes a dynamic metaphor for the resources transmitted across generations.

Spiritual Capital and Clergy Children: A Case Study

From 2001 until 2004, Douglas Davies and I conducted the 'Clergy and British Society' project, tracing the lives and influence of senior Anglican clergy from 1940 to 2000 (Davies and Guest 2007). A major part of this project concerned the adult children of these now retired Church of England bishops, their careers and religious convictions, focusing upon the extent to which they have taken on the values affirmed by and in their childhood clerical homes. Callum Brown, in his important rethinking of the secularisation problem, *The Death of Christian Britain* (2001), rightly emphasises the family as a key factor in determining the fate of Christianity as a significant social force. Further research has reaffirmed the importance of the family as an enduring shaping influence over the values individuals profess in adulthood (Bengtson et al. 2002). We do not exist as isolated late modern individuals, but within persistent networks – of family, friends and colleagues – that continue to shape our identities. In light of these findings, we asked whether there are patterns in the acceptance, rejection and evolution of values learnt through being a member of a senior clergyman's family.

These questions are easily reformulated in terms of spiritual capital – its generation, transmission, maintenance and evolution in different contexts. Indeed, one might see this project as a natural development of Bourdieu's work, especially given his pre-occupation with the religious capital vested in ecclesiastical hegemonies, and his own jointly authored study of power struggles among French bishops (Bourdieu and Saint Martin 1982). In our research, we move beyond Bourdieu's study, which examined the lives of celibate Roman Catholic bishops, by exploring how spiritual capital is passed on *via* the families of clergy who are married with children. Bourdieu's focus was upon how power is controlled and restricted by religious hierarchies. Our own concern has been with how the cultural resources nurtured by and around these hierarchies are transmitted outwards, through the next generation and into the wider social world. We work on the assumption that the family may serve not just as an enduringly influential shaper of social values, but also as a significant factor in the empowerment of individuals, who acquire stocks of capital by virtue of their upbringing – Bourdieu's 'familiarisation' – and through experiences and associations brought about through family roles and personal connections.

The project involved two major research techniques, developed with specific aims and objectives in mind. The need to gauge the demographic background and religious and career trajectories of respondents meant that a questionnaire survey was necessary, and we received detailed questionnaire responses from 225 individuals, including retired Anglican bishops, their wives and their adult offspring. The further need for a detailed examination of how bishops, their wives and children make sense of their identities in relation to the spiritual capital of the Church of England required extended interviews, and we conducted 51 recorded, semi-structured conversations with a sample from among our survey respondents. These allowed us to examine how these individuals currently reflect on their experiences as members of a clergy family, on family life, its peculiarities, benefits and problems, and how these relate to the subsequent development of outlooks and values which have become pertinent in the emergence of professional and religious identities. While we are enquiring about specific historical events and experiences, we have been asking individuals to recount them often many years after these events took place, and therefore through the inevitable filters of time and subsequent life experience. As such, we are not seeking to uncover causal historical relationships or determinative trends in generational value transmission. While our questionnaire data allows us to place our findings within a solid historical, ecclesiastical and cultural context, our interest has been primarily in the narrative and subjective construction of spiritual capital by the individuals who have taken part in our study.

Our analysis of questionnaire and interview data revealed that the experience of life within the clerical home – for the majority a vicarage, and later the bishop's residence – could be seen as the axis from which orientations towards religion and professional life later emerged. It was this experience that served as a persistent reference point for clergy children as they sought to make sense of their current attitudes to these topics.

We found that it was indeed possible to describe the most dominant characteristics of this upbringing in the clergy home using a capital framework. For example, while Anglican bishops are not paid high salaries, they are often accorded a sizeable and sometimes rather opulent residence, a luxury that was associated by their children with material comfort and a sense of status. Significant cultural capital was channelled into family life through the educational advantages enjoyed by the bishop, and often his wife also, and these advantages were often perpetuated by sending their children to prestigious schools, sometimes supported by a bursary for clerical children. In some cases, intellectual discussion of current affairs was introduced into family life so that their children entered adulthood with a distinctive theological and moral literacy. Of course, regular practical involvement in church life and liturgy also invested a certain 'embodied knowledge', augmenting this stock of what Bourdieu might call 'practical mastery' of a particular Christian tradition. The prestige and social standing vicariously accorded by virtue of their father's position also proved in some cases to be a valued source of symbolic capital, and the social capital accumulated through the bishop's local and national contacts appears to have secured some opportunities later in life. If there are advantages to be gained through having a familial connection to the spiritual elite, they are many, and complex.

All of these forms of capital were channelled through and influenced by the clergy household, and were recalled as positive and empowering experiences by the clergy children to whom we spoke. Many facets of this experience, however, also have a negative side. The moral and spiritual standing accorded to the father, for example, was often projected on to his children in a way that fostered unfair behavioural expectations, both at school where the vicar or bishop was sometimes well known, and in the parish, where the status of the 'clergy child' comes with an ambiguous set of associations. Some clergy children also felt that their individual spiritual identity was diminished because it was always perceived in relation to their father's status. This was not helped for some by the deferential behaviour of churchgoers towards the bishop, often perceived as confusing spirituality with hierarchical status, vestments and titles. Most striking, perhaps, were the ways in which the experiences of the clerical home were recalled, an emphasis placed on how it was predominantly a focus for the pastoral care of outsiders. This was recalled positively by some – as a model of altruism to be emulated later in life – but thoroughly negatively by others, who resented the fact that their needs always seemed to come second to the parish, that their father was often absent, and that the private boundaries of their home were frequently compromised.

In many ways the adult lives of the bishops' children of our study represent the successful transmission of the capital available to them by virtue of their upbringing. The vast majority had been to university and had been professionally trained in a particular field. Material advantages also extended into professional life, with many occupying lucrative, high status jobs in a variety of careers. Yet their orientation to their professional identities was distinctive, in many cases characterised by a commitment to the wider community and a tendency to measure professional output not by financial criteria but with reference to moral integrity. Indeed, this attitude is reflected in career choice, with over 50 per cent pursuing a career devoted to the care or nurture of others, such as teaching, social work or medicine, and only 20 per cent in private-sector business or commerce. A resistance towards a materialistic framework and a commitment to civic mindedness is also reflected in the high percentage of clergy children heavily involved in voluntary work. Our results suggest that the children of Anglican bishops are far more likely to engage in voluntary work than the average British citizen, especially where religious/church-related work is concerned.

In terms of religious identity, the picture is more ambiguous. The proportions of atheists and agnostics reflect the national picture; practically none, however, have gravitated into non-conformist, non-Christian or 'alternative' traditions. The majority (75 per cent) maintain that they have a Christian identity of some kind, and almost half claim they attend church at least once each week. However, follow up interviews and a closer inspection of the questionnaire returns suggests a huge diversity of 'Christian' orientations, including nominal Anglicans, uncertain seekers open to a range of spiritual resources, civic minded liberal churchgoers committed to their local parish, and left-leaning evangelical activists. Modes of religious practice appear to be as diverse as the moral and religious positions from which they supposedly emerge.

A more illuminating analysis emerges when we examine this population of clergy children not in terms of static categories, but in terms of the development of their spiritual careers, a proposal in keeping with Verter's understanding of spiritual capital as a liquid resource, open to development and transformation into different forms in light of changing life experiences. This approach, especially when facilitated by extensive narrative data gathered *via* interviews, allows for more interesting patterns to be identified, patterns suggestive of a negotiation of spiritual capital which is in large part a response to the ambiguous experience of being raised in a clerical household, as described above. The key factor here is that, within the clerical household, the boundaries of the worlds of work, religion and family are frequently and profoundly blurred, so that each field of life experience invades another. This is most evident in the recollections of the clerical home: a bounded domestic space, frequently compromised by its use by non-family-members, be they parishioners, other clergy or church officials, as if it were a public space. It was at the same time a home, a place for the father's work, and a context for the dispensing of pastoral care and spiritual guidance. This is an ambiguous legacy, and while some recall rich encounters with interesting and influential individuals, others focus on a sense of disorientation and alienation. Indeed, we may expect this blurring of boundaries to have been experienced as problematic, especially during formative years, when clergy children begin to learn that this arrangement is abnormal and counter to the dominant cultural trend. Indeed, as many have commented before, the predominant way in which religious life is managed in the UK is as a private matter, qualitatively distinguished and therefore separated from matters of professional life, and often from the home also.

Analysis of interview data suggests that many clergy children adopt a particular strategy in making sense of their current identities, focused on unravelling these boundaries and maintaining an arrangement that keeps them discrete. Thereby spiritual capital is negotiated in a way that harnesses its advantages, but within a life situation that maintains the home/religion/work boundaries these individuals have learnt as normal and desirable. For example, some respondents had sought to separate the notion of Christian faith from the institution of the Church of England. This allows them to account for their negative experiences during childhood as consequences of a flawed church rather than lay them at the door of Christianity as a whole. This also enables them to separate pressures on the family from Christianity itself, by associating them with professional pressures brought to bear on their father by the Church, thus freeing up Christianity as a palatable spiritual resource for appropriation in adult life and within the upbringing of their own children. Other respondents acknowledge the values they received because of their upbringing, and see a direct link to their father's vocation as a clergyman. They also embrace these values in their own lives, but make sense of their worth as moral, social or – in many cases – professional skills. They do their job as their father would do his job as a vicar, even though they are a corporate manager, teacher or civil servant. Hence, values are reconceived and rationalised as professional values, thus separating religion from professional life, while maintaining the spiritual capital acquired from being raised in a clerical household. Both of these instances serve as strategies for the negotiation of spiritual capital within the lives of individuals living in late modern Britain. In accordance with Verter's understanding, this conceives spiritual capital as a multi-faceted phenomenon, able to be transformed into other forms, but in dialogue with the boundaries established by early life experience.

Interestingly, some sons and daughters of Anglican bishops have, by contrast, taken the family model associated with their parents further. That is, they have adopted a more radical integration of the spheres of religion, work and family life, often in order to express a more counter-cultural form of Christianity. Some of these cases are conservative evangelical males who have rebelled against the more liberal Anglicanism of their fathers, or daughters who have married clergymen themselves. An inversion of spiritual capital is here in evidence, as individuals use their father's orientation to the church as a foil for their own emerging faith stance. One respondent's comments were particularly illuminating, suggesting his sense of independence as an individual and as a Christian depended on his defining himself in contradistinction from his father. Reflecting this point, he stated:

> My own faith was formed in an evangelical stable in a way my dad's wasn't, and really that became the way I think [I] expressed my own independence through my teenaged years. Dad and I were at our least close during my teens, and I became quite involved in the charismatic movement and became quite militant in my evangelicalism, and really thought my dad's liberal Catholicism was worthless. But my own sense of my values and my self as a Christian person were very much clearer for me ….

It is important to note that a process of resolution has since occurred between this individual and his father, so that his 'rebellion' may be interpreted as a necessary but temporary episode on a longer spiritual journey. Most importantly, as with many of the other cases we examined, a distinctive sense of identity was seen as emerging from a successful negotiation of the spiritual capital inherited, whether this is through a separation of life spheres, or by a more thoroughgoing integration of them.

Conclusion

To conceive of spirituality in terms of 'spiritual capital', as subject to the acquisition, development, maintenance and transmission of cultural resources, brings with it numerous advantages. It highlights issues of power inequality as shaped by, but not restricted to, religious institutions; it facilitates an analysis of religious identity in terms of a spiritual career, which pays greater attention to the flow of influences and resources acquired through the life course; it offers a theoretical way into the complex issue of non-institutional religion, as a matter of resources positioned within overlapping networks; and, most clearly within the context of the present study, it allows a clearer picture to be painted of religion as an inter-generational phenomenon.

While deploying the concept of 'spiritual capital' within the context of the 'Clergy and British Society' project revealed some valuable insights into its utility, it also exposed some theoretical limitations. Spiritual capital highlights the advantages of approaching religious identity in longitudinal terms, that is as a process of development and change, and subtle adjustment within the context of individual biographies, and draws our attention to the exchange of resources that invest power and influence. In this it invites particular research methodologies, and an examination of narrative in the construction of identity may be a fruitful way forward. However, our application of the concept also exposed certain lessons for the future. Not least, the example of clergy children highlights the importance of allowing that spiritual capital may not always be a uniformly or persistently positive resource for those who possess it. This is a useful illustration of how Verter differs from rational choice theorists Stark and Finke, who in their treatment of religious capital refer to 'mastery of and attachment to a particular religious culture' (Stark and Finke 2000: 120–25). Verter is right to criticise this model (Verter 2003: 158). It implies a fixed and orthodox appropriation of religious tradition; if one assumes mastery of a religious culture as a criterion for measuring religious capital, one indirectly aligns oneself with the authoritative version of that culture that emerges; alternative readings become at best shortfalls and at worst heresies. The example of clergy children brings to light the fact that that which is conceived as capital – as a resource for deployment – can be appropriated as a negative influence, so that emerging strategies for action and non-action are counter-reactions, grounded in discontentment rather than positive empowerment. Spiritual capital can be a source of struggle as well as a means to strength.

A second lesson relates to a shortcoming of capital theory generally, one that was exposed during the course of our project, and that relates to its in-built assumptions about human behaviour, assumptions that are heightened when set within Verter's vision of a deregulated late modernity. While Bourdieu talks of various forms of capital as residing in collective bodies, he does not speak of how capital may be deployed positively in the construction of them, in the forging of moral identities and in the ongoing development of moral communities. Capital, as our project discovered, is an essential factor not just in individual advancement, but also in the emergence and building of communities through genuine commitment to a greater order. (The significant commitment of the clergy children of our study to civic-mindedness and voluntary action may be an instructive example here). Capital does have the capacity to facilitate a positive expression beyond self-interest, and I would venture to say that this possibility includes, but extends beyond Putnam's claims about social capital as a social good. One way forward might point to the insights of the symbolic exchange theory ultimately derived from the classic sociology of Mauss (1954). This approach to social life, especially as recently developed in the work of people such as Jacques Godbout (Godbout and Caille 1998), is also premised on the idea of exchange, but acknowledges the importance of the quality of relationships through which this exchange take place, and suggests that the act of giving is as important as the advantage enjoyed by receiving particular commodities. A synthesis of these ideas generates some creative possibilities in the development of spiritual capital theory, and this argument is explored further in the volume emerging from the 'Clergy and British Society' project (Davies and Guest 2007).

Aside from the slipperiness and unanswered questions, 'spiritual capital' demands consideration, if only because it opens up some age-old questions inherited long ago from classical sociology. Just as spirituality depends upon institutionalisation for its continuance and consolidation into a 'tradition', so in the context of late modernity, does this 'spirituality' require a means of breaking out of its traditions in order to infiltrate assumed secular domains of social life. In other words, to explore 'spirituality' is to address the age-old Weberian tension between the originating experiences of religion and its later institutions, but to engage with the problem in reverse. That is, to take another Weberian model, we are not concerned with how charisma is routinised, but in how charisma breaks out of institutions in ways which pervade wider spheres of influence. Moreover, the emerging 'spiritual capital' is not a vague and rootless entity, following a peripatetic and voyeuristic tour amongst the various cynical outlets of the spiritual marketplace. Rather, it is a liquid flow of ideas and values that, while uprooted from their original institutional context, are nevertheless shaped by the traditions out of which they emerged, traditions that still steer their course, mould their practical expression and infuse the language in which they are affirmed, silenced or challenged.

Bibliography

Ammerman, N.T. (1997), *Congregation and Community*, New Brunswick, NJ: Rutgers University Press.

Becker, G.S. (1964), *Human Capital: A Theoretical and Empirical Analysis, with Special Reference to Education*, New York: National Bureau of Economic Research.

Beckford, J.A. (1989), *Religion and Advanced Industrial Society*, London: Unwin Hyman.

Bengtson, V.L., T.J. Biblarz, and R.E. Roberts (2002), *How Families Still Matter: A Longitudinal Study of Youth in Two Generations*, Cambridge: Cambridge University Press.

Bourdieu, P. (1977a), 'Cultural Reproduction and Social Reproduction', in J. Karabel and A.H. Halsey (eds), *Power and Ideology in Education*, Oxford: Oxford University Press, pp. 487–511.

Bourdieu, P. (1977b), *Outline of a Theory of Practice*, Cambridge: Cambridge University Press.

Bourdieu, P. (1985), 'The Forms of Capital', in J. G. Richardson (ed.), *Handbook Of Theory and Research for the Sociology of Education*, New York: Greenwood, pp. 241–58.

Bourdieu, P. (1987), 'Legitimation and Structured Interests in Weber's Sociology Of Religion', in S. Lash and S. Whimster, *Max Weber, Rationality and Modernity*, London: Allen and Unwin, pp. 119–36.

Bourdieu, P. (1991), 'Genesis and Structure of the Religious Field', *Comparative Social Research*, 13: 1–44.

Bourdieu, P. and J.C. Passeron (1977), *Reproduction in Education, Society and Culture*, London: Sage.

Bourdieu, P. and M. de Saint-Martin (1982), 'La sainte famille: L'episcopat francais dans le camp du pouvoir', *Actes de la Recherche en Sciences Sociales*, 44/45: 2–53.

Brewer, A. (1984), *A Guide to Marx's Capital*, Cambridge: Cambridge University Press.

Brown, C.G. (2001), *The Death of Christian Britain*, London: Routledge.

Coleman, J. (1990) *Foundations of Social Theory*, Cambridge, MA and London: Belknap Press of Harvard University.

Coleman, J. (2000), 'Social Capital and the Creation of Human Capital', in P. Dasgupta and I. Serageldin (eds), *Social Capital: Multifaceted Perspective*, Washington, DC: World Bank, pp. 13-39.

Davies, D. and M. Guest (2007), *Bishops, Wives and Children: Spiritual Capital Across the Generations*, Aldershot: Ashgate.

Durkheim, E. (1995), *The Elementary Forms of Religious Life* (trans. K.E. Fields), New York: The Free Press.

Foley, D. (1986), *Understanding Capital: Marx's Economic Theory*, Cambridge, MA; London: Harvard University Press.

Giddens, A. (1991), *Modernity and Self Identity. Self and Society in the Late Modern Age*, Cambridge: Polity Press.

Godbout, J. and A. Caille (1998), *The World of the Gift*, Montreal and London: McGill-Queen's University Press.

Guest, M. and S. Taylor, (2006), 'The Post-Evangelical Emerging Church: Innovations in New Zealand and the UK', *International Journal for the Study of the Christian Church*, 6(1): 49–64.

Heelas, P. (2002), 'The Spiritual Revolution: From "Religion" to "Spirituality"', in L. Woodhead, L., P. Fletcher, H. Kawanami and D. Smith (eds), *Religions in The Modern World*, London: Routledge, pp. 357–77.

Heelas, P. and L. Woodhead (2005), *The Spiritual Revolution: Why Religion is Giving Way to Spirituality*, Oxford: Blackwell.

Hervieu-Léger, D. (2000), *Religion as a Chain of Memory* (trans. by Simon Lee), Oxford: Polity Press.

Hirst, R. (2003), 'Social Networks and Personal Beliefs: An Example from Modern Britain', in G. Davie, P. Heelas and L. Woodhead (eds), *Predicting Religion: Christian, Secular and Alternative Futures*, Aldershot: Ashgate, pp. 86–94.

Iannacone, L. (1990), 'Religious Practice: A Human Capital Approach', *Journal for the Scientific Study of Religion*, 29(3): 297–314.

Jenkins, R. (1992), *Pierre Bourdieu*, London: Routledge.

Loury, G.C. (1981), 'Intergenerational Transfers and the Distribution of Earnings', *Econometrica*, 49(4): 843–67.

Lyon, D. (2000), *Jesus in Disneyland. Religion in Postmodern Times*, Cambridge: Polity.

Marx, K. (1970), *Capital*, London: Dent.

Mauss, M. (1954), *The Gift: Forms and Functions of Exchange in Archaic Societies*, London: Routledge and Kegan Paul.

Miller, D.E. (1997), *Reinventing American Protestantism: Christianity in the New Millenium*, Berkeley, CA: University of California Press.

Neuman, S. (1986), 'Religious Observance within a Human Capital Framework: Theory and Application', *Applied Economics*, 18: 1193–202.

Putnam, R. (2000), *Bowling Alone: The Collapse and Revival of American Community*, New York and London: Simon and Schuster.

Rey, T. (2004), 'Marketing the Goods of Salvation: Bourdieu on Religion', *Religion*, 34(4): 331–43.

Roof, W.C. (1999), *Spiritual Marketplace: Baby Boomers and the Remaking of American Religion*, Princeton, NJ: Princeton University Press.

Stark, R. and R. Finke (2000), *Acts of Religion: Explaining the Human Side of Religion*, Berkeley, CA: University of California Press.

Swartz, D. (1996), 'Bridging the Study of Culture and Religion: Pierre Bourdieu's Political Economy of Symbolic Power', *Sociology of Religion*, 57(1): 71–85.

Tipton, S.M. (1982), *Getting Saved from the Sixties: Moral Meaning in Conversion and Cultural Change*, Berkeley and Los Angeles: University of California Press.

Verter, B. (2003), 'Spiritual Capital: Theorising Religion with Bourdieu against Bourdieu', *Sociological Theory*, 21(2): 150–74.

Weber, M. (1978), *Economy and Society*, Berkeley, CA: University of California Press.

Woolcock, M. (1998), 'Social Capital and Economic Development: Toward a Theoretical Synthesis and Policy Framework', *Theory and Society*, 27(2): 151–208.

Wuthnow, R. (2000), 'How Religious Groups Promote Forgiving: A National Study', *Journal for the Scientific Study of Religion*, 39(2): 125–39.

Chapter 11

The Embodied Spirituality of the Post-Boomer Generations

Richard W. Flory and Donald E. Miller

We live in a world that is dominated by two significant and interconnected realities; we are bombarded with visual symbols virtually every minute of every day, and national cultures are increasingly converging into a global market culture. Music, movies, and television like MTV, its offspring and imitators, are shared across the globe, not only as avenues for artistic expression, but for the marketing of commodities, whether those commodities are Nike, Jesus, or individual identity.

But is this any different than 30 years ago? We think there is at least one significant difference: the current digital revolution has democratised access to information and images, and has made that access interactive rather than passive. Digital technology in computers, cameras, cell phones (with cameras), photography and filmmaking software is now relatively inexpensive and is in widespread use. Rather than being passive observers of the products of these digital tools, people are now active participants in producing, reproducing, and manipulating images, conversations such as on blogs, music, and the like. Music, television shows and movies are all swapped through digital networks, often with their content manipulated along the way. Digital cameras allow just about anyone to be able to make a movie, create a photo essay or exhibit, or just provide a more graphic way to display or sell goods (on the nature of the new digital media, see Manovich 2002; Stephens 1998; on effects of digital media, see Burnett 2005; Hansen 2004; Ryan 2003; Tapscott 1998).

The children of Baby-Boomers, whom we will simply refer to here as 'Post-Boomers', have come of age and had their consciousness shaped within this cultural context about themselves, what they believe, what counts as valid knowledge, and who – or what – has authentic cultural authority. As media theorist Douglas Kellner (1995: 1) has argued,

> A media culture has emerged in which images, sounds, and spectacles help produce the fabric of everyday life, dominating leisure time, shaping political views and social behavior, and providing the materials out of which people forge their very identities.

It is this new media culture, Kellner argues, that shapes worldviews, defining 'what is considered good or bad, positive or negative, moral or evil' (Kellner 1995: 1).

This has significant implications for religion and spirituality, especially for Post-Boomers who have 'native' digital knowledge. Despite the fact that they live in a symbolically saturated culture, Post-Boomers, particularly within large segments of Christianity, have had as their primary religious experience a symbolically impoverished environment. Churches look like warehouses with little if any religious imagery, 'worship' is organised around passive audiences that might raise their hands in praise to God, but rarely if ever interact with each other or the sacred in any form other than a sterile, cognitive recognition of the Other. Yet in the rest of their lives, Post-Boomers are actively producing and reproducing visual, aural, and physical experiences for themselves, and for and with others.

This chapter is based on a larger study of Post-Boomer religious activity in which we set out to discover the ways that Post-Boomers, given their cultural context and understandings, approach religion and spirituality.[1] Although we found several different forms of religious activity, including a relatively unreflective appropriation of cultural artefacts such as movies, digital/visual effects, and simulating a coffee house/club atmosphere for worship, as well as others who are actively resisting this type of cultural appropriation and view it as uncritically accepting of postmodern values, we also found many within the Post-Boomer generations who are actively seeking new forms of religious experience, from reinvigorating ancient symbols and rituals within their own religious traditions, to borrowing from other traditions and even creating their own rituals and symbols in the service of an embodied spiritual experience.

For this chapter, we discuss two emerging forms of Post-Boomer religion that are both engaging with the larger culture and are oriented toward the development of a deeper, more meaningful spirituality. First we discuss those we call 'Reclaimers', Post-Boomers who are discovering the liturgical traditions, such as the Anglican, Orthodox, and Catholic churches, and *reclaiming* ancient rituals and symbols in their quest for spiritual experience and expression. Second, we discuss 'Innovators', Post-Boomers who use digital technology, as well as more traditional forms of artistic expression, and other visual media in *innovative* ways in order to create a religious experience that utilises all of the senses, and in the process are reinventing rituals and symbols within their own context, often outside of established religious institutional settings. In each, these young people are rediscovering and creating new ways of experiencing the sacred that are rooted in both ancient practice and modern concern and desire.

Beginning with Robert Bellah's *Habits of the Heart* (1985), the dominant theme within the sociological study of spirituality in the USA has been the individual in pursuit of her or his own, often idiosyncratic, spiritual journey, especially as epitomised by 'Sheilaism'. This individualist theme has continued in such studies as Wade Clark Roof's investigations of Baby Boomer religion (Roof 1993; 1999; 2000), and Robert Wuthnow's studies of small groups (1994) and of spirituality since the

---

1   An earlier version of this chapter was published by the Alban Institute in its fall 2004 issue of Congregations magazine. For the larger study, see our *Finding Faith: The Spiritual Quest of the Post Boomer Generation* (New Jersey: Rutgers University Press, 2008).

1950s (Wuthnow 1998; 2001). Taken together, these studies suggest that particularly since the 1960s, spirituality has become decoupled from religion, with many people pursuing their own private, individualistic, and non-institutionalised form of spiritual fulfilment where the individual spiritual quest for fulfilment takes precedence over membership in, or commitment to, the religious community.

More recent work, however, has begun to show that there is more to the story of spirituality in America than these studies show. Historian Leigh Schmidt (2005) has shown that the individualistic strain of spirituality that Bellah traces to Ralph Waldo Emerson, Walt Whitman and the American transcendentalists has often included a commitment to public involvement, usually to progressive social and political goals, and can thus provide a model for linking spirituality and public involvement in the modern context. Similarly, Greg Stanczak and Donald Miller (2002: 23) have identified an 'engaged spirituality' in which they find that individuals have a personal spiritual commitment that includes active engagement in both transforming individual lives and larger social, civic and religious institutions in which they are active, and argue that 'spirituality, including private self-reflection, must be understood as engaged in, engaged by, and engaged within individual, interpersonal, and social contexts.

The two forms of Post-Boomer spirituality that we describe in this chapter are more similar to the latter examples of spirituality than the former, in particular in terms of their commitment to a religious community within which they seek a physical experience of the spiritual, and actively live out their spiritual lives as part of their commitment to both the religious community and surrounding community. Thus, this *embodied spirituality* is both personal and social – Post-Boomers seek individual spiritual experience and fulfilment in the community of believers, where meaning is both constructed and directed outward in service to others, both within the religious community and in the community where they are located. This experiential, community/other oriented spirituality makes sense in the context of what others have written about who we are calling Post-Boomers. For example, Richard Florida, in his study of 'the creative class' – which would include most Post-Boomers, certainly all we interviewed – emphasises their pursuit of various experiences, not as spectators and not as in pre-packaged experiences (such as tours, Disneyland), but as a product of their own creation (Florida 2002; see especially 166–7, 182–7). Similarly, different studies of the interactive nature of digital technology and image representation/production show that the observer – or better the co-creator or even re-creator – can participate in the creation, re-creation, manipulation, and dissemination of various digital media (see Hansen 2004; Ryan 2003; Tapscott 1998).

We argue that what we are finding can best be understood in contrast to Max Weber's 'inner-worldly asceticism', in which the individual eschewed emotional and sensuous enjoyment in favour of a rationally ordered life, and Robert Bellah's 'utilitarian individualism', in which the individual seeks both material success and personal fulfilment. In this, Post-Boomers represent a new religious type, what we are calling 'expressive communalism', in which they are seeking spiritual experience and fulfilment in embodied form through community and through various expressive forms of their spirituality, both private and public. By this we mean that the individual finds individual spiritual fulfilment through a physical experience – whether visual, aural, or physical – primarily in the context of the religious community, and further, that the primary goal is not necessarily individual fulfilment but living out, or embodying, their spiritual commitment publicly and in the larger community, through various types of service activities and cultural engagement with the community.

Methods

We began this project with some of the basic findings of our *GenX Religion* book as a starting place (Flory and Miller 2000) in particular such ideas as the experiential dimension of GenX religious activities, their entrepreneurial skills at establishing new and culturally savvy organisations, the extent to which their religious identity is rooted in the religious community, and their emphasis on 'authenticity' of one's life, outlook, and religious faith as being a primary component of how they view themselves and each other. We also utilised certain key informants that we had met either through our research proper, or as a result of the publication, and then began to follow the leads they provided us with, as well as many that we discovered and developed on our own. Although most of these were personal contacts, there was a good proportion that was Internet based – we made sure that we found as many websites as we could for various types of groups, starting with the sites of the groups we had already had personal contact with, and then following the links from those websites. This resulted in ten (physical) site visits to both congregations and events that drew participants from many different congregations, and approximately 100 interviews, all digitally recorded, both audio and video. The sites we visited were located in different urban areas throughout the US, including Los Angeles, Seattle, St Louis, Chicago, and New York.

Reclaimers

Our first form, Reclaimers, are Post-Boomers who are discovering the liturgical traditions of religions such as the Anglican, Orthodox, and Catholic churches, and are reclaiming as their own the ancient symbols, rituals and practices of these traditions in their spiritual quest. These are converts, either from other, non-liturgical forms of Christianity or from a non-existent or lapsed faith commitment. In this, the particular attractiveness of these traditions are the symbols, rituals, and smells of these churches, as well as the small communities of believers that they represent, and the connection to a larger historical tradition within Christianity that these traditions provide.

In our interview and visits to our respondents' churches, we found five primary characteristics of those who are reclaiming the liturgical rituals and traditions. First, there is an attraction to the visual and ritualistic elements of liturgical churches; second, they articulate a desire for a connection to a larger history of Christianity than that they had previously known in their spiritual lives; third, there is an attraction to and desire for a small religious community; fourth, they exhibit a desire for and commitment to a strict spiritual regimen, including confession, and cultivating spiritual disciplines; and finally, we find a desire for 'religious absolutes' and a set social structure which these Post-Boomers find within these congregations.

The attraction to the visual and ritualistic elements of the liturgical churches is at least partly self-evident in that these traditions have historically provided a visual link to Christian teachings – what one Episcopal priest we interviewed has termed, 'audio-visual aids to understanding the gospel' – which ranges from stained glass, icons and incense, to kneeling, genuflecting, and the kissing of icons and priest's garments. All of these elements were identified as being partially responsible for the attraction of these traditions; the visually compelling, embodied experience of the sacred that is available to the participants every time they attend a service at their church.

About 40 miles southeast of Los Angeles, the Episcopal Church of the Blessed Sacrament in Placentia, California, had become the spiritual home to over two dozen college students from a nearby evangelical Christian college. The Rector, Father David Baumann, was curious as to why. He identifies Blessed Sacrament as an 'Anglo-Catholic, high-Mass-on-Sunday church', and seemed genuinely amazed that young people from Baptist, Assemblies of God, Christian and Missionary Alliance, and other similar backgrounds, none with any experience in liturgical churches, would throw themselves so completely into parish life, transforming themselves and the church in the process.

According to Father Baumann, when he asked the students what had attracted them to the church and why they remained, the students responded in remarkably similar ways. Many of them first stated their dissatisfaction with their experiences in evangelical churches, and then in various ways expressed their attraction to the ritual, experiential, and visual elements that make up the mass at Blessed Sacrament, as well as the importance of the connection to a larger Christian history than what is usually emphasised in evangelical churches. Blessed Sacrament provided a completely different experience and context to the evangelical churches in which they grew up that in their view emphasised their relevance to the contemporary American context. The music, lectionary, rituals and the saints, all have a long and accessible history and supplied what they had not experienced in their churches before.

For example Emily, a sophomore at the college, stated that she had considered attending an Episcopal church because she was dissatisfied with the 'God is my teddy bear/best friend mentality of many evangelical churches'. Rebecca, also a sophomore, gave a similar response – 'I began looking into more liturgical styles of worship [because I] was fed up with the seeker-friendly Willow Creek movement, and remembering a missions trip to Russia, I looked into the Orthodox Church and other liturgical styles'. This is not to suggest that these two young women really understood beforehand what an Episcopal mass was going to be like – Emily, for instance, notes that she was at first a bit confused with all the liturgical activity taking place but, despite her confusion, she was 'wholly conscious of God's presence', and that over time, she began to 'understand through experience, what sacraments were, and what it meant to experience grace so tangibly'. She concluded that she is 'learning to experience God with my heart as well as my head'.

Overwhelmingly, these students – all between the ages of 18 and 23 – indicated that what they found at Blessed Sacrament was a combination of a Christian tradition that through its liturgy demonstrated a connection to a much larger history than their evangelical churches, and that the liturgy itself allowed them to experience God in ways they had never imagined. Some, like David, a senior at the college, simply made the case that Blessed Sacrament 'provides an atmosphere for me to worship God using my whole being - body, soul and mind. The liturgical style helps me to focus on my soul and mind by also engaging my body. This allows me to focus on God and remember his holiness in a real and meaningful way'. Becca, who is 20 years old, relates her attraction to the liturgy at Blessed Sacrament and compares it to her experience in Protestant churches:

> Finding reverence for God and order to the worship and something that didn't deny that you had a body .... It was exciting to find a church that just understood this and then had the tradition ... here's incense, which you smell and there's the wine and the bread, which you taste, and everything that you see. And then you hear the bells and you hear the songs and the organ, and you touch things. I mean it's a sensory overload ... you smell things and you hear things and touch things and you taste things, it's like, 'Oh,' suddenly you're in the part of the museum where you get to play with stuff.

Members of St Barnabas Orthodox Church located about 10 miles from Blessed Sacrament, expressed similar sentiments. Debra and Derrick Sanser, both in their mid-thirties and with three children, are typical in both their spiritual searching and their understanding of the Orthodox Church. They had previously been members of several Protestant churches such as the Vineyard and Calvary Chapel, yet always seemed to be searching for the permanence and richly textured experience they have finally found in the Orthodox Church. Debra said that on their first visit to St Barnabas '... the room was filled with incense and the choir just really inspired me .... when we walked in I was holding [our daughter] and we were standing in the back and she said, "Mommy, God is here"'. Derrick, contrasting St Barnabas to his experience in Protestant churches said, 'you see icons visually, you smell the incense, everything is sensory .... We're not sola scriptura [like the Protestants]. Jesus came in human form to restore human flesh, so being human is not a bad thing. It's actually being restored is a good thing, so we're actually holistic about that'.

In addition to their being attracted to the visual and aesthetic components of the liturgical traditions, all of our Reclaimers indicated a desire to place themselves within the larger scheme of Christian history than had previously been available to them, and which these traditions provided. Thus the ritual and liturgy itself, the music – decidedly not contemporary – the form and sequence of the church service and even the priestly status and role, all serve to provide a sense of belonging to a history that is not primarily contemporary and American in emphasis. This can manifest itself in a stronger form, usually among the Orthodox converts who frame all Protestant churches as having little or no history or set structure, and the Orthodox as being the most ancient, most authentic Christian tradition. Erin, a 20-year-old who attends St Barnabas and has recently become more actively committed to church and Christian faith says,

> I've realised that we can actually trace our church back to Antioch, which is where they were first called Christians, Christians (Acts 11: 26). Not many people can do that with their faith, and it doesn't change. It's the same liturgically, you know, through the years. Like the chanting and the prayers, it's not made up. The prayers that we pray and all the chants have been written down through the years by saints or monks or, you know, the forefathers all that.

Benny Wisenan, a 30-year-old schoolteacher whom we interviewed at St Barnabas along with his sister, Ruth Rutledge (he is a member of another Orthodox Church in the area), frames this in the sense of finding a new source of roots in an otherwise mobile and disposable culture that is southern California,

> You know, the oldest buildings are like the 1950s, so I never felt rooted, you know, and I became Orthodox and was in touch with cultures that are thousands of years old … the Greeks or the Antiochians, they have been Christians since Pentecost … and they have these deep traditions and now I'm a part of that. And it really gave me a sense of being part of something whereas before, I was kind of lost.

Lindsey, one of the college students at Blessed Sacrament, provides a somewhat softer version of this perspective, saying that she is drawn to the liturgy because, '… it's ancient. I mean in its earliest forms it comes from the early church hiding out in the Roman Empire and the Apostles …. It's passed the test of time, and it's carried the doctrines through'. Similarly, Becca says that

> [g]oing to a church that's been doing the same thing for almost 2,000 years, or the Episcopal church for 500 years … if you really engage in worship you realise that you're being led by millions of people before you who have said these things and who have done these things, and you're not just wandering around in your 20-something arrogance trying to plough your own path.

The desire for a small community within which they are known, are active, and to which they are responsible is a consistent desire for these young people. In some cases this almost becomes a total world, in that they seem to be spending the majority of their time in or at the church. But in general, the desire to be known and to know other parishioners in an intimate way, and to be a part of a spiritual family is the primary theme expressed. Debra Sanser sees the church as an extension of the family:

> As a church we're meant to be the body of Christ, not just a bunch of individuals with our own private relationship. Of course … God has to be personally real for us … He gives us a bit of himself and expects us to share it with each other and to be a community together …. If somebody's having a problem, people are there to help you …. I think that's so essential in life.

While Benny Wisenan sees it in more spiritual terms:

> In the Orthodox Church I have this sense that the whole community is helping me with my salvation. They pray for me. The saints intercede for me. We come to the liturgy all together in communion ... we're all interceding for each other. And so I feel like I'm not alone.

Similarly, Micah Snell, who attends Blessed Sacrament, and was one of the first of the students to begin worshipping there says that he and his wife were not looking for the sort of large church that could promote and support almost any activity, but 'the sense of family ... and a sense of belonging'.

The level of commitment needed to maintain the desired spiritual regimen required – or at least recommended – by these churches is quite high. It is a bit misleading to say that there is a spiritual regimen required by these churches; in fact, it is the young people themselves who are seeking out this sort of regimen, which is then provided by the priests and in the structure of the churches themselves. For example, among the converts to Orthodoxy that we have interviewed, the congregation has in many ways become the primary focus of their lives, meeting for various services three-to-four times per week (a number which is even greater during, for example the Christmas season or Pascha), and thus refocusing their lives within the congregation. They have also sought out their priests as spiritual mentors, who then impose certain regimens such as prayer and reading of sacred literature, whether the Bible or the Church Fathers, and the confession of sins. Further, at least for the Orthodox converts, the services themselves require significant physical stamina in order to make it through the entire two-to-three hour service – these are generally standing services, and most of those in attendance remain standing for the entire service. One parishioner told us that he views that physical sacrifice as a spiritual discipline.

Erin, at St Barnabas, says that although it is difficult

> To stay focused sometimes and to go to the services and to be fasting and to try and be steadfast. I think that I would not be as into the faith if I hadn't been Protestant before because I was able to compare and contrast the two. I had to say, 'I don't feel comfortable with the Vineyard, but I do believe in God. This is what I do believe. This is what I want.

Benny, while similarly acknowledging the difficulty of maintaining a rigorous spiritual life, has found help in his relationship with his priest – 'You have a relationship [with the priest] and you know you're accountable because if you're going to take it seriously you know that whatever you do you're going to have to reveal to this person'. At Blessed Sacrament, Father Baumann said that among the many young people who have been attending over the past few years, several are on a similar path of pursuing a rigorous spirituality:

> One of the things that they sought a lot is personal counselling, mentoring, spiritual direction, a good number of them are making their confessions; they're bringing in the real depth of their spiritual struggles. They are really seriously seeking deep sanctification.

The desire for a set social structure and religious 'absolutes' within the context of the visual and embodied spiritual elements that these churches provide was also almost universal in our interviews. In general, it seems that there is an elective affinity between the conservative natures of either the liturgical tradition into which one converts – Orthodoxy – or the particular congregation that one finds – Anglican – and the religious perspective of the Post-Boomer converts. The affinity is that both tradition/ congregation and individual tend to be quite conservative religiously, essentially finding a more culturally acceptable context for them to be 'fundamentalists', of a sort, but without the label.

Father Baumann reports that the young converts in his church are saying,

> We want absolute truth. We want the basic gospel. We don't want to be entertained, we want to be challenged. We want to be called to sanctity. We want to be challenged to the moral life. We want to learn how to pray.

Nate, one of the students at Blessed Sacrament, sees dangerous trends in some of the emerging forms of evangelical worship (which are not unlike what we have found in our 'innovate' form), that are sometimes framed as 'postmodern' worship, and that are being pursued at his school:

> I tried to explain to them why you need, you know, some kind of structure .... You cannot have four hours of worship without a point .... You need to have something to grasp on; you need a central concept. They're like, 'Well, God is the central concept.' And it seems like they've learned all different kinds of worship ... but it's a very nebulous form and there's nothing to grasp hold of.

His fellow student and Blessed Sacrament member, Lindsey, agreed and sees the structure of the liturgy as a guard against such changes:

> It's scary that post-modernism has crept into the church ... one thing I like about the structure of the liturgy and things like that is [that] it's ancient. It has passed the test of time and it's carried the doctrines through ... just the words themselves are so rich ... it makes it more [difficult] to deviate from it.

Through the various rituals and traditions of the liturgical churches, Reclaimers are finding an embodied spirituality in various ways. They are finding physical requirements such as kneeling, the sacraments, and even, in the case of some Orthodox services, standing for up to four hours, to be spiritually fulfilling. They are also finding communities of faith that are both contemporary and that reach back into history, and which provide resources for their spiritual journey they had not experienced before. These include spiritual disciplines such as fasting and confession, as well as examples from the lives of others in the same traditions.

Innovators

Our second type, Innovators, is so named because of the constantly evolving approach to religious and spiritual beliefs and practices that these groups exhibit. Many of these are newer, less established groups that are affiliated with the 'emerging church' movement; others are established churches and ministries that are innovating within their own traditions. These groups, whether newer 'emerging' churches or more established, frame their approach in contrast to what they see as an overly institutionalised and inwardly focused church to one that is focused on building community, both within the religious group and with the surrounding community, and as engaged in various ways with the larger culture. These churches are innovating in terms of their responses to the larger culture, introducing various forms of ritual and symbol into their worship services and new forms of religious and community life that emphasise communal belonging.

From among the congregations we visited and our interviews, we have found four primary innovator characteristics. First, there is a prevalence of visual representations and expressions of the sacred; secondly, most of these congregations tend to be small in size and high in commitment; thirdly, there is a general disinterest in established institutional forms of religion; and fourthly, an inward experiential and outward expression of the spiritual.

One of the first things that strikes you as you enter the space occupied by one of these groups is their emphasis on the visual representation and expression of the sacred. This can include some forms that are more traditionally religious such as crosses or icons, but more typical are the paintings, computer generated visual effects, photographs, and 3-D images that do not necessarily appear to be religiously oriented at first glance. These are often expressions of spiritual seeking or experience and can be as easily completed during a worship service, as they can be created beforehand to be used in the service, or perhaps as an exhibit in an art gallery that the church might operate. This emphasis is the result of the success of attracting members, conversant with cultural industries such art, design, and film and who are actively involved these. This is not to say that everyone who attends one of these churches is an artist or filmmaker, rather that there is a valuing of a visual aesthetic as a way to express and experience spiritual things.

For example, during worship services at the Bridge Communities in the ocean-side community of Ventura, California, just south of Santa Barbara, visually engaging, digitally produced images are projected on multiple walls of their meeting room, that also serve to provide a narrative as to what is happening at each part of the service. Various artworks set on easels and hanging from the walls that have been created for (or in) previous services also serve to set the visual context for the service. These are not, according to Greg Russinger, the 'lead missionary' (pastor) at the Bridge Communities, simply about putting on a show for others to watch. It is, instead, an integral part of the larger efforts at the Bridge to provide a context for people to talk with each other and to connect with God:

It's amazing when people begin to share life through paint, clay, sketching, whatever the case may be. The conversation that gets birthed from that is magical, I think. The reality that one can open up through the dynamic of what one has created, allowing other people to come in to talk with them about their life. I can come alongside and ask them, 'Why did you use that colour? Why did you paint the way you do? What is that telling me about who you are?'

This process of using artistic forms of expression to create conversations enables them to 'investigate the mystery of the gospel', in ways that words alone do not allow.

Visual art also has a significant role at Grace Brethren Church in Long Beach California, as well, through an active art gallery. The church has developed a programme that includes regular exhibitions in the gallery, commissioned artists and interns such as painters, musicians and dramatists, all emphasising the theme that the spiritual life properly considered is not only a cognitive affair, but must include the body and all of its senses. Lou Huesmann, the senior pastor at Grace, argues that 'it begins with creation, with God as creator' which opens up the possibility for art. He says that the church community has been shaped by the 'simple paradigm, creation, fall, redemption, restoration ... which has then been the umbrella under which the arts have developed' at the church. Ultimately, he sees the arts as a way to speak in a different way to current cultural sensibilities – 'my ultimate vision for all this is that in a culture like ours, you know, post-modern, post-Christian that we are becoming, especially here in southern California, I think the arts can be a tremendous way to speak to our culture about the beauty and integrity of Christianity'.

In contrast to the large, 'seeker' or 'mega' church model that has been the dominant form in the USA for the past 30 years, these churches are often intentionally small so as to facilitate a greater sense of community through more intensive face-to-face interaction. Their desire is not to grow for the sake of growing, but to limit their size so that they can in some way create the type of religious and spiritual community that promotes a sense of belonging to something bigger than just themselves. This is in part a reaction to the mega-church phenomenon in which there is a ministry for seemingly every life stage, but that can be somewhat alienating due to the sheer size of these congregations. It is also related to the desire among Innovators to have a personal connection with others in their religious community and to have more direct participation in the different programmes of the church and in its overall mission. Greg Russinger, who told us of his goal to split the Bridge into different congregations once the church got to 250 members, puts it this way:

I don't really see Jesus, you know, having a scorecard or a belt to put the notches [counting the number of church members]. Why do we live in the realm of church culture where the first question that comes up about church life is how many people are you running? Shouldn't it be how many people have you invested in this week? How many people have you engaged? I come from the philosophy of belief that I will never get caught up in the dynamic of largeness because I think largeness is not numbers as much as it's largeness of heart and what lives have been changed.

Andrew Jones, who works with several organisations throughout North America, Australia, Asia and Europe, 'in support of young people doing ministry in emerging culture', suggests that this denotes a value shift in how church ministry is being approached. He says,

> Much of the ministry that we were trained to do and we have been reproducing over the last few years, few decades, has been based on a very modern world view and a modern value system, which values things according to how long they lasted and how big they could become and the kind of impact and, actually, what's more institutional rather than relational or personal and not necessarily open to the supernatural or to spiritual things.

What he has seen develop over the last few years are instead churches that are more 'organic and local, committed to a local expression that's unique and makes sense for that smaller group of people'. He went on to add:

> Everywhere it seems that if we really value intimacy and powerful worship experiences that are fully interactive and if we value community on a deep level where we're really sharing life together and secrets and money, then we're looking at smaller groups than we're used to seeing.

Related to the emphasis on small size, we find a consistent and significant lack of interest in the institutional/organisational demands that larger churches must support. Most of these groups do not own any physical plant, rather they might rent or lease a building, or a room that they can use one or two days per week, or they might have struck a deal with a local pub or coffee house that allows them to meet weekly. They are not interested in owning real estate, building large institutional settings for their churches, or in having, 'a staff of thousands', and programmes to match as Karen Ward, the pastor of The Apostles' Church, a recently planted church in Seattle termed it.

The Apostles' Church meets in 'micro-churches' in various homes in the city throughout the week, and then comes together each Saturday evening for a 'mass gathering' of worship, sharing, a common meal, and then a going back into the community. Similarly, the Bridge originally met in a rented space in a light industrial area of the city, and has more recently moved into the old American Legion building in the downtown area, once it became available. The draw of the new location was the downtown area, the kitchen in the building from which they could provide community meals, and the central location for the community within the city.

A further indicator of their lack of interest in institution building is the size and conception of their ministerial staff. As with the congregation size, generally the staff is small as well – usually a lead person, and perhaps a support person. Although the lead person may from the outside appear to function as a 'pastor', this is not necessarily the term by which they are known, nor do they necessarily conceive of themselves as 'the person in charge'. Rather, they often operate as facilitators of both the religious experience of the congregation for any given meeting, and for the overall direction of the group, but even this can be understood as a function of the religious community. As Andrew Jones has observed,

The kinds of churches we're seeing are very organic, very decentralised .... They don't need a senior pastor. In some ways it's more like the early church in the book of Acts where you had elders, you had leadership and you also had wandering apostolic people speaking into different churches ... but you didn't have the business world, or outer structure, or all the priestly structure.

This makes for a relatively non-institutionalised and non-hierarchical authority structure for the community, which is not to say that these churches do not have elders or deacons, or other spiritual leaders, rather that even the way that they are organised is based on what they conceive as spiritual gifts rather than the requirements of the organisation. For example, Apostles' Church describes its leadership as such:

Church of the Apostles is a community led by the Holy Spirit (Romans 8: 14). We take seriously our birthing as children of God (by water and the spirit), and our royal priesthood (as disciples of Jesus Christ). Within a body of believers, God always provides those who have the *charisms* (gifts) of tending, nurturing, teaching and guiding.

Following this explanation is a listing of several persons in the church, all of whom, with the exception of the pastor, are laypersons in the congregation. The inward experiential and outward expression of the spiritual takes two primary forms, first, in the worship services, and second, in how they conceive of living out their religious commitments within the surrounding community and culture.

First, regarding the worship service itself, there are generally a variety of experiences that can take place, each of which emphasises and requires the interactive and physical, rather than the passive and (primarily) cognitive. There are likely to be many things taking place simultaneously; music and singing, opportunities for personal expression of the spiritual experience such as painting, or prayer stations, scripture readings, sharing in small groups within the larger service context, and the like. There is an order and structure to the service, but the emphasis is on both personal experience and expressing what that experience is to others within the community. At the Bridge, the services have what Greg Russinger calls a 'textural' quality. Thus, he reflects

Worship is not a vocal thing. Partly it's vocal but it's a very whole dynamic, it's very physical, either the expression of one's body through the brushing of paint, through the reading of poetry, we always allow moments engaged in song. We never put a minute to it, 25 minutes of this, 30 minutes of that, as much as it ends when God says it should end. And then we allow people to respond through what they've created, to talk about what that worship was for them. So, a lot of texture to it.

Second, for most of these groups, their conception of living out their particular religious commitments has not been limited to simply having religious and spiritual experiences and sharing them with each other. Rather, they have all, in one way or another, conceived of their responsibility and desire to live out their beliefs in the context of the surrounding/supporting community in which they are located. So, we hear them constantly talking about being 'in the middle of culture' or of 'serving the city', which means that they are not just getting together to share in a common religious experience, rather that they are developing various programmes and outreaches to their host city/town/city. When he first arrived at Grace Brethren, the church was, according to Lou Huesmann, 'inward focused'. One of the goals, through their different programmes in the arts and community activism, has been to live out their commitment to the idea that 'God has placed us here in Long Beach for a purpose, we're not just talking about individual evangelism, we're talking about being, serving the city, having Long Beach be glad that we're here, as Proverbs talks about the city rejoicing'. Similarly the goal at the Bridge is to be, as Greg Russinger says, 'as a rock that is dropped into water and it creates this circular rhythm of change. Our life in Christ should be that same dynamic of being in the midst or the middle, the centre of culture beginning to change [the culture]'.

Innovators have found sources for embodiment through various means, ranging from the use of new digital media to being active in small religious communities. In each, Innovators find an embodied spirituality by physically expressing and/or experiencing spiritual fulfilment, whether through painting, sharing in community with others, or through serving others as an expression of their spiritual commitments.

Embodied Spirituality

In the emerging social scientific literature on spirituality, analysts have largely framed 'spirituality' as a counterpart to 'religion', with the spiritual referring to the inner life, and the individualistic search for meaning, whether this is from within a particular religious tradition or traditions, or is a religiously unaffiliated 'spiritual but not religious' approach (for example Fuller 2001; Porterfield 2001; Roof 1993; 1999; 2002; Wuthnow 1998; 2001; 2003). Spirituality is thus alternatively framed as a *search* for meaning, a *quest* for spiritual fulfilment and/or development, or a move from an understanding of the spiritual as a place of 'dwelling' to one of 'seeking', or even 'shopping' (Roof 1993; 1999; Wuthnow 1998; 2001; 2003; Cimino and Lattin 1998). The individual and her/his spiritual journey is the referent, rather than the religious congregation or community, and the metaphor is one of movement, development, or choice as opposed to stability or constancy.

This individualistic questing, searching, seeking for spirituality and spiritual fulfilment does not necessarily connote a complete break with all commitments to religious communities of the past. Although some remnant of the more stable past remains for the individual, these forms of spirituality are primarily to be understood as involving an individual search, or quest, for spiritual growth, fulfilment, and understanding, with the religious community acting, to the extent that it has an active role, as a sort of non-essential aid, or context, to this journey.

Neither of the two types we have presented in this chapter would fall neatly into any of these characterisations. Both Reclaimers and Innovators are pursuing a spirituality that only makes sense in the context of the religious community and through demonstrating those spiritual commitments in the larger, surrounding community, rather than pursuing an exclusively – or even primarily – individualistic spiritual quest. Certainly both Reclaimers and Innovators represent a personal spiritual journey, perhaps even a quest, but there is much more to the story than just that. As different as these two types are, we find that these young people seek out smaller, more intimate communities of faith so that they can pursue their spiritual journey *within* those communities and directly contribute to the life of those communities, instead of constantly shopping for a better spiritual experience elsewhere. That is, their 'journey' is intended to take place within a particular community of faith, not as something they pursue as separate from their commitment to that community. Further, the spiritual journey is only partly introspective. That is, in addition to the personal desire and effort to grow or develop their spiritual lives, there is also an outward orientation that they understand as an integral part of their overall spiritual development. Thus we see not only public expressions of their spiritual and emotional states during a worship service, or a gallery exhibit that details a particular spiritual journey, but we see spiritual commitments channelled outward to the surrounding communities through various outreach initiatives.

In all of their spiritual efforts and activities, both personal/introspective and outward/community directed, the spirituality displayed is best understood as taking place in an *embodied* form through visual and physical manifestations of spiritual experience that are practised in and through a particular religious community. That is, spiritual experience takes place within a body of believers and is only meaningful as it is experienced in that context and as lived out through that body. Although Reclaimers and Innovators each find different contexts for embodied spirituality, Reclaimers looking to history and tradition, and Innovators developing combinations of the historical and the (post) modern, they each find it in very similar ways. Reclaimers are drawn to the ritual and symbols of the liturgy; Innovators participate in creating ritual and symbols for their worship services. Each is finding fulfilment in smaller religious communities as these are viewed as the best places for the commitment and involvement they seek. In each, these young people are not lone seekers; rather, their seeking is embodied in the community.

Embodied Spirituality as Expressive Communalism

How then can we make theoretical sense of these two approaches to spirituality – Innovators and Reclaimers – that we have found among Post-Boomers? Max Weber's famous typology of the different forms of asceticism and mysticism (Weber 1993), in particular his description of 'inner worldly asceticism' that has characterised the religious impulse of most of western Protestantism since the Reformation and the description of 'utilitarian individualism' and 'expressive individualism' provided by Robert Bellah et al. (1985), provide a beginning and points of departure.

For Weber, inner-worldly asceticism required the believer, while seeking the assurance of his or her salvation, to live a rationally ordered life rejecting 'everything that is ethically irrational, aesthetic [sic.], or dependent upon his own emotional reactions to the world and its institutions' (Weber 1993: 168). Ascetic Protestantism, according to Weber,

> Demanded of the believer, not celibacy, as in the case of the monk, but the avoidance of all erotic pleasure; not poverty, but the elimination of all idle and exploitative enjoyment of unearned wealth and income, and the avoidance of all feudalistic, sensuous ostentation of wealth; not the ascetic death-in-life of the cloister, but an alert, rationally controlled patterning of life, and the avoidance of all surrender to the beauty of the world, to art, or to one's own moods and emotions. The clear and uniform goal of this asceticism was the disciplining and methodical organization of the whole pattern of life. (Weber 1993: 183)

Thus the believer strove to live his or her life 'in the world, but not of the world', so to speak, operating within its constructs and confines, all the while rejecting its various measures of success, and sensuous enjoyment and fulfilment and instead focusing on a rationally ordered life and faith.

Bellah et al. (1985: 33) present what are essentially the secularised and almost completely individualised outcomes of this emphasis on the rational ordering of life, in their description of utilitarian individualism as 'a life devoted to the calculating pursuit of one's own material interest' and expressive individualism as the desire to 'cultivate and express the self and explore its vast social and cosmic identities' (Bellah et al. 1985: 35). The example of the former is Benjamin Franklin, famous for such aphorisms as 'a penny saved is a penny earned' and 'God helps them who help themselves', while American transcendentalist poet Walt Whitman, famous for poems such as 'Song of Myself', is the example of the latter. In each, the emphasis is on an individualism so encompassing that Bellah and his colleagues wrote two books worrying about what such an emphasis on individualism in American culture might mean for the future of American society (Bellah et al. 1985; 1991).

The embodied spirituality of the young people we have been describing here cannot be adequately described by any of these three types. In neither their spiritual pursuits nor in the development of their interests and abilities, have they rejected their moods and emotions, artistic expression or aesthetic enjoyment, or surrender to the beauty of the world. They exhibit both rational ascetic and non-rational expressive tendencies – they want a faith that makes rational sense to them and that is also an expressive, embodied spiritual experience.

Similarly, although they certainly pursue individual religious and spiritual experience, they do not seem to be so completely immersed in the forms of individualism identified by Bellah et al. (1985) that they have neglected the various communities within which they are active. Rather the young people profiled here intentionally pursue artistic expressions of various sorts, seeking and forming communities, and engaging in different forms of community outreach and involvement. This is not to suggest that they have somehow removed themselves from the individualism that pervades American society, rather that their individual spiritual quest is mediated through the communities in which they are active and in which they seek membership and a sense of belonging.

Thus, whether it is through the stained glass, icons, and incense of the liturgical traditions, or the creation of various art-works intended to express their particular spiritual experience, these only have personal meaning within the context of the religious community. These young people are not the spiritual consumers of their parents' generation, rather they are seeking both a deep spiritual experience and a community experience, each of which provides them with meaning in their lives, and each is meaningless without the other. Further, their community commitments are not necessarily restricted to just their own religious community, but generally includes social outreach to the surrounding community as a part of their spiritual commitments. This seems to be more true of our Innovators than it is the Reclaimers, but it does suggest an expansion of the idea of community for at least some segments of the Post-Boomer generations, and may signal a new commitment to a larger, more public engagement among religiously motivated post-boomers.

We believe that we are witnessing the emergence of a new form of spirituality, 'expressive communalism'. This new form is related to the individualistic forms of spirituality as described above, but is also distinct from them. Post-Boomers have embedded their lives in spiritual communities in which their desire and need for both expressive/experiential activities, whether through art, music, or service oriented activities, and for a close-knit, physical community and communion with others, are met. These young people are seeking out different forms of spirituality in response to the shortcomings they see as inherent in these other forms. They are seeking to develop a balance for individualism and rational asceticism through religious experience and spiritual meaning in an embodied faith.

Bibliography

Bellah, R.N., R. Madsen, W.M. Sullivan, A. Swidler and S.M. Tipton (1985), *Habits of the Heart: Individualism and Commitment in American Life*, Berkeley and Los Angeles: University of California Press.

Bellah, R.N., R. Madsen, W.M. Sullivan, A. Swidler and S.M. Tipton (1991), *The Good Society*, New York: Knopf.

Burnett, R. (2005), *How Images Think*, Cambridge, MA: The MIT Press.

Cimino, R. and D. Lattin (1998), *Shopping for Faith: American Religion in the New Millennium*, San Francisco: Jossey-Bass Publishers.

Florida, R. (2002), *The Rise of the Creative Class*, New York: Basic Books.

Flory, R.W. and D.E. Miller (eds) (2000), *GenX Religion*, New York: Routledge.

Fuller, R.C. (2001), *Spiritual But Not Religious: Understanding Unchurched America*, New York: Oxford University Press.

Hansen, M.B.N. (2004), *New Philosophy for New Media*, Cambridge, MA: The MIT Press.

Kellner, D. (1995), *Media Culture: Cultural Studies, Identity and Politics Between the Modern and the Postmodern*, New York: Routledge.

Manovich, L. (2001), *The Language of the New Media*, Cambridge, MA: The MIT Press.

Porterfield, A. (2001), *The Transformation of American Religion: The Story of a Late Twentieth-Century Awakening*, New York: Oxford University Press.

Roof, W.C. (1993), *A Generation of Seekers: The Spiritual Journeys of the Baby Boom Generations*, New York: HarperCollins.

Roof, W.C. (1999), *Spiritual Marketplace: Baby Boomers and the Remaking of American Religion*, Princeton, NJ: Princeton University Press.

Roof, W.C. (2003), *Bridging Divided Worlds: Generational Cultures in Congregations*, San Francisco: Jossey-Bass.

Ryan, M-L. (2003), *Narrative as Virtual Reality: Immersion and Interactivity in Literature and Electronic Media*, Baltimore, MD: Johns Hopkins University Press.

Schmidt, L. (2005), *Restless Souls: The Making of American Spirituality*, San Francisco: HarperSanFrancisco.

Stanczak, G. and D.E. Miller (2002), *Engaged Spirituality: Spirituality and Social Transformation in Mainstream American Religious Traditions*, Los Angeles: Center for Religion and Civic Culture, University of Southern California.

Stephens, M. (1998), *The Rise of the Image the Fall of the Word*, New York: Oxford University Press.

Tapscott, D. (1998), *Growing up Digital: The Rise of the Net Generation*, New York: McGraw-Hill.

Weber, M. (1993), *The Sociology of Religion*, Boston: Beacon Press.

Wuthnow, R. (1994), *I Come Away Stronger: How Small Groups are Changing American Religion*, Grand Rapids, MI: Eerdmans.

Wuthnow, R. (1998), *After Heaven: Spirituality in America Since the 1950s*, Berkeley and Los Angeles: University of California Press.

Wuthnow, R. (2001), *Creative Spirituality: The Way of the Artist*, Berkeley and Los Angeles: University of California Press.

Wuthnow, R. (2003), *All in Sync: How Music and Art are Revitalising American Religion*, Berkeley and Los Angeles: University of California Press.

Chapter 12

Visual Spirituality: An Eye for Religion

Kieran Flanagan

Sociological efforts to secure an understanding of the visual dimensions of spirituality might seem an unpropitious exercise, one doomed to failure. The two notions stand in contradiction to each other. The visual is an imperfect expression of what is invisible, what belongs to the ultimate, to the supernatural, to what is yet to be seen. Seeking to see beyond the limits of sight forces the gazer into realms of spirituality, areas where sociology fears to tread. Anyhow such dilemmas might seem proper to theological meditation and speculation; they hardly warrant sociological attention. The ambiguous relationship between the seen and the unseen seldom enters sociological realms, yet events change what needs to be understood in culture.

A law case held between the Florida Department of Highway Safety and Motor Vehicles and the applicant for a US driving licence might not seem of sociological interest. The complaint of Sultana Freeman was an exception. The Department refused her demand to be photographed for her driving licence wearing a *niqab* (the veil covering her face but leaving her eyes visible). Although supported by the American Civil Liberties Union, she lost her case at the Florida appeals court in September 2005.

In asserting her civil rights to appear in an identity but one not to be identifiable, Ms Freeman turned the politics of recognition on its head to make a statement of virtue in the public square. She used her *niqab* as a spiritual form of *Jihad* to deliver a visual snub to the vanity fair of cosmopolitan culture and its obsession with revealing all. The politics of veiling had become part of a cultural war, something Catholic nuns could never have envisaged when they cast off their habits to the fancy dress industry and to karaokes of *The Sound of Music*. Their medieval habits seemed culturally irrelevant and incompatible with the spirit of Vatican II and its encouragement of modernisation. Yet, times change, and what seemed useless to the modernising nuns four decades ago took on potent symbolic, spiritual and cultural uses for Ms Freeman. Her statement of self-effacement stands uneasily with the technological demands of a culture obsessed with the certification of identity. The spiritual basis of her inhibitions about revealing her face in public jarred with secular assumptions that all matters should be transparent, and certainly not hidden for religious reasons.

A year later, another event of inescapable significance occurred that also related to prohibitions on making images. In February 2006, a Danish newspaper published cartoons satirising the Prophet Muhammad. The publication generated a storm of Islamic protest. In solidarity, many European newspapers exerted their right to freedom of expression and reproduced the cartoons leading to what *The Times* (3 February 2006) headlined rather dramatically 'Cartoon wars and the clash of civilisations'. Similar, but less publicised, controversies occurred over the televising in 2005 by the BBC of an opera based on the life and times of the talk show host Jerry Springer. The presentation of Christ in a demeaning manner generated a minor Christian backlash, mainly from Evangelicals. Contrasting the differing levels of protest and the response of the mass media in the United Kingdom, a commentator suggested that when it comes to matters of iconography Christians are less than zealous in protecting their brand image, certainly compared to British Muslims. Somehow, Christians leave themselves open to the predatory blasphemies of the artistically challenged.

These events surrounding the *niqab*, the cartoons and Jerry Springer had one thing in common – they emerged from forms of religion marked by iconoclastic zeal. The protests were not only about what should not be shown, but also about what was vilified. At a time when the politics of representation seemed to hallow visual rights for all, these protests seemed a denial of these. Somehow, notions of inclusion had hit a boundary, an unexpected one in times of post-secularity, when public indifference suggested that blasphemy no longer offended and that few images could violate public sensibilities, least of all those in relation to religion.

The Islamic prohibitions on display of the face of God, of the Prophet Muhammad and indeed, of the virtuous woman, caught Western cultural sensibilities by surprise. Showing a face is embedded in cultural assumptions about character, trust and beauty. In a culture where all is on display, inhibitions about what can be seen seem bizarre to the secular mind. Yet, visual spirituality points to an ambiguity, one that marks a fundamental division between theologies that appeal to revelation. Should efforts be made to see the unseen? The question lies at the heart of visual spirituality.

Ocular Matters in Spirituality

No discipline likes oxymorons but the term 'visual spirituality' expresses well how these two elements could be combined in ways fit for sociological understandings. Visual spirituality is a term used by Chase in relation to Hugh of St Victor, the French medieval theologian who wrote a *Commentary on the Celestial Hierarchy of Saint Dionysius the Areopagite*. In this work, Chase suggests, 'visual spirituality' refers to a sacramental view of the world, one that involves a contemplation of images (Chase 2002: 187). The theological origins of visual spirituality can be traced to the Pseudo-Dionysius who treated relationships between heaven and earth in terms of a spiral from the visible into the invisible. Angels form a distinct part of his apophatic theology and this approach was used earlier in efforts to understand re-presentations in religious rituals (Flanagan 1991: 288–320). Using visual spirituality to envisage the other world, of the invisible and the unseen, might seem an odd turn to take for a discipline that has made many swerves of late in what it emphasises.

In his introduction to a series of volumes on world spirituality, Cousins drew together editorial understandings of the term 'spirituality'. It involves a quest for experience and understanding of the inner dimension of the individual, a core that entails 'prayer, spiritual direction, the various maps of the spiritual journey, and the methods of advancement in the spiritual ascent' (Cousins 1985:xiii). As the term visual spirituality would suggest, it is about the questing to see, the journeying in imagination that leads to absorption, a tasting of the joy to come that lies in the heavenly, whose reflection, as St. Paul said, can only be seen through a mirror darkly (1 Cor. 13: 12). In the end, as von Balthasar observed, 'the real significance of any particular mode of spirituality is in the fact that its source and authentication is in heaven' (von Balthasar 1989: 218). Faced with such dilemmas regarding visual spirituality, sociology might take to itself Hamlet's famous comment that 'there are more things in heaven and earth, Horatio, than are dreamt of in your philosophy'.

Visual spirituality deals with a strange paradox that the bodily eye and the spiritual eye cannot be open together, a point von Balthasar finds in Origen, whom he describes as 'the greatest theologian of the spiritual seeing' (von Balthasar 1991: 478–9; 1982: 380–407). Visual spirituality is a dimension of what Origen terms the 'spiritual senses', where embodiment links with the spirit and the intellect, to realise a seeing of the unseen, something that comes into fullness in heaven, but on earth is only seen indirectly through symbols, inner discernments and physical manifestations of the invisible. In this life, heaven is temporally curtained off from earthly view. This curtailment is a statement of the power of God. Those who bless the Lord come to wonder: 'who coverest thyself with light as with a garment, who stretchest out the heavens like a curtain' (Ps.104: 2). In the end, these matters return to conventional sociological queries: the examination of the construction of religious images, their reception and the modes of response they generate (Morgan 2005: 25–47). It is here that sociology engages with visual spirituality. In doing so, it confronts some unavoidable theological dilemmas.

Christianity is at best divided on the issue of seeing the unseen. In its severest form, Protestantism is afflicted with strains of iconoclasm. To make an image of God is presumptuous but also idolatrous. Like Islam, Protestantism places God at a distance where He abides unseen, remote and devoid of image save what comes in the Word and in revelation. In this visual impoverishment, Islam and Protestantism stipulate an asceticism of endeavour where images of consolation are denied. For them, visual spirituality would be a contradiction in terms, a violation of integrity and of the worth to be rendered to God.

By contrast, Catholic and Orthodox theologies, positively enjoin the use of images of the unseen God. These give witness to the Incarnation, to the revelation of the unseen God in the seen life of Jesus Christ. As long as what is seen is not confused with an unseen prototype, then visual spirituality is deemed to have an edifying dimension. Icons, paintings and sculptures form part of a rich repository of these theologies. These resources also form part of Western civilisation, but it is their uses as religious capital for the cultivation of visual spirituality that concerns this chapter.

Images give consolation to the eye, of hope for what lies beyond this vale of tears. But such forms of seeing have a duty of regard to the Incarnational. Visual spirituality gives witness to embodiment; only the angelic view the unseen in disembodiment.

Thus, visual spirituality has to have an external dimension to what is ultimately an act of contemplation in the interior where the grace of spiritual seeing is most fully realised. It is in this external dimension, of community, relationships, rituals, symbols and forms of representation that sociology gains a foothold on visual spirituality. In this social ambit to the visual spirituality, sociology has to accept also the theologies that endorse its nurture.

Forcing sociology to make theological choices is not new. Weber's approach to the genesis of capitalism was based on fine theological distinctions and these served to pick out the form, Calvinism, that was best suited for his case. Catholicism and the Orthodox traditions present theologies that enable sociology to explore visual spirituality in its fullness of paradoxes, contradictions and fruitful realisations. Protestantism is ill fitted to provide a theology that would sanction such sociological ventures. It concentrates on the Word, but also on the nurture of the inner self. It does not have a theology of aesthetics, bar one or two recent exceptions such as Paul Tillich. Oddly, the stipulations of Protestantism regarding the sanctity of the inner self as the dwelling place for spiritual endeavour inadvertently permit squatters' rights to be taken up by holistic spiritualities. The denial of avenues to the visual and social carries a price. If visual spirituality is knocking on the gates of sociology, an adjacent term, visual culture seems to have entered its portals.

Visual culture encapsulates an unprecedented shift in sensibility regarding matters of the visual. It has become a crucial ingredient of cultural expression, notably through images, spectacles, advertising and marketing that reflect powers of commodification to arrange what should be seen and recognised. The search engines of Google permit almost any image of almost anything to be conjured up. The Internet satiates the thirst to see. But as the visual has increased greatly in significance, digital culture has changed the social basis of seeing. Images no longer need to be made on the ground of culture; they can be assembled in virtual reality where resemblance is easy to confuse with an original. In this ocular feasting, the eye can easily be confused by facades, illusions and deceptions. The eye sees much but not necessarily with much discernment, for a condition of anomie seems to have descended on ways of seeing.

Seeing and being seen shape the interaction order in ways without precedence. Heightened awareness of the visual has become an added dimension of reflexivity, one whose significance sociology has yet to confront. But the vital issue which visual culture has brought to the fore, that is of crucial sociological importance is the relationship between the viewer and what is seen. A question of character lies in that relationship. The act of seeing has a moral dimension, but it is one masked in the context of the Internet. Its exemplary viewer, the voyeur lies hidden, disembodied, private and characterless. Seeing apart from the social, the voyeur is not seen to see. As seeing becomes privatised, and as spirituality in holistic forms is regarded as exemplary in its expression of subjective preference, these movements away from the social cannot be seen to be in the interests of sociology. Visual culture has changed its reflexive expectations.

Consider Goffman's notion of a social establishment. It was defined as 'any place surrounded by fixed barriers to perception in which a particular kind of activity regularly takes place' (Goffman 1959: 238). Through fortitude and the passage of fieldwork, the sociologist seemed bestowed with analytical powers to unfix these impediments to perception and to reveal all. But now the trumpet of technology has sounded and in a digital culture the walls impeding perception have fallen down. If boundaries that block the sociological gaze have fallen, other matters have been cleared away, even more germane to sociology.

The rituals of seeing, and the sites for viewing that incorporate the social seem oddly artificial to the voyeur who sees in a twinkle of the eye any image on his Google. He does not need to make untidy passage through the social to see an image. It can be conjured up instantly denying the possibility of sociological interventions. Yet, these outcomes are more ambiguous than they might seem initially. The voyeur's dilemma is that endless visual vistas are opened up, but so also are sites displayed that provide endless temptations to go and see images in their social milieu. The eye can grow tired of the miracle of the digital and might want to make a pilgrim's progress into the fields of culture to capture the freshness of sight that only a situated act of seeing can provide.

An effect of the Internet is to heighten awareness of what one should see. Sociology finds it difficult to handle this expansion of visual possibilities. Each viewer has his own agenda and set of subjective preferences. Often those who scroll on the Internet are deemed to be seeking forbidden pleasures. It is easy to find a bizarre range of websites that feed any imaginative need and desire. There is a strange democracy about the Internet. Any tale can be posted, and almost any image can be presented. Oddly, organised religion has been an unexpected beneficiary of the Internet.

In their steadfast affirmation of a spirit of secularity, the gatekeepers of the English mass media have performed an exemplary task of keeping religious activities out of public sight. Few galvanising images of spiritual endeavour pass through the gates. But with the expansion of the Internet, the visual treasures of organised religion are free to be displayed in plenitude and are available for view by any viewer unhindered by secular inhibitions. What is seen begs questions about their higher purpose, the spirituality that surrounds these hitherto forbidden sights. Here one encounters a paradox.

As sociology started to grasp the implications of visual culture, another movement also commenced in the mid-1990s of equal sociological importance: holistic spirituality. This is a shorthand term for an enormous range of new forms of spirituality. In simple terms, holistic spirituality is about first things – me; and the spirituality of organised religion is about last things – us. Between the two, there is a chasm. Oddly, the two movements, of visual culture and holistic spirituality stand in stark disconnection.

Holistic spirituality denotes an interior quest to integrate the body and soul in ways that tap spiritual powers of self-expression, capacities which institutional forms of religion are deemed to thwart. Whereas in the late medieval and early modern world, the lords spiritual and temporal ruled with authority in well cast divisions between the sacred and the civil (Principe 1983: 131), practitioners of holistic spirituality operate with disdain of these. For them, spirituality is to be democratised, to be removed from the orbits of obligation and authority in organised religion that kill the spirit. The techniques of holistic spirituality offer gifts of empowerment to the self to find the spirit within and to be a priest on its own powers of self-realisation. Holistic spirituality offers the glittering prize of self-affirmation, self-validation and self-containment, gifts of autonomy religion with its inconvenient God refuses to give. Does holistic spirituality escape the organisational clutches of religion? It might, but it always risks re-appropriation into a religion. Its point of weakness lies in the area of the visual.

Holistic spirituality needs to nurture a collective image, and in doing so, it faces the need to organise resources to realise a desired façade. This causes an aggregate of practices to slide into a religious form, whether virtual, implicit or invisible. In so organising, holistic spirituality risks the charge of being a quasi-religion. But there is a second weak point of holistic spirituality – its blindspot in relation to the visual. The concerns of holistic spirituality are interior and, in this pilgrimage within, no image cast in the external is needed, for the spirit sought has no form, no visible manifestation and no face. The subjectivisation of culture that is sacralised in holistic spirituality marks a property of choice open to the individual, who seeks an elective affinity with what he or she seeks to express. But that opening out of subjective preferences is not doomed to go down the cul-de-sac of holistic spirituality. Other sights are also available well fitted to fulfil expressive needs, and these can take other spiritual turns. By their definition elective affinities are never fixed; they are pliable. The subjective preference is an entity on the sociological table. It can move in many directions and take many turns in seeking. There is nothing stipulated in sociology that denies the allures of organised religion, especially in matters pertaining to visual culture.

Catholicism structures visual culture to envision the heavenly. Images, icons and architectural forms serve to nurture dispositions and practices of visual spirituality. Visual spirituality is about seeing to believe. But if the actor inhabits a culture where religion is disappearing from the landscape, and the eye increasingly can only focus with secular expectations, then the chances of petition for the gift of faith to see the unseen might seem diminished. Yet, the opposite is the case. Present forms of visual culture generate risks of ocular anarchy for the unwary over what to see that ultimately counts. The need to regulate ways of seeing has increased not decreased. This has inserted a property of self accounting in acts of seeing.

In holistic spirituality, the God who controls heaven is dethroned and the self takes to itself god-like powers to pull the curtain on the unseen and so to be the agent of its own self-revelation. No moral qualifications are required for such revelations. The introspection works from the prospect of strengthening and not from a platform of weakness. But in organised religion, seeing into the realms of the spiritual is subject to the refinement of character. The nurture of virtues is related to the capacity to see into the spiritual. This is well expressed in the famous assertion of St James, that 'pure religion and undefiled before God and the Father is this. To visit the fatherless and widows in their affliction, and to keep himself unspotted from the world' (James 1: 27). Duty to others and being unsullied by the world are the seedbeds of visual spirituality.

As visual culture expands in sociological significance, it exposes a paradox that the spiritual eye has diminished in ambition and use. Of course, such worries go back to Matthew Arnold, for whom utilitarianism and manufacture diminished the light of culture. But deeper worries have emerged, that the ways of seeing proper to notions of visual spirituality have become lost arts. As von Balthasar asked:

> Why should the liturgical sense of life, which is portrayed in the highest degree by Dionysius the Areopagite and is transmitted by him to the Middle Ages, be foreign to modern man, who measures so much and works with numbers and proportions? (von Balthasar 1991: 470)

The only certainty in life is death and this is a dimension of spirituality downplayed in holistic forms. The strengths of visual spirituality relate to its recognition of the weaknesses of embodiment. The body is frail; it suffers and dies. Anxiety about the afterlife gives force to the need to refine visual spirituality to seek to see what is to come that at present lies unseen.

The Other World and Visual Spirituality

The unseen, what is invisible and spiritual, seems to shrink in significance as digital culture lights up everything and increasingly governs what matters to be seen. In the end, digital culture is confined to what can be constructed on earth; the veil of heaven has not yet been torn apart and the eye still has not seen what it contains. Despite these limits, as indicated above, the Internet has opened out unparalleled opportunities for religions to display their visual wares. Contrary to expectations, the number of web pages on religion (combining Christianity, Church, faith, God, religion and theology) listed in 2004 is over double for those on sex (Højsgaard and Warburg 2005: 3).

Yet, oddly, this expansion of visual possibility occurs as Catholicism withers in Europe, unable to resist the acids of secularisation and the relativism and the indifference these fatefully seem to yield. Increasingly, religious practice in Europe is the calling of a diminishing minority who exercise a vicarious memory for the majority increasingly disconnected from the culture of Christianity (Davie 2000). As awareness of the visual culture of Catholicism expands, queries will emerge as to the significance of what is portrayed. One wants to know the story of the mysterious images of Catholicism and what they signify. Some narrative is needed to indicate why the unseen is not yet seen. This relates to a query put to Christ as to why he spoke in parables to those not given to understand the mysteries of the Kingdom. His purpose, he answered was that 'seeing they may see and not perceive' (Mark 4: 12). It is not just a matter of looking; one needs to nurture a capacity to see the unseen. Yet even if one wants to look, it seems that images of heaven and hell have vanished.

Few sociologists can imitate Bauman in his capacity to feel the instability of contemporary social life and the sense of flux and contingency it generates. He seldom comments on religious belief or its implications. In his extended interview in *Identity*, however, he reflects on attitudes to the sacred and on life where 'the "now" leaves no room for the eternal and no time to reflect on it' (Bauman 2004: 73). Later, he goes on to observe bleakly that 'bridges connecting mortal life to eternity, laboriously built over the millennia, are cast out of use. We have not been in a world deprived of such bridges before' (Bauman 2004: 75). It is this sense of emptiness and disconnection that makes the cultural circumstances shaping contemporary spiritual needs so unusual.

Those who suggest these concerns are not matters of sociological deliberation forget their place in Weber's *The Protestant Ethic* (1930). The salvation anxieties of the Calvinist emerged from a belief that solutions were to be found in this world, and not by reference to idolatrous representations of the other world that led to superstitious practices that seemed to distort Catholicism (Flanagan 2004: 162–9).

A difficulty lies at the heart of visual spirituality. Might those who seek to see, see what they want to see as against what they should see? Images of the afterlife are often cast in the expectations of the times. They are constructed to give comfort to the living on earth. As the curtain on heaven is yet to be pulled, what is yet to be revealed might be a matter of conjecture, the myopic projections of how life after death ought to be seen.

Images of the afterlife are of crucial importance in the exercise of visual spirituality. They bridge the gap between the invisible and the visible, but they also give a language of purpose to visual spirituality. Its dealings are less with the ultimate than ultimately with what happens in the afterlife. If the images are incredibly cast, then few will have the incentive to resort to visual spirituality. A slackening of the potency of these images, their capacity to command to look, has occurred in recent Catholic efforts to modernise its doctrines. Oddly, in seeking to make matters of faith more available, they seem to have become more unavailable if the indifference of present culture is a gauge of the effects of this strategy. In this project of modernisation, it might seem that the afterlife has been defenestrated of fear and judgement. Even in Catholicism, limbo has been shunted into the repository of dead theological formulations; purgatory just about remains as the belief of the nervous few. Hell is deemed empty, few having the capacity to commit a properly defined mortal sin (Fenn and Delaporte 2001: 336–60).

Even those who go to hell do not so much burn eternally as meditate in an existential quandary of total isolation. Indeed, it might seem hell has become the habitation of the individualism that has given rise to holistic spirituality, but clearly without the comforts. For some theologians, the capacity to commit mortal sin is confined to the few, who are able to meet its strict and restrictive criteria. A wit to sin is required to go to hell but in the proclamation of inclusiveness, it might seem that the witless of other religions than Catholicism are the beneficiaries of their ignorance of how to damn themselves. Pluralism applied to multi-faith circumstances seems to proclaim salvation for all. Inclusiveness is the spirit of the age, and the afterlife is re-ordered accordingly. Efforts to make theology relevant have become suffused with concerns to make its promulgations about the afterlife safe, sanitised and convenient and in this regard the spirit of secularity has triumphed. As the mantle of life in the hereafter is taken down and reveals an empty space filled with everybody, visual spirituality suffers. No galvanising images can be cast. Without a mobilising vision, the pallid properties of visual spirituality hardly serve to galvanise the pious on earth to look closely at their heavenly prospects.

This is not some sociological intervention in a fundamentalist mode. It lies at the heart of theological matters – what happens to the dead? Somehow, something has been lost of a sense of the need to fix the eye on heavenly matters. An art of looking seems to have fallen into decay. By contrast, in the medieval past, there was a genius for making images well fitted for exercises in visual spirituality. Its accomplishments, in cathedrals, art and architecture invite awe in a culture incapable of manufacturing such heavenly mirrorings. Such images are made no more. The present ground of culture permits no such sproutings to spring up for edifying gaze.

To find an image of heaven for his reflection on the afterlife, Saward had to use Quarton's altarpiece, *The Coronation of the Virgin* (1453–54). It was painted for a Carthusian monastery providing a window on heaven for the monks to see (2005: 15–16). Given their ascetic and celibate life of discipline, fasting, broken sleep, silence and enclosed isolation, it is perhaps not surprising that the monks looked closely at one of the few visual attractions available to give consolation to their eyes. Yet even they had to accept the limits to what the eye cannot see of a place where no telegrams about life there can be sent back to earth (1 Cor. 2: 9).

Orthodoxy in Catholicism is in the ascent and perhaps there is nostalgia for harsher times when spirituality had a bite and when the afterlife was not some democratic paradise for all, even for practitioners of holistic spirituality. In happier past times, sermons made the flesh creep unhappily at the thought of the fires of hell and the sadistic enjoyments of demons sent to torture the dammed. Such thoughts forced even the indolent into nugatory exercises in visual spirituality, into trying to visualise their fate in the afterlife. Liberal theologians of the late part of the twentieth century did their bit to extinguish such dark sides to religion. Yet, society itself has also changed in ways that secularise images of the afterlife.

The medical profession, undertakers and crematoria owners now order death and disposal. They order these matters in ways that take the fear out of what has become just another public service (Illich 1975: 122–50; Jupp 2001; 2006). Such burning matters that now exist relate to the operations in the crematoria and not in hell. Any fires connected to corpses are treated as earthly matters and not those of the afterlife. After service warranties relate to dust not to damnation. In a way, modernity has prised apart the relationship between death and the afterlife. In medieval times, death and the afterlife were far more closely connected in ways that gave immediacy and urgency to matters of visual spirituality.

In the medieval world, the smell of death was intermingled with the odour of sanctity in ways that might seem barbarous to the present pristine inhabitants of Western culture, whose notions of civilisation preclude such intermingling. Thus one might be surprised at the life of choirboys in the fourteenth century at Exeter cathedral whose dwellings were at the West End overlooking the cathedral green which Orme describes as 'a necropolis, an abode of the dead' with a charnel house, and graves possibly not dug (Orme 2001: 116). For the choirboys, this was their unexpected playground. But they too felt the fear of contagion of disease and death, and of joining others in their graves. It is easy to see medieval liturgies through rose tinted glasses; they were less respecting of the sacred than one might think. Nevertheless, death was part of the routine of life for the choirboys in the choirstalls. Shrouded in their long white surplices, in their angelic embodiments, the choirboys often sang sadly for the souls of the dead. They lived lives closer to the fact of death than the children of light. Dirges for the dead seemed woven into the spiritual fate of the departed in ways that could not be unstitched, that is until the vandalism instigated by the Reformation came to pass. In 1536, Exeter cathedral was cleansed of its idols and the bridge it manifested in symbolic form in its interior between heaven and earth was dismantled (Duffy 2001: 96–7).

The medieval world was rich in spiritual capital especially in the cathedral where visual culture was ordered to service the needs of visual spirituality. Ocular discipline emerged from ways of seeing, where piety mingled with expectation, where life and death were integrated and where seeing salvation was the dominant ambition for the projects of visual spirituality. But with the advent of the visual culture in its present frenetic form, the eye wanders, alert, but unfocused, feeding off the fruits of secularity and what other gods have consecrated as fit for new ways of seeing to be cultivated. These have undermined the need to cultivate alertness about the afterlife so central to visual spirituality. As seeing has become increasingly secularised and removed from a religious domain of expectation, a condition of blindsight has emerged. This refers to the capacity to see, but not to name or to be able to categorise (Flanagan 2007). This blindsight has particular ramifications for the exercise of visual spirituality. Those afflicted with blindsight need not look to decipher the symbols of secularity; secularisation affirms the indifference of the gaze; and the opening out of salvation to all takes the fear out of the need to be alert. The foolish virgins of today light their lamps to see for other purposes, and many of these are not cast in the direction of visual spirituality

Whether or not the spiritual senses of the choirboys of Exeter cathedral in medieval times were so well attuned to the needs of visual spirituality is a matter of conjecture, something for medieval historians to clarify. But from the vantage point of the present, their habitus would incline them to treat dirges with resonant respect, for what was sung related to evidences of death all around. One of the justifications for religion is its capacity to express the spiritual in some credible orderings in manifestations and symbols. In the medieval world, finesse was realised in description, naming and ranking hierarchies of the angels, in a complexity that present occupants of visual culture might find scarcely credible. Such a project is unlikely to attract the gaze of those in the sociology of religion; their eyes are cast elsewhere.

The Twilight Zone of Holistic Spirituality

One of Goffman's most important essays was aptly entitled – 'Where the action is'. This related to actions of significance, where character is tested, where fate operates and where gambling is requisite. The actor is seen to test and to be tested in such actions that affirm or deny a moral status (Goffman 1967). 'Where the action is' carries a property of excitement, of 'must see' and this seemed to denote the bias of sociology of religion towards cults and sects in the 1970s. They appeared to be far more exotic than the ordered patterns of institutional religion from which many sociologists wanted to escape. This generated a notion that institutional forms of religion were devoid of sociological interest. As a result few sociologists of religion seek today to understand the internal properties of ecclesial culture. Thus, little attention has been given to the spirituality that characterises this culture in its rituals, its schools and conventions. Not inclined to look at their mysteries, many sociologists direct their gaze to the outside, seeking to spot what is new. In consequence, new religious movements, New Age religions and new forms of spirituality seem to indicate 'where the action is' simply on the basis of their novelty. The implication is that nothing flourishing or new springs up in old time religions. Institutional forms of religion seldom look to sociology to validate or to uncover their forms of spirituality. Given their schools of spirituality, their traditions and centuries of practice, the virtuosi of ecclesial culture are most unlikely to look to sociology to validate their spiritual worth and its relationship to society. The result is that the spirituality of institutionalised religion does not belong in a sociological ambit; most sociologists would wish this. By default, it might seem that holistic spirituality is the only live act in town, and those who practise it have a self-evident justification.

These new forms of spirituality only came to be characterised as recently as 1997 in the USA (Heelas and Woodhead 2005: 1–2). They arise from distinctive needs and cultural circumstances. As Wuthnow notes, 'the current upsurge in spirituality appears, almost by definition, to be without roots' (Wuthnow 2003: 28). To that degree it reflects the needs of an age but is also a product of it. Because these new forms of spirituality operate outside organised religions, their authority cannot be appealed to for a definition to be secured. Sociologists had to take it upon themselves to supply one that seems authoritative for the purposes of their analyses. Thus, Roof suggested that these forms of spirituality provide 'a source of values and meaning beyond oneself, a way of understanding, inner awareness and personal integration'. He went on to add that 'what is at stake is a viable conception of the "self"' (Roof 1999: 35). There is a sense that the precipitating factors leading to holistic spirituality also reflect the insights, needs and aspiration of facets of sociology in its highest mode of reflection. Rootlessness, fragmentation, risk and anxiety, identity crises and above all the question of the self all became sociological matters of concern, and came to epitomise what was known as the condition of postmodernity, one most felt in the 1990s.

Liminality marks the course of life for many who inhabit a world where rituals resonate no more, and where God lives no more. All they are left with are the solaces of holistic spirituality and the endless interior inspections it licenses. All is presented as light and in the light there is no darkness. The spiritual forces are benign rather than malign, and the eye is not trained to distinguish these, for holistic spirituality is not given to seek such distinctions. What is the source of these spiritual powers, given there is no God to bestow them and no ritual to order them? What might seem liberation can contain a tragedy, and one of the few playwrights to discern this spectre was the Brian Friel in his play *Faith Healer.*

The play centres on the tragedy of Frank, the faith healer who has a strange spiritual gift given without grace. His calling was to 'a craft without an apprenticeship, a ministry without responsibility, a vocation without a ministry'. It was something he flirted with as a young man and it came to possess him (Friel 2001: 3). For him, the gift is mysterious, for he cannot fathom the source of its bestowal. All he has is a power to heal that is exercised almost serendipitously. His tragedy is that the one person who cannot be healed by these powers is himself. This failure affects those around him, not least his wife and baby, who die in the play. Taking powers of a god to himself, he lacks the compassion of a God who heals but also loves. His spiritual powers do not expand his humanity; rather they contract it. Instead of being about life and light, the play reeks of death and darkness. In the play one comes to realise that the main characters are dead, but they died in a time when God also seems to have passed away into an oblivion they share. In the play, one can discern some of the properties of sociological understandings of holistic spirituality, but the vision so yielded is far from comforting. Thus, Block suggests:

> *Faith Healer* presents a frightening picture of what happens to the world when post-Christian humanity recapitulates, fragmentarily and without comprehension, the rituals of identity, community and sacrifice of which the Incarnation, for some, still makes sense. (Block 2000: 202)

In his essay on the play, Block links Friel's concerns to those of Hans Urs von Balthasar in his collection, *Theodrama*. With reference to him, Block sees Friel constructing a theatrical space for the tragedy of reading 'God's "presence in absence"', the plight of postmodernity (Block 2000: 204). The play draws out a distortion in sociological characterisations of holistic spirituality, that they are seldom linked to issues of the apophatic that haunt postmodernity. The more one examines holistic spirituality the more one is struck by the degree to which it masks wider theological issues in culture.

What holistic spirituality manages to uncover is an emptiness one that impels the self to seek a deeper and more authentic identity, one fit for finding the ultimate. But in recognising an unseen order, there is no focal point, no narrative and no image, for the spirituality so nurtured flourishes on its opacity, its endless capacity to resist definition. All is about energising, amplifying experience and opening out in a vacuous way (Howard and Welbourn 2004: 35–47). Because it services the needs of the rootless and because it advantageously occupies no settled place, holistic spirituality can always reach for the widest of definitions. Thus, Wuthnow defined spirituality as consisting 'of all the beliefs and activities by which individuals attempt to relate their lives to God or to a divine being or some other conception of a transcendent reality' (Wuthnow 1998b: viii). Holistic spirituality offers allures for those in Wuthnow's apt characterisation, who move from dwelling to seeking, from habitation within institutional religion to a quest for the spiritual outside (Wuthnow 1998b: 52–84). This is why one attaches a property of the émigré to practitioners of holistic spirituality. They seem to be Weberian in their inward scrutinies, but blind to the tragedy of their social isolation. Like Weber, all they are left with is the prospect of finding their spiritual core within, for the landscape outside has been cleared of religious debris. Can the aggregate of holistic spirituality in its manifold forms, practices, borrowings, and techniques individually cast, avoid melting into the category of religion?

Fleeing Religion: The Escape Routes of Holistic Spirituality

Holistic spirituality has many attractions, not least in providing a diversity of techniques, practices and borrowings where picking and mixing is presented as an art open to the individual. As a consolation prize to émigrés from institutional religion, holistic spirituality offers an escape from its clutches. As Wuthnow suggests, it points to something beyond the ordinary where matters are free and unencumbered. By contrast, he suggests religion appears constraining, cold and structured (Wuthnow 2001: 306–7). A contrast is thus drawn between the liberating ethos of holistic spirituality and the constraining, supposedly deadening nature of institutional religion. In the context of the present cultural climate, some sociologists seem to feel that holistic spirituality reflects the spirit of the times in ways institutional forms of religion do not.

But this is to forget the argument of Simmel that such antinomies are endemic in modern culture and, indeed, characterise its basis in a particularly tragic form. Institutional forms of religion have a potential to be deadening, but are capable of redemption in the spirit (Heb. 9: 14). Simmel specifically considered religion in terms of its deadening potential. This consideration arises in his understandings of form and content.

Forms denote the objective enabling means through which some elusive content can be manifested. Content refers to the aesthetic, to properties of the spirit that required social ordering and manifestation. These expanded powers of encapsulation have a potential to kill the spirit when the apparatus of belief becomes an end in itself, the point that advocates of holistic spirituality would use against the apparatus of religion. But this would be to miss a wider point. Simmel's solution to the tragedy of culture does not lie in holistic spirituality, which he partly anticipated, but in theology. It was through the theology of Nicholas of Cusa that redemption of the tragedy of culture was to be found. From Cusa, Simmel affirmed the idea of a God that fused all contradictions but also transcended them (Simmel 1997: 36–44). This might suggest that the dream holistic spirituality offers of an escape from religion is one that leaves its followers blind to the replication of these deadening properties of form in the wider culture. The escape offered is illusory, for a theological solution to a sociological characterisation is denied. Holistic spirituality is the beneficiary of life in fragments; it is not a solution to these, for it bonds nobody and as a consequence offers no healing of a broken commonwealth. Despite these reservations, holistic spirituality presents itself to sociology with a lot of attractions.

There is a pioneering property to the questing and seeking that characterises holistic spirituality, one that fits well with liberal sociological values. It embodies American values of searching on a frontier for the roots of integrity. There is something self-evidently admirable about this lonely quest to find integrity within that accords with the Weberian values the discipline of sociology is supposed to incarnate, of seeking for the demons within to control them better. The ideal of autonomy, of a freedom to choose, mitigates for sociology the smorgasbord properties of holistic spirituality, where one picks and chooses at whim. In its most opaque form, holistic spirituality is inclusive, tolerant of individual endeavour, and affirming in the need for questing and journeying. The fact that nobody gives testimony of arrival at a definite point seems to worry few. It is the journeying not the arrival that arouses sociological sympathy, a trait that runs through Roof's pioneering work, *Spiritual Marketplace* (1999).

Advocates of holistic spirituality suggest that its disconnection from organised religion is a function of the postmodern times with its stress on individualism. Certainly these times might have greatly attenuated this disconnection, but such an outcome is not something accidental, but involves a strategy of imperialism and one with a history of efforts to offer an alternative to organised religion as *the* resource for realising spirituality. In the politics of spirituality, holistic spirituality runs some crafty campaigns.

In his account of seeker spirituality, Fuller provides a useful history of its emergence from an unchurched intellectual and cultural tradition peculiar to the USA (2001). Theosophy, pragmatism, and spiritualism all contributed to a notion that spirituality is something personal and private and that religion is public and by implication impersonal. More than anybody, William James legitimised the distinction between spirituality and religiosity.

Working from a psychological perspective, Fuller argues that James 'as a "highbrow" intellectual gave respectability to the long line of unchurched spiritual traditions he had inherited from the Swedenborgians, Transcendentalists, mesmerists and mind curists' (Fuller 2001: 134). But Fuller makes an equally useful point earlier when he indicates that James suffered from acedia, a spiritual malaise that reflected a sense of the absence of God (Fuller 2001:130–31). Acedia is a form of boredom or spiritual sloth. The term emerges in the context of early monasticism, as pioneered by the Desert Fathers (Flanagan 2004: 117, 119). Efforts to find quick fix solutions to acedia left their legacy in the lightness and sense of liberation holistic forms of spirituality affirm. But these solutions represent an escape from commitment and from the hard searching theology entails. Rather than rely on the Holy Spirit, the self seeks the spirit within to find its own solution. Such matters of choice complicate the response of sociology to matters of spirituality.

Bellah's study of individualism and commitment in American life introduced a term of lasting importance in debates on holistic spirituality. 'Sheilaism' was a term used to describe a young nurse who had been in therapy and in religious matters followed her own little interior voice (Bellah 1986: 221). Her efforts were directed to personalising religion. This involved striving to transform 'external authority into internal meaning' (Bellah 1986: 235). Such efforts came to fullness in the spiritual endeavours of those in New Age religions (Rose 1998). Its multitudinous adherents sought to find their own subjective religion in a culture that is both rootless and legitimises individualism (Possamaï 2000: 367; Heelas and Woodhead 2005). The spirituality so produced might well mirror the needs of the age, but its bears a price, a point Fuller recognised when he observed that 'in the long run, Sheilaism deprives us of a language genuinely able to mediate among self, society, the natural world and ultimate reality' (Fuller 2001: 159). On the other hand, Roof defends Sheilaism as an understandable form of spiritual rejuvenation, an effervescence that had its own self-evident justifications (Roof 1999: 146–9). But journeying within, alone, bears the risk of reaching too far into an interior and so leaving behind external references that would criticise and validate what was found. The risks of an overly individualised spirituality can also go in the opposite direction, as Wuthnow has indicated in his notion of 'multiphrenic spirituality'.

This refers to the burden of a plurality of religious identities in a biography that leaves an interior life unscrutinised and almost residual. Whereas in Sheilaism, identity is underdetermined, in 'multiphrenic spirituality' it is over determined. Thus, a woman who exemplified the condition in his essay could only affirm her belief 'in a cosmic self as an ultimate authority' (Wuthnow 1998a: 41). The pluralism of her religious affiliations leaves her singular and disconnected from her approach to spirituality. In this setting, her failure lies in a disconnection from the social and the lack of place in it for a stable spirituality. For Wuthnow, practice redeems those in this state. It relates to a morality and a commitment. Thus, he concludes that 'hucksters who sell cheap grace and who encourage facile spirituality need to be challenged, just as totalitarians do when they sell religious bigotry' (Wuthnow 1998a: 42–3). Thus, it can be argued, that whatever about a subjective turn in culture, the expressiveness that gives rise to the pursuit of holistic spiritually requires a social outlet, a site of manifestation, an arena for practice and realisation, where commitment is made and community is found.

Both sociology and spirituality seek a mean between the self and the social. While the Internet facilitates the emergence of certain forms of New Age religions and their spiritualities, it leads to endless networking and shopping around (Possamaï 2000: 369–70). Thus, the very entities that gave rise to holistic spirituality might also impair its reproduction. Heelas and Woodhead reflect on different scenarios in the Kendal study, one of which is an aging population in their sample, living off the 'sacred capital' of the Christianity they abandoned. They predict the holistic milieu will grow despite claims that the forms of transmission of holistic spirituality are weak. But in so arguing, they make an odd point that spiritual capital will be developed to replace that derived from Christianity (Heelas and Woodhead 2005: 132–4). Given the eclectic and individualised nature of holistic spirituality, it is hard to envisage how it can generate a spiritual capital without a communal religious affiliation to organise it. Spiritual capital presupposes investment, wagering and commitment, precisely the properties holistic spirituality claims are not required for its practice. The issue of transmission in regard to holistic spirituality is far more problematic than Heelas and Woodhead might indicate. In their contribution in this volume, Voas and Bruce suggest that forms of institutional religion and holistic spirituality *both* face similarly bleak outcomes and that neither can reproduce itself in a culture inimical to a concern with ultimate matters.

The diversity of forms and practices of holistic spirituality, and the individualism underwriting its basis, might well enable incorporation into religion to be resisted if not endlessly postponed. Even if some others are loath to turn the forces of holistic spirituality in a Durkheimian direction, others might have no such inhibitions.

If secularisation represents a form of theft from institutional religion, the appropriation of spirituality into the service of corporate religion might seem larceny on a grand scale. This emerges from circumstances Carrette and King rightly deplore whereby 'in a culture characterised by an addiction to buying and selling, "spirituality" has ... become the brand name for the act of selling off the assets of "old time" religion' (Carrette and King 2005: 125). This form of asset stripping can be used to service the needs of corporate religions. These build on the ethos of holistic spirituality. It supplies the petrol to run these virtual religions (Flanagan 2004: 14–41). Kunde (2002) offers a plausible vision of the notion of a corporate religion.

Kunde's account is littered with metaphors drawn from religion whose apparatus is re-dedicated to corporate ends. Products are endowed with images that are branded as iconic, the founders are designated as charismatic and the corporation is given a soul. In this context, spirituality becomes an instrument of management, a set of techniques harnessed for envisionment of goals, for the nurture of motivation and for the instillation of corporate bonding (Kunde 2002). This re-channelling of spirituality into a corporate tool suggests that its free-floating in one setting can be hijacked to service contradictory goals in another. As Carrette and King rightly argue, in reference to spirituality, 'the very ambiguity of the term means that it can operate across different social and interest groups and in capitalist terms, function to establish a market niche' (Carrette and King 2005: 31).

Ambiguity is often treated as a hallmark of the culture of postmodernity and the elusiveness of holistic spirituality, in definitional terms, might reflect that condition. But it also relates to an apposite remark of Oakes, that from Simmel one learns of a curious outcome to the evolution of culture, that 'as man becomes more cultivated, his life becomes more oblique and opaque' (Oakes 1980: 37). Somehow, the opacity of spirituality in holistic forms mirrors only too well the culture that gives rise to its popularisation. But the difficulty is that opacity permits any incorporation to be possible and almost any tag to be attached to spirituality. In that regard the rise of 'capitalist spirituality' might astonish Weber; it should not catch contemporary sociologists unawares.

Capitalism was supposed to be the gravedigger of the spirit of Calvinism. It was never to be envisaged that what Capitalism buried was to be disinterred and given the kiss of life as a resource for profit. Marx might have felt vindicated by an unexpected outcome where, as Carrette and King (2005: 17) observe, 'religion is rebranded as "spirituality" in order to support the ideology of capitalism'. The strange outcome is that spirituality, not religion, has become a form of false consciousness. In writing their study, Carrette and King sought to challenge this capitalist takeover of spirituality by 'rethinking the ethical and social dimensions of tradition' (Carrette and King 2005: 29). Not all takeovers of holistic spirituality are mendacious.

New forms of spirituality have had to be invented to fill a void left by the supposed demise of organised religion, but also to replace its functions. An example of this has emerged in the sociology of medicine, in particular in relation to nursing. There is an extensive sociological literature on the rehabilitation of spirituality as an important dimension of nursing roles. Spirituality offsets the pervasive intrusions of hospital bureaucracy while at the same time affirming the calling of nurses to heal and to care for *all* the needs of their patients. To cope with death, and the stresses of the calling, nurses have to confront spiritual issues in ways that arise in few other occupations. Again the form of the spiritual and its use is different to that appropriated to corporate ends. Facets of holistic spirituality emerge in this form cast for use in nursing, but in ways that differ. The spirituality so nurtured is geared to serve the Other, the patient and not the self. This new form of spirituality has an institutional setting and also a concern with reciprocity, with altruism and healing. It is serves to enhance a capacity to cope with compassion with those struggling with the implications of theodicy (Grant, O'Neil and Stephens 2004).

Post-secularity has generated an unexpected need to recover spiritual values and this occurs notably in relation to education and most particularly in relation to courses on civics and citizenship. There are other reasons to preserve spirituality in a definitional opacity. By keeping its definition opaque, spirituality serves as an ideal to shape and to justify a politics of inclusion. The opacity also services a prejudice, one which secularisation affirms. The prejudice is that spirituality contextualised in institutional religion sustains a sectarianism incompatible with civic values of inclusion. For that reason, it is thought desirable in schools to keep spirituality above religion and floating free from it.

Set in their highest form, the values of spirituality and religion converge. As Ashley argues, 'religious and secular spirituality have a great deal in common' and are less easy to separate in practice than many educationalists realise. In dealing with spirituality, some advocates seek a version devoid of reference to the supernatural, but others who incline towards a nexus that links humanist and secular values come to a common understanding of the importance of the idea of love, as an ideal value (Ashley 2000: 46–7). These concerns anticipate the subject matter of the first encyclical letter of Benedict XVI, *God is Love* (2006). Set to its highest concerns, this vision of love, nurtured within a nexus of theology, religion and spirituality seems a curiously apt statement for the times. The encyclical received widespread and approving comment in a surprised English mass media. It was as if it were unexpected that organised religion could address spiritual matters.

An inspection of the enormous diversity of beliefs and techniques that make up what is know as holistic spirituality might or might not justify the claim that it replaces organised religion. But whatever the outcome, advocates of holistic spirituality cannot just affirm the mythology that spirituality is detached in the practice of organised religion. As Hood has well indicated the majority of the population of the USA is religious *and* spiritual in terms of self-identification. He suggests that a vocal minority of academics argue otherwise (Hood 2003: 251–2). In debates on spirituality, it is easy to lose sight, as Hood suggests, of this majority whose practices of fusing both are oddly rendered atypical (Hood 2003: 261).

These comments return to a point of Simmel that religiousness is 'a form according to which the human soul experiences life and comprehends its existence ...' (Simmel 1997: 5). Thus, for Simmel, 'religion does not create religiosity, but religiosity creates religion' (Simmel 1997: 150). This urge of religiosity seeks a social means of making manifest spiritual sensibilities. Thus, the connection between spirituality and religion reflects a habitus, a disposition of the actor to meld these into a common form of expression, such as in ritual representations of the holy. In a crucial metaphor Simmel suggests that colour is the property that links religiosity and spirituality. This returns matters of spirituality to the visual. The form is *seen* to manifest a spiritual property and religion is the frame that enables it to be discerned. The social is what gives a focus to the expectation to see.

In surveying holistic spirituality, one is struck by the absence of concern with its visual expression. Celtic forms of spirituality and those derived from Hinduism are obvious exceptions to this point. As indicated above, the journeying holistic spirituality offers is to the interior. Ivakhiv has drawn attention to this neglect of the visual (what is seen in the exterior) in his account of New Age pilgrimage. He argues that an examination of New Age practices and texts 'reveals an overwhelming priority given to listening or "attunement" over the visual mode of engagement ...' (Ivakhiv 2003: 94). He suggests that pilgrim journeys to sites are less about travelling to see, where the visual gives relief, and more about visiting to untap spiritual energies and forces in the self. This might explain why he can assert that 'the role of visual imagery in New Age pilgrimage has rarely been studied' (Ivakhiv 2003: 102).

If it is correct to assert that holistic spirituality has a blindspot in relation to the visual, and as visual culture becomes more important, religions such as Catholicism, with a long tradition of handling its constituent elements, are likely to be the beneficiaries. The spiritual capital of Catholicism offers a rich resource for visual spirituality.

Spiritual Capital and Visual Spirituality

Sociologists were not alone in being taken aback by the paradigm shift in culture that revealed a displacement of spirituality away from institutional religion and into a marketplace. Traditional religions such as Catholicism seemed wrong-footed, being charged both with being spiritually bankrupt and being incapable of meeting the spiritual needs of the time. Again, one is faced with a puzzle that arises from the definition of spirituality. If spirituality is treated in holistic terms, then Catholicism by its nature cannot compete. This is not a form of spirituality Catholicism can or should supply. But there is a lingering worry, that a legacy of Vatican II left a Church seeking modernisation but in ways that diluted its spiritual capital. Forms of theology that sought to connect to the world, such as liberation theology or those emitting from feminism, seemed more concerned with overturning tradition than living within it.

The notion of the re-invention of tradition was not part of the vocabularies of these theologies. In these efforts to connect to the world, Catholicism lost its self-confidence to do so. Some of these supposedly radical theologies were recruiting sergeants for rivals, such as holistic forms of spirituality. As Bruce has suggested, 'the weakening of the once-all-pervasive Christian worldview permits the wide range of spiritual options on offer in the New Age' (Bruce 1998: 30).

More damaging, given the increasing vagueness surrounding access to the afterlife, the reasons for being a Catholic have become profoundly unclear. The purpose of being spiritual seemed to have been undermined. In seeking to reflect a spirit of modernity, Catholicism inadvertently mirrored the very indifference it was established to confound. Somehow, Catholicism seems to have mislaid not only a means of connecting to the cultural times, but also of supplying its spiritual needs, if the rise of holistic spirituality is indicative. How could this odd state of affairs come to pass, that sociology has to give instructions to theology over the forms of spirituality it *ought* to supply? Why the ecclesial hesitations about spirituality?

Spirituality only appears once in the index of the documents of Vatican II, adjective and in relation to the laity. Again, the term appears obliquely and once in the index in the 1994 *Catholic Catechism*. The reference is to 'spiritual direction'. Brief passing references to spirituality do appear in the section on prayer. There, spirituality is recognised in terms of a convergence of liturgical and theological currents that bear witness to an integration of faith. Reference is also made to different schools of Christian spirituality that share in living traditions of prayer (*Catholic Catechism* 1994: 572, para. 2685).

But the revised and definitive edition of the *Catechism* recognised the change in the significance of the term spirituality in popular culture. Listed in relation to spiritual life, spirituality was given headings on the Word of God, contemplation and prayer. It was also related to the Eucharist, linked to dogma and also to a diversity of forms of discipline or life (*Catechism* 2000). A need was recognised to re-set the term in its traditional understandings and to re-image it in more coherent ways that accorded with the needs of the times. A reinvention was required, but does sociology have a part in this project of ecclesial imperialism? Should sociology arbitrate between holistic spirituality and the spirituality of religion?

An unexpected outcome is that the issue of spirituality propels sociology in a theological direction. It is not a matter of just stipulating in a Durkheimian way a connection between spirituality and religion: an unavoidable issue of the source of this power emerges, and it is one that leads in a Weberian direction. The question emerges: who owns spirituality, what forms of channelling are legitimate and by what authority is it to be routinised and reproduced? This turns the issue of spirituality in the direction of Bourdieu, over the right to consecrate. But what is for him a metaphor returns to the issue of the original, when spirituality is set in a theological direction. Are these sociological matters? Strangely, support for a sociological intervention in these matters comes unexpectedly from the English sociologist of religion, Steve Bruce.

Famous for his sociological justifications of secularisation, he seems less than sanguine about its effects, notably in regard to the emergence of New Age religions.

In reflecting on their impact, Bruce accepts that it is 'not usually the job of sociologists to argue with the beliefs of those they study' (Bruce 1998: 23), yet he feels that New Age spirituality invites specific sociological criticisms. The anarchy of subjectivity underpinning individualism is endorsed by New Age spiritualities but the cost of this endorsement lies in the realm of the social order. To that extent, sociology has a view on their claims to authenticity. These spiritualities simply postpone consideration of problems of co-ordination of belief something religion functions to effect. Thus for Bruce, 'the need for social order is so fundamental to the human condition that to explicitly deny it is to exacerbate rather than to cure the ills of the modern world' (Bruce 1998: 35). Like Carrette and King, Bruce expresses sociological anxieties over the loss of the constraints in regard to spirituality. All three seem to veer to towards tradition and ordering as antidotes to what they perceive to be endemic *sociological* weaknesses in holistic spirituality. There is an implication that holistic spirituality in sociological terms is a form of false consciousness. Could these criticisms lead to a sociological endorsement of spirituality in its Catholic ambience? Whatever else it might do, Catholicism does stipulate an ordering to its belief. As a Church, it is not hesitant about exercising its authority in these matters, in relation to formulas of faith, morals, but above all in religion. But the authority is also cast in the direction of affirming the communal basis of the Church. Much play is made of it constituting a body with interdependent parts. Anything that tilts excessively towards the individual is to be discouraged.

This accounts for hesitations over spirituality as gifts of grace, given to individuals and expressed in forms of mysticism, ecstasy and charisma. The Church leans towards spirituality as located within channels of grace, such as sacraments and sacramentals. Its concerns are with the channelling of spirituality in routinised, stable and communal forms. In traditional form, therefore, spirituality involves seeking to overcome individualism 'through the purification of the heart from all passions, but also through the actual gathering of the Eucharist, which places creation in the movement – in space and time – toward its proper eschatological end' (Zizioulas 1985: 43). Exuberant self-proclaiming forms of spirituality that characterise holistic styles, whose mandate is drawn from a culture addicted to expressivism, would be wholly out of kilter with Catholic assumptions of practice and realisation. Its bias is towards the communal expressivism Flory and Miller uncover in the preceding chapter.

Spiritual practices are linked to the formation of character and the nurture of a life of virtue. Their pursuit involves a denial of the self, not its affirmation as in the case of rival holistic forms of spirituality. Zizioulas suggests in his account of the early Christian community that 'true spirituality always involves some form of death. The ascetic and the martyr are for this reason the true spirituals of the Church' (Zizioulas 1985: 39). Virginity is also deemed to reflect exalted spiritual values. The heroic virtue of sexual self-denial has long been considered advantageous for spiritual advancement. But in a strange way, virginity has a definite sociological purpose. In Late Antiquity, by standing against the social, virgins gave witness to another form of solidarity, one with the angels in heaven (Brown 1985: 427–43).

The link between discipline and the pursuit of spirituality is of course to be found in the spiritual exercises of St Ignatius. Principe suggests that the term spirituality is linked to piety and to exemplary ways of life that bear imitation. He draws attention to another obvious point that spirituality refers to persons whose lives are lived by the Spirit as against those whose carnal appetites form their guiding principles of life. The French seventeenth-century notion of spirituality related it to a life of quiet devotion and this became a dominant reference point for the term in Catholicism up to the early twentieth century (Principe 1983: 132–4). Alexander follows a similar line, of linking spirituality to piety and devotion, but notes the way the term bears on enthusiasm and unorthodoxy (Alexander 1980: 248–9). Both beg questions about the regulation of spirituality and fears concerning its unfettered forms. The briefest consideration of Catholicism and spirituality suggests a long tradition of handling irregular and rival forms such as those that are manifest in holistic spirituality. These concerns are by no means peculiar to the present culture but are endemic as ecclesial problems of separating out the authentic from the inauthentic. In this regard, wisdom rather than analysis wins.

Mysticism is often linked closely to spirituality and forms of religiosity. In looking at the link between religiousness and spirituality, Hood uses mysticism as a form of 'spiritual religion', one that can be traced back to theological formulations of faith (Hood 2003: 259). Yet, McGrath rightly indicates that reference to mysticism exasperates the terminological confusion over spirituality itself. He suggests that mysticism betokens something special, something exalted that makes it a particular and exceptional form of spirituality (McGrath 1999: 5–7).

If spirituality is to be successfully attached to religion in sociological terms, it is in its forms of routinisation that these attachments are to be found. As Cottingham suggests, the lifeblood of religion, its spiritual basis, derives not from the 'visionary and ecstatic discoveries of the mystics on the one hand', nor from the 'cataphatic disquisitions of the theologians on the other', but from repeated practices of prayer and worship. In liturgy can be found the place of the integration of the spiritual into tradition and community in an exemplary form of practice (Cottingham 2005: 163–4). Liturgy might be considered the exemplary site for the exercise of visual spirituality. It is in the deciphering of symbols that important facets of spirituality are to be found. This relates to Weber's notion to office charisma. It involves the capacity and authority to decipher symbols and to that degree can be linked to the routinisation of spiritual expectations and realisations.

Reference to Weber reverses the notion that spirituality only has a subjective, individualised dimension. Instead, one can argue that spirituality in its ritual channelling has an objective side, but one in which subjectivity flourishes. Spirituality has an external dimension, in the social, but it is one that is not fated by the cultural times to be disconnected from the internal. Surely, in the simplest of sociological terms, that notion of disconnection is incredible. What is in the external is internalised and appropriated within, and in that sense both are fused in enactment and self-appropriation. Secondly, reference to routinisation avoids the implication that institutional religions cannot reproduce their own forms of spirituality.

Because spiritual experience can deceive, or reflect an unhealthy exuberance, Catholic authority has a long tradition of sorting the pious from the impious and in a well-established balancing act, the subjective preferences of the individual with the more objective needs of the community. The whole notion of spiritual direction so fundamental to monasticism affirms this point. In the end, in this setting, spirituality does return matters to the individual, but not to the individualism that precipitates the need to explore in the mode of holistic spirituality.

Bouyer's *Introduction to the Spiritual Life* (1960), marked an important change of emphasis in Catholic understandings of the implications of spirituality. His interests lay 'in the link between the objects of faith and the reactions aroused by these objects in the religious consciousness' (Principe 1983: 137). In arguing that the total context of spirituality needs to be taken into account, Principe (1983:139–40) explicitly inserts an expectation that sociology is required to read this properly. This expectation is implicit also in Alexander's three theological dimensions to spirituality. These refer to how people live their faith; the affective side of religion for *homo religiosus*; and finally, the heuristic and analytical basis of the concept (Alexander 1980: 253–4).

It seems almost obvious to affirm a cultural dimension to spirituality. This dimension relates to issues of experience, expectation and regulation, to capacity for discernment, and to forms of recognition that shift with changing cultural mileux. These have definite but indeterminate effects on how spirituality is not only linked to religion but also to theology. Within Catholicism, these have a triangular relationship, but one that can come adrift. The detachment of theology from spirituality worried von Balthasar. These worries were expressed in a famous essay on 'Theology and Sanctity'. This referred to an evolution where 'theology at prayer was superseded by theology at the desk' (von Balthasar 1989: 208). It is the loss of a reflective dimension to theology that concerned von Balthasar. His project, as Walker indicates, involved a 're-theologising theology' (Walker 2005: 517–23).

Sociology's one testimony to theology is to give witness to the social dimension of spirituality. A mandate for this comes from an observation Burns makes regarding St Augustine's views on community. Burns argues that 'the social dimension of grace challenged the assumption that access to God could be best attained through solitary ambition and withdrawal from society' (Burns 1985: 342). It is in the milieu of the social that grace is to be found; it is also where spirituality is to be nurtured. Even though spirituality relates to the cultural ground, what emerges still eludes. As von Balthasar observed:

> No mission, and no spirituality is capable of being defined in its living centre. They all come from the infinite variety of the divine life, which always exceeds the compass of the human mind. Ultimately, then, we cannot project the geometry of heaven on to the earthly plane, or draw up a system of spirituality. (von Balthasar 1989: 226)

His point is that states of life with their own spiritualities are diverse, but similar in their self-giving to each other. In this sharing they imitate Rublev's icon of the Holy Trinity. In this sharing, the social bond is healed and strengthened.

This concern with sharing receives timely sociological expression in Putman's *Bowling Alone*. His worries relate to more negative aspects of individualism, the weakening of commitment to society in general and to groups in particular. Social capital, the cousin of community, as he aptly describes it, refers to social networks and civic virtue is entwined in these 'reciprocal social relations' (Putman 2000: 19). For him, religion is an enormously important resource in American society for the development of social capital. Not surprisingly, however, reflecting on church statistics, he observes that 'privatised religion may be morally compelling and psychically fulfilling but it embodies less social capital' (Putman 2000: 74). This shopping around effects an expansion of the secular sphere but also a contraction of what can be termed spiritual capital, a concept Guest has also explored in Chapter 10.

Verter's concept of spiritual capital stands against the individualism of holistic spirituality. It refers to embodiment, material and symbolic commodities and the powers of churches to legitimise 'an arbitrary array of religious goods' and to promote their use (Verter 2003: 159–60). Spiritual capital builds on Bourdieu's approach to cultural, religious and symbolic capital (Flanagan 2007). Most importantly, for this chapter, spiritual capital provides a conceptual basis for sociological understandings of visual spirituality.

Habitus supplies the notion of a disposition to accept ways of seeing proper to the authentic use of spiritual capital and the theological stipulations regarding reception and appropriation. The recognition Bourdieu gives to agents on the cultural field to designate and to consecrate (paintings and sculpture) applies also to those objects on the religious field, however much he might decry the authority and power so used. The process of defining is similar in both fields, but in the case of visual spirituality the use and ends are different, for the use of the spiritual capital is not just to please the eye, but also to give it access to something unseen. Dispositions relate to inclinations to see, forms of acceptance that tilt over into the yielding that characterises faith. Sociologists might balk at this formulation, yet it encapsulates a contradiction endemic in Bourdieu's sociology of culture. The notion of *illusio* refers to a letting go to invest in the game, but this acceptance of a yielding has to be placed against a bracketing of what is denoted as the content of the game, what embodies issues of taste, aesthetics, and religion that give it a language of designation, as a play with matters of ultimate value (Bourdieu and Wacquant 1992: 98). This ultimate value can refer to what is marked as spiritual. A denial of *illusio* precludes the sociologist from entering the spirit of the game. To live in the brackets is to preclude going forward from form into content, of making the leap that is inherent in Simmel's approach to religion.

If sociology is to proceed, it has to work out its analytical salvation through notions of mimesis and transformation, so that in relation to visual spirituality, habitus is married to *illusio* and a disposition is nurtured to utilise spiritual capital to cultivate the sight characteristic of the spiritual senses. The discipline has to operate with a belief that seeing can change and re-constitute social relationships, even if the envisioning operates on a borderland with the unseen. In that regard, there is a property of liminality in visual spirituality. This reflects a comment of von Balthasar that 'for man in his full reality "experience" as an immediate perception of reality, is to be found at both extremes of his being ...'. He goes on to add that 'the experience of the senses, however, appears to be hopelessly worldly and mystical experience, on the contrary, hopelessly unworldly and non-sensory' (von Balthasar 1982: 366–7). Finding a visual mean in this liminality might seem totally elusive; yet many have sought in the light and found it.

Seeing into the light of Being, the ultimate source of the unseen, relates to a raft of theological and philosophical issues, raised by Plato, the neo-Platonics, Origen, the Pseudo-Dionysius and St Hugh of Victor to name a few, that are far beyond the remit of sociology to evaluate. But what is of the light, of heaven, is something whose image needs to be manufactured on earth. What is prone to anthropomorphism is redeemed by heavenly responses. von Balthasar expresses this well when he suggests that the angels have a vital theological task of making 'visible the social character of the Kingdom of Heaven, into which the cosmos is to be transformed' (von Balthasar 1982: 674–5). Strangely, the coming of the angels in an era of post-secularity marks a divide between holistic spirituality and the conventions of spirituality of Catholicism.

Jacob's Ladder: On Envisaging the Rungs

Jacob had a dream of a 'ladder set up on the earth, and the top of it reached to heaven and behold the angels of God ascending and descending on it' (Gen. 28: 12). Now it could be said that belief in angels, never mind seeing them disappearing at the top of a ladder, are hardly expected concerns for the exercise of a sociological imagination. Apart from Comte's eccentric affirmation of the angels in his Positivist religion, that incorporated sociology into its vision, these supernatural messengers hardly penetrate sociological consciousness, or indeed, unconsciousness. Yet, there is one signal exception to this – Peter Berger's *A Rumour of Angels.*

Berger's critique was directed against the trivialising tendencies of radical theologians who sought to legitimise the secular consciousness of the age (Berger 1971: 97). Contrary to its title, Berger in his concluding remarks to the book indicated that it had not been about angels, though 'at best, it might be a preface to angelology, if by that one meant a study of God's messengers as His signals in reality'. His study was a reflection on 'a situation in which transcendence has been reduced to a rumour' (Berger 1971: 119). It was set against a notion of the spiritual adventure of modern man '*un*learning any conceivable metaphysical terror' (Berger 1971: 16). Fundamental to his account is that faith is rooted in experience and that 'every ordering gesture is a signal of transcendence' (Berger 1971: 72). This stress on the inductive basis of religion was prophetic in terms of drawing attention to the cultural terrain upon which belief emerges and upon which signals of transcendence are 'heard'. Yet, in this setting, there are risks of mishearing these signals. As Berger indicated, 'the denial of metaphysics may be identified with the triumph of triviality' (Berger 1971: 96). But then, he argued that each age must seek to find signals of transcendence uniquely its own (Berger 1971: 100). This makes the emergence of holistic spirituality and its concerns with the angels all the more perplexing.

In the late 1960s, few might have predicted that Berger's sociological testimony to a rumour of angels would be expanded into a flood of testimonies in the 1990s. Three out of four Americans believe in angels and these beliefs are endorsed in a growing volume of popular works on experiences of the angelic visions and presences (Wuthnow 1998b: 115; 120–21). But Wuthnow goes on to observe that 'the most recent literature suggests that angels are rather ill-disposed toward institutional religion, that they transcend religious and theological distinctions, and that they simply appear to good-hearted people who need them' (Wuthnow 1998b: 128). In short, their visitations serve to give comfort to the anxious and the distressed. Not surprisingly, he suggests that in America, institutional religious leaders regard these manifestations as 'more consistent with consumer culture than with theology' (Wuthnow 1998b: 131). Are these angels messengers from God or are they manifestations of spiritual powers available to each and all, so that everybody gets the angel they need and deserve? Oddly, an unexpected dimension of holistic spirituality has been opened up, one that clearly belongs to matters raised by visual spirituality. How is sociology to cope with these visitations? Does it have a disciplinary preference for the feathery creatures of holistic spirituality, or the very masculine angelic manifestations that marked the Annunciation, Incarnation and Redemption in the New Testament?

These interests in angelic dimensions to holistic spirituality are by no means confined to the USA. In one English magazine there are advertisements for angelic medicine, 'guardian angel meditations' and an 'angel love guide' (Urquhart 2004). Celestial messages seem to have come to England too. Testimonies to angelic visitations are written in compelling ways (Gallagher 2004). Innocuous in their appeal, non-judgemental in their visitation and demanding no price of commitment, these angels are messengers of solace, trainers and healers, that seem far more attractive to the angst-ridden than the sterner breed populating traditional religion who come with all manner of inconvenient theological baggage.

Public interest in the supernatural has been fuelled by Evangelical concerns in the USA, but also by television series such as *Buffy the Vampire Slayer* and its spin offs *Angel* and *Touched by an Angel?* (Clark 2003: 46–74). Again, exhibiting traits noted elsewhere, Clark indicates, these programmes tell 'stories of a spiritual battle between good and evil with an almost complete disinterest in organized religion' (Clark 2003: 47). Clark argues that many facets of these interests in the supernatural exhibit the commodification of a Protestant imagination regarding the afterlife. As she suggests, these programmes play ambiguously on the dark side of evangelicalism (Clark 2003: 24–45). Her study illustrates the dangers of failing to regulate visual spirituality so that the light and dark side of life here and in the hereafter are kept in a healthy balance. Chase supplies an indication of how this might emerge in his account of angels and spiritual direction (Chase 1997).

In its more recent and zealous evangelical forms, Protestantism invokes the Word to draw the individual to a responsibility for a good life and the avoidance of damnation. But such strictures emerge from a theology suspicious of image making, and for Protestants visual spirituality is replete with idolatrous risks. The outcome of this restriction on the making of images of the afterlife is a vacuum which the entertainment industry fills with glee, commodifying that which Protestantism as a religion is inhibited from either producing or regulating. As Clark rightly indicates, the entertainment media have commandeered 'what if' speculations about life on the other side and has exploited a culture that questions authority and the right to define a truth of ocular and spiritual affairs (Clark 2003: 221–2).

These extra-mural apparitions of angels have perplexed Catholic theologians. Just before Vatican II and in the spirit of its implementation, angels appeared as unwanted images, impediments to the project of modernising theology and liturgy. They belonged to a sentimental, immature form of theology unfit for presentation in a world that had grown beyond such matters. Thus, more adult forms of theology downplayed the angels as a sort of embarrassed secret of Catholicism. There were other theological reasons for relocating angels away from the main altars. As White well indicates, the angels as a facet of salvation were pared down in terms of image and complexity to assert a Christ-centred theology. So angelic hierarchies were dismantled on earth to reveal notions of heaven more fitted to the times when science and reason ruled the cultural roost. But as White concluded, in a climate of scepticism 'this could all too easily degenerate into a narrow, rationalistic demythologisation, and hence in the sidelining, if not in the outright rejection, of more mysterious or emotive Catholic doctrines with a consequent impoverishment of Christian life' (White 2005: 570). Oddly, as in so many areas, what the Church ejected in the interests of modernisation became the ingredients for the seeking of enchantment in the postmodernity that followed (Flanagan 1996).

A strategy of reductionism, a paring down to a noble simplicity was implemented with rigour after Vatican II. At a time when a culture was expanding its cultural capital to feed the imagination, many in the spirit of Vatican II were pursuing a policy of its contraction. Nowhere was this reductionism accomplished with greater zeal than in the case of liturgy. Somehow, there was a belief that if the sanctuary was cleared, the spiritual view would be better, even if there was little to see. Images of the angelic, in choirs and in altarpieces were casualties of an iconoclasm that crippled the aesthetic imagination of the Church in the immediate post-Vatican II period. In seeking to connect to culture, the Church managed to accomplish a stunning disconnection. As it modernised with a ruthless and authoritarian zeal, all supposedly done in the name of liberalism and a need to open to the world, the Church managed to dispose of many facets of cultural, symbolic and spiritual capital. With its spiritual capital somewhat depleted, it might seem that there is little hope for exercises in visual spirituality. But a theology with a tradition has a rich store of memory and unexpected affirmations spring up as testimonies of grace.

Russian society in the fourteenth and fifteenth century hardly seems a site for brilliance and innovation in visual spirituality, yet it produced a set of painters whose icons, as Jenkins indicates, were of unequalled depth of feeling and spiritual awareness (Jenkins 1998: 11). Often works of great religious beauty emerge from cultural times of strife and cruelty. These themes formed the basis of a brilliant film by Tarkovsky on perhaps the most significant of these icon painters – *Andrei Rublev*.

The film sets his life in episodes, where the monk Rublev travels across a country ridden with instability and cruelty. These tempestuous and unstable times contrast oddly with the serenity and love so beautifully and unexpectedly caught in his icons. The film is shot in black and white, colour being left to the end, when the camera lovingly moves over his icons, almost touching them. But these windows on heaven have no protection against civil strife and one of the most graphic scenes of the film shows a cathedral under siege. Many who have taken refuge in the cathedral are slaughtered. The roof has been taken off the cathedral. Rain runs down the icons on its walls and the faces weep at what they see. The price of their compassion is the staining of their beauty.

Protecting a young woman from being raped, Rublev kills a man. Guilt-ridden, he takes a vow of silence and abandons his gift of icon painting as a penance. His sin has disqualified him from making images of the holy. For him visual spirituality has become a dead art. But visual spirituality is also about seeing and doing in ways that act as channels of grace, that transform what is possible and that almost capriciously reverse tragedy. One sees a glimpse of such grace in the final sequences of the film.

A young man, whose father was a maker of bells, valiantly takes charge of re-casting the cathedral bell the Tartars have destroyed. He claims to be using his father's casting formulae, but this is a deception, for he was too selfish to pass the secret to the son. When the bell finally rings true, clear and well, the young man crawls away from the cathedral and falls on a muddy track. He is nearly destroyed by the exertions of his labour, for the casting process involved many helpers and he had taken it upon himself to lead them. If all had gone wrong, he would have been killed. As an artist who also experienced the anguish of getting close to God, Rublev sees the young man's plight and comes to cradle and comfort him. In this act of love, he is given back his sight to make images of the unseen. Mercy and redemption give him again a place in visual culture and his character is released to paint for posterity again. He can show his face again, or rather the face of the One he loves. He returns to see again the truth of what he was taught, that prayer facilitates the making of images of the invisible. It is the means through which visual spirituality operates.

As visual culture begs a complementary dimension, one that visual spirituality offers, it is impossible not to reflect back on the medieval world that constructed so many images of the ethereal in architecture and liturgy. Interest in medieval culture has blossomed in British and American universities. It provided ways of seeing the unseen that a culture of post-secularity can no longer produce. Wuthnow regards this trend as illusory and as a 'serious mistake' (Wuthnow 2003: 246). Unlike in the USA, where the medieval is constructed in imitation and on websites, English society is littered with vestiges of these advanced times of visual spirituality. Tourists gaze at these remains in awe as outsiders on a visual spirituality whose accomplishments present culture has no way of imitating. Yet this would be to miss a point, one Berger noted some time ago. He declared:

> The theological decision will have to be that, 'in, with, and under' the immense array of human projections, there are indicators of a reality that is truly 'other' and that the religious imagination ultimately reflects. (Berger 1971: 65)

From the beginning, Christians were warned to beware of misreading the times. Thus it is written: 'Beloved, do not believe every spirit, but test the spirits to see whether they are of God; for many false prophets have gone out into the world' (1 John 4: 1). The verse below adds 'they are of the world, therefore what they say is of the world, and the world listens to them' (1 John 4: 6) and if sociology tears its disciplinary clothing at this utterance, let it remind itself that it was around dilemmas of affirming this world, or living in denial of it to view better the other world that Weber's template for the discipline was formed in *The Protestant Ethic*. It contains a theological dilemma which the secularised mind of sociology seldom inspects. It generates a question sociology has forgotten; one visual spirituality poses. On which world does it wish to set its disciplinary gaze – this one or the other? Whatever the answer, the consequences are remarkably different.

In regard to visual spirituality, sociology suggests that religion is the spectacle frame that holds the theological lenses. In the end, no one views alone, for each set of sights seen contains tales to be told of what enraptured the eye. The more elusive, the more fleeting and the more mysterious the sightings, the greater is the incentive to tell others. In seeing something that animated the spirit, the telling becomes an urge to give testimony of the effects of *that* sight in *that* unexpected situation on the self. The less one understands what one saw, the more one reflects on it. In the little epiphanies of life, grace can be fleetingly discerned. At its best, visual spirituality carries a property of conversion. One looks at life, at what is framed for edification in a new light. A shift in perspective has been made and in seeing the self is enlarged. Perhaps the shepherds who came in haste to the stable to see in wonder are the exemplary actors of visual spirituality. They journeyed; they saw with their own eyes; and they came back to tell tales of what they had seen. On their return, they showed their face to others, who wondered too. Perhaps, that is where the task of sociology lies in relation to visual spirituality, in chronicling the untold tales of those who journeyed to see and were amazingly enlarged by what they saw. Even in sociology, the light can shine in the darkness, but perhaps that is the tale of visual spirituality itself.

Bibliography

Alexander, J. (1980), 'What do Recent Writers Mean by Spirituality?', *Spirituality Today*, 32: 247–56.

Ashley, M., (2000), 'Secular Spirituality and Implicit Religion: The Realisation of Human Potential', *Implicit Religion*, 3(1): 31–49.

Balthasar, H. von (1982), *The Glory of the Lord. A Theological Aesthetics. I: Seeing the Form* (trans. J. Fessio and J. Riches), ed. E. Leiva-Merikakis, Edinburgh: T. and T. Clark.

Balthasar, H. von (1989), *Explorations in Theology I: The Word Made Flesh* (trans. A.V. Littledale with A. Dru), San Francisco: Ignatius Press.

Balthasar, H. von (1991), *Explorations in Theology II: Spouse of the Word* (trans. A.V. Littledale with A. Dru), San Francisco: Ignatius Press.

Bauman, Z (2004), *Identity: Conversations with Benedetto Vecchi*, Cambridge: Polity.

Bellah, R.N., R. Madsen, W.M. Sullivan, A. Swidler and S.M. Tipton, (1986), *Habits of the Heart: Individualism and Commitment in American Life*, New York: Harper and Row.

Benedict XVI (2006), *God is Love*, London: Catholic Truth Society.

Berger, P.L. (1971), *A Rumour of Angels: Modern Society and the Rediscovery of the Supernatural*, Harmondsworth: Pelican.

Block, E. (2000), 'Brian Friel's *Faith Healer* as Post-Christian Christian Drama', *Literature and Theology*, 14(2): 189–207.

Bourdieu, P. and L.J.D. Wacquant (1998), *An Invitation to Reflexive Sociology*, Cambridge: Polity.

Bouyer, L. (1960), *Introduction à la vie spirituelle*, Paris: Desclée.

Brown, P. (1985), 'The Notion of Virginity in the Early Church' in B. McGinn, J. Meyendorff and J. LeClercq (eds), *Christian Spirituality: Origins to the Twelfth Century*, New York, Crossroad, pp. 427–43.

Bruce, S. (1998), 'Good Intentions and Bad Sociology: New Age Authenticity and Social Roles', *Journal of Contemporary Religion*, 13(1): 23–35.

Burns, J.P. (1985), 'Grace: The Augustinian Foundation', in B. McGinn, J. Meyendorff and J. LeClercq (eds), *Christian Spirituality: Origins to the Twelfth Century*, New York: Crossroad, pp. 331–49.

Carrette J. and R. King (2005), *Selling Spirituality: The Silent Takeover of Religion*, London: Routledge.

Catechism of the Catholic Church (1994), London: Geoffrey Chapman.

Catechism of the Catholic Church (2000), Popular and definitive edition, London: Geoffrey Chapman.

Chase, S. (1997), 'Angels: The Classical Christian Tradition and Contemporary Spiritual Direction', *Listening: Journal of Religion and Culture*, 32(2): 91–103.

Chase, S. (2002), *Angelic Spirituality: Spirituality: Medieval Perspectives on the Ways of the Angels* (trans. S. Chase), New York: Paulist Press.

Clark, L.S. (2003), *From Angels to Aliens: Teenagers, the Media and the Supernatural*, Oxford: Oxford University Press.

Cottingham, J. (2005), *The Spiritual Dimension: Religion, Philosophy and Human Value*, Cambridge: Cambridge University Press.

Cousins, E. (1985), 'Preface', B. McGinn, J. Meyendorff and J. LeClercq (eds), *Christian Spirituality: Origins to the Twelfth Century*, New York: Crossroads, pp. xi–xiv.

Davie, G. (2000), *Religion in Modern Europe: A Memory Mutates*, Oxford: Oxford University Press.

Duffy, E. (2001), *The Voices of Morebath: Reformation and Rebellion in an English Village*, New Haven, CT and London: Yale University Press.

Fenn, R.K. and M. Delaporte (2001), 'Hell as a Residual Category: Possibilities excluded from the Social System', in R.K. Fenn (ed.), *The Blackwell Companion to Sociology of Religion*, Oxford: Blackwell, pp. 336–60.

Flanagan, K. (1991), *Sociology and Liturgy: Re-presentations of the Holy*, Basingstoke: Macmillan.

Flanagan, K. (1996), *The Enchantment of Sociology: A Study of Theology and Culture*, Basingstoke: Macmillan.

Flanagan, K. (2004), *Seen and Unseen: Visual Culture, Sociology and Theology*, Basingstoke: Palgrave Macmillan.

Flanagan, K. (2007), *Sociology in Theology: Reflexivity and Belief*, Basingstoke: Palgrave Macmillan.

Friel, B. (2001), *Faith Healer*, London: Faber and Faber.

Fuller, R.C. (2001), *Spiritual but not Religious: Understanding Unchurched America*, New York: Oxford University Press.

Gallagher, M. (2004), 'I Rescued My Granny Thanks to a Christmas Vision', *Spirit and Destiny*, December: 14–15.

Goffman, E. (1959), *The Presentation of Self in Everyday Life*, New York: Doubleday Anchor.

Goffman, E. (1967), 'Where the Action Is', in E. Goffman (ed.), *Interaction Ritual*, Harmondsworth: Penguin, pp. 149–270.

Grant, G., K. O'Neil and L. Stephens (2004), 'Spirituality in the Workplace: New Empirical Directions in the Study of the Sacred', *Sociology of Religion*, 65(3): 265–83.

Heelas P. and Woodhead, L. (2005), *The Spiritual Revolution: Why Religion is giving way to Spirituality*, Oxford: Blackwell.

Højsgaard, M.T. and M. Warburg, 'Introduction: waves of research', in M.T. Højsgaard and M. Warburg (eds) (2005), *Religion and Cyberspace*, London: Routledge, pp. 1–11.

Hood Jr, R.W. (2003), 'The Relationship between Religion and Spirituality', *Religion and the Social Order*, 10: 241–64.

Howard, S. and D. Welbourn (2004), *The Spirit at Work Phenomenon*, London: Azure.

Illich, I. (1975), *Medical Nemesis: The Expropriation of Health*, London: Calder and Boyars.

Ivakhiv, A. (2003), 'Nature and Self in New Age Pilgrimage', *Culture and Religion*, 4(1): 93–118.

Jenkins, S. (1998), *Windows into Heaven: The Icons and Spirituality in Russia*, Oxford: Lion.

Jupp, P.C. (2001), 'Virtue Ethics and Death: The Final Arrangements', in K. Flanagan and P.C. Jupp (eds), *Virtue Ethics and Sociology: Issues of Modernity and Religion*, Basingstoke: Palgrave, pp. 217–35.

Jupp, P.C. (2006), *From Dust to Ashes: Cremation and the British Way of Death*, Basingstoke: Palgrave Macmillan.

Kunde, J. (2002), *Corporate Religion,* London: Prentice Hall.

McGrath, A.E. (1999), *Christian Spirituality*, Oxford: Blackwell.

Martin, D. (2005), *On Secularization: Towards a Revised General Theory*, Aldershot: Ashgate.

Morgan, D. (2005), *The Sacred Gaze: Religious Visual Culture in Theory and Practice*, Berkeley: University of California Press.

Oakes, G. (1980) 'Introduction', in G. Simmel (ed.), *Essays on Interpretation in Social Science*, Manchester: Manchester University Press, pp. 3–94.

Orme, N. (2001), *Medieval Children*, Yale: Yale University Press.

Possamaï, A. (2000), 'A Profile of New Agers: Social and Spiritual Aspects', *Journal of Sociology*, 36(3): 364–77.

Principe, W. (1983), 'Toward Defining Spirituality', *Studies in Religion*, 12(2): 127–41.

Putman, R.D. (2000), *Bowling Alone: The Collapse and Revival of American Community,* New York: Simon and Schuster.

Roof, W.C. (1999), *Spiritual Marketplace: Baby Boomers and the Remaking of American Religion*, Princeton, NJ: Princeton University Press.

Rose, S. (1998), 'An Examination of the New Age Movement: Who is Involved and What Constitutes its Spirituality', *Journal of Contemporary Religion*, 13(1): 5–22.

Saward, J. (2005), *Sweet and Blessed Country: The Christian Hope for Heaven*, Oxford: Oxford University Press.

Simmel, G. (1997), *Essays on Religion* (ed. and trans. H.J. Helle with L. Nieder), New Haven, CT: Yale University Press.

Verter, B. (2003), 'Spiritual Capital: Theorising Religion with Bourdieu Against Bourdieu', *Sociological Theory*, 21(2): 150–74.

Urquhart, R. (2004), 'Someone to Watch over Me ...', *Prediction*, December: 12–16.

Walker, A.J. (2005), 'Love Alone: Hans Urs von Balthasar as a Master of Theological Renewal', *Communio*, 32, Fall: 517–40.

Weber, M. (1930), *The Protestant Ethic and the Spirit of Capitalism* (trans. T. Parsons), London: Unwin.

White, D. (2005), 'Are Angels Just a Matter of Faith?', *New Blackfriars*, 86(1006): 568–83.

Wuthnow, R. (1998a), 'Morality, Spirituality, and Democracy', *Society*, 35(3): 37–43.

Wuthnow, R. (1998b), *After Heaven: Spirituality in America Since the 1950s*, Berkeley: University of California Press.

Wuthnow, R. (2001), 'Spirituality and Spiritual Practice', in Richard K. Fenn (ed.), *The Blackwell Companion to Sociology of Religion*, Oxford: Blackwell, pp. 306–20.

Wuthnow, R. (2003), *All in Sync: How Music and Art are Revitalising American Religion*, Berkeley: University of California Press.

Zizioulas, J.D. (1985), 'The Early Christian Community', in B. McGinn, J. Meyendorff and J. LeClercq (eds), *Christian Spirituality: Origins to the Twelfth Century*, New York: Crossroad, pp. 23–43.

Conclusion

Kieran Flanagan and Peter C. Jupp

Of late, sociology has taken many turns, for example, into the cultural and the subjective. For some, a turn in the direction of spirituality might seem a rotation too far. Yet, increasingly, spirituality, however opaque, has become a matter of public concern, over its forms of expression, its status as a desirable ingredient in institutions and what it signifies of the quality of culture. To sociologists, spirituality might seem like a dense fog that has come in off Dover beach. Orthodox religion might have gone out with the cultural tide, but with its ebbing spirituality has rolled in unexpectedly as a sort of replacement. Is it part of an increasingly invisible religion or a phenomenon to be treated in its own right, or is it an entity that only makes sense when attached to a theology? The multiplicity of settings in which matters of spirituality are emerging seem without a pattern that makes sociological sense. Even less helpfully, as already observed by many in the collection, spirituality is a term difficult to define and is one peculiarly resistant to sociological encapsulation. Yet, despite its nebulous nature, as a topic, spirituality has attractions for sociology.

It offers escape from earlier concerns with sects and secularisation, and reverses a worry of Beckford, that still has some justification, that the interests of the sociology of religion lie at the edge of the discipline of sociology (1985). Whatever its demerits, spirituality certainly belongs to the agenda of sociology as a whole and all the contributors to the collection affirm this important point. Yet, as Holmes indicates in his survey of spirituality in academic disciplines in Chapter 1, sociology seems late in coming to grasp its significance. What sociology discerns is not a spirituality that emerges from the activities of ecclesial culture, but an extra-mural activity that springs up from the questing circumstances of a culture designated as increasingly characterised by individualism but also rootlessness. In the dislodgements and the fractures of the social, issues of the ultimate have emerged. As social capital becomes depleted in terms of communal commitment, increasingly the self walks alone, seeking answers to the needs of expressiveness often in interior questings.

In Chapter 1, Holmes provides a useful overview of the place of spirituality in seven academic disciplines. His extensive bibliography points to a burgeoning literature on spirituality and its increasing academic significance. For Holmes, the academic landscape is changing radically to assimilate notions of spirituality. But as this process evolves, difficulties of definition become more self-evident. He is not hopeful that an umbrella form of definition can be found, and the strength of his chapter is to suggest that any self-understandings of spirituality are likely to be peculiar to particular disciplines. He also makes an important point that some academic disciplines, such as psychology, have been the beneficiary of what they have propagated, that spirituality is a matter of self-concern and exploitation and one to be contemplated in detachment from organised religion. The scale of academic interest in spirituality will surprise many readers. Is holistic spirituality overblown in the significance ascribed to it and will it suffer from the forces of secularity the same fate as organised religion?

These were some of the issues Voas and Bruce pursue in their contribution in Chapter 2. The weak points of holistic spirituality are: its definitional opacity that affects indeterminately its relationship to religion, but also the quest for the sacred; the methodological difficulties of calibrating its incidence of practice and affiliation; and the question of its transmission where, as with organised religion, demography conspires against effective reproduction between generations. The issue of what counts as spiritual forms a critical theme of this chapter.

In his vigorous response to these criticisms, in Chapter 3, Heelas provides a defence of the methodological accomplishments of the Kendal project and the numerical significance of the practice of holistic spirituality. But his most significant section relates to the growth of the holistic milieu whose expansion propels holistic spirituality to a position of a replacement for organised religion. Certainly, he makes a good case for indicating the scale of its expansion and diversity. He sees young people as increasingly shaping their spiritual lives by reference to notions of subjective well-being. Heelas affirms the worth of holistic spirituality as an autonomous practice that nurtures interior virtues as benign forces, whose flourishing bears fruit in the social. For him, the questing is benign and to be given sociological affirmation.

Reflecting on the Kendal project on which she worked with Heelas, in Chapter 6, Woodhead examines the issue of women in relation to holistic spirituality. Why are they so predominant as consumers? The value of her contribution is to introduce a purely sociological and structural explanation, one that relates gender to the need for space for assembly of self-questioning but also forms of healing and recognition that holistic spirituality distinctively supplies. It offers languages and forms of expression to those who are denied public recognition in worlds of work and leisure where the female feels alien before perceived notions of masculine hegemony. The dignity and self-affirmation forms of holistic spirituality supply also cause Woodhead to affirm its sociological worth and significance.

The issue of how organised religion responds to the emergence of these unexpected new forms of spirituality is pursued by the two contributions from The Netherlands. They suggest that connections between secularisation and the sacred, and between holistic spirituality and organised religion, are less clear-cut than might seem to be the case for sociologists such as Heelas. Secularisation generates new relationships to the sacred, and that is what they find in the case of The Netherlands.

In Chapter 4, Droogers reflects on the methodological implications of these new relationships, making a sound case for the complementary use of qualitative and quantitative methods. But his strong point is to draw attention to the historical and Protestant basis of individualism in The Netherlands. This cultural and theological inheritance facilitates the growth of holistic forms of spirituality, but also the spirit of secularity that sustains their emergence as a matter of private choice and appropriation. Rights of autonomy in religious and cultural matters are deemed sacred in The

Netherlands. The loss of membership to the forces of secularisation is well covered, but also the loss of ecclesial authority in a religious marketplace where the making of binding commitments is problematic. It might be argued that individual repertoires of religion are simply eclectic assemblies of belief, matched to subjective preferences whose exercise weakens the social bond and depletes the spiritual capital of organised religion. Appropriations of holistic spirituality affirm a denial of commitment to the communal base of religion itself. In the divisions, it is weak before forces of secularisation and reduces difference to a matter of opinion. The picking and mixing forms a receptive climate for holistic spirituality but Droogers hesitates over how far the findings of the Kendal study apply in The Netherlands, where he suggests matters are more complex and, indeed, are often contradictory.

The contribution from Versteeg, in Chapter 5, builds on the approach from Droogers and supplies a novel view of holistic spirituality from within organised religion, generating questions of reception and accommodation that are rarely pursued. More interestingly, the sites for his research are Catholic and monastic, and these have their own traditions of spirituality. Some of the issues he raises regarding the mixing of Catholic notions of spirituality with rival holistic versions can be usefully compared with the insights in Chapter 9 in the contribution from Giordan. His contribution draws attention to the politics of spirituality and conflicting expectations it generates. The status of this pick and mixing within wider Catholicism might be further explored.

Holistic spirituality might well be something pervasive in life and times after postmodernity, when many patterns of bonding have unravelled, but there are other responses, as Chambers reminds us in his contribution in Chapter 7.

Subjectivity is like the diviner's rod; it has an odd habit of switching directions as it moves across the same cultural field. Islamic responses to the same culture that facilitates holistic spirituality, point to a movement in the opposite direction, an individualism accepted as a civil right, but subsumed to the needs of collective identity, and cast in conformity to the symbolic needs of a highly organised religion. The rights of expressiveness that underpin life in civil society, are used to defend the wearing of the *hijab*, a covering of the face and one that paradoxically, nullifies the expressivism European culture affirms. Chambers shifts spirituality from the individualised concerns of holism to its symbolic significance as a boundary-maintaining instrument that sustains a collective identity within a decidedly flourishing organised religion. The construction placed on spirituality is tooled for use in a direction that contradicts the tenets of holistic forms. Resistance, not capitulation marks the Islamic response of these veiled women and their spirituality is deeply embedded in their religion. The contrast between the differing responses of women in the Kendal project discussed in Chapter 6 and those in Chapter 7 is striking. The rootlessness that generates holistic spirituality also provides a contrast with other forms of spirituality that emerge from those who are decidedly rooted in their own beliefs. The cultural ground that realises spirituality seems ambiguous in the contrasting forms it generates.

The value of Varga's contribution in Chapter 8 arises in three areas. First, he provides a thorough reading of Simmel that brings into focus his concerns with spirituality, as they emerge in notions of religion and religiosity. The bridging property of religion in relation to the objective and the subjective is well noted. As Varga observes, Simmel's attitude to religion is complex. Varga shows why this is so. Secondly, Varga places Simmel's approach to religion and spirituality in the context of his sociological interests in individualism. Varga amply indicates the way many contemporary facets of debate on spirituality were well anticipated by Simmel and this relates to the third point. Simmel's approach to spirituality provides a useful means of understanding postmodernity and Varga reflects on this well. His chapter demolishes the notion that spirituality is something alien and alienating in the sociological milieu. From his extensive reading, and using German source material, Varga shows how a purely sociological characterisation of spirituality can be found in Simmel's analysis of religion.

A turn in the direction of theology marks Giordan's assessment of sociology and spirituality in Chapter 9. Like Droogers, he argues that present understandings of spirituality seem artificial if detached from their traditional forms of use and understanding. Many of the dilemmas raised by spirituality and its practices have been confronted over the centuries in Catholicism. More importantly, he rehabilitates the significance of religion in the setting of popular culture as a form of resistance to holistic spirituality. It operates on the periphery of Italian Catholic culture but is not quite incorporated into its distinctive version of an implicit or invisible religion. Catholicism penetrates Italian culture too much to permit such dalliances.

Giordan touches on a point that needs considerably more research. There is an implication in his paper that Protestantism supplies a milieu that is receptive to the use and recognition of holistic spirituality. Now it is true Versteeg's contribution contradicts this point. His milieu for the reception of holistic spirituality is Dutch Catholicism, but this might be atypical. Surrounding Protestantism, in its liberal forms, is a charge of capitulating to secularisation. There is also the added issue of membership of cults and sects. Might the same arguments apply to holistic spirituality? Writing on the Kendal Project, new spiritualities and subjectivisation, Martin wrote:

> Put dramatically, Protestantism destroys its capacity to reproduce and retain its vital memory, not because of some problem with the scientific world-view or rationalization, but by going completely inward, personal and inarticulate. (Martin 2005: 84)

Might the inwardness cultivated in Protestantism supply an elective affinity with holistic spirituality in ways that do not apply to Catholicism? Giordan's contribution points to a wider issue that needs further investigation. What are the spiritualities of Islam, Buddhism, Judaism and Christianity and how do these relate to the paradigm of holistic spirituality? To follow the point of Holmes regarding academic disciplines, are some organised religions more at risk than others to loss of membership to practitioners in holistic spirituality?

Working from a different sociological angle to others in the collection, Guest moves spirituality away from the connection with individualism that marks holistic versions, and into a more organised form – spiritual capital. The concept presupposes a location in organised religion and the strength of spiritual capital lies in the light it throws on effective forms of transmission. The concept evolves from other forms of capital in Bourdieu's sociology of culture. The contribution of Guest reverses the notion that located in organised religion spirituality is something dead, devoid of capacity and is best detached for re-creation in the ambit of holistic spirituality. As a resource, access to spiritual capital gave to the children of the study he undertook with Davies, definite traits of altruism, of reaching out, and thus offsetting the individualism and the interior channelling that characterises holistic forms of spirituality. There is a property of out-reach to the form of spirituality Guest explores in his chapter, one whose utility is to be understood by reference to sociology, not theology.

Flory and Miller, in their contribution in Chapter 11, provide a persuasive account of spiritual questing as conceived in terms of two ideal types – the Reclaimers and the Innovators. Unexpectedly, this seeking does not occur in a holistic milieu, as one would expect to find in a sociological account from California, but largely in setting of organised religion: Christianity. Their chapter supplies what Drooger's would want to affirm: the need to use qualitative methods in the study of spirituality. Interesting testimonies and tales of questing emerge from the respondents in these two categories in this chapter. The individualism that enables holistic spirituality is treated as disabling in terms of the types of spirituality chronicled in this chapter. Like Chambers, their subjects seek spirituality *within* structures that effect and sustain bonding, hence the common emphasis on small size church groups that offer communal support. Secondly, they introduce a useful new concept, expressive communalism and this draws attention to the collaborative basis of spiritual seeking and mutuality of regard it generates. Another facet, and one that links to Chapter 12 by Flanagan, is their concern with spiritual embodiment in its visual dimensions. The forms of spirituality that emerge in this chapter are responses to the expansion in significance of visual culture and the re-casting of expectations of seeing new technologies generate.

Flanagan's concern with visual spirituality marks limits which sociology faces in dealings with spirituality. Images of the afterlife so important to visual spirituality depend on the authority and stipulations of theology. Sociology has little control over these matters, yet they can have profound implications for the credibility of visual spirituality and the seeking to see the unseen it nurtures. His chapter mirrors notions of expressive communalism mapped out in the preceding contribution. Flanagan's concern is with the rehabilitation of ways of seeing best fitted to visual spirituality, and these can be found in an exemplary form in the medieval Church. It cultivated capacities to see images in ways where the needs of the eye of perception could be reconciled with the desire to nurture the inward spiritual gaze (Hamburger and Bouché 2006). He argues that the demands of visual culture are incompatible with the inwardness cultivated in holistic spirituality. This is a claim that might deserve further sociological exploration.

Whatever their differences, all contributors seem to agree that spirituality has distinct capacities to illuminate matters of religion, the self and culture in ways other concepts cannot. Many vistas of sociology are opened up by the concept of spirituality, however difficult it is to define. The collection has a property of a tug of war between those who place spirituality outside organised religion and those who seek to wrest it back. In this pulling and tugging of two entities notoriously difficult to define, sociology is placed in the middle as a sort of umpire. Holistic spirituality yields a distinct set of concepts, in relation to the individual, subjectivity, expressivism and responses to the rootlessness postmodernity expands. Forms of spirituality within organised religion point to a different sociological agenda, of tradition, ritual, symbol, external authority and communal practices within which the individual operates. Clearly both differ in the gods and God they acknowledge. Is questing a purely interior act, or does it inevitably have an exterior manifestation? Or might it be the case in the conventions of sociology, that both dimensions are vital. The question of the interior and exterior dimensions of spirituality echoes earlier debates in sociology on the relationship between action and structure. Symbolic interaction supplies some points of relief for these arguments.

Is an alternative form of spirituality to what is customarily understood in organised religion something 'new', something viable and something that reflects a response to changing cultural circumstances? Holmes and Heelas might answer in the affirmative. Yet, might holistic spirituality suffer the same fate as organised religion before the powers of secularisation as Voas and Bruce argue? Or might it be the case that the spirituality of organised religion is also a viable proposition, even in times of post-secularity? Flory and Miller, and to some extent Giordan and Flanagan might suggest this point, and possibly also Droogers. The implication is that culture is both permitting and producing new forms of spirituality and these can also be found within organised religion to a greater degree than some sociologists might imagine. Flanagan and Chambers might converge in suggesting that tradition and memory provide old precedents that can be made fit for new cultural circumstances. A matter of contention, one that emerges in Versteeg, relates to how organised religion perceives rival holistic forms of spirituality. Should it accommodate to these, or should it dismiss holistic spirituality as alien to its own forms? This relates to theological issues of authority outside sociological powers of arbitration. Varga's contribution on Simmel well indicates the complexity of such issues. Spirituality, in the form of religiosity, might lie antecedent to religion, but it still requires this form to manifest its expressive needs, a point that can be linked to the contribution from Flory and Miller.

Finally, how is sociology to handle spirituality? Is a purely sociological appraisal of its basis possible? This might seem to be the case in the contributions of Woodhead and Guest, even if they differ greatly in the forms of spirituality they use. For both, spirituality provides resources and capacities to cope in relation to structural needs and constraints. But again the difference is notable. One form, that explored by Woodhead is directed to spirituality as a coping mechanism that shores up unsettled interiors of the self, whereas the other, that of Guest, looks at spirituality almost in a Durkheimian way as facilitating altruism and a yielding of the self to the demands of others. One set, perceives spirituality as a compensation for being short-changed in relation to social capital, whereas the other points to forms of investment in it, but in strategies that are distinctively to be understood by reference to spirituality.

A question not pursued in the collection relates to the vexed matter of reflexivity. Does the study of spirituality have distinctive reflexive implications for sociology? This relates to matters of choice, of ultimate values over which form of spirituality is to be legitimised for sociological purposes. Do these have purely analytical uses, or do they relate to the biographical sensibilities of the sociologist? Might the study of spirituality have reflexive implications that might lead to a form of spiritual renewal in the discipline? If so, does sociology have a preference for one form over another? Most contributors to the collection do not seem to have a reflexive stance, or exercise an elective affinity over which type of spirituality marks their own personal preferences. Two exceptions are Heelas and Flanagan, who seem to occupy polar ends in their endorsement of contrasting forms of spirituality – holism and Catholicism.

Reflexivity suggests that the expansion of subjectivisation that facilitates the rise of holistic spirituality can also be applied to sociology itself. Increasingly, reflexivity marks the disembodied sociologist as scarcely credible. If reflexivity forces sociology to consider degrees of embodiment in sociological analyses, how might this emerge in studies of spirituality?

The sociological study of spirituality, as an emergent property of a rapidly changing Western culture, generates distinctive forms of theodicy, issues the embodiment within holistic spirituality does not seem to handle. Although spirituality can be domesticated within life-styles and in this form has an uneasy overlap with leisure and therapy, concern with the well-being of the body can mask its frailty and contingency, in short that it suffers and dies. To that degree there is always a postponed facet to spirituality: the supernatural and the future of the dead in an afterlife. These considerations seem too often to be put on the back burner of sociology.

Yet, sociologists of death suggest that changes in belief and practice about death and afterlife have also helped to prepare the soil for a flourishing of spiritualities about death and dying which traditional Christianity would have found heterodox. For Jupp, Parliamentary reforms in the United Kingdom were, in retrospect, a critical stage in the secularisation of death. In the 1850s, Parliamentary legislation closed churchyards in cities and replaced them by publicly owned cemeteries. This fractured the Church of England's monopoly of the rite, site, mode and conduct of disposal. Local government authorities held no remit for the religious interpretation of being dead, only supplying space for dead bodies. This secularising was further extended when cremation, with symbols neutral as regards Christian belief, was successfully promoted as an alternative to burial (Jupp 2006).

Christian funeral rites faced further competition when the Burial Laws Amendment Act, 1880, specified that funerals could be conducted according to any religious rites or none. This would undergird the rise of secular funeral rituals especially after the dominance of cremation from the 1960s. By the 1990s, only 8 per cent of people believed in the resurrection of the body, supported by a reincarnationist variant which held that 'we come back as someone or something else' (12 per cent). Forms of immortality were more popular – 34 per cent believed that 'our souls pass on another world' (Davies and Shaw 1995: 86–101; Davies 1997).

So what happened here? The fragmentation of the Christian consensus on the afterlife is the product of a complex combination of factors as the Churches responded to rapid development in the understanding of human and social identity, and to changes in community life. New patterns of social and geographical mobility, the exodus of the middle classes and women from the pews and the collapse of Sunday Schools undermined the Church's authoritative position as a guide to belief and morals. All these have fractured the transmission of collective memory and have left a vacuum for alternative world views to expand in response to continuing human needs about death. Meanwhile, the expansion of educational, career and leisure opportunities, the rise of prosperity and of consumer choice can be set in a frame of lengthening longevity which puts a premium on issues of health, illness and the importance of the body. These serve to privilege individuals as consumers of experience and self-gratification, shaping their world views by reference to notions of subjective well-being.

Such developments help to shift the individual's gaze from matters eternal to matters transitory, from postponed gratification to immediate satisfaction. This process affects attitudes to mortality. Whilst death is a statistical certainty, actuarial science demonstrates that its incidence today bears so small a measure of probability it can be realistically discarded as an everyday risk. And when death comes in 'a good old age', it is no longer surrounded with religious sanctions. Meanwhile, this is an era when the realities of the Holocaust and of nuclear threat have given way to more local fears of violence and terrorism. There is now far more awareness of the threat of early, violent death. The film industry exposes our fears on the screen. Hollywood has the technology to portray all conceivable variants, not only on dying but also on an afterlife existence. Our imagination thus feeds on the fears and fantasies that film technology can recreate in endless new forms (Knox 2006).

In traditional religions, divine revelation spoke to human needs. Today, whatever is projected, nothing seems revealed. In the absorbing spectacles feeding today's spiritualities of death, there seems no Plato who will escape from the cinema of his cave, nor any Dives to be certain that his return from the dead might be credible.

Increasingly, there is a growing recognition of the significance of religion in the United Kingdom, notably in the strategies for future funding as marked by research councils. For instance, the Economic and Social Research Council and its counterpart in Arts and Humanities are now linking religion to ethnicity and identity. A decade ago, such linkages would have been inconceivable. As such research ventures grow, the issue of the type of spirituality being researched is also likely to grow in significance. Dealing with spirituality marks two obvious divides between holistic forms and organised religion, and between forms of well-being and those that recognise a supernatural dimension. It is perhaps likely, that as the link between ethnicity, religion and identity is pursued, the importance of spirituality in the setting of organised religions that deal with the supernatural is likely to increase. Ethnicity is associated with organised religions that treat the afterlife as a matter of crucial theological significance. There are many differing forms spirituality operating even within one organised religion. This point was well illustrated in a recent research study of Generation Y in the United Kingdom (Savage et al. 2006)

Generation Y is defined as the Millennial Generation. It refers to those who have grown up in a globalised society who inhabit a milieu of information and communications technology that shapes their cultural perspectives (Savage et al. 2006: 7). The study makes a valuable distinction between formative and transformative spirituality. The former version relates to notions of invisible or implicit religion and refers to an implicit appreciation of spiritual values in social relationships, the arts and nature. The latter version is narrower in scope, more directed to the theological, more overtly 'religious' dimensions and more aware of experience of the spiritual. Unfortunately, in their use the researchers accept holistic forms of spirituality, as outlined by Heelas and Woodhead in the Kendal study, as transformative (Savage et al. 2006: 12–13). This is odd, as the value orientation of their study of Generation Y is geared to further an Evangelical Christian perspective in mission and conversion.

The findings of the study revolve around a notion of 'happy midi-narrative', the story line of the sample (Savage et al. 2006: 37–8). Whereas the narratives of Flory and Miller move in a questing direction in relation to religion, Generation Y in this portrayal seem models of contentment, inhabiting a formative unchallenging and unchallenged spirituality. Only in a small number of cases does transformative spirituality matter. Thus, set against the hopes of a vision for wider things, the study gloomily concluded that 'Generation Y tends to work with a much shorter view, for the central concerns of religion and spirituality are beyond its horizons' (Savage et al. 2006: 150). In this regard, Voas and Bruce might take comfort from the findings of the study. The disconnection with Christianity, in this case Anglicanism stands starkly as a central image and outcome of the study.

In looking at the study, the centrality of the Word is affirmed, but little attention is given to the specific forms of spiritual and cultural capital needed to reconnect youth back to the Anglicanism. It might be suggested that strategies of café style spirituality, and efforts to re-cast ecclesial culture into an image and likeness of the milieu in which Generation Y operate expressively are only likely to confirm them in their disconnection. By affirming their milieu in strategies of evangelisation, Generation Y are affirmed where they are and not where they should be, questing into the transformative spirituality of the Evangelical tradition of Christianity. In short, in its desperation to connect, such Anglican strategies seem only to affirm disconnection. The bareness of the proclamation of the Word, at the end of the study, presented as a spiritual solution stands starkly to the excitements of the cultural milieu. No spiritual capital and no cultural wrappings are acknowledged that would move the subjective preferences of Generation Y in a wholly different spiritual direction.

The mixing of holistic forms of spirituality with the traditional assumptions of organised religion can yield an explosive mixture, a case in point being the tragedy of a religious order of nuns in California in the 1960s, when the imperative to engage with the world and to modernise was at its most uncritical point. The contrast between their case and the passive acquiescence of the religious orders in Versteeg's account in Chapter 5, illustrates how the politics of spirituality change according to culture, site, and era.

The nuns of the Immaculate Heart of Mary, in Los Angeles, under the leadership of a zealous mother superior, sought to open to the world through the use of therapy and encounter groups that affirmed the self and its expressive rights. The outcome was that the order fell apart, the majority of nuns abandoning their vows, leaving a minority behind who still exist and offer post-graduate degrees in spirituality with feminist emphases. Normally such irruptions would be of little sociological significance, but in this case the matter had profound implications. The nuns formed a case study for a psychiatrist, Carl Rogers, who wished to use encounter groups to free up identities in education. This exercise occurred as the nuns fell into dispute with Cardinal MacIntyre of Los Angeles (and Rome) over their path to renewal and modernisation. The mother general at the time, 1963–69 has written her defence of her stewardship in this era (Caspary 2003).

Claims were made that the introduction of self-directed forms of expressiveness was at odds with an authority system that was other directed, and for some, might involve life in denial of a culture of self-expression. A Catholic psychologist involved in the programme retracted his support for these exercises in humanist psychology in 1993, and claimed it enhanced sexual awareness among the nuns and served to liberate them from living lives of celibacy. The reverberations of the row marked a divide between humanist psychology, loosely connected in values to those of holistic spirituality and the authority of an ecclesial culture that stipulated the link between the ascetic and the spiritual. Values of self-affirmation and self-denial collided, as did the differing spiritualities upon which these were based. By deferring to the authority of the former, the religious order, in effect, disintegrated (Kugelmann 2005). Why does one form of spirituality permit a flourishing, and the use of another generate disintegration?

In a strange and ironic turn, traditional forms of spirituality received vigorous affirmation from Scientologists and their 'Citizens Commission on Human Rights'. Their hostility to the intrusion of psychiatry into matters of religion reflected a struggle for power to purify mental states with their techniques rather than those drawn from psychiatry. The case of the nuns was treated as an exemplary example of the dangers of psychiatry, therapy and other forms of treatment of the self.

This crisis in California alerted Catholicism to the dangers of alternative and unregulated forms of spirituality. But then Catholicism has a long history of coping with such matters. The conflict over this religious order suggests that issues of holistic spirituality do not just emerge from the circumstances of indifference that characterise secularisation. Spirituality might not be susceptible to tight definitions, but when mixed in competing forms, adherents know the differences.

The collection has generated far more questions than it answers. A vista worthy of sociological exploration has been opened out and in the study of spirituality new issues, new interpretations and new characterisations of culture and religion emerge. The opacity of the term spirituality facilitates a diversity of approaches to its sociological study and many of these are revealed in this collection.

Bibliography

Beckford, J.A. (1985), 'The Insulation and Isolation of the Sociology of Religion', *Sociological Analysis*, 46(4): 347–54.

Caspary, A.M. (2003), *Witness to Integrity: The Crisis of the Immaculate Heart Community of California*, Collegeville, MN: The Liturgical Press.

Davies, D.J. (1997), *Death, Ritual and Belief*, London: Cassell.

Davies, D.J. and A. Shaw (1995), *Reusing Old Graves: A Report on Popular British Attitudes*, Crayford, Kent: Shaw and Sons.

Hamburger, J.F. and A.M. Bouché (eds) (2006), *The Mind's Eye: Art and Theological Argument in the Middle Ages*, Princeton, NJ: Princeton University Press.

Jupp, P.C. (2006), *From Dust to Ashes: Cremation and the British Way of Death*, Basingstoke: Palgrave Macmillan.

Knox, S. (2006), 'Death, Afterlife and the Eschatology of Consciousness: Themes in Contemporary Cinema', *Mortality*, 11(3): 233–52.

Kugelmann, R. (2005), 'An Encounter Between Psychology and Religion: Humanistic Psychology and the Immaculate Heart of Mary Nuns', *Journal of the History of Behavioural Sciences*, 41(4): 347–65.

Martin, D. (2005), *On Secularisation: Towards a Revised General Theory*, Aldershot: Ashgate.

Savage, S., S. Collins-Mayo, B. Mayo with G. Cray (2006), *Making Sense of Generation Y: The World View of 15–25-year-olds*, London: Church House Publishing.

Index